Late Modernism and
the Poetics of Place

Late Modernism and the Poetics of Place

Neal Alexander

Edinburgh University Press is one of the leading university presses in the UK. We publish academic books and journals in our selected subject areas across the humanities and social sciences, combining cutting-edge scholarship with high editorial and production values to produce academic works of lasting importance. For more information visit our website: edinburghuniversitypress.com

© Neal Alexander 2022, 2024

Edinburgh University Press Ltd
The Tun – Holyrood Road
12(2f) Jackson's Entry
Edinburgh EH8 8PJ

First published in hardback by Edinburgh University Press 2022

Typeset in 10.5/13 pt Sabon LT Pro
by Cheshire Typesetting Ltd, Cuddington, Cheshire, and
printed and bound by CPI Group (UK) Ltd, Croydon,
CR0 4YY

A CIP record for this book is available from the British Library

ISBN 978 1 4744 8440 4 (hardback)
ISBN 978 1 4744 8441 1 (paperback)
ISBN 978 1 4744 8442 8 (webready PDF)
ISBN 978 1 4744 8443 5 (epub)

The right of Neal Alexander to be identified as the author of this work has been asserted in accordance with the Copyright, Designs and Patents Act 1988, and the Copyright and Related Rights Regulations 2003 (SI No. 2498).

Contents

Acknowledgements	vi
Introduction	1
1. David Jones: The Sites of History	21
2. Basil Bunting's Regional Modernism	52
3. W. S. Graham: Between Places	81
4. Lorine Niedecker: Life by Water	111
5. Charles Olson's Mappemunde	142
6. Gwendolyn Brooks: From Bronzeville to the Warpland	171
Conclusion: After Late Modernism	199
Notes	208
Bibliography	244
Index	264

Acknowledgements

No one ever writes a book on their own, no matter how solitary the process may sometimes seem. During the writing of this book, I benefitted from two six-month periods of research leave from Aberystwyth University, in 2017 and 2021, which enabled me to begin and then finish the work needed. For their help in making this possible, I am very grateful to Anwen Jones, Louise Marshall, Sarah Prescott, and Sarah Wydall. During the first of those periods, I spent a lot of time working in the National Library of Wales, or simply staring at the sea from its windows, and was impressed by the generosity and professionalism of the staff there. Over the years, I have learned a great deal from conversations with colleagues and friends, including David Cooper, Sarah Davison, Dominic Head, Sheila Hones, David James, Matt Jarvis, Richard Marggraf Turley, Jim Moran, Julie Sanders, Nathan Waddell, Danny Weston, and Emma Zimmerman. Matthew Francis, Gavin Goodwin, Jamie Harris, Luke Thurston, and Tim Woods all read draft chapters of the book, and their comments pushed me to explain myself better, consider alternatives, extend tentative lines of argument, and read things that hadn't occurred to me. Any errors or deficiencies that remain are down to me. Two anonymous readers for Edinburgh University Press confirmed my sense of the project's potential but also made me think harder about its scope, inclusiveness, and ultimate purpose – which was exactly what I needed. At Edinburgh, Jackie Jones was willing to take a second look at my plans and gave me valuable encouragement at a key stage in the research. More recently, Susannah Butler, Fiona Conn, Caitlin Murphy, and their colleagues have steered me through the production and design processes with patient expertise and good humour. Aidan Cross's meticulous, sharp-eyed copy-editing has improved every aspect of the book's effort to communicate clearly with its readers. Most important of all has been the boundless support and encouragement and care that my family have given me. Thank you Colin, Barbara, and Gareth Alexander; Doreen

Phillips and Neil Wright; Hywel Phillips and Elaine Edwards; Barry and Pauline Phillips; Steven, Emma, Ariana, and Meira Davies. Finally, words can't express how much I owe to, and am sustained by, the love of Tina, Seren, and Fflur Alexander. Mae'r llyfr hwn ar eich cyfer chi, gyda fy holl gariad.

Versions of Chapter 1 and Chapter 2 of this book have previously been published as: 'History, Geography, Poetry: David Jones's Late Modernism', *Modernism/modernity* 26.4 (2019), 869–92; and 'The Idea of North: Basil Bunting and Regional Modernism', in Neal Alexander and James Moran, eds, *Regional Modernisms* (Edinburgh: Edinburgh University Press, 2013), pp. 200–20.

Introduction

This book undertakes a detailed literary geography of late modernist poetry in the three decades following the end of the Second World War. Its focus is upon the work of a diverse group of mostly second-generation modernists who were active on both sides of the Atlantic during the second half of the twentieth century, long after the death of modernism had been proclaimed. Part of my purpose is to contribute to a wider critical reappraisal of the literary history of Anglophone modernism, with particular attention to its later manifestations. A familiar and much-rehearsed literary-historical narrative traces the origins of Anglophone modernism to 1890 or 1900, identifies its zenith in the golden age of the 1920s, and chronicles its terminal decline during the Depression years of the 1930s.[1] According to this account, modernism came to an end with the twin disasters of James Joyce's *Finnegans Wake* (1939) and the invasion of Poland by Nazi Germany on 1 September 1939. One problem with this tale of literary modernism's rise and fall is that it ignores the tenacious survivals of late modernism well into the post-war period. In particular, the three decades from 1945 to 1975 marked a major new phase of experiment and achievement in Anglophone modernist poetry, an aspect of late modernism that has received little serious critical attention to date. This period saw the publication of such important (though often neglected) late modernist texts as William Carlos Williams's *Paterson* (1946–1958), Wallace Stevens's *The Auroras of Autumn* (1950), Lynette Roberts's *Gods with Stainless Ears* (1951), David Jones's *The Anathémata* (1952), Melvin Tolson's *Libretto for the Republic of Liberia* (1953), W. S. Graham's *The Nightfishing* (1955), Hugh MacDiarmid's *In Memoriam James Joyce* (1955), Louis Zukofsky's *"A" 1–12* (1959), Marianne Moore's *O to Be a Dragon* (1959), Charles Olson's *The Maximus Poems* (1960), H. D.'s *Helen in Egypt* (1961), Charles Reznikoff's *Testimony: The United States (1885–1900)* (1965–1968), Basil Bunting's *Briggflatts* (1966), George

Oppen's *Of Being Numerous* (1968), Gwendolyn Brooks's *In the Mecca* (1968), Lorine Niedecker's *North Central* (1968), and Brian Coffey's *Advent* (1975). Furthermore, New Directions published the first nearly complete edition of Ezra Pound's *The Cantos* in 1970, though the poem was begun more than half a century earlier.[2]

Given this remarkable late flourishing of Anglophone modernist poetry in the decades following the Second World War, the more interesting question is not when modernism came to an end, but rather how it persisted and transformed itself during the second half of the twentieth century. In this regard, I take my bearings from Raymond Williams, who observes that the term 'modernism' has habitually been used retrospectively since the 1950s, thereby 'fix[ing]' the moment of modernism in the period 1890 to 1940.[3] For Williams, this non-historical fixation of modernism's historical unfolding is symptomatic of a failure of the critical imagination that is ideological in character. Accordingly, he critiques the canonisation of modernism, by which he means the critical construction of 'a highly selective version of the modern which then offers to appropriate the whole of modernity', because it facilitates its integration with the new capitalist world order that emerged after the Second World War.[4] Against this ideological tendency to regard modernism as 'fixed' rather than formative, Williams argues that 'we must search out and counterpose an alternative tradition taken from the neglected works left in the wide margin of the century'.[5]

The collective labour of identifying and delineating alternative traditions of modernist writing, art, and culture has been a characteristic feature of the new modernist studies for several decades now, particularly through its 'transnational turn'. Critical work in this vein challenges the Eurocentric biases of older models of internationalism by attending to the imperial and postcolonial contexts of modernism's literary production, and 'emphasizes a variety of affiliations within and across national spaces' rather than regarding modernism as inherently deracinated.[6] In this context, the 'wide margin of the century' is understood in terms of a major spatial expansion of the ambit of literary modernism, what Andreas Huyssen calls 'modernism at large'.[7] At the same time, however, scholars of modernism have begun to reconfigure its temporal parameters, partly as a result of the recognition that modernism happens at different times in different places and under different conditions of modernity.[8] The 'neglected works' upon which I focus attention in this book are poems written and published during a period when the very term 'modernism' had come to refer to a literary movement that was over, apparently consigned to the past. Nonetheless, I will show that they are distinctively modernist in character, sensibility, and form, instances of the living on of modernism in the late twentieth century.

Periodising Late Modernism

Simplifying a little, there are two main ways of defining late modernism: one relates a story of decline and obsolescence that is keyed to larger narratives of historical change; and the other tells a tale of survival and persistence long after modernism is supposed to have passed on. The first kind of critical definition is exemplified by Tyrus Miller, who regards late modernism as a phenomenon of the late 1920s and 1930s, 'a distinctly self-conscious manifestation of the aging and decline of modernism' that also 'strongly anticipates' the emergence of postmodernism.[9] Miller's examples are eclectic and deliberately non-canonical, including fiction and non-fiction texts by Wyndham Lewis, Djuna Barnes, Samuel Beckett, and Mina Loy. Late modernism differentiates itself from high modernism in a number of ways: through its use of satiric or parodic laughter; its eschewal of aesthetic autonomy and 'strong symbolic forms'; its erosion of the distinctions between subject and object; and its preoccupation with grotesque bodies.[10] In Miller's influential account, then, late modernism belongs to the interwar years and fits within the conventional period boundaries ascribed to modernism as a whole (1890–1940), though it also constitutes a sort of counter-tradition that brings modernism to an end. Late modernism is the undoing of modernism, a reaction against some of its defining aesthetic priorities that accomplishes modernism's ultimate dissolution. Following Miller, but adjusting his periodisation slightly (1928–1945), Cheryl Hindrichs further amplifies this elegiac interpretation, arguing that the 'lateness' of late modernism derives from an historical awareness on the part of writers of 'being at a moment of ending and judgement', when the novelty of high modernism has become either impossible or obsolete.[11]

Those critics who characterise late modernism in terms of aging and decline usually adopt a relatively conservative periodisation, treating it chiefly as a phenomenon of the 1930s and 1940s. They also tend to associate late modernism with a waning of modernism's aesthetic and political radicalism. For example, John Whittier-Ferguson's *Mortality and Form in Late Modernist Literature* (2014) focuses upon the later works of four canonical modernist writers – Virginia Woolf, T. S. Eliot, Gertrude Stein, and Wyndham Lewis. He argues that these texts are not only preoccupied with death and endings during an historical period overshadowed by economic depression and global war, but also mark a 'new phase' of development, a stage of formal or stylistic reinvention that 'comes after the writing for which each artist first became famous'. Key examples include Woolf's turn towards 'writing that attends primarily to externals, to facts' after the radical interiority of *The Waves* (1931), and Eliot's 'doctrinally conservative' but aesthetically 'resourceful' Anglo-Catholic poetry.[12] Whittier-Ferguson's chief interest lies in what Edward Said calls the 'late style' of certain modernist writers in middle or later age. However, where Said follows Theodor Adorno in characterising late style in terms of 'intransigence, difficulty, and unresolved contradiction', Whittier-Ferguson's version of late modernism gravitates towards the conditions of 'serenity and maturity' with which artistic lateness has conventionally been associated.[13] In the late works of Woolf, Eliot, Stein, and Lewis, he implies, most of the elements that were most aesthetically, morally, or politically disturbing to readers in their earlier, high modernist texts have been tempered or superseded all together.

A more nuanced and historicised conception of late modernism is offered by Jed Esty, who situates it in the wider historical and political context of the dissolution of the British Empire during the 1930s and 1940s. Discussing late works by Eliot, Woolf, and E. M. Forster in detail, he describes Anglo-American late modernism as 'a major literary culture caught in the act of becoming minor', one engaged on a project of 'cultural salvage' that manifests itself chiefly through an anthropological interest in English national culture and traditions.[14] In Esty's formulation, the waning of aesthetic novelty and significance ('becoming minor') that distinguishes late modernism is the price that writers must pay for the revival of a sense of cultural wholeness and national integrity. Late modernism is also, on this account, a more insular and locally embedded literary formation than the metropolitan high modernism that precedes it. Esty notes the 'cosmopolitan privilege' that accounts for modernism's 'general capacity to rise above, while incorporating, the local materials of any given cultural tradition'.[15] By contrast, the aesthetic of late modernism is predicated on a perception of 'cultural boundedness, unity, and knowability' that stubbornly refuses such transcendence of local particulars.[16] The broad contours of Esty's argument trace a shift away from international or transnational horizons towards the narrower bounds of national culture and identity in a period of post-imperial decline. Similarly, Marina MacKay regards Britain's post-imperial condition as the key context for late modernism during the Second World War, observing that all of the major modernist writers supported the war effort as part of a 'guilty compromise' with the established centres of political power.[17] We can identify a number of important differences between some of the main critical definitions of late modernism here.

For, where Miller sees late modernism as a last gasp of modernist avant-gardism, both Esty and MacKay describe a phase of modernist writing that is both aesthetically and politically conservative in temper, preoccupied with questions of identity, custom, and tradition. Moreover, while Miller's study is deliberately international in focus, Esty and MacKay both concentrate more exclusively upon late modernism in England.

Beneath their differences, what all of the critics considered so far agree upon is that late modernism is primarily a phenomenon of the first half of the twentieth century, originating during the interwar years and brought to a conclusion by the end of the Second World War in 1945.[18] There is, however, another critical definition of late modernism, one that emerges significantly earlier and has a wider cross-disciplinary basis, that understands it as the continuation of a distinctively modernist aesthetic well into the post-war period, when modernism's moment was thought to have passed. For instance, the architectural historian Charles Jencks argues that it was not until the 1960s that the dominance of the Modern Movement in architecture – exemplified by Le Corbusier, Walter Gropius, and Ludwig Mies van der Rohe – began to wane, leading to the rise of both Late-Modern and Post-Modern styles. Although they emerged roughly simultaneously, Jencks argues that each of these styles is characterised by a different kind of response to the perceived failures of Modern architecture's utopian social ambitions. Post-Modernism is 'double-coded', 'one half Modern and one half something else (usually traditional building)', whereas Late-Modernism is distinguished by its 'extreme' elaboration of certain Modern traits, 'exaggerating the structure and technological image of the building in its attempt to provide amusement or aesthetic pleasure'.[19] Among Jencks's examples of Late-Modernism are Norman Foster's Sainsbury Centre, Norwich (1974–8) and Richard Rogers and Renzo Piano's Pompidou Centre, Paris (1971–7), each of which exaggerate elements of circulation, structure, lighting, and space in ways that emphasise both beauty and technical mastery.

Fredric Jameson was the first to see the potential for adapting Jencks's definition of late modernism to literature and music. However, where Jencks associates Late-Modern architecture with an extremist intensification of modernist stylistic traits, Jameson characterises late modernism as a mode of stubborn or even heroic persistence, 'the last survivors of a properly modernist view of art and the world after the great political and economic break of the Depression'. He continues:

> Jencks's late moderns are those who persist into postmodernism, and the idea makes sense architecturally; a literary frame of reference, however, throws up

names like Borges and Nabokov, Beckett, poets like Olson or Zukovsky [sic], and composers like Milton Babbitt, who had the misfortune to span two eras and the luck to find a time capsule of isolation or exile in which to spin out unseasonable forms.[20]

The 'unseasonable' or untimely nature of late modernism is evident from its awkward temporal positioning, situated as it is between, but also partly overlapping, the 'two eras' of modernism and postmodernism. Indeed, Jameson adjusts Jencks's periodisation, considering that 1960 is too late a date for the beginning of late modernism in literature and the arts. Instead, he implies that it is best understood as a phenomenon of the immediate post-war decades when the emergence of a US-dominated consumer capitalist society was still taking its course. Perry Anderson develops the historical logic of this line of argument further when he observes that it is too simplistic to suppose that the avant-gardist impulses of modernist art came to an abrupt end in 1945. Noting the vital experiments of the Situationists, the American abstract expressionist painters, and the films of Jean-Luc Godard, he argues:

> The quarter century after the end of hostilities thus seems in retrospect an inter-regnum, in which modernist energies were not subject to sudden cancellation, but still glowed intermittently here and there, within an inhospitable climate. It was not until the turn of the seventies that the ground for an altogether new configuration was prepared.[21]

Although Anderson does not use the term himself, his postulation of an 'inter-regnum' during the quarter century following the War's end offers a compelling historicisation of late modernism as, in Jameson's terms, the survival or persistence of a properly modernist aesthetics into the second half of the twentieth century. It is upon this periodisation of late modernism that I propose to build, chiefly by showing how 'modernist energies' live on in the work of a loose group of British and American poets who published their most important texts in the three decades from 1945 to 1975.

It is worth noting, however, that Jameson's subsequent discussion of late modernism in literature and the arts employs a very different critical definition. In *A Singular Modernity* (2002), he echoes Williams by describing the formation of a powerful 'ideology of modernism', which centres on the doctrine of 'the autonomy of the aesthetic' and finds its most influential expression in the New Critics' formalism and the art criticism of Clement Greenberg.[22] This cultural ideology corresponds to the historical and political conditions of the Cold War, in which the possibility of revolution or some utopian transformation of society as a whole is neutralised by the spread of consumerism and market values, at least in the capitalist West. According to Jameson, 'late modernism' is the mode of artistic practice that, in the post-war period, embodies and exemplifies the ideology of modernism. Late modernism is not, on this definition, the survival of a properly modernist aesthetic sensibility, but refers instead to the domestication of modernist experiment, which is transformed during the post-war years into 'an arsenal of tried and true techniques, no longer striving after aesthetic totality or the systemic and Utopian metamorphosis of forms'.[23] As examples of late modernism, Jameson mentions abstract expressionism in painting and the poetry of Wallace Stevens, both of which illustrate the characteristically late modernist preoccupation with 'art about art, and art about the creation of art'.[24] Whatever its artistic achievements, then, late modernism would seem to equate to a decline in aesthetic and political radicalism, a falling away from modernism's utopian potential. The problem with Jameson's second definition of late modernism, however, is that it generalises on the basis of a very small number of literary and artistic examples, taking the abstraction, idealism, and autotelic reflexivity of Stevens's poetry to be characteristic of late modernism as a whole. It also overlooks, or chooses to ignore, the late modernist texts of Beckett, Olson, Zukofsky, and others that he had earlier acknowledged, and which are certainly less amenable to the ideology of modernism as Jameson describes it.

I want to argue that there are good critical and literary-historical reasons for preferring Jameson's initial definition of late modernism as the survival of modernist aesthetics well into the post-war inter-regnum. We have already encountered a number of examples in architecture (Foster and Rogers), painting (the abstract expressionism of Jackson Pollock or Barnett Newman), film (Godard and *La Nouvelle Vague*), and music (Babbitt), as well as literature that would seem to justify employing the term in this way. It is particularly apposite, I contend, with regard to the historical dynamics of Anglophone modernist poetry. For example, Tim Armstrong remarks upon what he calls 'the afterlife of modernism' in the work of a cluster of poets – George Oppen, Basil Bunting, Thomas MacGreevy, and Brian Coffey – all of whom had 'interrupted careers'.[25] Each of these poets published their earliest texts in the 1920s or 1930s, then apparently fell silent for decades before resurfacing in the 1960s or 1970s with their major works: Bunting's *Briggflatts* and Oppen's *Of Being Numerous*, for instance. Such interruption or intermittency clearly forms a pattern in the work of some late modernist poets (Lorine Niedecker is another example), but it is not necessarily the rule. Other poets – such as William Carlos Williams, H. D., and Hugh MacDiarmid – established their reputations in the early decades of the twentieth century but continued to write and publish long after the War had ended in 1945. Both Pound and Zukofsky were engaged for much of their careers in writing long poems 'intertwined with a life and a life-time', so that their processes of composition spanned the two halves of the century.[26] Finally, although they each forged important personal and working relationships with first-generation modernists such as Eliot, Pound, and Williams, Lynette Roberts, Charles Olson, and W. S. Graham only began to publish their work in the early 1940s.

There is, then, a variety of routes to late modernism in Anglophone poetry; but one of its common features is a broad margin of overlap with the preceding phase of 'high' modernism. Moreover, while the contention that modernism's 'moment' is accurately situated between the late nineteenth and mid-twentieth centuries might make good literary-historical sense in the case of narrative fiction, it is significantly less persuasive where modernist poetry is concerned.[27] Indeed, Matthew Hart remarks that 'many poets would have disagreed with the proposition that modernism itself came to a close around mid-century', giving Bunting's genealogy of modernism from Yeats and Pound to Zukofsky and David Jones as an example.[28] Anthony Mellors adds further weight to this revisionist account of modernism's literary history in his 2005 study, *Late Modernist Poetics*, where his focus is also upon the post-war period. Arguing that late modernist poems 'remain true to the modernist imperative that eclecticism and difficulty form a hermeneutic basis for cultural renewal', Mellors also notes that they tend to eschew the 'unifying or totalising gestures' that are characteristic of high modernist forms.[29] In this regard, late modernism is both an agent of modernism's immanent self-critique and the extension or persistence of modernist aesthetics into an era marked by anti-modernist retrenchment. Accordingly, Mellors defines late modernism as 'the continuation of modernist writing into the war years and until at least the end of the 1970s', mentioning Bunting's *Briggflatts*, Jones's *The Anathémata*, Williams's *Paterson*, and Zukofsky's *"A"* as key examples.[30] Instead of surveying a wide range of late modernist poetry, however, Mellors focuses more narrowly upon a small group of texts – chiefly Olson's *The Maximus Poems*, and J. H. Prynne's *The White Stones* (1968) – in which the reactionary politics of an older generation (represented by Eliot and Pound) are rejected, but their 'mythic values' are upheld 'against perceived threats to selfhood and community'.[31] Nonetheless, the general characterisation of late modernist poetics that Mellors elaborates obviously have wider applications, providing the foundations for a critical understanding of late modernism as the mode of survival or persistence of modernism after its supposed end. As Hart observes, the narrative of late modernism's relationship to earlier manifestations of modernism is 'a real story of complex continuity', one marked by gaps, inconsistencies, and intermittency, but also by tenacious survivals.[32] Consequently, late modernism remains a significant, if occluded and marginalised, force in poetry throughout much of the second half of the twentieth century.

Placing Late Modernism

Late modernist poetry is a diverse but compact and surprisingly cohesive literary formation. It is predominantly Anglophone in language and transatlantic in geographical distribution, comprising a body of poetic texts informed by modernist aesthetics and published in the three decades from 1945 to 1975. In my usage, late modernist poets are typically those who had begun to publish before the end of the Second World War and continued to do so for a significant period thereafter, bridging two distinct periods of literary history. The majority of these poets were born in the first two decades of the twentieth century, though a few (including MacDiarmid, Jones, and Tolson) are slightly older. Many of them knew each other personally and they often published their work in common networks of little magazines and small presses. In this regard, Basil Bunting is a particularly important mediating figure: a close friend and neighbour of Pound's at Rapallo during the 1930s, he socialised with Williams, drank whisky with MacDiarmid, and kept up a lively literary correspondence with Zukofsky for over three decades. He also championed the work of David Jones and visited Lorine Niedecker in Wisconsin in 1967.[33] Like Gwendolyn Brooks and W. S. Graham after him, he published his work in Chicago's *Poetry*, a pioneering modernist little magazine, which continued to feature late modernist poetry long after the Second World War.[34] After Fulcrum Press published Bunting's magnum opus, *Briggflatts*, in 1966 they went on to bring out volumes by Niedecker and Jones as well as work by a younger generation of modernist poets, including Ed Dorn, Roy Fisher, and Gary Snyder.[35] It has sometimes been suggested that the term 'late modernism' can be extended to the work of these younger poets, who are variously associated with the San Francisco Renaissance (Snyder), Black Mountain College (Dorn), and the British Poetry Renaissance (Fisher).[36] However, for the purposes of this study, I consider these younger poets – most of whom were born in the late 1920s or 1930s – as neo-modernists; and, in my conclusion, I trace some of the lines of influence deriving from late modernist poetry in their work.

Having clarified what I mean by 'late modernism', I want to identify three key features of late modernist poetry. Not all of these features will be present in every late modernist poem, though they often appear in combination. The first is the prevalence of longer forms – sequences, serial poems, mid-length and long poems – even where there is a marked tendency towards the lyrical, as in the cases of Brooks, Bunting, Graham, and Niedecker. There is a strong thread of continuity here with earlier modernist traditions, for Robert Hampson and Will Montgomery observe that 'the non-narrative long poem' has been 'central to modernism from Pound and Eliot through to the present day'.[37] A number of late modernist poems, including Zukofsky's "A", Olson's *The Maximus Poems*, and Reznikoff's *Testimony*, are sprawling, multi-volume epics partly modelled on Pound's *The Cantos*, with its open-ended construction and conflicting impulses towards comprehensiveness and fragmentation. Others, however, more closely resemble what C. D. Blanton calls the 'intensive' epic, a poem that seeks to include the historical totality by techniques of condensation and allusive reference, for which Eliot's *The Waste Land* (1922) provides the key exemplar.[38] This kind of elliptical suggestiveness is a central feature of late modernist poems such as Roberts's *Gods with Stainless Ears*, Tolson's *Libretto for the Republic of Liberia*, and Bunting's *Briggflatts*, all of which also follow the poem-with-endnotes format of *The Waste Land*. Falling somewhere between these two extremes are a cluster of mid-length epic poems, among them Williams's *Paterson*, Jones's *The Anathémata*, and H. D.'s *Helen in Egypt*. Serial poetry differs from these variants on modernist epic by virtue of the extent to which formal fragmentation becomes, paradoxically, an organising principle. According to Rachel Blau DuPlessis, the serial poem offers 'one way of extending a lyric into a long poem but without grandeur, without any necessary continuous narrative nor any *systematizing* philosophical position'.[39] Paratactic and fragmentary in form, the serial poem combines a sense of scope and opportunities for pattern-making with a flexible approach to thematic content, voice, and argument. Late modernist examples include Niedecker's 'Lake Superior', Graham's 'Implements in Their Places', and Oppen's 'Of Being Numerous'. By comparison, poetic sequences such as Brooks's 'The Anniad', Graham's 'Seven Letters', or the Roman poems in Jones's *The Sleeping Lord and Other Poems* (1974) tend to consist of a group of distinct but related lyric poems arranged to imply some kind of narrative order.

The second feature of late modernist poetry I want to highlight is the complexity of the geographical imaginations to which it gives expression, particularly through a concern with the poetics of place. Texts such as Brooks's *In the Mecca*, Bunting's *Briggflatts*, Jones's *The Anathémata*, and Olson's *The Maximus Poems* are each characterised by an intense immersion in the histories and geographies of particular places. At the same time, they reveal a conception of place as open and in process, subject to the changes wrought by time and constituted by their relations with other places at a range of spatial scales from the local to the transnational. By the poetics of place I mean something similar to what Jim Cocola calls 'topopoiesis' or 'place making', the imaginative creation of place in and through language but also referring, ultimately, to 'the world exceeding signification'.[40] Although the poetic imagination plays a crucial role in the process of placemaking, as Cocola conceives it, the places depicted in poems are understood as more than merely imaginary, for poems are also particular engagements with actual places and contribute to the layers of meaning that such places accrue. Indeed, because of their nuanced uses of language and form, poems are able to explore, interrogate, and invent the meanings of places with a level of eloquence and sophistication rarely encountered elsewhere. From the perspective of phenomenology, 'place' is conceived as both primal and essential, the very ground of being and human experience. 'To exist at all,' writes Edward Casey, 'is to have a place – to be *implaced*, however minimally or imperfectly or temporarily'.[41] In epistemological terms, however, place can be defined as 'space invested with meaning in the context of power'.[42] That is, places – in all their stubborn, material particularity – are instances of what Henri Lefebvre calls 'social space', for they are at once productive of and produced by social relations in given historical contexts: '*(Social) space is a (social) product*'.[43] What I am chiefly concerned to examine in this book is the variety of ways in which late modernist poems contribute to the wider social processes whereby particular places are invested with meaning.

One of the striking characteristics of many late modernist poems is the prevalence of geographical terms – 'place', 'space', 'site', 'locality', 'land', 'city', 'map' – in their conceptual vocabularies. 'Place' features prominently in texts by Niedecker and Graham: the epigraph to Niedecker's 'Paean to Place' reads 'And the place / was water'; while the speaker of Graham's 'The Nightfishing' observes that 'this place finds me / And forms itself again'.[44] In both examples, place is depicted as fluid or shifting, but is nonetheless regarded as a formative matrix for subjective experience. Jones's later work is deeply informed by his admiration for James Joyce, whose commitment to 'the particular, to place, site, and locality' he regards as exemplary.[45] Williams prefaces *Paterson* with an affirmation of 'local pride' and also acknowledges the influence of Joyce's *Ulysses* (1922) during the period when he was writing the poem.[46] For Olson, 'space' is a more significant and resonant term than 'place': space is 'the central fact to man born in America, from

Folsom cave to now'; and yet, in *The Maximus Poems*, he is concerned to document 'the geography of it all' through an obsessive record of American experience in one particular place, the city of Gloucester, Massachusetts.[47] Over the course of her career, Brooks's poetry moves from chronicling the everyday lives of African Americans in Chicago's Bronzeville to depicting the 'Warpland' of racial divisions and class conflicts that is post-Civil Rights America.

It is also worth noting that late modernist poetry is often informed by its authors' familiarity with various kinds of geographical thought and knowledge. For instance, Olson met the historical geographer Carl Sauer in 1947 and was profoundly influenced by his research on pre-Columbian and Pleistocene America.[48] Jones and Niedecker respectively studied the geology and geomorphology of Britain and the Lake Superior region in order to write their late poems, *The Anathémata* and 'Lake Superior', thereby placing geographical knowledge at the heart of their creative practice.[49] Jon Hegglund has argued that modernist literature can productively be read 'as geography by other means', and this approach seems especially apposite with regard to late modernist poetry.[50] Modernism's absorption with the problems of time and 'time consciousness' has been overstated, and its geographical dimensions are increasingly widely acknowledged.[51] I argue that the geographical bent of many late modernist poems is particularly significant, bringing historical experience into focus through the texts' multi-faceted engagements with a range of real and imagined places.

The third key feature of late modernist poetry is its tendency to foreground the cultural significance of peripheral and non-metropolitan places. Modernism has been described as essentially 'an art of cities', one that derives its cultural energies and formal experimentalism from the metropolitan, polyglot milieu in which it was formed.[52] Noting the impact of the 'urbanisation of consciousness' on modernist writing, Andrew Thacker contends that 'developments in the material space of the city' during the late nineteenth and early twentieth centuries 'revised how people lived, experienced and thought about the places in which they lived'.[53] Consequently, the geography of literary modernism was frequently urban if not metropolitan, and the image of the city is central to many modernist texts of the 1920s and 1930s, from Eliot's *The Waste Land* to Woolf's *Mrs Dalloway* (1925), John Dos Passos's *Manhattan Transfer* (1925), and Hart Crane's *The Bridge* (1930). Although the city remains significant as both place and idea in some late modernist poems, including Brooks's *In the Mecca*, and Olson's *The Maximus Poems*, it is less often central and rarely metropolitan. In this regard, Williams's *Paterson* set a pattern that several younger poets would follow. Rather than New York or even suburban Rutherford, Williams chose to depict daily life in the provincial, industrial city of Paterson, New Jersey, remarking that: 'New York was too big, too much a congeries of the entire world's facets. I wanted something nearer home, something knowable'.[54] Nearer home, but not home itself; Williams's orientation towards Paterson as a 'knowable' place remains charged with a degree of unfamiliarity. Moreover, as Jameson observes, the 'fundamental spatial provincialism' of *Paterson* is held in tension with its ambitious use of 'the larger framing apparatus of an epic', whereby the city of Paterson is figured as a synecdoche for some ultimately ungraspable totality.[55] 'The province of the poem is the world,' writes Williams in Book III, reconceiving 'provincialism' as an expression of the text's global imaginative scope.[56] This tension is also present in the work of other late modernist poets, where there is an even more emphatic shift away from metropolitan centres and a corresponding imaginative investment in apparently marginal places: Bunting's Northumbria; Jones's Welsh mountain valleys; Niedecker's Black Hawk Island, Wisconsin; Graham's Clydeside and West Penwith. None of these places is conceived as rigidly bounded or self-sufficient, however, and in their texts these poets typically explore the local and particular from perspectives that are informed by mobility, displacement, and contacts with other cultures.

No matter how deep or enduring their attachments, modernist texts are rarely fixed in one place only. Rather, they are typically formed within, and responsive to multiple, overlapping spatial frames: local, regional, national, and international. 'Modernism looks quite different depending on where one locates oneself and when,' observes David Harvey, noting that 'the particularities of place' provide a crucial index to 'the diversity of the modernist effort'.[57] However, it is not just that modernism is geographically diverse when considered as a whole, but also that spatial complexity is often intrinsic to the very forms and styles of individual modernist texts. This is what Thacker means when he remarks upon the 'polytopic character of modernist writing', whereby radically different spaces and geographical scales are brought into relation with one another, creating distinctive effects of disorientation in the experience of the reader. Such effects call for more supple and geographically-attentive modes of reading, and the development of a critical practice that locates modernist texts 'within the movements between and across multiple sorts of space'.[58] Similarly, Rebecca Walsh argues that modernist poetry from Walt Whitman to H. D. exhibits a distinctively '*anachoristic* attitude', developing paratactic formal strategies 'that "mix up" conventionally distant and culturally, nationally, or racially different locales on the globe'.⁵⁹ In this way, modernist poets produce texts that either complicate or imaginatively reconfigure existing geopolitical relations and alignments. Both of these critical accounts of the geography of literary modernism underline the relational character of place as it is conceived in such texts. If, as Doreen Massey contends, space is the product of social relations (or disconnections) – 'a simultaneity of stories so far' – then places are 'collections of those stories, articulations within wider power-geometries of space'.⁶⁰ A 'global sense of place' therefore entails grasping place not as a bounded or static entity but in terms of its relations with what lies beyond it, as 'a particular constellation of social relations, meeting and weaving together at a particular locus'.⁶¹ This understanding of place as porous and dynamic, constituted by its relations with other places and always linked to wider spatial contexts is an important element in the geographical imaginations of late modernist poems, even when the same poems also articulate a more nostalgic view of place as a focus for authentic belonging.

But why is there such a preoccupation with place – and with particular places – in late modernist poetry? One possible answer to this question concerns the far-reaching social, political, and economic changes occurring during the post-war period, which redrew existing geopolitical relationships and seemed to threaten the distinctiveness of places as meaningful environments for human lives. The most important of these historical shifts include: the establishment of US hegemony and the spread of American-style consumer capitalism; a wave of national liberation movements resulting in a global process of decolonisation; the looming threat of nuclear annihilation under Cold War conditions; and the creation of a range of transnational organisations (from global corporations to the United Nations and the World Bank) capable of bypassing the sovereignty of nation-states.⁶² Consequently, Giovanni Arrighi argues that during the post-war decades the United States oversaw the emergence of a new world system in which 'non-territorialised spaces-of-flows' began increasingly to displace 'the conventional spaces-of-places' associated with nation-states and territorial modes of belonging.⁶³ On the one hand, as Tim Cresswell observes, this increased sense of mobility and global flows (of people, commodities, and information) has 'led some to perceive an accelerating erosion of place' whereby the world has grown more homogeneous. On the other, local distinctiveness remains an important feature of contemporary experience in even the most cosmopolitan of societies, suggesting 'the continuing salience of place, even in a mobile world'.⁶⁴ In a world system founded upon spaces-of-flows, the spatial relations within and through which places are constituted have become immeasurably more complex, but this does not mean that places as such have disappeared. Jahan Ramazani contends that modernist poetry is keenly attuned to this complex situation, for its geographical imaginations are both 'responsive to local or national conditions' and 'inseparable from modernity's intensified global flows'.⁶⁵ I argue that this is particularly true of those late modernist poems written and published in the three decades after the end of the Second World War. Late modernist poetry can be understood both as an imaginative response to the perceived eclipse of place in human experience during the second half of the twentieth century, and as a resistant or nostalgic affirmation of its continuing significance in a reconfigured world system predicated upon spaces-of-flows.

Late Modernism and Literary Geography

Literary history and literary geography can and should mutually inform one another. To that end, Thacker argues persuasively for a more detailed 'spatial history of modernism', one that would give 'an account of the precise historical fashion in which particular spaces and places were conceptualised and represented'.⁶⁶ The burden of my argument in this book is to demonstrate the (hitherto under-appreciated) significance of late modernist poetry for such a spatial history of modernism. In doing so, I draw extensively upon the critical resources of literary geography, an interdisciplinary field of research at the interface between human geography and literary studies.⁶⁷ The origins of literary geography are roughly contemporaneous with those of Anglophone modernism: the term was coined in 1904 by the novelist and journalist William Sharp (aka Fiona Macleod), and subsequently used by Virginia Woolf in a 1905 review of two books on Thackeray and Dickens, respectively.⁶⁸ Human geographers have long been interested in what literature can teach them about the relationships between humans and the non-human environment; and a similarly well-established strand of literary criticism studies the role of place, region, and landscape in literary texts.⁶⁹ However, these two bodies of scholarship tended to develop in parallel and remain largely within their disciplinary boundaries until the 1990s, when the effects of the spatial turn in the humanities and the corresponding cultural turn in the social sciences encouraged new interdisciplinary dialogues.⁷⁰ Nonetheless, Sheila Hones observes that, as a scholarly field, literary geography remains a somewhat 'unruly, multicentered, and multinetworked academic space-time', notable for the variety of ways in which it is conceived and practised rather than any coherent, shared methodology.⁷¹

For some critics, literary geography means generating maps from quantitative data in order to correlate genre with geography or to trace the lineaments of a particular narrative trajectory. This is the approach pioneered by Franco Moretti, whose central concern is to illustrate 'the *ortgebunden*, place-bound nature of literary forms' using visual diagrams – principally maps.[72] Moretti's method is effective in revealing large-scale spatial structures and relations in literary texts, but one of its major drawbacks is its inability to respond to nuance and ambiguity at the level of language and style.[73] For other critics, such matters are crucial, so that literary geography examines the complex relationships between material and metaphorical spaces, actual and imagined geographies. In his outline for a critical literary geography, Thacker conceives of such relationships dialectically, arguing that: 'We should reconnect the representational spaces in literary texts not only to the material spaces they depict, but also reverse the movement, and understand how social spaces dialogically help fashion the literary *forms* of texts.'[74] This methodological principle seems particularly apposite for any study of the geographies of literary modernism. Consequently, in the main chapters of this book I examine both how late modernist poems create distinctive representations of specific places and how the material spaces in which the poems were written shape and condition their forms. I also concur with Thacker in regarding literary geography as a 'process of reading and interpreting literary texts by reference to geographical concepts'.[75] For my purposes here, literary geography is a geographically informed mode of literary criticism, rather than 'the study of literature by geographers'.[76]

It is worth noting, however, that Thacker has been justly criticised by Hones for largely ignoring the work of human and cultural geographers, so that his version of literary geography is less geographically informed than it ought to be.[77] In turn, Hones's version of literary geography, in which she conceives of the literary text as a 'spatial event', 'something which happens at the intersection of agents and situations scattered across time and space', is firmly situated within a tradition of geographical analysis, however interdisciplinary.[78] Hones is concerned to examine the full range of contexts and actors that co-create any given text as 'an always emerging geographical event', from its composition and publication to its dissemination and reception by readers, with particular attention to where and when the processes of literary production and interpretation play out.[79] However, she explicitly regards literary texts chiefly as 'case studies' through which to broach problems of 'theory and method in cultural geography'.[80] By contrast, although I share Hones's sense of the significance of geographies of literary production, my primary concern is with the interpretation and analysis of literary texts using concepts and ideas adapted from cultural geography (and elsewhere). Moreover, I follow Adorno in regarding 'contemplative immersion' as necessary for any immanent critique of artworks, including late modernist poems, which seeks to grasp meaning in terms of 'the enactment of antagonisms that each work necessarily has in itself'.[81] For instance, the ways in which contradictory experiences of belonging and alienation, settlement and mobility, or boundedness and porosity are interwoven, but never wholly resolved in poetic figurations of place.

Another widely-influential approach is Bertrand Westphal's geocriticism, a 'geocentered' method of critical reading in which place is given priority instead of particular authors or texts.[82] Rather than simply analysing Williams's poetic depictions of the city, the mountain, and the river in *Paterson*, for instance, a geocentered reading would examine the representation of Paterson, New Jersey in as wide a range of textual depictions as possible, by various authors, from different periods, and across a range of genres. The methodology of geocriticism is fundamentally comparative, therefore, and seeks to apprehend the commonalities and differences between multiple literary figurations as facets of an open-ended and intrinsically heterogeneous textual assemblage. Westphal calls this mode of analysis 'multifocalization', contrasting its potential for articulating 'a network of perspective' with the more restricted parameters of author-centred studies.[83] Suggestive as it is, Westphal's methodology is not wholly suitable for a study such as this, which focuses upon a particular literary-historical phenomenon in which the relationships of poets to places are typically singular rather than shared. A key weakness of geocriticism is its inability to recognise that a single author, or even an individual text may disclose multiple, contradictory, densely layered representations of a given place. This is precisely what I try to demonstrate in the author-focused chapters that make up the core of this book. Moreover, as Robert Tally observes, Westphal's geocentric approach 'fails to encompass the full range of spatial representations' in literary texts, which often effect disorienting fusions of the 'real', the 'fictional', and the 'fantastic'.[84]

One of the central ideas informing this study of late modernist poetry is that literary texts are not simply objects but also subjects of geographical knowledge, or what John Kirtland Wright calls 'geosophy'. As Tim Cresswell explains, Wright argued that geographers could benefit from studying the geographical knowledge accrued and developed by ordinary people: 'He suggested that geographers need to know how people know their world. He argued for an exploration of their geographical imaginations'.[85] Literary texts are particularly rich sources of such geographical knowledge, as geographers have long recognised; and my argument in this book is that the geographical imaginations that are given expression in late modernist poetry repay particularly close attention. In part, this is because modernist texts often synthesise various kinds of academic and non-academic discourses in their attempts to know the world. Jessica Berman argues that the central concerns of geographers such as Ellen Churchill Semple, Harold Mackinder, and Paul Vidal de la Blanche – with location, mapping, centre and periphery, race and identity – also occur in many works of high modernist fiction.[86] I argue that this geographical bent is even more intense and explicit in the work of late modernist poets, including Jones, Niedecker, and Olson, in the second half of the twentieth century. Marc Brosseau suggests that literary critics and geographers alike should 'consider more closely how the literary text may constitute a "geographer" in its own right as it generates norms, particular models of readability, that produce a particular type of geography'.[87] Late modernist poetry not only discloses its own particular geographical imaginations but also often engages reflexively with geographical terms and concepts as part of its ongoing inquiry into how the world might be known. In this sense, many late modernist poems can usefully be considered 'geographers' in their own right.

There is a case for undertaking further critical work on the late works of first-generation modernist poets, including Williams's *Paterson*, H. D.'s *Helen in Egypt*, and the later volumes of Pound's *The Cantos*, as a means of tracing the tenacious survival of modernist aesthetics in the post-war period. However, my focus in this book is upon a group of lesser-known, second-generation modernists and their often neglected or under-appreciated texts. In the chapters that follow, I develop detailed literary-geographical readings of the work of six late modernist poets, three from Britain – David Jones (1895–1974), Basil Bunting (1900–1985), and W. S. Graham (1918–1986) – and three from the United States of America – Lorine Niedecker (1903–1970), Charles Olson (1910–1970), and Gwendolyn Brooks (1917–2000). For the most part, my focus is upon their major late works, often published near the end of their careers or posthumously, between 1945 and 1975. Each of these poets has received critical attention individually – to a greater or lesser extent – but they have rarely, if ever, been considered together in a comparative perspective that is transatlantic in scope. This 'transatlantic' frame is integral to the structure of the book and the selection of the poets and poems for discussion; though it is also an important element of the geographical contexts in which the latter have their being. For instance, the itinerant Bunting spent most of 1938 and 1939 in New York and Los Angeles, before returning to England to enlist following the declaration of war with Nazi Germany. He also published his second collection, *Poems 1950*, with Cleaners Press, which was run by a disciple of Pound's, Dallam Flynn, from Galveston, Texas.[88] Niedecker, who received a copy of Bunting's *Poems 1950* as a Christmas gift from Zukofsky, rarely travelled beyond Wisconsin, though her poems circulated much further afield.[89] In 1968, her pivotal collection *North Central* was published by Stuart Montgomery's London-based Fulcrum Press, which released Bunting's *Collected Poems* in the same year and brought out Niedecker's *Life by Water: Collected Poems* in 1969.[90] Graham lived in New York for nine months in 1947–8, while Olson made an extended visit to England and Germany in 1966–7.[91] Brooks also crossed the Atlantic in 1971 to visit Tanzania and Kenya, and again in 1974 to travel in Ghana, experiences that deepened the Afrocentric turn that characterises her later poetry.[92] Although by comparison Jones's life-story is relatively sedentary, at least following his military service during the First World War, sea voyages – particularly in the Mediterranean and North Atlantic – are a key feature of his poetics of place, as they are also for Olson, Bunting, and Graham.

In Chapter 1, I argue that Jones's profound historical sense is grounded in and given expression by a geographical imagination that foregrounds the concepts of place, site, and locality. However, his poetry's emphasis upon cultural integrity and the bounded character of authentic places is frequently in conflict with their fragmentary and heterogeneous forms. Chapter 2 contends that Bunting's *Briggflatts* has too often been misread as a poem that is elementally 'rooted' in the poet's home region of Northumbria, for it is also profoundly concerned with experiences of displacement and transience, foregrounding vagrancy as a characteristically modern mode of being-in-the-world. Born in Greenock, Scotland, W. S. Graham spent most of his life at the other end of Britain, in Southwest Cornwall. In Chapter 3, I argue that this displacement crucially shapes his poetry, which moves imaginatively between different places, collapsing spatial and temporal distances as well as ontological distinctions in the condensed geographies of language and the printed page. Similarly, Chapter 4 shows that the defining existential condition for Niedecker's poetics of place is the fact that she lived by water, for edges are paradoxically central to her poems, which return obsessively to the meeting places between terrestrial and aquatic worlds. The interface between land and sea is a crucial place in Olson's epic, *The Maximus Poems*, which focuses upon the port city of Gloucester, Massachusetts but also spans the Atlantic Ocean across several millennia of human history. In Chapter 5, I argue that cartography plays a central imaginative role in Olson's text, which can itself be read as an eccentric world map of westward migrations. The migration of African Americans to northern cities during the early twentieth century, along with new forms of racialised spatial segregation within those cities, are the fundamental geographical forces that converge in Brooks's Bronzeville poems, which are the focus of Chapter 6. Although it is tightly circumscribed by racial and class divides, Brooks depicts Bronzeville as a place-in-process where the throwntogetherness of everyday urban experience is a source of cultural vitality as well as tension. Finally, the conclusion considers the lasting influence of late modernist poets and texts upon a younger generation of neo-modernist writers from Britain, the United States, and the Caribbean, most of whom began to publish during the 1960s and 1970s.

Chapter 1

David Jones: The Sites of History

History and geography, place and memory, territory and myth are intricately intermeshed in the poetry of David Jones. Jones's distinctive historical sense – his perception 'not only of the pastness of the past, but of its presence' – is grounded in and given expression by a geographical imagination in which the concepts of place, site, and locality are of central importance.[1] He explicitly characterises the poet's role as that of a 'rememberer' whose business is 'to keep open the lines of communication' with the past, and describes poetry itself as an act of 'recalling' or 'anamnesis'.[2] This act of anamnesis by which history is both recalled and represented is predicated upon an engagement with the material and symbolic qualities of particular places. Hence Jones's conception of the poet as a kind of archaeologist and bricoleur, whose synthesising creative imagination draws upon the cultural materials that 'happen to be lying about the place or site or lying within the orbit of [his or her] "tradition"'.[3] The particular places and cultural traditions with which Jones's poetry is most deeply concerned are those of Britain, and especially Wales; although his aesthetic sensibility is broadly congruent with that of European modernism. Neil Corcoran argues persuasively that Jones's major literary achievement derives from his success in 'localising, or domesticating, in a specifically British context, a modernist sense of the relation between a poet and his "tribal" history'.[4] However, it is important to note that his imagination is also temporally and spatially expansive, taking in the whole of Western Europe from the time of the Roman Empire to the middle of the twentieth century, and ranging from the Eastern Mediterranean to the continent's North Atlantic archipelago. Indeed, Jones's most ambitious long poem, *The Anathémata*, reaches far back into prehistory and geological time in its exploration of the fundamental links between art and religion, culture and place.

Although he claimed to be a poor scholar, Jones's formidably erudite and allusive long poems are informed by wide-ranging and eclectic research, including a keen amateur interest in the disciplines of geography, oceanography, and geology.[5] His library, now held at the National Library of Wales, includes volumes such as John Gorton's *Topographical Dictionary of Great Britain and Ireland* (1833), Halford Mackinder's *Britain and the British Seas* (1902), L. Dudley Stamp's *The World: A General Geography* (1940), and A. E. Trueman's *Geology and Scenery in England and Wales* (1961), among many others.[6] Jones owned eighteen maps (mostly of Wales and England), five atlases (of Britain, Palestine, and the classical world), and a sea-chart showing the Bristol Channel and Lundy Island. Moreover, he annotated his Ordnance Survey *Map of South Wales showing the distribution of long barrows and megaliths* (1936) to delineate the course taken by the hunt for the giant boar, Twrch Trwyth, in the medieval Welsh tale 'Culhwch and Olwen', which is a key inter-text for his poem, 'The Hunt'.[7] This instance of practical 'literary cartography' underlines a more fundamental point about the character of Jones's geographical imagination.[8] His late modernist poetics of place is underpinned by a longstanding interest in and knowledge of geographical terms and concepts; while the topographical and toponymic exactitude that distinguishes many of his texts derives from his habitual use of maps, charts, and atlases.

Jones was born in Brockley, Kent, in 1895 and spent most of his long life in various London boroughs and suburbs – Brockley, Chelsea, Kensington, and Harrow – with only occasional periods outside of the city. The most notable of these is the three years that he served as a private in the Royal Welch Fusiliers in France, Belgium, and Ireland during the First World War.[9] However, from an early age Jones strongly identified with his father's patria, Wales, and developed a life-long interest in Welsh culture and the Welsh language. 'From about the age of six,' he writes in an autobiographical essay, 'I felt I belonged to my father's people and their land, though brought up in an entirely English atmosphere'.[10] This identification was profound and life-long, but also willed and therefore precarious. The periods that Jones spent living in Wales, at Capel-y-ffin in the Black Mountains and on Caldey Island off the Pembrokeshire coast, from 1924–1927, were arguably crucial for his career, marking 'a new beginning' both personally and artistically.[11] Nonetheless, Jones was also painfully aware of his own cultural, linguistic, and geographical alienation from his imaginative homeland for much of his writing life, describing himself as 'an English monoglot' and 'a Londoner' – at best, a writer 'of Welsh affinity'.[12] There is, then, in Jones's work, a pervasive contradiction between his intense imaginative engagement with Wales and sense of irremediable alienation from the land, people, and culture with which he identifies.

Another major contradiction arises from the relationship between form and content in Jones's poetry, which is experimental and linguistically innovative but articulates a politically conservative world-view. Like T. S. Eliot, Ezra Pound, and W. B. Yeats, Jones might be regarded as an 'anti-modern' modernist, one who values tradition, idealises rural communities, and regards the 'megalopolitan technocracy' of the modern age as a baleful agent of social and cultural decline.[13] In this respect, Jones shares Eliot's bleak perception of contemporary history as an 'immense panorama of futility and anarchy'.[14] His critique of modernity is frequently undertaken via an extended historical analogy with the dominating force of the Roman Empire in the Celtic world. Jones's attitude towards the Roman heritage of Britain is deeply ambivalent, though, in part because from 1921 he was a practising Catholic and in part because he regards Roman influence on British culture as formative as well as destructive.[15] Commenting on the tension between his 'tradition-oriented ideological convictions' and 'experimental, even *avant-garde*, poetic practice', Elizabeth Ward argues that Jones's imagination is characteristically 'mythopoeic', gravitating towards 'pre-existing archetypal patterns' that are inherently dualistic in nature.[16] However, Ward exaggerates the extent to which such dualities harden into static oppositions in Jones's work. Rather, Jones's poetry bears out Theodor Adorno's contention that every artwork is 'a force field, a dynamic configuration of its elements', which are constellated in relations of tension or contradiction with one another.[17] Consequently, it is crucial to attend not just to the ways in which Jones's poems establish symbolic oppositions between Romans and Celts, modernity and tradition, metropolis and locality, and so on, but also to the ways in which their formal and linguistic complexities render such dichotomies dynamic or unstable.

Across Jones's varied oeuvre as a poet, several places and times recur more or less frequently and are invested with particular symbolic significance. Firstly, the scarified landscapes and battlefields of Northern France and Belgium during the First World War, particularly the uncanny 'stranger-world' depicted in *In Parenthesis* (1937), widely regarded as the most important modernist depiction of the war.[18] Secondly, Palestine during the time of Christ's Passion, which is not only central to the elaborate symbolism of *The Anathémata* but takes on a more detailed material presence in the Roman poems of *The Sleeping Lord* (1974), especially 'The Fatigue'. Thirdly, the Roman Empire during the period of its incipient decline, especially the North-western peripheries of the Roman sphere of influence, where Romans, Gauls, and Celts come into contact – as, for instance, in the sinister 'Teutoburg Wood' of 'The Dream of Private Clitus' or, more positively, the 'differentiated sites' of 'The Tutelar of the Place'.[19] And finally, the island of Britain both during and after its Roman occupation, with particular emphasis upon the cultural importance of Wales within the wider British context, and on London's civic and maritime histories, which take the fore in the 'Redriff' and 'Lady of the Pool' sections of *The Anathémata*.

Although each of these spatio-temporal fields is distinct and assumes a different level of significance in particular poems, the tendency is for them to overlap or intersect, thereby creating a shifting web of historical and geographical connections. In this regard, Jones's poetry exemplifies what Andrew Thacker calls the 'polytopic quality of modernist writing', its propensity to bring different places, spaces, and geographical scales into relation with one another.[20] Remarking on Jones's 'typological mode of perception', Kathleen Henderson Staudt observes that his texts typically discover or posit 'hidden correspondences among myths, rituals, and actual events in history'.[21] I would argue that such hidden correspondences are also a significant feature of Jones's geographical imagination. For instance, the allusions that Jones makes throughout *In Parenthesis* to Aneurin's *Y Gododdin* not only create historical analogies between medieval and modern warfare. They also produce and sustain a geographical parallel between the entrenchments of Northern France and the battlefield at Catraeth (Catterick, North Yorkshire) where the proto-Welsh Gododdin were defeated by the Angles of Deira.[22] More complex still are the 'Mabinog's Liturgy' and 'Sherthursdaye and Venus Day' sections of *The Anathémata*, which respectively retell the life of Christ in the Welsh forms of mabinogi and Boast, and depict Christ's Passion by way of a toponymically dense panorama of Welsh rivers and mountains: 'to make virid Gwenfrewi's glen, Dyfrdwy / to crystal his ferned Hodni dell'.[23] Notice that in both of these examples, Jones's historical analogies and geographical correspondences direct the reader's attention to the matter of Britain, which is the affective centre of his poetics of place.

Waste Lands

Perhaps the most striking confluence of Jones's historical sense with his geographical imagination occurs in his recurrent use of the spatial trope of the waste land, which he partly adapts from T. S. Eliot. However, two further literary sources are crucial to Jones's distinctive versions of the waste land trope: Thomas Malory's account of the desolation of King Pellam's land in *Le Morte D'Arthur* (1485); and 'Culhwch and Olwen', one of the Welsh Arthurian tales collected in *The Mabinogion*, which depicts the destruction caused by the boar Twrch Trwyth in Ireland and Britain. In his preface to *In Parenthesis*, Jones alludes directly to Malory in order to characterise the battlefields of the First World War as 'the Waste Land', remarking that 'that landscape spoke "with a grimly voice"'.[24] Moreover, the central section of Jones's text is titled 'King Pellam's Launde' and in the formal Boast that is its centre-piece, Dai Greatcoat affirms: 'I was the spear in Balin's hand / that made waste King Pellam's land'.[25] Dai here assumes the role of the aggressor, but he is a victim too, and his performative role in the context of the Boast is that of the archetypal soldier, in all times and places.[26] In fact, Jones more commonly depicts his Welsh and cockney soldiers of the Western front as suffering inhabitants of a strange 'wilderness' they have not willed into being, but in which they are 'pent like rodents all the day long; appointed scape-beasts come to the waste-lands'.[27] The connotations of sacrificial ritual here, combined with a network of literary and mythic allusions, indicate that Jones's use of the spatial trope of the waste land is not simply resonant in the context of modern mechanised warfare, but also a crucial means by which to articulate his broader historical vision of modernity.

Jones's conception of history is at once pessimistic, cyclical, and – in some of its expressions – apocalyptic. In Jones's view, the modern age has enacted a disastrous 'break' with 'past shapes of society' and is experienced as a thoroughgoing 'metamorphosis' in 'the liaisons with our past'.[28] In particular, modernity is characterised by a technological and bureaucratic prioritisation of the 'utile' over the 'gratuitous', and a corresponding waning in the potency of symbolic forms. Accordingly, the signmaking capacities that Jones regards as a defining existential trait of humankind are threatened, and with them all human culture of any value. In modern life, 'Technological Man' is alienated from his 'creaturely' nature and from 'the thought-modes of Man-the-Artist'.[29] Jones's views on history and modernity were strongly influenced by the thought of Oswald Spengler, whose *The Decline of the West* (1926–1928) he read and annotated in 1941–1942. From Spengler and Christopher Dawson, Jones derived a cyclical or spiral conception of history where the vitality of local cultures is gradually displaced by metropolitan civilisation, which in turn grows decadent and enters a phase of decline.[30] Although he rejected Spengler's positivistic determinism and racist overtones – 'his cheapness and brutality and inhumanity' – Jones echoes Spengler's negative characterisation of modernity as a period of dissolution and decay.[31] For instance, in his preface to *The Anathémata* he claims to be writing 'in a late and complex phase of a phenomenally complex civilization'.[32] And in his essay, 'The Myth of Arthur', Jones adopts an explicitly

Spenglerian vocabulary to lament the abandonment of 'long-standing cultural ways of life', remarking:

> We do not know what songs may yet be possible or what shape our myth will take, but it looks as though the waste land before us is extensive; and it is certain that in our anabasis across it we shall have reason to keep in mind the tradition of our origins in both matter and spirit.[33]

The allusions in this passage are not only to Spengler, but also Malory, Eliot, and Saint-John Perse, whose *Anabasis* was translated into English by Eliot in 1930 and influenced Jones deeply.[34] The more important points to make here are two-fold: firstly, that the spatial trope of the waste land is here explicitly linked to Jones's historical vision of modernity; and secondly, that Jones retains a degree of optimism, in spite of his pessimistic historical diagnosis, that both 'songs' and 'myths' will remain possible for inhabitants of the waste land, even if their forms of expression remain unpredictable.

Critics of Jones's work have noted the significance of the waste land trope to his depiction of modern war in *In Parenthesis*. For instance, Thomas Dilworth argues that it is a key feature of the poet's 'secular mythos', symbolising 'the degradation of human life' in both social and personal terms.[35] What is less widely recognised, however, is the extent to which this trope recurs in Jones's later work, often in new contexts and with different shades of meaning. The opening pages of *The Anathémata* provide a good illustration, focusing on the figure of a priest celebrating Mass, which for Jones is the most potent of humankind's signmaking rituals, in a spatio-temporal situation that threatens both religion and art with insignificance:

> The cult-man stands alone in Pellam's land: more precariously than he knows he guards the *signa*: [. . .] the tokens, the matrices, the institutes, the ancilia, the fertile ashes – the palladic fore-shadowings: the things come down from heaven together with the kept memorials, the things lifted up and the venerated trinkets.[36]

The allusion to Malory provides a strand of intertextual continuity with *In Parenthesis*, but here the representative inhabitant of the waste land is not the figure of the soldier but that of the artist-priest, who 'guards the *signa*' and struggles to transmute the 'dead forms' of modern civilisation into 'anathemata': 'the profane things that somehow are redeemed'.[37] As Staudt observes, *The Anathémata* is a characteristically self-reflexive modernist text that 'repeatedly displays itself as material and sign shaped by the history of humanity as a sign-making species'.[38] Indeed, through the ambiguous figure of the 'cult-man' – who is both artist and priest – in the waste land, Jones's poem dramatises at its outset its own conditions of possibility, placing the question of the poem's origins at the beginning of its ambitious historico-geographical enquiry into origins and beginnings. Moreover, where Spengler's philosophy of history underscores the inevitable subordination of art to 'technics', *The Anathémata* both acknowledges present decline – 'the stream is very low' – and affirms the continuing relevance and durability of art: 'This man, so late in time, curiously surviving'.[39]

Different again is the version of the waste land trope that figures in one of Jones's last poems, 'The Sleeping Lord', which depicts King Arthur as a sleeping giant whose mutilated body is identified with the polluted and despoiled landscapes of industrial South Wales. Towards the end of the poem, Jones incorporates his own version of the hunt for Twrch Trwyth by Arthur and a composite war-band drawn from across Britain, Ireland, and France, freely adapting the original account in 'Culhwch and Olwen'. What is striking about Jones's version, however, is the extent to which it emphasises the damage done by the giant boar, not just to human dwellings but also to the natural ecosystems of Wales, particularly its forests and woodlands:

> Not by long-hafted whetted steel axe-blades
> > are these fallen
> that graced the high slope
> > that green-filigreed
> the green hollow
> > but by the riving tusks
> of the great hog
> > are they felled.
> It is the Boar Trwyth
> > that has pierced through
> the stout-fibred living wood
> > that bears the sacral bough of gold.
> > It is the hog that has ravaged the fair *onnen* and the hornbeam and the Queen of the Woods.[40]

Jones's passing allusion to J. G. Frazer's *The Golden Bough* (1922) in these lines forges a link between the waste land trope and ancient fertility rites that inevitably recalls Eliot's *The Waste Land*. However, the fate of the Queen of the Woods also sets up echoes with the final section of *In Parenthesis*, where a maternal nature goddess cuts 'bright boughs of various flowering' for the dead soldiers of Mametz Wood and modern chemical weapons are described as having 'more riving power than ever Twrch Trwyth'.[41] Where *In Parenthesis* aligns the allegorical destructive force of Twrch Trwyth with mechanised warfare, 'The Sleeping Lord' depicts the 'hog-wasted *blaendir*' of South Wales as a waste land created by modern industrial production and its technologies.[42] As Jones knew, widespread deforestation was a consequence of the burgeoning iron and lead industries in South Wales, which relied on charcoal for smelting, before switching to coal in the late eighteenth century.[43] What is also distinctive about 'The Sleeping Lord' is the way in which it employs the waste land trope in the context of an incipient environmental politics. Dilworth exaggerates when he claims that Jones's text is 'the first ecological poem and the greatest of the twentieth century'.[44] Nonetheless, it is certainly possible to discern in 'The Sleeping Lord' a profound imaginative response to the effects of human destructiveness upon the natural world as well as a lyrically precise description of the biodiversity that has been lost. To the extent that it both dramatises the consequences of ecological damage and makes the non-human world a significant presence, Jones's poem exhibits several of the key features that Lawrence Buell ascribes to the 'environmentally oriented work'.[45]

The Matter of Britain

If, as I have claimed, the matter of Britain is the affective centre of Jones's poetics of place, then it is important to recognise that Jones's conception of 'Britain' is deeply idiosyncratic. There are four key features that are worth foregrounding. Firstly, Jones tends to regard Britain as embodying a pre-modern cultural unity that might be recovered by the artist and opposed to the mortifying displacements of modernity. Hence his preoccupation with the half-forgotten 'heritage' of Britain, which is preserved in 'the actual land itself, its sites and rooted communities'; and his affirmation that 'the unity of the island' remains to be discovered on its 'Celtic fringe'.[46] In this way, Jones characteristically translates history into geography, regarding the peripheral spaces of the island of Britain (particularly Wales) as repositories of the cultural forms of the past. Secondly, despite this concern to recover a lost cultural unity, Jones also conceives of British culture as inherently diverse and heterogeneous, a mixed inheritance that is at once multi-lingual and multi-ethnic in character. Tracing the word 'Britain' back to its etymological roots in the Old Welsh '*Priten*', which he glosses as 'speckled, mottled, variegated', he goes on to remark: 'Not only is our land a most mottled, dappled, pied, partied and brindled land, but so is our character,' and 'so also in a curious way is our art'.[47] There is a profound and productive tension in Jones's conception of Britain between its projection as a cultural unity and its constitution by 'things of very mixed derivation'.[48]

Jones's Britain is radically eccentric in the sense that it displaces the dominating centrality of England within the wider matrix of Britishness in favour of Wales and Welsh culture, thereby imaginatively reconfiguring existing relations between core and periphery. Corcoran argues that Jones's pervasive use of Welsh words and forms in his poetry, as well as his extensive allusions to Welsh history, mythology, and literature lend his work an 'alienating otherness' that makes the reader 'painfully aware of the cultural, political and linguistic diversity' that the concept and polity of Britain comprehends.[49] Finally, Jones tends to focus upon the geographical fact of Britain's insularity, rather than the political unions upon which the British state is founded, as the source of its cultural wholeness and integrity. In the preface to *In Parenthesis*, he describes the mixed group of Londoners and Welshmen among whom he served during the First World War as representatives of 'the genuine tradition of the Island of Britain'.[50] Subsequently, he characterises *The Anathémata* as a 'necessarily insular' poem because it is the creation of 'a person whose perceptions are totally conditioned and limited by and dependent upon his being indigenous to this island'.[51] Simplifying a little, we might say that Jones's emphasis on the insular character of Britain reinforces his tendency to posit an occluded cultural unity, whereas his prioritisation of Wales within the British context is of a piece with his affirmation of cultural diversity and internal difference.

Jones's poetic figurations of the matter of Britain are informed by a dialectic of identity and otherness that manifests itself both at the level of content and in the language and forms of his texts. Up to a point, Jones's poetry participates in the wider 'anthropological turn' that Jed Esty identifies in the work of Anglophone modernists during the 1930s and 1940s whereby faith in the radical autonomy of art is replaced by new interest in and enthusiasm for 'national culture'.[52] Esty characterises this anthropological concern for national culture and native customs on the part of modernist writers as a response to the waning of the British Empire and a related 'crisis of European cosmopolitanism', the combined effects of which stimulated a process of 'national retrenchment' and enabled an imaginative transformation of 'insular culture'.[53] Jones's poetry, with its profound interest in the culture, folk customs, and native myths of the island of Britain, might be regarded as a particularly intense and complex expression of the anthropological turn in late modernism that Esty describes – though Esty fails to mention Jones's work in his study. Moreover, Jones's stress on the significance for Welsh culture of 'the whole tie-up of ancient duration with site and locality' has obvious affinities with the process of 'demetropolitanization', whereby 'place' is affirmed as 'a sign of cultural unity' that Esty sees at work in texts such as T. S. Eliot's *Four Quartets* (1943) and Virginia Woolf's *Between the Acts* (1941).[54] But here a major difference also emerges, for while Jones affirms the centrality of Wales to the cultural tradition of Britain as he conceives it, Esty is almost exclusively concerned with England and English national culture in late modernist writing. Consequently, Esty's critical paradigm cannot fully account either for the deliberate eccentricity of Jones's preoccupation with the matter of Britain, nor for the fundamental tension between unity and diversity, identity and difference that is integral to the meaning of 'Britain' in his texts.

Of course, as Jones himself was painfully aware, by birth and by virtue of the language in which he writes, he is an English rather than a Welsh writer. Indeed, René Hague dismisses Jones's 'attempts to Cambrianize his work' as superficial and unconvincing, arguing that he is best understood and evaluated within the context of 'the English tradition'.[55] However, this is to radically underestimate the extent to which not only the content of Jones's texts, but also their distinctive forms and modes of linguistic expression, are fundamentally bound up with the culture and history of Wales. Jones consistently affirms that the forms and materials used by the poet derive from 'the particular cultural complex' to which he or she belongs, and the poet's art entails 'the embodiment and expression of the mythus and deposits comprising that cultural complex'.[56] Moreover, although he acknowledges that readers may find his Welsh historical and cultural references obscure, he is explicit in regarding Wales as the repository of 'the more venerable culture in that hotch-potch which is ourselves'.[57] The 'hotch-potch' that is British culture finds its formal correlative in the densely macaronic character of Jones's language, in which a weft of Welsh and Latin words or phrases, with the addition of some French, German, and Greek terms, is interwoven with a warp of supple English that is by turns formal and colloquial, descriptive and figurative. Corcoran observes that the 'densely allusive language' of Jones's poetry 'is a constant, living reminder, in the very texture of the work, of the metamorphoses of our linguistic inheritance'.[58]

Consider, for example, the following passage from the 'Angle-Land' section of *The Anathemata* in which an anchorite ('ancra-man') in the fenlands of Lincolnshire hears the speech of native Britons as a Babel of unfamiliar and incomprehensible tongues:

Past where the ancra-man, deeping his holy rule
in the fiendish marsh
      at the *Geisterstunde*
     on *Calangaeaf* night
heard the bogle-*baragouinage*.
       Crowland-*diawliaidd*

> *Waelisc*-man lingo speaking?
>   or Britto-Romani gone *diaboli*?
> or Romanity gone *Waelisc*?[59]

In these lines, Jones both draws upon and thematises the mixed linguistic inheritance of Britain, its bewildering 'complex' of different cultural forms of expression and perception: Welsh (*'Calangaeaf'*, *'diawliaidd'*), Roman (*'diaboli'*), Anglo-Saxon (*'Geisterstunde'*, *'Waelisc'*), and Norman-French (*'baragouinage'*). The promiscuous intermingling of different linguistic cultures in these lines – which is underlined by the prevalence of hyphenated words, often straddling two languages – provides a formal analogue for the historical transition in Britain from Roman rule to the establishment of Anglo-Saxon kingdoms in the fifth and sixth centuries (and looks ahead to the Norman invasions of the eleventh century). Jones himself remarks that the 'fractured and fused forms' of these lines are an attempt to approximate in language something of the 'historic situation' he describes.[60] However, the complexity and obscurity of this passage also serves to defamiliarise the English language itself by bringing it into dialogue with the heterogeneous sources from which it has historically emerged. In this way, the English monoglot poet masquerades as a '*Waelisc*-man lingo speaking'.

A crucial source for Jones's conception of British culture as hybrid and multi-lingual is the shared complex of Welsh and Arthurian myth. In the preface to *In Parenthesis*, Jones describes 'the Celtic cycle' of myths and legends that finds its most important expression in *The Mabinogion* as 'a subterranean influence' lying 'under every tump in this island'.[61] Elsewhere, he claims that the Arthurian legends may be regarded as 'an *Iliad-Aeneid* of the Celtic-Germano-Latin Christian medieval West', the definitive epic of 'the matter of Britain'.[62] As Jones's rather cumbersome hyphenated adjective seeks to acknowledge, the Arthurian tales are a composite body of texts written in a variety of medieval languages, including Latin, Welsh, Breton, and French, as well as English. Jones is careful to stress that the 'composite weave' of the Arthurian myth complex 'is its essential characteristic'; yet he also claims that Arthurian myth is culturally significant because it is 'equally the common property of all the inhabitants of Britain'.[63] Notice that Jones's understanding of Arthurian myth is informed by the same dialectic of unity and diversity that I have argued is central to his conception of British culture as a whole.

This dialectic is given concrete expression in the figure of Arthur himself in Jones's poem 'The Hunt', which depicts the hero-king both as a living embodiment of the land of Britain and as a wounded shape-shifter whose identity is radically metamorphic:

> Like the breast of the cock-thrush that is torn in the hedge-war when bright on the native mottle the deeper mottling is and brighting the diversity of textures and crystal-bright on the delicate fret the clear dew-drops gleam: so was his dappling and his dreadful variety
>   the speckled lord of Prydain
> in his twice-embroidered coat
>   the bleeding man in the green
> and if through the trellis of green
>   and between the rents of the needlework
> the whiteness of his body shone
>   so did his dark wounds glisten.[64]

The identification of Arthur's wounded body with the landscape and natural environment is developed still further in 'The Sleeping Lord', but what is striking about these lines is the way in which they bring together Christian and pagan analogues in the multi-faceted figure of Arthur, who is at once a scourged and bleeding Christ and a primal nature spirit or fertility god. Moreover, in keeping with the motif of mottled or dappled hues and textures, Jones weaves together his retelling of 'Culhwch and Olwen' with a range of other intertextual allusions, most significantly to Gerard Manley Hopkins's 'Pied Beauty': 'Glory be to God for dappled things'.[65] Appropriately, then, Jones's Arthur is a composite textual figure of 'diversity' and 'dreadful variety', as much as he is a unifying mythic figurehead for the island of Britain.

Seas, Islands, Coasts

Jones's favourite epithet for Arthur is 'the Bear of the Island', recalling the origins of his name in both the Greek 'Arktouros' ('Guardian of the Bear') and the Welsh 'arth' ('bear'), but also emphasising the specifically insular character of the myth complex for which he is the focus.[66] This is something of a strategic simplification, for it side-lines the Breton and French Arthurian tales, though it is consistent with Jones's geographical conception of Britain as an island and with his stress on its ancient cultural unity. The geographical qualities of islands are ambiguous, however, providing a further articulation of the dialectic of unity and diversity that I have described. Pete Hay notes that, as distinctive kinds of places, islands are bounded on all sides by a continuous shoreline, and this characteristic of boundedness enables the formation of strong 'island identities' and unified communities. Nonetheless, because islands are of necessity integrated into wider circuits of communication, travel, and trade, their boundaries are permeable: 'Connectedness describes the island condition better than isolation'.[67]

Despite his tendency to conceive of Britain in terms of a lost or occluded cultural unity, Jones's work also acknowledges the connectivity of insular spaces through its pervasive concern with rivers, waterways, and sea voyages. In the preface to *The Anathémata*, he remarks that: 'In Britain, "water" is unavoidably very much part of the *material poetica*'; and in a 1952 letter to Jim Ede, Jones claims that 'one *cannot begin* to consider Britain without being straight away involved in the sea and all the sea meant both in the domain of fact and in our whole poetic tradition'.[68] Even more significant is a remark Jones makes in his important essay, 'The Myth of Arthur': 'The folk tradition of the insular Celts seems to present to the mind a half-aquatic world – it is one of its most fascinating characteristics – it introduces a feeling of transparency and interpenetration of one element with another, of transposition and metamorphosis.'[69] What is striking here is the way in which Jones simultaneously grounds his image of Britain in the 'folk tradition of the insular Celts' and associates it with fluidity, metamorphosis, and inter-relatedness. Jones's geographical conception of Britain as an island (among islands) and his emphasis upon the social and cultural significance of the sea suggests his affinities with what John Brannigan calls 'archipelagic modernism'. In Brannigan's definition, archipelagic modernism refers to writing from the Irish and British archipelago in the period 1890–1970, which 'prioritises a locational focus upon islands, coastlines, and the sea', by contrast with the metropolitan orientation of high modernism.[70] Moreover, archipelagic modernism foregrounds the cultural diversity and hybridity of the North Atlantic archipelago, acknowledging that it is 'plural, diverse, and abounds in local particularities'.[71]

The Anathémata is the most extensive and important instance of archipelagic modernism within Jones's oeuvre. No fewer than five of this long poem's eight sections – 'Middle-Sea and Lear-Sea', 'Angle-Land', 'Redriff', 'The Lady of the Pool', and 'Keel, Ram, Stauros' – feature ships and sea voyages among the islands, coasts, docks, and seaports of Britain and Europe. In 'Middle-Sea and Lear-Sea', Jones dramatises the historical emergence of a specifically British cultural identity by way of a voyage narrative, which begins in the Eastern Mediterranean of Classical antiquity and culminates off the South-western coast of Britain. Jones refers to this voyage proleptically as a 'wanderers tall tale to tell / anabasis / by sea, by land', but the tale he goes on to tell concerns at least two different journeys: that of a Greek ship sailing towards

Phaleron, the ancient port of Athens, in the fifth century BC; and that of a ship manned by Phoenicians and Phocaeans sailing from Phaleron to the coast of Cornwall, part of the ancient trade in tin, perhaps in the second millennium BC.[72] The conflation of these two sea voyages, with their different trajectories and time-frames, allegorises the transmission of Classical culture from the Mediterranean to the island of Britain and the wider archipelago of which it is a part. From the perspective of the Greek sailors, this process of cultural transmission and interfusion entails a near-miraculous journey 'out of our *mare* / into their *See*'; which is to say, not just the passage from one sea to another but also a linguistic and cultural encounter with others and otherness on the far side of the known world.[73]

Jones's voyage narrative becomes both gripping and densely textured as the Phoenician-Phocaean ship nears the storm-swept coast of Southwest Cornwall, plunging his mariners into a turbulent confluence of mythological currents – Greek, Celtic, and Scandinavian:

> Now north by east
>   over the nine white grinders
>   riding the nine daughters of the quern of islands
> kouroi from over *yr eigion*
>   making Dylan's *môroedd*
>   holding on towards
> Igraine's *dylanau*
>   the eyes of her
> towards the waters
>   of the son of Amblet's daughter.[74]

In these lines, the ship passes by a group of skerries ('the quern of islands') battered by the nine daughters of the Norse sea-god Ægir, while the crew of the ship are transfigured as Greek 'kouroi', marble statues associated with Apollo, from over the deep ocean ('*yr eigion*'). Their course is set for the seas ('*môroedd*') belonging to Dylan, the Welsh sea-god who appears in the Fourth Branch of the Mabinogi, and whose name aligns his nature with that of an ocean wave. Hence the subsequent reference to 'Igraine's *dylanau*': the waves of Igraine, mother of Arthur, who is in turn referred to obliquely as 'the son of Amblet's daughter'. Just as the waters of the Bay of Biscay, the Celtic Sea, and the English Channel mingle off the South coast of Cornwall, so in Jones's lines a variety of languages, mythologies, and cultural imaginaries are brought into constellation with one another without eliding their differences or distinctive origins.

By the end of 'Middle-Sea and Lear-Sea', the Phoenician-Phocaean ship has sighted 'Bolerion' (Land's End) and is steering toward its 'port of call', St Michael's Mount; but whether or not it ever arrives is left an open question – 'Did he berth her? / and to schedule? / by the hoar rock in the drowned wood?' – as though to emphasise the dynamic process of voyaging itself rather than its ostensible end.[75] Indeed, several critics have remarked on the pronounced allegorical or archetypal character of sea voyages in Jones's poem, whether as a figure for 'the journey of the human soul' or 'the experience of the Church in the world'.[76] Certainly, there is evidence for such a reading, particularly in Jones's depiction of the scurrilous, drunken ship's captain as a kind of thalassic Christ-figure – 'Ischyros with his boots on' – and, in 'Keel, Ram, Stauros', his merging of this figure with that of the artist-priest: 'Pious, eld, bright-eyed *! marinus*'.[77] However, Jones's archipelagic modernism is most engaging when such archetypal or symbolic elements are grounded in, and modified by nautical, topographical, and historical particulars. For instance, 'Angle-Land' begins by describing another sea voyage along the southern and eastern coasts of Britain during the early Middle Ages, when those regions were being settled by Jutes and Angles. Employing a series of interrogative sentences, Jones tracks the ship's progress eastwards through the English Channel, naming landmarks and topographical features that would enable navigators to chart their positions: 'Vecta Insula' (the Isle of Wight), 'South Sand Head', 'the Flats and the Brake', 'the Gull', 'the Foreland', 'the Elbow', and so on.[78] Jones's notes gloss many of these toponyms and thereby aid the reader in grasping the text's shifting literary geography, which combines detailed topographic description with layered mythological and historical allusions. Crucially, the sea voyage once again functions to represent the process of social and cultural change in a multi-ethnic Britain. For instance, as the ship passes the fog-bound coast of the Thames estuary, Jones views the history of the British landscape from the perspective of the sea, describing how the field systems of the invaders ('broad Angle hidage') are displacing those of the native Celts ('the lightly furrowed *erwau* / that once did quilt Boudícca's royal *gwely*').[79]

'Angle-Land' culminates in one of those 'scale-bending' representations of space that Jon Hegglund regards as characteristic of the modernist geographical imagination, moving abruptly from a local, situated perspective to an aerial or 'cartographic overview that places the narrative scene in a new, disjunctive context'.[80] Following the course of an imagined ship up the East coast of Britain, Jones's narratorial consciousness enacts a sudden shift of scales to evoke a panoramic vision of Britain's eastern rivers meeting and merging in the North Sea:

> all our easting waters
> are confluent with the fathering river and tributary to him: where Thamesis,
> Great Ouse, Tyne from the Wall's end, de-marking Tweed, Forth that winds
> the middle march, Tummel and wide looping Tay (that laps the wading files
> when Birnam boughs deploy toward Dunsinane – out toward the Goat Flats).
> Spey of the Symbol stones and Ness from the serpentine mere
> all mingle Rhenus-flow
>   and are oned with him
> in Cronos-*meer*.[81]

Moving gradually from South-east England to North-east Scotland, this passage is at once dense with local particulars – the names of rivers, places, and topographical features – and geographically expansive, describing how the waters of British rivers mingle with those of the Rhine ('Rhenus-flow'), the mightiest of all Western European rivers, in the sea of Cronos. In this way, Jones depicts the sea as a common and connective element for the peoples of Western Europe and the North Atlantic archipelago, a '*Brudersee*' and an 'arena of transnational interchange'.[82] However, *The Anathémata* was largely written in the years immediately following the end of the Second World War, and Jones's poem also refers explicitly to 'the fratricides / of the latter-day', when the North Sea was patrolled by German submarines. Such recent instances of international conflict are, in turn, closely linked to the strategic use of cartography in modern warfare, for 'the greyed green wastes' of the North Sea are represented by grids and numbers and quadrants 'on the sea-green *Quadratkarte*', thereby reconfiguring it as a battlefield.[83] There is a tension, then, in Jones's poem between an imaginative effort to conceive of the relations between local places and transnational spaces, which regards the sea as a medium of connections rather than a barrier, and the geometrical abstractions of cartography, which are aligned with violent attempts at world domination and the obliteration of local differences.

Known-site and World City

Jones's later poetry is preoccupied to a remarkable degree with the threat that is posed to local places, cultures, and communities by modern capitalism, especially in its urban, industrial, and technological manifestations. His distinctive mode of poetic localism also finds expression in a politicised antipathy towards all forms of authoritarian rule and exploitation. As Paul Robichaud observes, Jones's poetry is 'consistently anti-imperialist and antitotalitarian', despite his political conservatism and ambivalent attraction to fascist ideas during the 1930s.[84] Jones strongly objects to what he regards as the levelling and homogenising influence of modernity and modern technology, which elides or ignores the differences specific to each place and culture. In correspondence with Aneirin Talfan Davies, Jones bemoans the 'subordination of the things of site & locality' to 'the requirements of the new technocracy'; and, in his preface to *The Anathémata*, he argues that the creative power of the artist is vitiated by the contemporary destruction of local cultures, 'when where was this site and were these foci there is *terra informis*'.[85] Through its pervasive concern with locality and place, Jones's poetry exhibits what Adorno calls art's inherent 'tendency toward radical particularization', though his comments on art also suggest a highly developed awareness of the 'dialectic of the universal and the particular'.[86] In this regard, Jones considers the work of James Joyce – and particularly *Finnegans Wake* (1939), his 'paradigm of literary art' – to be exemplary.[87] Not only is Joyce's work intrinsically bound up with his imaginative attachments to 'place, site, and locality', but his writing succeeds in making 'the universal shine out from the particular'.[88] Indeed, Jones contends that it is precisely because Joyce's work entails 'absolute fidelity to a specified site, and the complex historical strata special to that site' that it is able 'to express a universal concept'.[89] Of course, in discussing Joyce, Jones is also describing his own aesthetic project, which foregrounds the importance of 'the contactual and the particular' in conveying the reality and meaning of experience.[90]

In several respects, Jones's prioritisation of place, site, and locality within his wider poetics bears resemblance to certain features of the contemporaneous thought of Martin Heidegger – though there is no concrete evidence of any direct or indirect influence. Certainly, Jones and Heidegger are in broad agreement about the extent to which the displacement and objectification consequent upon technological modernity alienates humankind from its own nature and authentic being. For instance, where Jones critiques modern technocracy for obliterating the differences and differentiation that make local cultures meaningful, Heidegger charges 'technological production' with 'level[ling] every *ordo*, every rank, down to the uniformity of production' so that 'the holy, the hale and the whole, seems to be effaced'.[91] Elsewhere, Heidegger describes the modern predicament as one of being 'unfree and chained to technology', which, in its instrumental and utilitarian guise, treats nature itself as no more than a 'standing-reserve' of energy for human exploitation.[92] Jones and Heidegger also concur on the central importance to art (especially poetry) of close attachments to intimately known places. In his 1955 'Memorial Address', Heidegger asks rhetorically: 'does not the flourishing of any genuine work depend upon its roots in a native soil?', going on to warn that modernity threatens 'the *rootedness*, the *autochthony*, of man [. . .] at its core'.⁹³ Heidegger's explicitly chthonic vocabulary of 'roots' and 'soil' renders his place-based ontology vulnerable to criticism because of its perceived affinities with the 'Blut und Boden' ideology of the Nazis; and Jones has also been criticised for what Jeremy Hooker calls 'the limitations of his idea of blood and soil'.⁹⁴

Less controversial and more widely influential is Heidegger's conception of 'dwelling' as a fundamental mode of authentic being. In 'Building Dwelling Thinking', he explores the etymological links between 'dwelling' and 'being', elaborating an essentially sedentary conception of the relationship between people and places. To dwell, Heidegger affirms, is 'to remain, to stay in place': 'To say that mortals *are* is to say that *in dwelling* they persist through spaces by virtue of their stay among things and locations'.⁹⁵ Dwelling concerns the kind of rooted being that may overcome difference and disparity, promoting a mode of belonging and coexistence that is founded upon primal oneness. Yet here an important difference between Jones and Heidegger becomes clear, for Jones's profound imaginative attachments to place and locality do not proceed from a secure and intuitive sense of belonging but rather from a condition of dislocation and self-division of which he was painfully aware. As Jonathan Miles remarks, Jones's veneration of place and site in his poetry is deeply at odds with the humdrum reality of his 'nomadic' life in various London suburbs; and Hooker argues that it is precisely this state of 'uprootedness' that gives rise to his intense engagement with 'the matter of Wales'.⁹⁶ In this regard, Jones more closely resembles the exile Joyce writing obsessively about Dublin from Trieste, Zurich, and Paris than Heidegger, the philosopher of Being, dwelling in his Black Forest hut.

Jones's later work, particularly the shorter poems and fragments collected in *The Sleeping Lord*, repeatedly explores the unequal and uneven relationships between local cultures and global powers – or, in Jones's vocabulary, 'known-site' and 'world city'. Jones's use of these terms, and their several variations, is idiosyncratic and potentially misleading, so a brief gloss may be helpful. Edward Casey remarks that, by contrast with the relational depth and dynamic character of 'place', 'site' connotes simplicity, fixity, and isolation: 'Site is place reduced to being "just there"'.⁹⁷ Jones's use of the term 'site', which probably derives from his reading of archaeological sources, is less precise and is not clearly distinguished from 'place' or 'locality', with which it is often roughly synonymous. At most, 'site' is differentiated from the more encompassing 'place' by its reference to specific topographical features such as hills, tumuli, and river valleys; but even this usage is not consistent. 'World city' is adapted directly from Spengler, referring both to the metropolitan hub of an imperial system (usually Rome and/or London) and to the global reach of that system's institutions and power structures.[98] For instance, in 'The Wall' a soldier patrolling the city walls of Jerusalem at the time of Christ's passion reflects on the malign influence of Rome – a sprawling 'megalopolis that wills death' – by describing how he walks 'in the shadow of the labyrinth of the wall, of the world, of the robber walls of the world city'.[99] As this example illustrates, there is a pronounced positive-negative polarity to the distinction that Jones makes between the local and the global, sometimes amounting to a structural antagonism or opposition. Ward argues that 'London and Wales, metropolis and hinterland' figure in Jones's work as 'paradigms of opposition'; and Dilworth identifies a pervasive symbolic antithesis between 'rural place', which Jones associates with cultural vitality, and the destructive influence of the 'engulfing, dehumanising city'.[100] Nonetheless, while Jones's imaginative and political sympathies are almost always with place and locality, such archetypal oppositions are never wholly reified in the poems themselves but rather dynamic and open to deconstruction.

The antagonistic or antithetical relationship between the local and the global, 'known-site' and 'world city', is dramatised most fully in two poems at the centre of *The Sleeping Lord*, 'The Tribune's Visitation' and 'The Tutelar of the Place', which are best understood as a dialogic pair. Much of 'The Tribune's Visitation' is given over to the dramatic monologue of a Roman Tribune, a representative of imperial power and political pragmatism, addressing a fatigue of soldiers stationed in Palestine during the first century AD. The fatigue itself is composed of a 'mixed bunch' of recruits 'from all parts', both metropolitan Rome and the Germano-Celtic peripheries of the empire.[101] The ideological purpose of the Tribune's monologue is to fashion this heterogeneous group, with their various local attachments and allegiances, into a cohesive and unified body whose corporate and individual identities are oriented in accordance with 'the world-plan' of imperial conquest and administration.[102] Styling himself as 'a man speaking to men', he disparages the significance of 'small localities' and their modes of communal identity, extolling the martial duty of creating a uniform world order:

     It's the world-bounds
 we're detailed to beat
     to discipline the world-floor
 to a common level
     til everything presuming difference

and all the sweet remembered demarcations
>					wither
to the touch of us
>					and know the fact of empire.[103]

In these lines, the Tribune performs the role of spokesperson for the homogenising force of modernity and empire, denigrating all appeals to the remembered past or the particularity of local cultural traditions in favour of present conditions and the omnipotence of what he calls 'contemporary fact'.[104] The rhetorical force of his monologue implicitly acknowledges J. E. Malpas's point that 'the structure of subjectivity is given in and through the structure of place'.[105] By seeking to destroy or at least diminish the affective power of local places and cultures in the minds of his men, he is engaged in a discursive attempt to remould their identities and interpellate them as compliant subjects of a global empire. However, Jones both complicates the character of his monologist and implies the stubborn persistence of local attachments when he has the Tribune recall his own native place of Albanus and 'the remembered things' of his childhood there, even as he disavows them publicly.[106] Ironically, the Tribune's speech is most eloquent not when he calls to mind imperial ambitions and power, but when he is describing the manifold local differences and identifications that Roman hegemony would obliterate and subsume.

Where 'The Tribune's Visitation' explores the conflictual relationship between local cultures and global power from the perspective of the metropolitan centre, 'The Tutelar of the Place' approaches the same topic from a position that is aligned with the geographical and cultural margins of empire. The central opposition dramatised in 'The Tutelar of the Place' is that between a Celtic culture of place and locality, defined in terms of its 'holy diversities' and presided over by a female tutelar or guardian spirit, and a Roman civilisation characterised by the 'rootless uniformities' of imperial rule, which are embodied in the figure of a male dictator known as the Ram.[107] The poem begins by invoking and celebrating a goddess of place and 'known-site' who is at once a universal figure and a profoundly local deity known by different names in different places:

> She that loves place, time, demarcation, hearth, kin, enclosure, site, differentiated cult, though she is but one mother of us all: one earth brings us all forth, one womb receives us all, yet to each she is other, named of some name other . . .[108]

This maternal, protective spirit of place is 'a rare one for locality', capable of shielding her children and devotees 'against the world-storm' of modern technocracy.[109] Accordingly, the second half of the poem takes the form of a sustained prayer for intercession, pitting the familiar milieux of local communities against the global ambitions of an alien and despotic imperium:

> Queen of the differentiated sites, administratrix of the demarcations, let our cry come unto you.
> In all times of imperium save us when the *mercatores* come save us from the guile of the *negotiatores* save us from the *missi*, from the agents
> who think no shame
> by inquest to audit what is shameful to tell
> deliver us.[110]

Here, the military, legal, and bureaucratic power of a metropolitan civilisation is conceived as an immediate threat to the vitality and continuity of local traditions – 'the diversities by which we are'.[111] Repeatedly, the poem's speaker equates locality with difference, diversity, and otherness, addressing the tutelar (with a characteristic echo of Hopkins) as 'patroness of things counter, parti, pied, several'.[112] By contrast, the world of urban, industrial modernity is conceived in terms of its deadening uniformity and materialism, crystallised in the image of displaced villagers populating 'the rectangular tenements' of an industrial city and labouring 'in the houses of the engines that fabricate the ingenuities of the Ram'.[113]

'The Tutelar of the Place' illustrates with stark power the antithesis between rural place and urban deracination that Dilworth describes, and this antithesis runs in parallel with several other oppositions between: the Roman Empire and the Celtic world; modern civilisation and traditional culture; masculine and feminine principles. However, a close reading of the poem and its contexts shows that these oppositions are undermined, or at least rendered dynamic, by its formal and thematic concerns with difference and diversity. For instance, Jones describes the speaker of the poem's dramatic monologue as 'a Celt in the Roman army who is thinking of his homeland', thereby revealing that experiences of displacement and divided loyalties inhabit the very voice that utters its hymn to hearth and home place.[114] This dramatic situation makes it possible to understand the poem's idealised depiction of rural communities and local customs as arising from the psychology of exile and self-estrangement. It is also worth noting that the form of the poem – its rendering as a complex soliloquy or dramatic monologue – complicates the antithesis between masculine and feminine principles that its imagery and themes establish. At the centre of the poem, the speaker ventriloquises the part of a grandmother ('our gammer') calling children to bed and leading them in a prayer to 'Sweet Jill of our hill'.[115] As Dilworth remarks, the narrator of this poem is 'psychologically androgynous', a persona who combines the symbolically masculine qualities of objectivity and analysis with the feminine attributes of subjectivity and intuition.[116] We might regard 'The Tutelar of the Place' as an example of the 'blending of male and female personages' that Anne Price-Owen argues characterises Jones's poetry and art as a whole.[117] Most importantly, it is clear that the feminine tutelar who is described and invoked repeatedly in the poem is a thoroughly hybrid, composite figure, embodying elements of Celtic mythology, Roman religion, and Catholic iconography. Among her many aspects are those of an earth goddess; a genius loci or spirit of place; and the Queen of Heaven or 'Mother of Flowers', names given to the Virgin Mary.[118] The sheer number of names and identities by which she is known – 'sweet Jill of the demarcations / arc of differences / tower of individuation / queen of the minivers' – underline her protean character and the diversity-in-unity for which she stands.[119] However, because the tutelar's identity derives in part from the very imperial civilisation against which she is invoked, she actually bridges the opposition between metropolis and locality, Roman and Celtic worlds.

This complex and contradictory expression of localism is further evident at the level of the poem's dense linguistic texture and self-conscious exploration of the language of place. Like that of several other late modernists, Jones's poetry strongly emphasises 'the materiality of the signifier', both through the inclusion of inscriptions or engravings and through its macaronic, multi-lingual forms.[120] However, as I have argued above, what is distinctive about Jones's linguistic experiments is the way in which they illustrate the diverse linguistic and cultural inheritances of Britain at the level of form and diction. In his preface to *The Anathémata*, Jones argues that the poet's imagery, meanings, and perceptions derive from the 'mythus and deposits' comprising his 'particular historical complex', and that this entails 'the employment of a particular language or languages [...] at an especially heightened tension.'[121] Consequently, his English-language poems are studded with untranslated words from Latin and Welsh. In 'The Tutelar of the Place', many of these non-English words refer to particular kinds of places, settlements, or landforms. For instance, in the following passage:

> Yet, when she stoops to hear you children cry
>   from the scattered and single habitations
> or from the nucleated holdings
>   from towered *castra*
>   paved *civitas*
>   treble-ramped *caer*

> or wattled *tref*
> stockade *gorod* or
> trenched *burh*
> from which ever child-crib within whatever enclosure
> demarked by a dynast or staked by consent
> wherever in which of the wide world-ridings
> you must not call her but by that name
> which accords to the morphology of place.[122]

In these lines, the morphology of place is manifested through the morphology of the English language and its various precursors. '*Castra*' and '*civitas*' are both Latin terms, referring to military camps and the Roman city-state respectively; '*caer*', '*tref*', and '*gorod*' are Welsh words, meaning 'fort', 'hamlet', and 'hiding place'; while '*burh*' is the Old English name for a fortified settlement. At the level of content, this passage posits a singular relationship of correspondence between language and place through acts of naming – which is ironic enough, given that the poem includes no place-names whatsoever. Indeed, Jones himself remarks that this poem in praise of the local and the particular 'belongs to no special time or country', for 'such suffrages may go up from so many different sorts of habitations and under so many differing circumstances'.[123] At the level of form, however, the very fluency with which the speaker moves between the language of metropolitan power (Latin) and that of local resistance (Welsh) implies a sophisticated linguistic cosmopolitanism, and calls into question the opposition between Roman and Celt that its rhetoric and imagery constructs. This multi-lingual texture and the finicky exactitude of the poem's language are intrinsic to its effects, and 'The Tutelar of the Place' ultimately gives expression to a powerful but internally contradictory mode of late modernist localism.

Ward has argued, controversially, that 'The Tutelar of the Place' is only the most explicit example of the deep political conservatism informing Jones's poetry, arguing that its 'commitment to idealised values of primitivism and irrationalism' is broadly compatible with the blood-and-soil ideology of fascism.[124] In my view, the poem is more persuasively read as an attempt to voice the resistance of colonised peoples to imperial rule from within a specifically British historical and cultural context; and as a prescient critique of the homogenising effects of economic and cultural globalisation in the mid-twentieth century. Fredric Jameson has described two distinct positions on globalisation: 'a postmodern celebration of difference and differentiation' and a more pessimistic apprehension of 'increasing identity (rather than difference)', which is evident in the 'standardization of culture' and 'the destruction of local differences'.[125] Jones's poetry, which perceives both modernity and empire as levelling, homogenising forces, tends very strongly towards the latter position. Indeed, there are even some striking affinities between Jones's poetics of place and the politics of left-wing 'place-based' movements described by Michael Hardt and Antonio Negri, in which 'the boundaries of place (conceived either as identity or as territory) are posed against the undifferentiated and homogeneous space of global networks'. For Hardt and Negri, such a position on globalisation is ultimately inadequate because it 'rests on a false dichotomy between the global and the local'; and Ward argues that Jones's poetry suffers from a similar tendency towards dualistic thought and simplifying abstractions.[126] However, as I have tried to show, Jones's sophisticated experiments with form and language significantly complicate the rhetoric and imagery of his poems, rendering their oppositions between local cultures and metropolitan civilisation, difference and deadening uniformity dynamic and liable to reconfiguration.

The Geological Imagination

Like that of several other late modernist poets – including Hugh MacDiarmid, Charles Olson, and Lorine Niedecker – Jones's poetics of place is informed by a keen amateur interest in and understanding of geology. His library contains a surprising number of books on geology and earth science, including I. O. Evans's *The Observer's Book of British Geology* (1950), W. G. Fearnsides and O. M. B. Bulman's *Geology in the Service of Man* (1950), W. W. Watts's *Geology for Beginners* (1929), and five volumes in the *British Regional Geology* series (South Wales; North Wales; the Welsh borderland; the South of Scotland; London and the Thames Valley).[127] Moreover, the frequency with which Jones makes use of geological terms, both descriptively and as metaphors, in his poetry and prose writings is remarkable. At times, he uses recondite scientific terms derived from his reading and research with precision; more often, though, Jones freely adapts terms that have specific meanings and applications in the discipline of geology but are also current in general usage. For example, he remarks that *The Anathémata* is centrally concerned with 'the complex deposits of this Island'; and claims that all effective poetic images are 'drawn from the deposits of a common tradition'.[128] Elsewhere, Jones notes that 'the Welsh deposits' of British culture are closely 'linked with locality, terrain and site'.[129] In geology, 'deposition' is 'the constructive process of the laying down of any kind of loose rock material', such as mud, sand, or calcite.[130] But a 'deposit' is also something set down or stored away for safe-keeping;

and Jones's flexible metaphorical use of the term – always in the plural form – seems to refer to the constituent elements of a particular culture, as though that culture were formed, shaped, and eroded over time by analogy with a physical landscape. Other examples of Jones's recourse to geological metaphors when speaking of art and culture might be multiplied. One of the things that Jones most admires about Joyce's work is its ability to give expression to the 'complex historic strata' that are sedimented in Dublin; and he describes Joyce himself as 'a master of the metamorphic'.[131] Metamorphic rocks are those whose character has been fundamentally altered by the effects of heat and pressure, an appropriate analogy for Joyce's experiments with language in *Finnegans Wake*; while 'strata' are layers of sedimentary rocks. What Jones's recurrent use of these geological metaphors implies, then, is that he conceives of culture as both composed of many different layers and as subject to profound transformations over time.

On closer consideration, however, it becomes clear that Jones is attracted to geology and geological modes of thought for contradictory reasons. Geology is, as its name indicates, the science of the earth, its structures, processes, and history; it studies the relations between physical features of the earth and the ways in which their constituent elements change over time.[132] In this regard, geology plays an important role both in Jones's dynamic conceptions of place or 'site' and in his depictions of large-scale historical processes. On the other hand, Jones often employs geological metaphors as a means of giving expression to certain spiritual or mythical fundamentals, which are conceived of as essentially ahistorical and unchanging. For instance, while the findings of the physical sciences are 'necessarily mutable', Jones affirms that 'the poet, of whatever century, is concerned only with how he can use a current notion to express a permanent mythus'.[133] This contradiction between mutability and permanence is illustrated powerfully and concisely in a passage from the 'Middle-Sea and Lear-Sea' section of *The Anathémata*, which describes the birth-pangs of Western culture in the Eastern Mediterranean via a complex geological metaphor:

> The adaptations, the fusions
> the transmogrifications
>   but always
> the inward continuities
>   of the site
>   of place.[134]

Commenting on this passage, Corcoran observes that it gives expression to 'the theme of an underlying unity, or continuity' that Jones believes can be discovered or uncovered in 'the apparent discontinuity of our present cultural situation'.¹³⁵ There is, however, a significant tension in these lines between their semantic content and the form in which that content is given expression. For, whilst the movement of the sentence is from an initial awareness of mutability and confusion towards a deeper apprehension of inner continuities, Jones's use of enjambment, indentations, and broken or half-lines contribute to a sense of displacement or fragmentation under great pressures. It is by prolonging and deepening rather than resolving this contradiction between mutability and permanence that Jones's poetry is able to depict places, in Doreen Massey's words, 'not as points or areas on maps, but as integrations of space and time; as *spatio-temporal events*'.¹³⁶ The science of geology offers a sophisticated array of terms and concepts with which to articulate such a dialectic of settledness and flux, continuity and change.

Jones might be regarded as a late modernist example of what Jacques Rancière has called 'the geological or archaeological poet' who emerged contemporaneously with the new science of geology at the turn of the nineteenth century, and whose role is to give expression to the idea that everything speaks, even mute things like rocks and fossils.¹³⁷ Corcoran, for instance, speaks of Jones's 'poetry of geological transformation'.¹³⁸ However, where Rancière's geological poet is chiefly concerned with the phenomena of the social world, Jones's poetry also displays a more thoroughgoing imaginative engagement with the actuality of geological processes. In this regard, Jones's geological imagination is most active and inventive in the 'Rite and Fore-Time' section of *The Anathémata*. This opening section of Jones's long poem begins with the rite of the Mass, then goes on to recall three moments of origin and emergence within the wider narrative of God's Creation: the beginnings of art in Western Europe; the evolutionary origins of humankind as a distinct species; and the shaping of the landscapes and places inhabited by prehistoric humans, with a particular focus on Britain during and after the Pleistocene glaciations. There is, as Miles observes, a dual emphasis throughout this section upon demonstrating 'the mutability of the created world' and affirming 'the presence of God' as a supreme source of continuity and meaning.¹³⁹ Jones refers to God the Creator as 'the Master of Harlequinade, himself not made, maker of sequence and permutation in all things made', the ultimate cause of geological metamorphoses but also of patterns, structures, and meaningful configurations of matter. However, Jones's unorthodox epithet for the Supreme Being provocatively associates the divine plan of the Creation with both variegation and the performative buffoonery of pantomime. Appropriately, Jones goes on to imagine the irregular sequence of glaciations and warmer periods of the Pleistocene Era as a '*Vorzeit*-masque' or plainsong performed by a cosmic choir:

> *Col canto* the piping for this turn.
> Unmeasured, irregular in stress and interval, of interior
> rhythm, modal.
>   If tonic and final are fire
> the dominant is ice
>   if fifth the fire
> the cadence ice.[140]

Rather than adapting geological terms to describe the social world of art and culture, these lines employ the specialised vocabulary of music ('tonic', 'dominant', 'fifth', 'cadence') as part of an extended metaphor that depicts vast geological processes and fluctuations in the earth's climate. Nonetheless, there is a certain analogical correlation posited in the fact that the phrase 'irregular in stress and interval' might be understood to refer, self-reflexively, to Jones's distinctive mode of free verse composition as well as to the sequence of glaciations and thaws that is the ostensible subject of his lines.

In 'Rite and Fore-Time', Jones also reprises the matter of Britain by exploring the metamorphoses its folded and faulted material fabric has undergone in the most recent geological epochs. In doing so, he both illustrates the antiquity and perdurance of individual national territories within the island of Britain (especially that of Wales) and demonstrates the extent to which such identities have been subject to far-reaching alterations and rendered interdependent. For instance, in another scale-bending panoramic vision of Britain's western coast, Jones depicts the glacial displacement of land masses from the Southern Uplands of Scotland into the Irish Sea and further south to North Wales:

> Before, trans-Solway
>   and from over Manannan's *moroedd*, the last debris-freighted floes
> echeloned solid from Monapia to Ynys Fôn [sic]
>   discharged into Arfon *colles*
> what was cargoed-up on Grampius Mons.
>   Off the 'strath' into the *ystrad*
> out of the 'carse' on to the *traeth*.
> Heaped amorphous
>   out of Caledonia
> into Cambria
>   bound for Snowdonia
> transits Cumbria.[141]

Appropriately for a passage that describes the creation of Welsh landforms from rocks carried by glaciers from Scotland, these lines are a macaronic fusion of different languages and geographical imaginaries in which place-names and topographical terms predominate. Jones creates toponymic rhymes by juxtaposing 'Monapia' (Pliny's name for the Isle of Man) with 'Ynys Fôn' (Ynys Môn, the island of Anglesey), 'Arfon' (the heart of the medieval Welsh kingdom of Gwynedd), and 'Grampius Mons' (the Roman name for the Grampian Mountains). Similarly, the Scots terms 'strath' and 'carse', meaning a broad river valley and the alluvial land by a river respectively, find their near-equivalents in the Welsh '*ystrad*' (dale) and '*traeth*' (beach or shore).

The broken lines of this passage also create a sequence of rhymes and off-rhymes between 'Caledonia' (the Latin name for Northern Scotland) and 'Snowdonia' (a mountainous region of North Wales), 'Cambria' (a Latinised name for Wales) and 'Cumbria' (a county in North-west England, whose name is linked etymologically to 'Cymru', the Welsh name for Wales). Jones's intricate but irregular use of indentations and variation of line lengths combine with his multi-lingual correspondences to produce a formal analogue for the geological processes of displacement and convergence that his poem describes. Much of 'Rite and Fore-Time' is taken up with a detailed and sometimes formidably complex exploration of such metamorphoses in the physical structure of the earth, and with the prehistoric emergence of the human inhabitants of its landscapes and terrains. Jones's purpose is to show how all such upheavals and transmogrifications are encompassed and preceded by the 'New Light' of God's Creation, which shines on and illuminates everything: 'Through all the metamorphs or whatever the pseudomorphoses'.[142] And yet, this climactic discovery of the informing purpose and ultimate constancy of the divine Logos is only possible because of the poem's radically particular representation of metamorphoses and mutability, wherein places are conceived as open and in process rather than static or self-enclosed.

Jones's geological imagination is also powerfully manifest in the last poem he completed, 'The Sleeping Lord', a late 'fragment' that was first published in 1967.[143] This poem returns to and enlarges upon a motif that runs through Jones's oeuvre, that of sleeping figures identified with the landscape awaiting some future awakening. For instance, in *In Parenthesis*, slumbering soldiers are described as 'sleeping like long-barrow sleepers, their dark arms at reach'.[144] In his long note to this passage, Jones refers to 'the persistent Celtic theme of armed sleepers under the mounds', including those legends concerning 'Arthur sleeping in Craig-y-Ddinas or in Avalon or among the Eildons in Roxburghshire'.[145] 'The Sleeping Lord' is Jones's most ambitious and sustained elaboration of this theme, combining myth and history with a detailed survey of the physical, economic, and social geographies of South Wales. It begins with a series of interrogative questions concerning the giant sleeping figure of Arthur, whose 'bed deep on the folded strata' is at once the geological foundation of the South Wales landscape and, via a bilingual pun, a grave ('bedd' in Welsh).[146] In this regard, Jones's giant sleeper inevitably resembles the figure of Finn in Joyce's *Finnegans Wake*, whose prostrate 'brontoichtyan form' is 'outlined a-slumbered' and identified with the physical fabric of Dublin and its hinterlands.[147] What is striking from the outset of Jones's poem is the way in which it combines this mythic material with both topographical exactitude and the scientific vocabulary of geology:

> Is the Tump by Honddu
>   his lifted bolster?
>   does a gritstone outcrop
> incommode him?
>   does a deep syncline
>   sag beneath him?
> or does his dinted thorax rest
>   where the contorted heights
>   themselves rest
> on a lateral pressured anticline?
> Does his russet-hued mattress
>   does his rug of shaly grey
> ease at all for his royal dorsals
>   the faulted under-bedding.[148]

Bed and bedrock, figure and landscape, interior and exterior spaces are conflated in these lines, which use anaphora and alliteration to knit its varied images together but also break the sense of its two complex sentences across multiple enjambments and deep indentations. The language of anatomy ('thorax', 'dorsals') is brought into apposition with that of earth science ('gritstone outcrop', 'faulted under-bedding'). A 'syncline' is a trough fold in stratified rocks, and an 'anticline' is its opposite, an arch created by lateral or upward pressure. Although these lines focus upon an inert mythical figure in a state of apparent repose, then, Jones's geological vocabulary calls the reader's attention to the effects of violent tectonic forces which have shaped the mountainous landscapes of South Wales in the distant past.

The long middle section of 'The Sleeping Lord' describes Arthur's court and the prayer of his hall priest, who recalls the dead and departed 'of the entire universal orbis / from the unknown beginnings / unguessed millenniums back / until now'.[149] In the final pages of the poem, though, Jones returns to the giant sleeping figure of Arthur to explore the relationships between the geological structure of South Wales and its twentieth-century social geography. Perhaps the most striking geological feature of this region is its carboniferous deposits or coal measures, the basis of much of its industrial character since the mid-nineteenth century.[150] In Jones's poem, the wounded body of Arthur is identified implicitly with that of the crucified Christ and explicitly with the scarred and polluted landscapes of the industrial south Wales valleys:

> Is the Usk a drain for his gleaming tears
> who weeps for the land
>   who dreams his bitter dream
> for the folk of the land
> does Tawe clog for his sorrows
> do the parallel dark-seam drainers
>   mingle his anguish-stream
> with the scored valleys' tilted refuse.
> Does his freight of woe
>   flood South by East
> on Sirhywi and Ebwy
>   is it southly bourn
> on double Rhondda's fall to Taff?[151]

In these lines, the names of Welsh rivers ('Usk', 'Tawe', 'Sirhywi', 'Ebwy', 'Rhondda', 'Taff') compose a kind of topographical litany that sweeps across the whole of the South Wales coalfield, from the borderlands of Gwent to Swansea in the west. However, these rivers carry refuse and poisons, by-products of industrial processes, into the water system and so contribute to the bitterness and anguish of Arthur, the anthropomorphic embodiment of the land itself. Given that the poem was begun in November 1966, it is not implausible to read the line 'with the scored valleys' tilted refuse' as an oblique reference to the Aberfan disaster of 21 October 1966, when a spoil tip collapsed and buried a local school, killing 144 people, including 116 children.[152] A few pages later, Jones also alludes to the Torrey Canyon oil spill off the coast of Cornwall in March 1967, when he describes a 'dying gull / on her sea-hearse / that drifts the oily bourne'.[153] As these references to contemporary historical events indicate, 'The Sleeping Lord' is a sustained meditation on the human and ecological consequences of industrial capitalism on a particular, intimately described landscape and the communities that it supports. To adapt Adorno's phrase, in Jones's poem the South Wales valleys figure as a 'cultural landscape' that is 'etched by the real suffering of the past' and its continuing effects in the present.[154] Characteristically, this cultural landscape is depicted by means of a geological imagination that seeks to penetrate beneath its surface and understand the large-scale processes of change and persistence within which the events of human history take place.

Jones's fascination with geology, evoking the deep past through the bones of the landscape, is one manifestation of the wider convergence of history and geography that I have been tracing in his poetry. His pessimistic, anti-modern historical vision finds powerful expression through the spatial trope of the waste land, which recurs across his oeuvre from *In Parenthesis* to 'The Sleeping Lord'. Jones contrasts the alienation and decadence of metropolitan modernity with the integrity and authenticity of local cultures, particularly via a series of antitheses between Roman imperialism and Celtic tradition, urban and rural spaces, masculine and feminine principles. However, close attention to the language and forms of Jones's reveals such oppositions to be profoundly unstable, while his engagements with the matter of Britain acknowledge and draw creative impetus from its cultural difference and diversity. Nowhere is this clearer than through his poetry's profound but also deeply conflicted imaginative alignments with Wales, a country that he regarded as his homeland and yet from which he also felt irremediably displaced by his circumstances of birth and upbringing. By insisting on the cultural centrality of Wales, Jones renders the history of Britain radically eccentric, strange to itself. Moreover, his archipelagic late modernism is repeatedly drawn to the marginal and littoral spaces of the island of Britain, its seacoasts and islands, as sites in which its layered histories of conquest and settlement, encounter and hybridisation can be imagined or recovered.

Chapter 2

Basil Bunting's Regional Modernism

Basil Bunting's poetic representations of place are shaped by a geographical imagination that thrives on contradictions. His regional modernism is characterised both by the imaginative centrality of northern landscapes and cultural paradigms to his writing, and by the refraction of such local and regional attachments through a self-consciously international modernist poetics. Bunting's major work, *Briggflatts* (1966), explores its twin themes of dislocation and homecoming through an intense imaginative engagement with the history, geography, and linguistic textures of the North-east of England. However, Bunting's poem is also a deliberately eccentric poetic autobiography that both enacts the expression of a securely 'northern' regional identity and suspends any such existential anchoring through its formal disjunctions and dense collage of incommensurable spaces and times. If the poem can be regarded as celebrating locality and belonging in a cherished regional landscape, it also attests to experiences of displacement and encounters with otherness, foregrounding vagrancy as a characteristically modern mode of being-in-the-world. In part, this world-view derives from Bunting's own personal experiences, for his idiosyncratic career as a poet, journalist, interpreter, diplomat, and MI6 agent entailed temporary residences in France, Italy, the United States, the Canary Islands, and Iran, before his return to his home place, Northumberland, in 1952, more than thirty years after his first departure in 1919.[1] However, Bunting's emphasis upon mobility, journeying, and transience in his later poems is also integral to his reflections on modernity, echoing György Lukács's claim that 'transcendental homelessness' is characteristic of the modern condition.[2] My purpose in this chapter is to demonstrate the extent to which regional, national, and international horizons are articulated together in his poetics of place, with particular reference to *Briggflatts* as a paradigmatic example of regional modernism.

Region and Nation

At first sight, the phrase 'regional modernism' appears oxymoronic, its two terms – adjective and noun – pulling in opposite directions. A well-rehearsed and widely accepted narrative about literary modernism defines it as an essentially metropolitan phenomenon with an emphatically internationalist character. Most of the major Anglophone modernist writers – including Ezra Pound, T. S. Eliot, James Joyce, and Gertrude Stein – were exiles or émigrés whose texts are conspicuously polyglot, multi-form, and composed of diverse cultural materials. Moreover, Malcolm Bradbury describes modernism as 'an art of cities', noting that the dynamic energies of urban life in the major European capitals are given expression in the fractured, discontinuous forms of modernist writing.[3] By definition, modernism is liberated from provincialism and local allegiances, caught up in an ambivalent but creatively productive relationship with the alienating currents of modernity and modernisation. In Marshall Berman's influential account, Paris, London, Berlin, St Petersburg, and New York are the principal centres of the modernist maelstrom, and the city street is modernism's paradigmatic space, 'the medium in which the totality of modern material and spiritual forces could meet, clash, interfuse and work out their ultimate meanings and fates'.[4] The problem with such critical and literary-historical accounts is that they strategically over-simplify the involved, multi-scale geographies of literary modernism, thereby underplaying the significance of regional and local affiliations for the geographical imaginations of many modernist writers, particularly those from Britain and Ireland.[5] To take just three obvious examples: Joyce's European stature is founded upon his intense imaginative engagements with Dublin, a provincial, colonial city that could only ironically be regarded as 'the Hibernian Metropolis' in *Ulysses* (1922); D. H. Lawrence's major novels, *Sons and Lovers* (1913), *The Rainbow* (1915), and *Women in Love* (1920), find their characteristic terrains among the farmlands, towns, and mining country of the Nottinghamshire-Derbyshire border; and Hugh MacDiarmid spearheaded a distinctively Scottish version of modernism during the 1920s and 1930s, first from the provincial town of Montrose and subsequently from remote Whalsay in the Shetland Isles.[6] In such instances of regional modernism an internationalist or cosmopolitan sensibility arises from, and is given direction by, contexts that are distinctively local or regional in character. At the same time, regional modernism's commitment to an aesthetic of the new also recasts conceptions of regional identity in more flexible, relational forms.

It is in the context of this model of regional modernism, wherein different spatial scales of personal, political, and creative affiliation overlap, that the distinctive achievements of Bunting's later, post-war poetry can best be understood. More usually, though, his work is considered under the rubric of 'British modernism', a national literary phenomenon that has proven difficult to characterise or define accurately. Modernism has had an uneven career in British poetry, in part because of the persistence of anti-modernist attitudes in both critical discourse and 'mainstream' poetic practice during the second half of the twentieth century.[7] Nonetheless, as Peter Howarth observes, it is clear that 'British poetry has been irrevocably changed by modernism' and this is true both for the contemporary avant-garde and, in a different way, for the line of poets that descends from Thomas Hardy through Philip Larkin to Andrew Motion.[8] One distinctive feature of Bunting's poetry that he shares with other British late modernists, such as W. S. Graham, David Jones, Hugh MacDiarmid, and Lynette Roberts, is its emphasis upon the particularities of place, apparently grounding the transcultural or exilic aesthetic of high modernism in specific and intimately-described landscapes. Neil Corcoran notes that Bunting and Jones both cultivate difference through their respective affirmations of locality and regional culture, demonstrating in their work 'how an English national culture was only one among many in the British Isles'.[9] Similarly, Robert Crawford shows how MacDiarmid's assertive and self-conscious internationalism was complicated, but never compromised, by 'an interaction with the minutely local.'[10]

To varying degrees, all three writers eschew the dominant national frameworks for identity, conjoining the local and the international in a manner that exposes the variegated plurality underlying the very idea of a unified 'British' culture. Indeed, as William Wooten remarks, 'British modernism tends to be most characteristically British when it is at its most resistant to dominant notions of Britishness or the British State.'[11] This paradoxical formulation certainly accords with Bunting's agonistic sense of Northumbria's social, cultural, and linguistic distinctiveness, as well as his abhorrence of centralised authority. For instance, in a 1946 letter to Dorothy Pound, he wrote: 'I am for thwarting the government – all the governments, especially the more powerful and effective ones'; and Richard Burton notes that Bunting consistently expressed his contempt for 'the prevailing national political culture' of Britain throughout the 1970s and early 1980s.[12] Unlike those of many first-generation Anglophone modernists, such as Eliot, Pound, and W. B. Yeats, Bunting's politics were markedly left-wing and anti-authoritarian throughout his life, and this informs the significance that his poetry grants both to marginal places or cultures and to humble, everyday things.

There is, however, a danger that by emphasising the regional or national characteristics of modernist poetry from Britain a form of domestication may be effected, and the singularity or eccentricity of these writers' texts assimilated to the values of the dominant culture. For example, one of Bunting's most vocal champions, Donald Davie, places *Briggflatts* at the centre of the canon of post-war British poetry, commending what he sees as its 'deeply ingrained Englishness' over and above its cosmopolitan tendencies, which are dismissed as superficial.[13] In this way, the intrinsic cultural hybridity of Bunting's late modernism is underplayed so that he can be made a pillar of the English poetic tradition. Against such strategies of recuperation and appropriation, Drew Milne argues that the work of British modernist poets should be understood in terms of its 'possible cosmopolitan solidarities' rather than its espousal of familiar geopolitical identities.[14] In Bunting's case, such cosmopolitan solidarities are apparent in his friendships and correspondence with a diverse group of European and American modernists, including Constantine Brancusi, Karl Drerup, Mina Loy, Lorine Niedecker, Ezra Pound, Tibor Serly, William Carlos Williams, and Louis Zukofsky. Bunting's aesthetic cosmopolitanism is also apparent in the preface he wrote for his *Collected Poems* (1968), where he acknowledges the influence of Dante, Horace, Malherbe, Villon, Manuchehri and Ferdowsi alongside Wordsworth, Wyatt, Whitman, Spenser, Pound, and Zukofsky.[15] In this regard, Bunting follows the example of his sometime mentor Pound, who insisted that any thorough knowledge of literature entails 'knowledge of various tongues' and espoused translation as 'good training' for apprentice poets.[16] Accordingly, throughout his career, Bunting wrote and published a diverse group of poems that he called 'overdrafts', translations or adaptations of texts from their French, Italian, Latin, and Persian originals. Indeed, with Pound's encouragement, Bunting taught himself classical Persian in order to translate Ferdowsi's epic poem, *Shahnameh*, after discovering an incomplete version in French at a quay-side book stall in Genoa in 1930.[17] Alongside his more widely-recognised attachments to Northumbria, Bunting's intense interest in the literature, culture, and landscapes of Persia/Iran is a key element of his distinctive geographical imagination, which precludes any straightforward assimilation of his poetry with a continuous English tradition.[18]

Given the significance of such cosmopolitan solidarities, there is a danger of restricting the range and invention of Bunting's modernist poetics by prioritising his local and regional attachments. Dennis Brown voices a similar concern when he remarks that the full scope of Bunting's 'achievement' has been limited by 'what appears to be regional loyalty' among some of his critical supporters.[19] However, Milne's polemical focus upon the centrality of 'geographical displacements' to British modernist poetics is also potentially limiting in another way.[20] For, Bunting's material and emotional attachments to specific places and regions in the north of England are a significant component of his work's imaginative texture and should not be dismissed or ignored. What is needed is a more dialectical understanding of the way in which local and international concerns inter-animate in Bunting's poetry, beginning with an appraisal of the respective claims made for both his regional roots and his cosmopolitan modernism.

Rootedness and Spatial Relations

Late in life, Bunting liked to play the role of the Old Man of the North, affirming that: 'A poet is just a poet, but I am a Northumbrian man. It has always been my home, even when I've been living elsewhere'.[21] Such assertions of regional pride are apparently sincere but can mislead readers by implying that his texts posit a more straightforward set of relations between 'home' and 'elsewhere' than is actually the case. Similarly, critics who commend Bunting's espousal of a marginal cultural identity at odds with the hegemony of the metropolitan centre often fail to acknowledge sufficiently the complexity of his poetic representations of place. This is especially the case when they have recourse to the organicist rhetoric of 'roots' and 'rootedness', which Theodor Adorno identifies as a key component of the 'jargon of authenticity' employed by existentialist thinkers, particularly Martin Heidegger.[22] Eric Falci, for instance, describes *Briggflatts* as 'an intensely rooted poem'; and for Richard Caddel and Anthony Flowers, Bunting's poem is significant primarily because it is 'deeply rooted in the North of England'.[23] Samuel Rogers develops this idea further when he identifies the combination of 'rootedness in landscape' and 'historical depth' as defining features of the British modernist long poem, taking Bunting's *Briggflatts* as his key example.[24] Each of these observations has some critical value; but, by foregrounding permanence and continuity as essential to the experience of place, through the shared metaphor of 'rootedness', each obscures the importance of journeying, wandering, and exile to the thematic concerns and symbolic forms of *Briggflatts*, a poem that does not simply hymn its homeland but, crucially, traces the intersecting arcs of several departures and returns. As an autobiography of sorts, *Briggflatts* draws upon the itinerant trajectory of Bunting's own life, which took him from Scotswood to Wylam by way of London, Paris, Rapallo, Berlin, New York, the Canary Islands, Tehran, and Isfahan. To speak of roots is to risk neglecting the importance of these elsewheres for Bunting's conception of home, and to underplay the significance of the various cosmopolitan solidarities that inform his aesthetic. Mobility, which Tim Cresswell defines as 'the dynamic equivalent of *place*', is as much a feature of Bunting's geographical imagination as is the topographically specific, situated character of many of his most important poems.[25]

Rather than an elemental rootedness, then, Bunting's most characteristic work is informed by a vagabond poetics, wherein the dialectical tension between place and displacement is a central, animating force. The term 'vagabond' derives from two Latin words: 'vagus', meaning 'to wander'; and 'proprius', meaning 'one's own way'. By wandering freely on his or her own way, the vagabond also embodies a subversive or rebellious counterpower to established social orders and hierarchies.[26] The term was first used in the early modern period in Europe to refer to those 'landless men' and emancipated serfs who moved from place to place in search of work or lodgings during the transition from feudalism to mercantile capitalism. As Tim Cresswell observes, the vagabond was frequently criminalised because his 'wayward travels meant that he always had traces of elsewhere about him', so that his very presence 'disturbed those who had chosen a settled and rooted existence'.[27] In several respects, Bunting fits the profile of the modern vagabond, and his poetry is certainly informed by an affinity with wandering, wayward, and socially marginal figures. In particular, he was attracted to the work of the fifteenth-century vagabond-poet François Villon, partly through the influence of Pound but also because of their shared experiences of imprisonment and criminalisation, which are refracted through one another in Bunting's first important poem, *Villon* (1930).[28] There is also a distinctly nautical bent to Bunting's vagabondage: during the 1930s he worked on boats in Italy and the United States, trained as a sailor at Nellist's Nautical Academy in South Shields, and briefly pursued a career at sea.[29] Moreover, sailors, boats, and sea voyages recur across his oeuvre, from 'the men of the sea / who have neither nation nor time' (8) in *Villon* to his final ode, published in 1980, where an aging sailor apostrophises his boat: 'Soon, while that northwest squall wrings out its cloud, / cutter, we'll heave to / free of the sands' (133). Indeed, this ode, which begins with the line 'Now we've no hope of going back' (133), elaborates on a theme first established in *Briggflatts* – 'No hope of going back' (44) – and augments the earlier poem's use of nautical figures. In Bunting's work, the sailor is a counterpart of the vagabond poet, while in *Briggflatts* the boat's wake supplies a metaphor for reading and writing poetry: 'Flexible, unrepetitive line / to sing, not paint' (46).

A key problem for any critical reading of *Briggflatts*, and for several of Bunting's other mid-length poems, is the question of how the text's regional and international elements inter-relate. Is Bunting a regionalist who adapts the techniques of international modernism to his subject matter? Or a modernist who happens upon regional topics because of the accident of his birth in North-east England? Keith Tuma contends that Bunting gives Poundian modernism 'a Northumbrian signature'; but he also goes on to describe how the 'Northumbrian core' of *Briggflatts* is 'set in a field of international influences and traditions'.[30] In Tuma's first reading, then, a regional 'signature' inflects but does not fundamentally transform Bunting's recognisably modernist aesthetic; in his second, regional identity provides the irreducible 'core' of the poem, which resonates decisively among more cosmopolitan influences and contexts. Such critical equivocation reflects the way in which Bunting's focus shifts restlessly between local, regional, national, and international horizons, which are intricately coordinated but rarely cohere in a single representational frame. The geographer John Tomaney registers something of this complex situation when he observes that Bunting's representations of Northumbria are 'rooted in a sense of place that is both territorial and open to the world'.[31] Tomaney's emphasis, however, falls more heavily on rootedness and territoriality than openness to larger historical and geographical contexts, and he argues that *Briggflatts* is principally concerned with the theme of 'dwelling' and with depicting 'a spiritual and poetic homeland'.[32] As I have argued, such an emphasis upon dwelling and the 'spiritual' significance of the poet's homeland oversimplifies the involved interplay between home and elsewhere, the local and the international in Bunting's geographically and culturally diverse text. If, as Martin Heidegger remarks, to dwell is 'to remain, to stay in place', then Bunting's vagabond poetics eschews such a sedentarist metaphysics, foregrounding the importance of journeys in time and space, and dramatising the dynamic construction of selfhood through encounters with other peoples, cultures, and places.[33]

Bunting's ambivalent, self-conscious attitude towards dwelling and belonging is evident in 'Chomei at Toyama', a poem composed in the early 1930s which is as much concerned with the themes of dwelling, home, and the relationship between self and place as is *Briggflatts*. Bunting's poem is a verse adaptation – part translation, part condensation – of *Hōjōki*, a thirteenth-century Japanese prose text by Kamo no Chōmei, describing the author's retirement from public life in Kyoto to live as a Buddhist hermit in the hills above Toyama. Bunting, who admitted to knowing 'no Japanese and nothing about Japan', worked from an Italian prose translation by Marcello Muccioli, mediating between three languages and transforming the form of the original text.[34] Victoria Forde notes that 'Chomei at Toyama' is centrally concerned with 'the mutability of life which underlies all that seems permanent', a theme that is explored through the leitmotif of the house that Bunting threads through the whole poem.[35] In the first half of the text, Chomei recalls a series of disasters – a fire, a whirlwind, famine, an earthquake – that devastated Kyoto, which was then the capital city of Japan, during the late twelfth century. In particular, Bunting highlights the destruction of the city's built environment – 'a thunder of houses falling' (67) – and has Chomei remark dryly: 'Men are fools to invest in real estate' (66). At the same time, through references to 'Sixth Avenue' (66) and 'Riverside Drive' (67), he encourages the reader to see parallels between ancient Kyoto and New York during the Depression years. The second half of the poem describes Chomei's pastoral hermitage on the slopes of Mount Hino with humour and gentle irony. Crucially, while the old man expresses his satisfaction at having escaped the 'Hankering, vexation and apathy' (73) that characterise worldly, urban life, he deliberately embraces the mutability and impermanence of existence, observing: 'This is the unstable world and / we in it unstable and our houses' (68). Importantly, Chomei's hut (or 'hōjōki') is 'a lodging not a dwelling' (69) and without any sure foundation, a temporary shelter against the elements that can be abandoned or moved to another place when necessary.

In 'Chomei at Toyama', impermanence is posited as an existential condition, an idea that echoes through many of Bunting's poems. For instance, in 'Villon' the poet-speaker remarks that 'We are less permanent than thought' (7); and a late ode, 'At Briggflatts Meeting House', concludes with the image of clouds dancing 'under the wind's wing' as 'leaves / delight in transience' (132). For Bunting, being in the world entails living amid uncertainty, instability, and to inhabit place has less to do with the security of 'rootedness' than it has with experiencing the eventful character of places, their unique manner of taking place in the flow of time. As Edward Casey describes it, 'place is not entitative – as a foundation has to be – but eventmental, something in process, something unconfinable to a thing. Or to a simple location'.[36] What this means is that places are neither static objects nor self-enclosed entities, but open to change over time and produced through their relations with other places. Where Tomaney reads *Briggflatts* as disclosing an image of Northumbria that is bounded, stable, and distinct, 'the evocation of a home-world', I suggest that Bunting's poem is better understood in terms of 'the relational region', a conception of place that emphasises the region's implication in networks of spatial relations that extend far beyond its boundaries.[37] According to this perspective, regions comprise 'a series of open, discontinuous spaces constituted by social relationships which stretch across them in various ways'.[38] Far from being enclosed and self-sufficient, the region can be understood as a point of intersection or convergence for an array of social, historical, and economic processes. Or, as Doreen Massey argues, places are always 'meeting places', 'articulations within the wider power-geometries of space.'[39]

Tomaney's concern is that such an emphasis upon networks and spatial relations will subordinate local particularity and the scale of lived experience to the alienated transactions of global flows. However, this need not necessarily be the case. For Henri Lefebvre, the experience of place always partakes of what he calls the 'hypercomplexity of social space', whereby spaces and places interpenetrate one another at a range of scales from the local to the global:

> The national and regional levels take in innumerable 'places'; national space embraces the regions; and world space does not merely subsume national spaces, but even (for the time being at least) precipitates the formation of new national spaces through a remarkable process of fission. All these spaces, meanwhile, are traversed by myriad currents.[40]

Social spaces are entangled and implicated in one another, maintaining a semi-autonomous existence but also sharing in an ambiguous continuity. In such circumstances, the local and the regional, the national and the international overlap without ever simply being reduced one to the other. Lefebvre's account of spatial hypercomplexity provides a useful framework for understanding the co-presence of regional and international concerns in Bunting's poetry because of the way it suggests how particularity and socio-spatial relations might be thought together in representations of place.

The North-east and the Middle East

The distinctive 'northernness' of Bunting's poetry, particularly but not exclusively *Briggflatts*, is at once pervasive and elusive, begging several questions. Is Bunting's North the modern region of Northumberland or the ancient kingdom of Northumbria, which stretched from the Humber to the Firth of Forth and west as far as Cumbria? Can it be restricted to the North, or North-east, of England, or is it fundamentally separate from any English polity? Where do its borders begin and end? For Peter

Davidson, 'north' names the direction of an idea as much as it designates a geographical location, while both location and idea partake of a fundamental ambiguity. 'As a descriptor of place', he argues, '"north" is shifting and elusive, yet, paradoxically, it is a term that evokes a precise – even passionate – response in most people'.⁴¹ Similarly, Katharine Cockin notes that the North, as both space and representational paradigm, 'is not fixed, but is rather still forming or becoming', a creative process that is particularly visible in literary texts.⁴² The North of England is frequently defined in opposition to 'the South' – itself an idea that subsumes a host of local and regional differences – but the boundary separating the two is difficult to draw with any confidence.⁴³ Historians and geographers disagree as to whether the North should be regarded as beginning at the Humber, the Don, the Trent, or at an imaginary line drawn between the Severn and the Wash. At times little more than a synonym for Yorkshire, 'the North' can expand to include as many as eleven English counties.⁴⁴ These ambiguities are not resolved by focusing upon Bunting's version of his native Northumbria, in which the cultural and historical associations of an autonomous seventh- and eighth-century kingdom are superimposed upon a modern British region. Moreover, Bunting's conception of Northumbrian identity is never straightforwardly Anglian or, indeed, English, but rather tends to emphasise its heterogeneous, hybrid character.

In a lecture on the seventh-century *Codex Lindisfarnensis* (The Book of Lindisfarne), Bunting entertains the hope that contemporary artworks produced in the North-east might preserve and develop 'the impulse of Northumbrian culture' by forsaking imitation of Roman, European, or Southern English models and instead 'trying to discern what is our own'. His use of the first-person plural possessive pronoun ('our') is telling here, underlining Bunting's conscious alignment of his own poetics with the history and cultural traditions of a distinct region. Nonetheless, Bunting is careful to stress that he is referring to 'a fusion of cultures' in which Anglian, Celtic, and Norse elements combine.⁴⁵ While he articulates a desire for cultural continuity, Bunting also conceives of Northumbria as a site of intersection and cultural encounter; it is the unique mixture or 'fusion' of different traditions that combine in Northumbrian culture to make it distinctive. Such openness and hybridity aptly reflects Northumbria's historic 'position at the crossroads of northern Europe', the Humber and the Clyde each serving as 'highways to wider worlds'.⁴⁶

Following Bunting, the North can be understood as a meeting place that illustrates the hypercomplexity of social space: its location and extent are elusive or at best ill-defined; its borders are porous and shifting;

and its culture is a fusion of heterogeneous elements. The aesthetic required to represent such a place adequately must combine a focus on the particular with an awareness of manifold spatial relations. Bunting's poetics of place is informed by his conviction that art should attend to complexity and particularity, resisting wherever possible the temptations of generalisation or abstraction. 'Go in fear of abstractions', warned Pound; and Bunting explicitly approved of the elder poet's 'stress on the immediate, the particular, and the concrete'.[47] Moreover, in a 1932 essay he writes: 'Simultaneity, interdependence, continuous self-references and absence of simplification are characteristic of all fact, whether physical or mental or emotional.'[48] It is striking, then, that Bunting should find an appropriate formal model for representing such complexity and interdependence – which is historical and social as much as spatial – in the 'utterly abstract' visual art of the *Codex Lindisfarnensis*, an art that is 'complex to an extraordinary degree, without ever losing its unity and its proportion.' In the 'perpetual crisscross of lines' decorating the carpet pages of its illuminated Gospels, Bunting perceives a mode of formal patterning that might encompass both microcosmic and macrocosmic perspectives, demonstrating the mutual implication of things in a compressed and stylised manner.[49] Interestingly, he recognises something similar in the structural forms of Pound's *Cantos*, which elaborate 'an extraordinarily complex system of related images, changing as fluidly as the data of life and thought themselves'.[50] Dark Age latticework and modernist kaleidoscope: these formal structures provide the templates for Bunting's articulation of local, regional, national, and international concerns in *Briggflatts*, and inform the poem's imagery through the repeated trope of the woven fabric, the text of the world. Indeed, Peter Makin remarks that: '"Weave" may perhaps be *Briggflatts*'s main image for the cosmos.'[51]

Any exclusive focus upon Bunting's attachments to Northumbria or the supposedly "rooted" character of his poetry risks distorting the distinctive character of his regional modernism. In this regard, Julian Stannard rightly notes that 'Bunting's commitment to the north never precluded an enthusiasm for wider international perspectives'.[52] Arguably the most important of these international perspectives derives from his long-term engagement with Persian poetry and culture, which began in 1930 and continued until his death in 1985. Indeed, Bunting's twin enthusiasms for Northumbrian and Persian culture come together memorably in Part III of *Briggflatts*, which recasts an episode from Ferdowsi's *Shahnameh* in which Alexander the Great/Sekander encounters the Angel Israfel.[53] The outcome of this encounter between military commander and angel of death is to check Alexander's hubris, end his imperial campaigns, and send him homewards. 'What Alexander learns,' remarks Bunting, 'is that man is contemptibly nothing and yet may live content in humility'.⁵⁴ However, Alexander's return with his men to Macedonia, 'to end in our place by our own wars' (52), clearly also serves as a mythological parallel for the poet-protagonist's return, in a state of humility, to Northumbria, the 'acknowledged land' (56) from which he, too, has long been absent. At the centre of *Briggflatts*, then, a poem that is intimately bound up with the history, geography, and cultural traditions of Bunting's native Northumbria, is an episode concerning a Greek warrior king adapted from a tenth-century Persian epic poem. Nor is this an isolated instance of the convergence between Bunting's regional attachments to Northumbria and his more exotic affiliations with Persia. For instance, in Part II the focus shifts abruptly from rock pools on the Northumbrian coast to the wildlife of the Persian desert: 'Asian vultures riding on a spiral / column of dust / or swift desert ass startled by the / camels' dogged saunter' (49). Similarly, in Part IV the speaker's contemplation of ancient battlefields in the North of England is interrupted by a powerful sensory memory of 'ibex guts steaming under a cold ridge, / tomcat stink of a leopard dying while I stood / easing the bolt to dwell on a round's shining rim' (55). Such images cannot easily be assimilated with a reading of *Briggflatts* that foregrounds its 'rootedness' in a singular, bounded region; but nor can they simply be ignored, for they are an integral part of the poem's complex poetics of place.

Bunting's acquaintance with Persian poetry began with Ferdowsi in 1930, but over the course of his career he translated nearly two dozen poems and fragments of larger works by Hafez, Manuchehri, Rudaki, and Saadi. In 1953 he told Zukofsky, with some justification, that he was 'more widely read in Persian than most of the Orientalists in the British and European universities'.⁵⁵ Initially, Bunting's knowledge of Persian culture was gleaned entirely from books; but in 1942 his ability to read classical Persian led to his being deployed as an interpreter for the RAF in Iraq and then Iran, working closely with the Bakhtiari tribe, who claim descent from Shah Fereydun, a character in Ferdowsi's *Shahnameh*.⁵⁶ In the desert landscapes of South-west Iran, Bunting found that literature and reality, history and myth were tightly interwoven. In 1944 he joined the Combined Intelligence Centre in Baghdad but served as a diplomat in Isfahan, a city he loved and which left a lasting impression on his imagination.⁵⁷ Keith Alldritt observes that: 'For Basil Bunting the city came to have the same sort of importance that Byzantium had for Yeats'.⁵⁸ By 1947 he was based at the British Embassy in Teheran and had responsibility for Political Intelligence across nearly the whole of the Middle East, occupying a position at the heart of the British Intelligence community with which he was not always at ease.[59] Bunting left the Foreign Office in 1948 following his marriage to a Kurdo-Armenian girl from Isfahan, Sima Alladadian, who was more than thirty years his junior, but remained in Iran as a correspondent for *The Times* until 1952, when he was expelled by the Prime Minister, Mohammad Mossadeq.[60] For almost a decade, then, Bunting was an important figure in the volatile political circles of the Middle East and he developed a profound knowledge and understanding of Persian history and culture during his time in Iran. By contrast, his return to Northumberland was inglorious and involuntary, and the decade that followed was characterised by poverty, precarious employment, and a demoralising decline in his poetic creativity. Burton aptly describes this period as 'Bunting's empty years'.[61]

Bunting's knowledge and personal experience of the Middle East, especially Iran, is given fullest expression in *The Spoils* (1951), a mid-length poem that also draws upon his war-time experiences in the Mediterranean, North Africa, and Western Europe. Indeed, while its atmosphere, imagery, and themes are different, Alex Niven argues that *The Spoils* 'preempts the expansive rhetorical mood of *Briggflatts* and that work's emphasis on place and a distinctive geographical *mise-en-scène*'.[62] There are also similarities in terms of the parallels that both poems draw between moments in the distant past and the present of personal experience or remembrance. *The Spoils* is divided into three parts, though it was originally conceived as four.[63] It opens with two epigraphs, one in Arabic from the Koran – '*al anfal li'llah*', which Bunting translates as 'The spoils are for God' (537) – and the other from the Book of Genesis, which describe the sons of Shem, mythical ancestors of the Semitic peoples, both Arabs and Jews.[64] The poem gives expression to what Bunting regarded as a characteristically Semitic view of life as a 'journey', on which death is a necessary and even welcome 'companion' (26). The real enemy of life is not death but servitude, particularly the kind of unfreedom that is created by economies of money and commerce. In Part I, the Jewish tax-gatherer and merchant, Asshur, is occupied with 'ringing and weighing coin' when he encounters a stranger, a soldier standing in his doorway, and assumes the other man's critical perspective of his occupation:

one stood in the door
scorning our occupation,
silent: so in his greaves I saw
in polished bronze
a man like me reckoning pence,
never having tasted bread

where there is ice in his flask,
storks' stilts cleaving sun-disk,
sun like driven sand. (26)

Catching his own reflection in the soldier's polished armour, Asshur is jolted out of his mundane task and granted a vision of another possible life, one of danger and hardship but also lyrical beauty in the soldier's desert camp. Similarly, the Bedouin Arpachshad describes his life of wandering the desert sands as 'apt to no servitude' (27), offering scant comfort but rare freedom. Throughout *The Spoils*, the Arabian and Persian deserts are associated with freedom and the pleasures of a life sharpened by the ever-present threat of death. By contrast, Aram, the romantic Zionist, creates a memorable image of debased commercial culture in the figure of 'David dancing before the Ark' as his audience 'toss him pennies' (28). Here, the King of Israel is depicted as little more than a vaudeville performer or busker, while the most sacred of objects, the Ark of the Covenant, is implicated in a milieu that is both profane and exploitative.

Although *The Spoils* draws most of its images and allusions from the Middle East, especially Iraq and Persia, Bunting's criticisms are directed against a culture of money and avarice that he associates primarily with the West. Against this, the poem poses the major achievements of Persian culture past and present, which exemplify grace, complexity, and artistic vitality. Part II begins by describing the architectural splendour of the Jāmeh Mosque (Masjid-e-Jāmeh) in Isfahan, 'where Avicenna may have worshipped' (30), then moves on to celebrate Iran's contemporary cultural vigour in the miniatures of Hajji Masavvor, the music of Naystani, Taj, and Moluk-e-Zarabi, and the storytelling of Sobhi, which keeps 'boys from their meat' (31). Finally, in Part III Bunting returns to the theme of soldiering introduced in Part I, amplifying it to take in the whole theatre of conflict during the Second World War, thereby connecting East and West explicitly. Indeed, as Stannard observes, the poem's title suggests both 'the spoils of war' and the ruination caused as a result of the fighting.[65] One striking passage describes abandoned vehicles and destroyed arms in the desert landscapes of Egypt and Libya – 'a tank's turret twisted skyward, / here and there a lorry unharmed / out of fuel or the crew scattered' (34) – which Bunting claimed to have witnessed during a month-long journey from Basra to Tripoli in 1943.[66] In its final lines, the poem shifts focus to the seas and coastlines of Northern Europe, depicting an air raid on Glasgow and concluding with a panorama that is geographically expansive but anchored by carefully chosen topographical details:

> From Largo Law look down,
> moon and dry weather, look down
> on convoy marshalled, filing between mines.
> Cold northern clear sea-gardens
> between Lofoten and Spitzbergen,
> as good a grave as any, earth or water.
> What else do we live for and take part,
> we who would share the spoils? (35)

The intricate patterns of alliteration, assonance, and rhythmic variation in these lines are perhaps modelled on 'the mosaic pattern of Eastern poetry', as Forde suggests, but the imagery of 'Cold northern clear sea-gardens' is in striking contrast to the date groves and desert landscapes with which the poem begins.[67] Nonetheless, there is also a deeper symmetry between the poem's beginning and its end. In this stanza, Largo Law on the east coast of Scotland is linked, via convoys bound for the Arctic, to the Norwegian islands of Lofoten and Spitzbergen, and the journey northwards picks up and recasts the metaphor of life's journey, where death is 'No ill companion' (26), with which Part I opens. Indeed, the rhetorical question posed in the final lines implies that it is precisely this journey through life in the company of ubiquitous death for which 'we live'. Like *Briggflatts*, then, *The Spoils* might best be understood as a poem about journeys and journeying, both actual and metaphorical, that lead far from home.

The Music of Place

A decade and a half separates the first publication dates of *The Spoils* and *Briggflatts*, during which time Bunting was living in Northumberland and struggling to support his family as a journalist. This exhausting drudge-work, combined with the refusal by Faber to publish his *Poems 1950* (1950) in Britain, produced a sense of creative paralysis in Bunting that would not dissipate until Tom Pickard, a young Tyneside poet, visited him at Wylam in 1963 and encouraged him to read his work to new audiences at the Morden Tower in Newcastle.[68] What followed, according to Burton, was a major 'creative resurgence' resulting in 'the biggest event in the world of poetry (in English at least) since the publication of *The Waste Land* in 1922, *Briggflatts*'.[69] More modestly, Bunting claimed that *Briggflatts* was written during his train journeys to and from work as 'a lesson' for Pickard on how to write a long poem, which he meticulously pared down from about 20,000 lines to just 700.[70] By doing so, Bunting was following his own advice. In his *ABC of Reading*

(1934), Pound attributes the bilingual adage 'Dichten = condensare' to Bunting, describing it as his 'prime contribution to contemporary criticism'; and Bunting himself remarked that 'most good work, whether in poetry or in music or in drawing, is a matter of condensation as far as the immediate technique is concerned'.[71] *Briggflatts* is not a long poem by comparison with Pound's *Cantos*, Zukofsky's *"A"*, or even Williams's *Paterson*. Whereas those three modernist epics take the extended forms they do because of their collage-like structures, which enable them to include and assimilate very diverse materials, the scope and ambition of *Briggflatts* is paradoxically apparent in its fragmentary narrative, compressed diction, and the dense aural effects of its language. In this regard, *Briggflatts* exhibits some of the features of what C. D. Blanton calls the 'intensive' mode of modernist epic poetry, which is characteristically elliptical and allusive rather than accumulative and 'extensive'. For Blanton, this technique is exemplified by Eliot's *The Waste Land*.[72]

Briggflatts is a poem immersed in the intricacies of the material world, attending to the interplay of history and topography, human cultures and non-human environments, 'excepting nothing that is' (55). Subtitled 'An Autobiography', it nonetheless maintains a characteristically modernist impersonality, deferring the use of first-person pronouns until Part II and employing them sparingly thereafter, usually in contexts that involve self-questioning or doubt. Moreover, as Matthew Hart observes, the poem's fragmented account of the growth of a poet's mind also opens onto a more far-reaching 'biography of a place and a language'.[73] Accordingly, *Briggflatts* begins by describing a northern landscape transfigured by the arrival of spring:

> Brag, sweet tenor bull,
> descant on Rawthey's madrigal,
> each pebble its part
> for the fells' late spring. (41)

This initial conjunction of poetry, place, and music sets the tone for much of what follows. Bunting thought of *Briggflatts* and several of his other long poems as 'sonatas', texts that rework a common theme across several movements, each with their own shifting patterns of sound and sense.[74] As Adorno remarks, the 'unity' of the sonata form is 'a clearly differentiated manifold, with development and reprise', and this is true also of the form of Bunting's poem.[75] In its opening lines, the bull's tenor voice is heard against the polyphonic trickling and gushing of the river, and the whole landscape is made to sing in intricate counterpoint. This conceit is repeated and varied many times throughout the poem, providing a thread that links different places, times, and ecosystems. On the high moors of Stainmore 'becks ring on limestone, / whisper to peat' and Eric Bloodaxe, last king of Northumbria, is recalled through 'Baltic plainsong speech' (42); a rock pool pulses to 'a galliard by William Byrd'; the wildlife of the Persian desert 'figures sudden flight of the descant / on a madrigal by Monteverdi'; even the lowly rat, alter-ego of the poet, 'has daring / to thread, lithe and alert, Schoenberg's maze' (49). Ian Gregson has remarked on *Briggflatts*'s importance as a 'nature poem', demonstrating that 'experience can best be understood through detailed examination of the physical world'.[76] What is particularly striking in these examples, however, is the blending of nature and culture that occurs in the music of place.

From its first stanza, *Briggflatts* is engaged in creating what Murray Schafer calls a 'soundscape', the distinctive 'acoustic environment' that is associated with a particular place or landscape.[77] Bunting does not distinguish sharply between the 'aestheticized noise' of music and the 'lived sonic experience' of the natural world, but rather dramatises their correspondences.[78] For instance, the slowworm's song which closes Part III is repeated by 'every bough' of the surrounding woodland (54); and the sonatas of Domenico Scarlatti echo in 'stars and lakes', while 'the copse drums out his measure' (56). In Part V, a full orchestra accompanies the appearance of the first constellations in the northern sky:

Young flutes, harps touched by a breeze,
drums and horns escort
Aldebaran, low in the clear east,
beckoning boats to the fishing. (59)

Over the course of the poem, the bull's bellowing on the fellside and the River Rawthey's madrigal are incorporated into a shifting soundscape that emphasises the inherent connectedness of things, and their coexistence in places that remain distinct but are nonetheless implicated in one another.

The music of place is a central theme in *Briggflatts* that has its formal counterpart in the poem's own intricate soundscape of acoustic effects and flexible rhythms. For Bunting, poetry is first and foremost a pattern of sounds, whether harmonious or dissonant. In the preface to his *Collected Poems*, he writes: 'With sleights learned from others and an ear open to melodic analogies I have set down words as a musician pricks his score, not to be read in silence, but to trace in the air a pattern of sound that may sometimes, I hope, be pleasing' (555). Throughout his career, Bunting affirmed that '[p]oetry, like music, is to be heard'; he even claimed that 'poetry can exist without troubling itself to have any meaning at all' so long as it creates a sufficiently engaging complex of sounds and rhythms.[79] Accordingly, the language of *Briggflatts* is dense with sonic textures, full of clotted rhythms and ringing alliteration, hard consonants, open vowels, off-kilter rhymes. Extensive use of elision gives an impression of terseness and compressed power that is enhanced by the text's modern recasting of Old English alliterative verse and Welsh *cynghanedd*.[80] Although not written in dialect, *Briggflatts* employs a distinctively 'northern' vernacular that comes to the fore when the poem names domestic items ('skillet', 'girdle', 'settle'), plants and animals ('may', 'peewit', 'spuggies', 'gentles'), and topographical features ('fells', 'saltings', 'skerry'). In one of his half-serious notes to *Briggflatts*, Bunting pointedly observes: 'We have burns in the east, *becks* in the west, but no brooks or creeks' (538). Language, then, is both a marker of identity – to say 'burn' or 'beck' is to connote northernness, even as an East-West divide is acknowledged – and the medium through which the meanings of place are construed. Moreover, the very sounds of these northern words for places and things are important to the soundscape of the poem, the 'music' of which, Bunting (in)famously claimed, would be 'mauled' by 'Southron' accents and speech habits (538).

Commenting on the relationship between language and place, Peter Quartermain argues that the distinctive sound-patterns of Bunting's poetry 'combine to suggest something of the Northumbrian landscape'.[81] This is an attractive idea, but one that is difficult to illustrate conclusively given the looseness of the analogy, not to mention the variety of sounds and landscapes in question. However, it is notable that the language of *Briggflatts* tends to become more thickly textured when the writing of place is an explicit preoccupation, as in the lament for a drowned Viking warrior in Part II:

> Wind writes in foam on the sea:
>
> Who sang, sea takes,
> brawn brine, bone grit.
> Keener the kittiwake.
> Fells forget him.
> Fathoms dull the dale,
> gulfweed voices . . . (46)

The dead man – a singer or poet – is commemorated in these lines through a word-music that combines the sounds of waves, wind, and gulls, human and submarine voices. The use of paired double stresses ('brawn brine, bone grit'), alliteration ('Fells forget him'), internal and slant rhymes in combination with strenuously condensed syntax creates an initial impression of turbulence that gradually ebbs and subsides towards the concluding ellipsis. As often happens in *Briggflatts*, sound is foregrounded over meaning: in a sense the sound *is* the meaning of these lines. Forde notes the degree to which Bunting's poetry exemplifies what Pound called *melopœia*, 'wherein the words are charged, over and above their plain meaning, with some musical property, which directs the bearing or trend of that meaning'.[82] However, the ellipsis, which graphically denotes silence, an absence of sound as voices fade out of hearing, also serves to remind the reader of the poem's essentially *written*, textual character. For, an ellipsis leaves a mark without making any sound. If writing is figured as ephemeral in these lines, no more than the traces of wind on water, then those traces are less negligible than the metaphor suggests; in fact, they constitute much of the poem's substance.

Bunting's poetics is explicitly 'phonocentric', in Jacques Derrida's sense of the term, to the extent that he prioritises speech over writing and affirms the 'absolute proximity of voice and being'.[83] Repeatedly in his scattered remarks on poetry, he stresses the vital importance of speech and song, and affirms that sound is fundamental to the poem's very being. For instance, in conversation with Eric Mottram, Bunting explains: 'I've never said that poetry consists *only* of sound. I said again and again that the *essential* thing is the sound. Without the sound there isn't any poetry'.[84] And in a 1934 letter to George Marion O'Donnell, he remarks that: 'Language is speech first and last, it is only a set of written symbols between whiles'.[85] Nonetheless, *Briggflatts* implies that poetry is also unavoidably textual, bound up with an economy of writing and inscription. Indeed, Hart contends that the 'key synthetic vernacular irony of *Briggflatts* lies in the fissure between its nostalgia for a "musical" past and the undeniable literariness of its media and method'.[86] The poem incorporates this very 'fissure' between song and writing into one of its central networks of imagery, conjoining the symbolic figures of the mason and the lark in an equivocal allegory of poetic labour:

> A mason times his mallet
> to a lark's twitter,
> listening while the marble rests,
> lays his rule
> at a letter's edge,
> fingertips checking,
> till the stone spells a name
> naming none,
> a man abolished.
> Painful lark, labouring to rise!
> The solemn mallet says:
> In the grave's slot
> he lies. We rot. (41)

In lines such as these, *Briggflatts* continues and develops an association of writing with death that informs Bunting's poetry from his first major poem, 'Villon', where 'DEATH is written over all' (6). Linked to the materiality of rocks and earth, and involving both craft and physical labour, the mason's inscriptions contrast sharply with the apparent freedom of the lark's sky-borne melodies, in which vitality and transcendental aspiration are combined.

At least initially, there is also a lyrical prioritisation of sound in these lines, for the mason's mallet strikes are synchronised with the rhythms of the bird's song, implying that nature calls the tune for cultural labour. Moreover, it is the lark that 'labours' to rise, while the mason is pictured listening for the resonance of the stone he carves. However, as the lark's singing becomes 'painful' the transience and insubstantiality of such 'twittering' is contrasted with the relative permanence of the mason's art. The headstone he is making will bear the name of 'a man abolished', thereby 'naming none', its chiselled letters persisting in the absence of the mortal being whose finite existence they record as a name and a date. As the mason subsequently exclaims: 'Words! / Pens are too light. / Take a chisel to write' (43). Paradoxically, writing aspires to a permanent record of impermanence, just as the emphatic full rhyme of the stanza's final couplet underlines the inevitability of decay and disintegration, the loss of integrity. But, of course, neither song nor writing is immune from the erosive effects of time: 'Name and date / split in soft slate / a few months obliterate' (44).

With the bull's tenor voice and the River Rawthey's madrigal, the lark's twitter belongs to a network of motifs in *Briggflatts* concerned with what I have called the music of place, which combine to produce a soundscape that thematically and formally foregrounds the aural character of poetry. However, Bunting also elaborates upon the metaphors of carving and inscription associated with the memorial mason's labour throughout the poem, as if creating a textual counterpoint to its emphasis on music and song. For example, when the mood of Part I modulates from adolescent sensuality and fulfilment to loss and bitter self-reproach, the private catastrophe is figured in terms of a failure of writing and making, as 'shame deflects the pen' or 'jogs the draftsman's elbow' (44). Similarly, the failure of language to assuage traumatic experience is imagined in terms of sculpting and carving words themselves: 'Brief words are hard to find, / shapes to carve and discard' (44). The same metaphor recurs in extended form in Part II, when the poet-protagonist has left Northumbria for Italy, where he wanders stone-yards and cemeteries and comes to think of himself as a poet-mason undergoing a difficult apprenticeship:

> No worn tool
>   whittles stone;
> but a reproached
>   uneasy mason
>
> shaping evasive
>   ornament
> litters his yard
>   with flawed fragments. (48)

The loss of creative power described in these lines hinges on the 'evasion' and 'reproach' that attend the protagonist's Italian exile, for he has forsaken both his young lover and his homeland in the North of England. Yet, the obvious self-reflexivity of the passage also encourages the reader to recognise elements of the poem she reads in these 'flawed fragments'. Indeed, whilst *Briggflatts* strives for completion and fullness it also repeatedly registers its own textual insufficiency:

> It looks well on the page, but never
> well enough. Something is lost
> when wind, sun, sea upbraid
> justly an unconvinced deserter. (47)

Death, desertion, loss, and failure: the connotations of writing in *Briggflatts* are predominantly negative, corresponding with Bunting's explicitly phonocentric bias. As Derrida observes, 'writing, the letter, the sensible inscription, has always been considered by Western tradition as the body and matter external to the spirit, to breath, to speech, and to the logos'.[87] Nonetheless, it is worth noting that Bunting's poem also, particularly in its later sections, deploys the metaphors of carving and inscription more positively to describe natural processes. In Part IV, for instance, profane violence is perpetrated in disregard for 'the text carved by waves / on the skerry' (55); and in Part V the Northumbrian coastline is again figured as a material text or monument, blades of surf 'shaping the shore as a mason / fondles and shapes his stone' (59). Whatever its supposed shortcomings, writing is an integral part of the texture of place in *Briggflatts*, just as sound and song convey the patterns of its meanings.

Weaving Times and Places

The threads of image and metaphor that I have been tracing are braided and knotted together over the course of the poem, and the formal structure of plaiting or weaving is essential to its conjunction of incommensurable times and places. Andrew Duncan aptly describes the symbolic structure of *Briggflatts* as 'shimmering, persistently evading resolution', and this formal irresolution is reflected in the poem's unsettled and unsettling representations of place.[88] In a characteristically reflexive passage, Bunting foregrounds the challenge that the woven fabric of reality poses for interpretation:

> Can you trace shuttles thrown
> like drops from a fountain, spray, mist of spiderlines
> bearing the rainbow, quoits round the draped moon;
> shuttles like random dust desert whirlwinds hoy at their tormenting sun?
> Follow the clue patiently and you will understand nothing. (55)

The restless sliding of one image into another in these lines, and the rapid shifts in focus and scale – from spiders' webs and water droplets to dust devils and celestial bodies – illustrates the complexity of material relations while acknowledging the limitations of poetic representation and human knowledge. The guiding metaphor of the 'shuttle', which occurs twice in these lines, neatly illustrates the poem's basic technique, which is to bring disparate images and ideas together by means of association or juxtaposition, working them into patterns of sense that are dynamic rather than fixed.

As Bunting has it, *Briggflatts* registers 'the loveliness of things overlooked or despised' but maintains an attitude of humility towards the world, admitting that 'we know neither where we are nor why'.[89] Such uncertainty regarding both location and causation is related to the text's acute sense of the implications of place, whereby meaning resides not in spaces but in spatial relations, which are necessarily subject to change over time. Through its elaboration of musical motifs, *Briggflatts* rhymes the sounds of a Cumbrian fellside with Baltic plainsong and hears Monteverdi in a Persian desert. Similarly, whilst walking in the countryside of northern Italy, its Northumbrian protagonist translates sound into writing, present into past, imagining the surrounding landscape illustrated in 'a text whose initial, / lost in Lindisfarne plaited lines, / stands for discarded love' (48). By invoking the bards Aneurin and Taliesin, Bunting reveals historical, cultural, and linguistic ties between Northumbria and the ancient poetry of Wales. The saints Aidan, Cuthbert, Columba, and Columbanus attest to the North-east's significance within the archipelagic culture of early Christianity. Bloodaxe's symbolic prominence emphasises the region's Viking heritage, and his status as 'king of York, / king of Dublin, king of Orkney' (44) laconically sketches a network of spatial relations that inform the particularities of place in *Briggflatts*.

In all of these ways, Tony Lopez remarks, *Briggflatts* 'contests the definitions of "English" culture' whilst remaining 'anchored in the cultures of the British Isles'.⁹⁰ Perhaps 'anchored' is too strong a metaphor here, though it is apt given the importance of sea voyages in Bunting's poem, and *Briggflatts* might be regarded as challenging the validity of 'British' as well as 'English' frameworks. If, as Raphael Samuel contends, 'British' is 'a term which seems to reaffirm the historic and geographical unity of the British archipelago' then it sits ill with Bunting's sharp sense of regional particularity and refusal of centralised homogeneity.⁹¹ Indeed, *Briggflatts* is a product of the period characterised by what Tom Nairn calls the break-up of Britain, driven by 'the slow foundering of the British state' during the 1960s, and Bunting himself anticipated that foundering with some relish.⁹² In a 1984 letter to Jonathan Williams, written in the midst of the Miners' Strike, Bunting wrote: 'If England goes to hell via Thatcherian economics, as it may, we might eventually escape, and Hugh MacDiarmid and I will share a bottle of celestial malt to celebrate the break-up of Great Britain into a new heptarchy'.⁹³ If Bunting's poem can be said to embody devolutionary energies through its emphasis on regional distinctiveness, then such break-up or fragmentation is also paralleled by an intuition of the broader Atlantic and Northern European contexts through which such distinctiveness must inevitably be understood. Fiona Stafford's observation that the affirmation of local work 'depends, paradoxically, on encounters that take place far from home' applies with particular force to *Briggflatts*.⁹⁴ Bunting's poet-protagonist only comes to recognise the value of his Northumbrian homeland by first experiencing the 'squalor' and inauthenticity of London's Tottenham Court Road (45) and by 'sweat[ing] in the south' during his Italian sojourn (46). So, whilst Burton Hatlen is right to say that 'it is the very intensity of Bunting's engagement with Northumbria that makes him an international poet', the opposite is also true: it is the intensity of his international engagements that makes Bunting a Northumbrian poet.⁹⁵

Briggflatts takes its name from a hamlet in the Rawthey Valley on the Cumbrian edge of the Yorkshire Dales, where Bunting spent vacations as a boy, pursuing an adolescent romance that forms a central strand of the poem's narrative.⁹⁶ It is also the location of a seventeenth-century Quaker meeting house where, according to the agnostic Bunting, the silence of the meeting allows those present to 'detect the pulse of God's blood in our veins'.⁹⁷ Neither of Bunting's parents were members of the Society of Friends, though they sent their son to Quaker schools – Ackworth in Yorkshire, then Leighton Park in Berkshire – and Bunting took the Quaker ethos of pacifism sufficiently seriously to be jailed as a conscientious objector in 1918.⁹⁸ Late in life, he described himself as 'a Quaker by upbringing', though he stressed that he had 'no use for religion conceived as church forms'; rather, Quaker spirituality appealed to him because it seemed to give understated expression to 'a kind of reverence for the whole creation'.⁹⁹ Given this ambivalent attitude to religion and spirituality, the significance of Brigflatts for Bunting's poem has less to do with its importance in the history of the Society of Friends than with its personal associations and symbolic status as a meeting place, a space that affords opportunities for interpersonal relationships, romantic union, and communion with the natural world. The place name itself reinforces this idea of meetings and encounters, for 'Brigflatts' derives from the Old English '*brycg*', meaning 'bridge', and '*flēot*', meaning 'inlet' or 'stream': it is a ford, causeway, or crossing place.¹⁰⁰ This remote settlement, which falls outside the modern region of Northumberland but within the ancient kingdom of Northumbria, serves as a focal point for the text's proliferating itineraries, linked to a whole network of regional, national, and international places: the fells of Garsdale and Lunedale; Redesdale and Coquetdale further north; the Northumbrian seaboard and the holy island of Lindisfarne; the North Sea with its trade routes to Scandinavia and the Scottish Northern Isles; Ireland and Wales; Italy, the Mediterranean, and the Middle East. Brigflatts thereby becomes an unlikely but symbolically potent centre for the tracery of routes, relations, and interdependencies that Bunting's poem elaborates.

Journeys of various kinds and extents occur throughout *Briggflatts*, emphasising the contiguities of place through travel and movement. When we first encounter the young lovers in Part I they are embracing on the mason's wagon as it begins its journey eastwards from Brigflatts to Wensleydale: 'In Garsdale, dawn; / at Hawes, tea from the can' (42). At the opening of Part II, the protagonist is already in London discovering the rhythms of modernist poetry in traffic noise, counting 'beat against beat, bus conductor / against engine against wheels against / the pedal' (45). And in the first of the two dream sequences that make up Part III of *Briggflatts*, Alexander leads his men on an expedition to the ends of the earth, where 'bevelled downs, grey marshes', and pestilential 'saltings' feature in a nightmarish version of Northumbrian landscapes (52). Alexander's hubris provides a mythological parallel for the poet-protagonist's own ambition and vagrancy, and his return trajectory shares something of the impulse of Alexander's men who, weary and homesick, pine for the 'rocky meadows' of Macedonia, desiring only to 'end in our place by our own wars' (52). Makin elaborates on these parallels to argue that the poem's central plot elements of departure and return hinge on the affective polarity of North and South: 'What is clear in *Briggflatts* is that the abandoning of the girl belongs also with the abandoning of the North for the South, which is also the abandoning of a hard field for an easy one'.[101] According to this reading, the protagonist's return to Northumbria entails the assumption of mature responsibilities as well as providing the familiarity of hearth and home. However, while his homecoming in Part IV is heralded by the sun rising 'on an acknowledged land', the accompanying images of ease and sated desire – 'hunger is stayed on her settle, lust in her bed' – are soon dispersed and this part of the poem concludes as its anti-hero steers 'towards a taciturn lodging amongst strangers' (56). Moreover, the poem's enigmatic Coda ensures that *Briggflatts* ends on a note of inconclusion and uncertainty, forsaking land once more to embark on a sea voyage into the unknown: 'Blind, we follow / rain slant, spray flick / to fields we do not know' (61). As a result, place emerges in Bunting's text not as a stable point of origin grounding lyric expression but as a field of often conflicting associations and identifications, at once bounded and porous, traversed by human itineraries and historical forces.

Thus far I have focused on the conjunction of diverse spatial contexts and relations in Bunting's poetry, especially where regional and international affiliations intersect, but *Briggflatts* is also a text much preoccupied with questions of time and memory. Its modernist character is immediately apparent in the way it engages with 'notions of temporality which overlap, collide, and register their own incompletion'.[102] Bunting's poem is also an important example of what Edward Said calls 'late style', the distinctive idiom of works created towards the end of an artist's life or career, which Said associates with an 'increasing sense of apartness and exile and anachronism'.[103] Bunting was in his mid-sixties when he wrote *Briggflatts*, and a significant impetus for the poem's composition was his backward look on experiences that took place fifty years previously. Moreover, the poem's autobiographical strands are interwoven with the diverse histories of Northern Britain, and Bunting pays special attention to those temporary continuities or recurrences that manifest themselves amidst the general condition of flux and change. As Wooten observes, the poem favours synchronic over diachronic time, creating collage effects through 'temporal juxtapositioning' and 'anachronisms which allow different periods to co-exist'.[104] For instance, the mason's 'copper-wire moustache' and 'sea-reflecting eyes' identify him as an avatar of Bloodaxe, the ninth-century Viking king (42); while the '[c]lear Cymric voices' of Aneurin and Taliesin lamenting the fallen at Catraeth and Argoed Lwyfain ring out across contemporary Teesdale and Wensleydale (55). At its climax in Part V, as winter burgeons into spring and the seasonal cycle is completed, the poem's various pasts and presents coalesce in the here-and-now of a Northumbrian pastoral, as 'shepherds follow the links' leading 'demure dogs / from Tweed and Till and Teviotdale':

> The ewes are heavy with lamb.
> Snow lies bright on Hedgehope
> and tacky mud about Till
> where the fells have stepped aside
> and the river praises itself,
> silence by silence sits
> and Then is diffused in Now. (59)

Echoes abound in these lines, for the River Till's song of self-praise inevitably recalls the Rawthey's madrigal in the poem's opening lines, and the pregnant silence of these fells in the Scottish Borders reprises the moment when 'all sounds fall still' (42) on the uplands of Stainmore in Part I. Snow on the dark slopes of Hedgehope also creates a visual echo of white may-blossom clinging to the black flank of the dancing bull at Brigflatts. These visual, sonic, and spatial correspondences contribute to the poem's construction of an epiphanic present, which, Andrew Lawson argues, seeks to cancel temporal distance in a manner that 'magnifies time into space'.[105] However, the self-reflexivity of the text's autobiographical register ultimately places any such diffusion or repletion under erasure as history returns and the partiality of memory is acknowledged.

The temporal coincidence of Then and Now, past and present in *Briggflatts* is contingent upon the vagaries of memory, which play a significant role in the poem's depiction of place. As Hatlen observes, the dominant theme in Bunting's poem 'is, in a word, memory – or, since it is not the faculty but the process that is at issue, perhaps I should say "remembering"'.[106] Certainly, remembering is a central concern in *Briggflatts*, but it is also acknowledged to be painful and difficult, at times almost impossible: 'It is easier to die than to remember' (64) claims the narrator in Part I. Perhaps this difficulty of remembering, as much as Bunting's commitment to a modernist poetics of impersonality, accounts for the text's deliberate refraction of autobiographical experience through a third-person narrative perspective. Hatlen is also right to stress that the *process* of remembering, which is both fallible and necessarily open-ended, is foregrounded in the poem. According to Walter Benjamin, 'the important thing for the remembering author is not what he experienced, but the weaving of his memory, the Penelope work of recollection'.[107] I have already noted that the metaphor of weaving is crucial to both the thematic preoccupations and the form of Bunting's poem, and the complex, reiterative structures of the text might be thought to mimic the shuttling rhythms of memory as a process. The intricacies of past experience retain their fascination for the poet-protagonist even in moments of regret and self-reproach, for they encode the possibility of reparation and reconciliation in the future.

Memory in *Briggflatts* is also intricately articulated with the 'mosaic' (44) of places that the text composes in tracing the trajectory of an individual life and the history of a region. Peter Middleton and Tim Woods observe that places are 'loci of memory; reference points of narratives, propositions and emotions; signs of the passing of time and the histories that mark it.'[108] *Briggflatts* is emphatically a poem that grounds remembered experience in particular places, recognising that such places are subject to the contrary movements of time and its effects. The unabashed adolescent sexuality that provides the focus of Part I is informed by its geographical context, an uplands northern landscape where 'stone white as cheese / jeers at the dale' (63), and it is on a bed of local stone that the girl and boy first embrace. Similarly, the 'unconvinced deserter' of Part II indulges his senses 'where the ramparts cuddle Lucca' and composes poetry aloud, in Yeatsian mode, 'on the ridge / between marine olives and hillside / blue figs, under the breeze fresh / with pollen of Apennine sage' (67). In both these examples, richly sensuous memories of past experience are situated exactly and deliberately in their proper places, which thereby become loci of memory. Yet, if the Penelope work of recollection in *Briggflatts* weaves time and space together, in doing so it serves to bring out their multiplicity rather than their essential unity, admitting the co-presence of radically different places and temporalities.

In a typically terse note to *Briggflatts*, Bunting warns the unwary reader that his text is: '*An autobiography*, but not a record of fact. The first movement is no more a chronicle than the third. The truth of the poem is of another kind' (538). The 'truth' of autobiographical memory, then, is acknowledged to be at odds with the record of fact. Consequently, like much else in the poem, the reconciliation between Then and Now is to be understood as an artistic fiction, and one that recognises its own provisional character. It must be weighed against the retrospective anguish that dominates the last stanzas of Part I, where 'amputated years ache' and the breach between present and past appears absolute: 'No hope of going back' (44). Furthermore, the full presence of the remembered past is called into question in Bunting's complex metaphor of navigating by the light of dead stars in Part V:

Each spark trills on a tone beyond chronological compass,
yet in a sextant's bubble present and firm

places a surveyor's stone or steadies a tiller.
Then is Now. The star you steer by is gone,
its tremulous thread spun in the hurricane [. . .]. (60)

The light and music of the stars is beyond any human measurement, yet these shifting constellations nonetheless provide a means of orientation in space, whether on land or at sea. As a sailor who owned his own boat and sextant during the late 1930s, Bunting had practical experience of navigating by the light of the stars.[109] Delayed travelling across the void, starlight unites past and present in the moment of its visual perception, much as the practice of life writing conveys an immediate apprehension of past experience only by way of 'the autobiographer's present judgement "Now"'.[110] Immediacy is mediated; presence is represented. What is more, 'the star you steer by is gone' and so too is the reality of the past, which lives on only as an afterglow threaded into the woven fabric of present experience, as something 'tremulous' and evanescent. Just as its elaborate sonata form complicates and cuts across the unfolding of autobiographical narrative, in *Briggflatts* time does not flow in an orderly, linear fashion; but nor is it absolutely frozen in synchronic stasis. Rather, for Bunting, human experience is, in the words of Michel Serres, 'polychronic, multitemporal, revealing a time that is gathered together, with multiple pleats'.[111] So time passes and does not pass; continuity and transience coexist in temporal experience; the past is present and absent all at once.

This involved coordination of different times – personal and cosmological, historical and mythical, linear and cyclical – is, as I have argued, closely connected with the text's vagabond poetics of place. *Briggflatts* attends fastidiously to the particularities of regional identity and culture, but is also committed to the idea of Northumbria as a crossroads or meeting place in which a multiplicity of spatial trajectories, historical experiences, and geographical relations are knotted together. To speak of the poem's 'rootedness' in place is therefore to neglect its grasp of the dynamism of place itself, its manifestation of change in the here-and-now, and to underestimate the entanglement of local, regional, national, and international affiliations to which it attests. *Briggflatts* eschews the rhetoric of rootedness and dwelling for metaphors of weaving, braiding, and ravelling through which the networks of association and implication that make locations meaningful for human purposes might be intuited. In Part V, flocking shorebirds create shifting, ever-changing patterns in the air and 'sinews ripple the weave, / threads flex, slew, hues meeting, / parting in whey-blue haze' (58). These lines figure the experience of place in terms of meeting and parting, flexing and rippling, a restless process of inter-animation that also plays itself out in the text's carefully orchestrated form. In this way, Bunting imparts a sense of the hyper-complexity of social spaces, whereby disparate spatial scales ranging from the local to the global overlap. It is not just that his late modernist aesthetics are grounded in the specificities of a familiar regional locale, for the regional sensibility of *Briggflatts* only comes into focus through a range of international or cosmopolitan points of reference. The archetypal modernist dichotomy of dwelling and exile is clearly invoked by the structure of departure and return that the poem elaborates. Yet, it is also complicated by the theme of restless displacement that plays within the very modes of inhabiting and being that the text depicts. Appropriately, in the final lines of the Coda, the poem's twin concerns of place and identity give rise to profound epistemological uncertainties: 'Who, / swinging his axe / to fell kings, guesses / where we go?' (61). In this way, Bunting's regional modernism figures place as a destination as much as a point of origin, emphasising the significance of wandering and journeying to modern experiences of being-in-the-world.

Chapter 3

W. S. Graham: Between Places

W. S. Graham's poetics of place is closely bound up with his intense preoccupation with language, its possibilities and limitations in the event of the poem. Born and raised in the shipbuilding port town of Greenock, twenty miles west of Glasgow on the banks of the Clyde, Graham spent most of his writing life living at the other end of the archipelago, in South-west Cornwall. Across a career of nearly four decades, memories of Greenock and its hinterlands infuse many of the poems written in Cornwall, so that displacement becomes a recurrent theme of Graham's poems as well as one of its existential conditions. Moreover, a distinctive feature of his poetry is the way in which it moves imaginatively between places, collapsing spatial and temporal distances in the condensed geographies of the word. Especially in his later work, Graham finds suggestive correspondences between the landscapes, seascapes, and industrial histories of Clydeside and Cornwall, without eliding their differences and distinctive characters. His poetry also moves fluently between representations of real places that are known and familiar, and imagined or constructed spaces in which his poetry stages encounters with the unknown. These include the ice-bound landscapes of polar explorers and the equally white and silent space of the page on which his poems leave their marks. Characteristically, the kinds of places and landscapes to which his poems obsessively return are those in which land and sea, terrestrial and maritime worlds interact.

One of the most flexible spatial tropes in Graham's poetry is that of the journey or voyage, which Tony Lopez characterises as chiefly 'a voyage of self-discovery'.[1] For Matthew Francis, however, Graham's recurrent theme of journeying or voyaging is more persuasively understood as a figure for the 'movement from writer to reader' in the poem's fraught and uncertain act of communication.[2] Graham's handling of the trope of voyaging – from land to sea, present to past, self to other, writer to reader – is supple enough to accommodate a variety of critical interpretations, and I want simply to note its importance as one manifestation of his distinctive geographical imagination. Geographical terms and concepts such as 'place', 'space', 'journey', 'map', 'distance', and 'land' are remarkably common in Graham's poetry; but because they are often closely connected to his apparently primary concerns with language and communication, the significance of material places for his work has been undervalued. Graham's richly patterned and inventive poetics of place is distinctive for the way in which it frequently folds attention back upon the poem itself as a virtual space of turnings and equivocations, dialogues and silences. However, this late modernist self-reflexivity is wedded to a profound interest in bodily engagements with place, through work, walking, and a heightened sensory awareness of the things of the world. Part of my purpose in this chapter is to show the extent to which Graham's original and sophisticated ideas about language are informed by his affective and imaginative relations with place, or rather places.

Language and Place

Although he was born (in November 1918) more than three decades after the first generation of Anglophone modernist writers, Graham's poetry constitutes a late and complex expression of modernism's characteristic linguistic self-consciousness. Fredric Jameson has argued that aesthetic modernism is characterised by a 'commitment to language' as its 'fundamental point of reference', not only in poetry or fiction but also in music, architecture, and the visual arts.[3] Seeking to identify the social basis for this modernist commitment to language, Raymond Williams contends that in the polyglot metropolitan milieux of the early twentieth century, modernist writers came to perceive language itself as no longer 'customary or naturalized, but in many ways arbitrary and conventional', and therefore as 'a medium that could be shaped and reshaped'.[4] Graham spent time living in the bohemian quarters of Glasgow and London during the 1940s, and visited New York for about nine months in 1947–8, but his defining attachments are with non-metropolitan places and regions: Greenock and the Firth of Clyde, the West Penwith peninsula in Cornwall.[5] Nonetheless, his formative literary influences – Arthur Rimbaud and Gerard Manley Hopkins, T. S. Eliot, James Joyce, and Ezra Pound – encouraged him to adopt as his own the kind of sensitivity to linguistic conventions and will to experiment that Williams describes. Writing to Edwin Morgan in 1950, Graham notes that he has been studying the poetry of Pound and Eliot, remarking that their use of 'different textures of thought and idiom' entails 'a widening of the possibilities of what a poet may say'; and he goes on to make an emphatically modernist statement of purpose: 'I want my poems to be more than ever a valid extension of the possibilities of the language'.[6] In subsequent letters, Graham speaks repeatedly of seeking to create 'disturbance in the language' and of the importance for the poet of remaining 'open to the possibility of fresh grammatical shapes'.[7] At the same time, he is acutely aware of the resistance that language offers to the poet and to poetry's acts of communication, for as a medium it is both malleable and recalcitrant, conventional and unpredictable in its effects.

Aside from his letters, Graham's most important and coherent statement on poetry and poetics is his short essay, 'Notes on a Poetry of Release', which was first published in *Poetry Scotland* in 1946. By turns elliptical and highly suggestive, Graham's essay articulates in compressed form most of the ideas on language that will be elaborated and reworked in his mature poetry, four of which are particularly significant. Firstly, Graham affirms that a poem is fundamentally 'a successful construction of words', that language is the material from which it is made: 'The most difficult thing for me to remember is that a poem is made of words and not of the expanding heart, the overflowing soul, or the sensitive observer'.[8] The most difficult thing to remember, but also the most important: here, Graham explicitly subordinates a neo-Romantic conception of poetry as expressing the spontaneous overflow of emotion to a late modernist aesthetic that acknowledges the capacity and materiality of language as the medium of speech, writing, and thought. Graham would likely endorse Alain Badiou's remark that the poem 'presents itself as a thing of language, encountered – each and every time – as an event', though he would demur at Badiou's claim that the poem 'has nothing to communicate'.[9]

Secondly, Graham conceives of language as 'obstacle and vehicle at the same time', at once the primary medium of communication and a barrier or screen between the writer and the reader that must be negotiated anew in every act of writing and reading. On the one hand, Graham regards language as radically mutable, capable of being reshaped by each individual speaker every time that it is used, so that: 'Each word changes every time it is brought to life. [. . .] You cannot twice bring the same word into sound'.[10] In this regard, language is a paradigmatic model of Heraclitean flux because repetition or iteration cannot help but produce new meanings.[11] On the other hand, language is intrinsically social and never belongs wholly or solely to any individual speaker. In Graham's words, language is 'scored and impressed by the commotion of all of us since its birth', and the poet must work with the inherited meanings and conventions of the language in which she writes, even as she seeks to extend its possibilities.[12] In this way, argues Theodor Adorno, 'language mediates lyric poetry and society in their innermost core', thereby undermining the withdrawal into individual subjectivity with which lyric has long been associated and lending an irreducibly social character to every poem.[13]

Graham's poetry also emphasises the constructed and inherently changeable character of the poetic self as it is articulated in and through language. In 'Notes on a Poetry of Release', he revises the modernist poetics of impersonality by presenting himself as 'the poet writing in a disguise of the 1st person', a formulation that foregrounds the intrinsically performative character of lyric enunciation. Graham also figures the act of composition as an 'involuntary war' between the poet and his or her 'material and immediate environment' of words, language itself.[14] As the poet seeks to shape words and phrases into the verbal artifact of the poem, he or she is altered by each encounter with language. In a letter of 1949, Graham adapts Heraclitus's aphorism on rivers to express the poet's mutability: 'I am a river flowing past a point, not the man I was a second ago, but what is the point? What is the one me?'[15] Throughout Graham's poetry, the problem of 'the changing self' is a source of fascination and perplexity.[16]

Finally, Graham explicitly deprioritises authorial intention as a source of meaning in the poem, and instead conceives of the 'release' of meaning in terms of the reader's active engagement with the poem as a thing made of words, or with the 'space of continual meanings behind the words'.[17] In this regard, Graham conceives of the poem as what Roland Barthes calls a 'writerly text', one that requires the productive (writerly) participation of the reader to become meaningful: 'It is brought to life by the reader and takes part in the reader's change'.[18] This means that both poem and reader are changed in and by the act of reading, which is understood as an event with unforeseeable outcomes. Although Graham regards his poems as attempts to communicate, and therefore as informed by authorial intention to some degree, he also insists that '[his] poem is not a telephone call. The poet only speaks one way. He hears nothing back'.[19] Hence, the haunting and surreal image of a 'telephone ringing deep / Down in a blue crevasse' that occurs in 'Malcolm Mooney's Land'; or the speaker's painful awareness, in 'Approaches to How They Behave', of how his words 'Go out into a silence I know / Nothing about'.[20] Ultimately, Graham conceives of the poem as a construction of words with which the reader will collide or connect, and make use of according to his or her own purposes.

Towards the end of 'Notes on a Poetry of Release', in a passage that is usually overlooked by critics, Graham adopts an explicitly geographical register to posit an analogy between the creation of a poem and the construction of a mountain by vast geological processes: 'A poem is a mountain made out of the containing, almost physical language, and with the power to release a man into his own completely responsible world larger than that outward solid geography.'[21] In a 1944 letter to William Montgomerie, he rehearses the same metaphor, contending that: 'After each poem there should be such an apparent addition to the world that it will be as obvious as a new over-4000ft mountain added to the Grampians. [. . .] It's almost as physical as a geographical change.'[22] Besides giving an index of Graham's ambition as a young poet, these statements illustrate the extent to which his thinking about poetry is informed by geographical thought and the metaphors it suggests. Although the imaginative 'world' of the poem is given primacy over that of real places and landscapes – 'outward solid geography' – the analogy between poem and mountain implies some meaningful relationship between the two (the poem is 'an addition to the world') and is itself motivated by Graham's actual engagements with the physical geography and landscapes of Scotland.

As an adolescent and young man living in Greenock, Graham was a keen amateur hill-walker, often making forays into the surrounding mountains or setting out for the more imposing peaks of the Southern Highlands which lay within a day's hike across the Firth of Clyde.[23] These mountains and others further afield find their way into his early poems – Beinn Narnain (3, 59, 60, 64), Ben Cruachan (12, 25, 75), Goatfell (25), Sgùrr nan Gillean (4) – not only as evocative place-names but as affective points of reference, nodes of connection between the world of language and that other, outward geography that the poet knows. For instance, in 'Since All My Steps Taken', Graham figures his speaker's determination to become a poet as a journey on foot ('With hobnail on Ben Narnain') away from the safety and security of the family home and into the mountainous terrain of language itself: 'All journey, since the first / Step from my father and mother / Towards the word's crest' (59). In another hill-walking poem, 'The Hill of Intrusion', Graham's speaker rows up Loch Long to the foot of Beinn Narnain and describes feeling the winds of inspiration blowing from the summit into:

The silence between
My heart and those
Elements of nature
That are my food (64).

If the poem is a construction of words, then these lines imply that the silent space between inner experience and outward realities is its necessary pre-condition, and that the 'elements of nature' provide the poet with physical, emotional, and imaginative sustenance for the work of writing. Moreover, if the poem itself can be understood as a hill of intrusion that would disturb the language, then its own crafted and constructed world of language is not purely autonomous or self-enclosed. Rather, it is in turn intruded upon by remembered experiences – the 'Wrecked pile of past / Events' (63) – that are intimately connected with a network of real places and solid geographies.

Language and place are closely inter-related across the whole of Graham's career, as the titles of many of his books illustrate: *Cage Without Grievance* (1942); *The Seven Journeys* (1944); *The White Threshold* (1949); *The Nightfishing* (1955); *Malcolm Mooney's Land* (1970); *Implements in Their Places* (1977). Even in his most abstract late poems, Graham conceives of the poem as a constructed object with its own idiosyncratic spatiality, a 'public place / Achieved against subjective odds and then / Mainly an obstacle to what I mean' (162). Nonetheless, it might be argued that Graham's geographical imagination is subordinate to his over-riding obsession with language, and that the various places and landscapes that his poems describe are no more than convenient figures for the strange world of words in which poetry has its being. Lopez comes close to this position when he argues that in his early poems of walking, sailing, and journeying 'Graham is moving in "language" as much as any real landscape'; and Francis similarly emphasises the 'metapoetic' dimension of Graham's poetry, which frequently 'takes itself as its own object of reference'.[24] Graham's friends and contemporaries also underscore the primacy of language in Graham's poetic imagination. David Wright observes that '[w]ords, their weight, resonance, ambiguities, affinities and associations were his obsession'; and Edwin Morgan contends that 'Graham's continuing faithfulness to the Word is what gives his whole work its integrity'.[25] However, there is a danger of rendering Graham's body of work more limited and one-dimensional than it actually is if language is taken to be the ultimate referent of all, or nearly all, of his poems' varied signs and images. Paul de Man argues that modern lyric poetry is characterised by 'the ambivalence of a language that is representational and non-representational at the same time', and this ambivalence seems crucial to the effects of Graham's poetry, which typically moves restlessly between representation and allegory, literal and metaphorical meanings.[26] Consequently, 'place' in Graham's poetry refers simultaneously to a range of real-and-imagined places or landscapes and to the space of language itself as it is encountered by the writer and the reader in the event of the poem. In what follows, I propose to adopt a kind of critical double vision, attending to Graham's subtle and ingenious explorations of language through metaphors of place and space, while also appraising his use of poetic language to reveal the existential and social significance of engagements with material places.

Remembering Greenock

The most significant focus for Graham's poetics of place across the whole of his writing career is Greenock, an industrial port town situated among hills and sea-lochs in the western reaches of the Firth of Clyde. Before 1800, Greenock was the home base for the largest herring-fishing fleet in the West of Scotland; during the industrial revolution, it became a centre for shipbuilding, sugar refining, engineering, and transatlantic trade.[27] Graham's childhood home was a top-floor tenement flat at One Hope Street, which had views of the shipyards and sugar docks that feature in many of his poems. For instance, although Greenock is never mentioned by name in 'Listen. Put on Morning', the poem's speaker imagines his readers lying in their beds awake 'Under the tenements / Under the sugar docks / Under the printed monuments' (60); and in 'The White Threshold', the speaker recalls himself 'as a child in tenement-top' looking down on 'his loud Clydeside / Down on derricks donkeymen / Caulkers platers from the blacksoap timbered cradles' (95). Economically and socially, Greenock was essentially an outlier of Glasgow by the early twentieth century, but its proximity to the hills, the firth, and the surrounding Renfrewshire countryside is important to Graham's sense of the town's hybrid character, its propensity for bringing together urban, industrial, and natural environments in a single, complex place. Lopez observes that Graham's 'seaming together of industrial and rural material' in his early poems is 'no more than a view of Greenock and its surrounding hills', albeit refracted through the modernist lens of Rimbaud's *Illuminations* (1886).[28]

Graham's father worked as a journeyman engineer and, after leaving school aged fourteen, Graham was apprenticed as a draughtsman to a Glasgow firm of structural engineers. This was in 1933, when a crippling economic depression spread across Clydeside and unemployment in Greenock affected twenty per cent of the workforce.[29] During his five-year apprenticeship, Graham began attending evening classes on art and literature at Glasgow University and, in 1938, he was awarded a bursary to study at Newbattle Abbey, an adult education college near Edinburgh. At Newbattle, he took courses in English literature, Scottish literature, and philosophy, met his wife Nessie Dunsmuir, and began his life-long commitment to poetry.[30] Nonetheless, Graham's training in draughtsmanship and background in industrial Greenock informed and influenced his conception of the craft of poetry, and of the poem itself as a successful construction in words. George Barker claims that Graham's poems may be considered 'a marvellous branch of Glasgow engineering: his poems are as lucidly and imaginatively constructed as anything that ever emerged from the Greenock shipyards'.[31] Graham also sometimes employed metaphors drawn from industrial manufacture to describe his personal experience of poetic creation. Writing to Michael Schmidt in 1978, he describes the psychological struggle to write in the following terms: 'What makes me be able to bear making my once-young brain from the lovely burnish of the Firth of Clyde hammer out the laborious words'.[32] While these comments suggest that Graham's recurrent depictions of docks and shipyard gantries in his poems might be read as metaphors for the workshop of the poetic imagination, it is important to recognise the extent to which his personal familiarity with industrial labour on Clydeside had a formative influence on his approach to *poiesis*, the making of poems from the materials of language.

In 1943, Graham went to live in a caravan in Germoe, Cornwall with Mary Harris, the mother of his daughter, Rosalind; when the relationship with Harris broke up Graham remained in Germoe and was joined by Dunsmuir in 1944.[33] The couple would never live in Scotland again, though they often considered returning; South-west Cornwall would be their adopted home for most of the rest of their lives.[34] As a poet and as a man, Graham's relationship with Scotland was deeply ambivalent. He always regarded himself as a Scot, albeit one living in self-imposed exile at the other end of Britain, and saw his poetry as indelibly marked by his Scottish origins. For instance, in 1949 he observed that: 'The more I go on in my work the more Scotch I find I am'; and in 1970 he claimed that 'although I don't write in the Lallans, my verse has a Northern hardness and texture which is Scots'.[35] Not only is Graham's poetry concerned with Scottish places, landscapes, and communities – especially Greenock and Clydeside – but its language and forms are often emphatically un-English, though rarely self-consciously 'Scots'.[36] Graham's use of Scots words and phrases – in lines such as 'The caaing thresher in his splendid blood' (92) or 'For the gale will skelp upon the firth' (144) – is habitual and pervasive enough to justify the inclusion of a glossary in his *New Collected Poems* (2004), but hardly a major obstacle to comprehension for non-Scottish readers.

Nonetheless, Graham's self-identification as a Scottish poet complicates his relationship to the English language, which is characterised by a mixture of fascination and estrangement. Jacques Derrida argues that the condition of 'being-at-home [*être-chez-soi*] in language' will always remain in question for every speaking or writing subject, for 'there is no natural property of language'. Accordingly, my language never belongs wholly or straightforwardly to me, nor I to it, for it is always (originally) 'the language of the other'.[37] Although Derrida claims that this condition of estrangement affects every relation to language, his formulation helps to explain Graham's profoundly self-conscious use of the English language – a self-consciousness that suggests a degree of alienation – particularly well. Several of Graham's late poems play variations on the conceit of the poet frustrated or outwitted by a language over which he has only limited control. For instance, in 'Language Ah Now You Have Me' the poet-speaker presents himself as 'hiding in / The jungle of mistakes of communication' (207); and in 'Implements in Their Places' he exclaims with comic exasperation: 'Dammit these words are making faces / At me again' (248). Graham also plays with the idea that English is at once a native and a foreign language to him, as in a late notebook poem where the speaker describes himself as 'a flying translator translating / English into English' (300).[38] These lines imply that, for the Scottish poet writing in English – or, at least for Graham – writing is always a kind of translation, for the English language is non-identical to itself.

Graham's self-identification as a Scottish poet is itself complicated, however, by his openly antagonistic attitude towards the contemporary Scottish literary scene, and particularly the cultural nationalism of the Scottish Renaissance, which was spearheaded by Hugh MacDiarmid. As Margery Palmer McCulloch observes, many of the writers most closely associated with the Renaissance during the 1920s and 1930s – MacDiarmid, Neil M. Gunn, Edwin and Willa Muir, Catherine Carswell, and Lewis Grassic Gibbon – were strongly influenced by Anglo-American and European modernism. These writers sought to reconcile nationalist and internationalist cultural visions, which in poetry chiefly meant a renewed focus on Scottish subject-matter and, following the example set by MacDiarmid, the 'revival of the Scots vernacular as a modern, avant-garde medium'.[39] Although he maintained a friendship with MacDiarmid throughout their careers, and shared his enthusiasm for modernist experimentation, Graham was dismissive of what he called 'Plastic Scots' and suspicious of the 'National bias' that led his Scottish contemporaries to forget that poetry is 'made of words instead of heather and homerule and freedom'.[40] By 1949, he had consciously adopted the role of the exiled prophet without honour in his own land: 'I now consider myself banished, more or less, from the Scottish Lit Scene, which I don't hold with and seems to get more embarrassing with its playing bards glumerin lufts keekin wi sna'.[41] What Graham objects to is less the manifest artificiality of MacDiarmid's or Sydney Goodsir Smith's poems in synthetic Scots than the implicit claims their language makes concerning its ability to express an authentically Scottish identity, an identity founded on a conception of place that Graham regards as embarrassingly sentimental. Rather than a guarantor of identity, Graham consistently conceives of poetic language as a means of encountering otherness and of estranging oneself from one's home. Perhaps the most memorable expression of this alienating power of language for the writer's sense of self and place occurs in 'The Nightfishing':

> Each word is but a longing
> Set out to break from a difficult home. Yet in
> Its meaning I am. (108)

Language, and particularly the language of the poem, both expresses the 'longing' for, and the desire to 'break' away from the constraints and security that 'home' represents. The line break between 'longing' and 'Set out' serves to reinforce this crucial ambiguity. Home is at once the focus of the speaker's identification ('in / Its meaning I am'), and at some level the underlying motivation for the words he speaks or writes. Yet, each word of the poem also displaces him from the home place, and ultimately it is in the 'break from a difficult home' that the 'meaning' of his selfhood is to be found.

In Graham's poetry, the affective ties and meanings of 'home' are strongly aligned with Greenock, or rather with its various fictional manifestations. At the same time, his poems are often predicated upon a fundamental condition of displacement or alienation from the home place, so that Greenock and its hinterlands can only ever be returned to through memories, dreams, and the powers of the imagination. Francis describes this contradiction in terms of a central tension in Graham's work between his conflicting allegiances to community – home, family, and place – and to writing. His commitment to writing, and to being a poet, has 'separated him from his family both symbolically, by imposing its distances and barriers between them, and pragmatically, because he had to abandon the values of his family in order to practise it'.[42] According to Francis, Graham seeks to overcome this contradiction by conceiving of language as 'in some sense a form of community in itself'; language resembles community to the extent that it is a collective, social entity, one that both resists and responds to his individual will.[43] Moreover, Graham sometimes conceived of language as a kind of second home. In 1967 he wrote to Ruth Hilton to say that: 'The thing is to find or create (in this case the same thing) a language, a timbre of thought or voice, which I will live in'.[44] Equally important to Graham's attempts to overcome the sense of displacement from home and community that writing entails is the work of memory that features so prominently in his Greenock poems, from *The White Threshold* onwards. Paul Ricoeur remarks that: 'It is on the surface of the habitable earth that we remember having travelled and visited memorable sites. In this way, the "things" remembered are intrinsically associated with places'.[45] In many of his Greenock poems, Graham employs memory as a means of temporarily re-inhabiting a place in which he no longer lives, and which he can visit only through his immersion in the community of language.

Memories of Greenock and of Graham's family are powerfully evoked in 'Three Letters', which comprises poems addressed 'To My Brother', 'To My Father', 'To My Mother'. The dedication – '*In memory of my mother / Spring 1948*' – explicitly marks this three-fold text out as a work of remembrance as well as remembering. The opening lines of 'To My Brother' foreground Graham's interwoven concerns with writing, memory, and place in the context of family relationships:

> Alastair approach this thirty
> Lines with a homing memory.
> Each step speaks out the springtime.
> Our Clydeside merges home. (98)

Foregrounding the poem's epistolary character, Graham's speaker seeks to activate his brother's 'homing memory' by offering a written record – 'thirty / Lines' – drawn from his own. The spatial and emotional distance separating the two brothers is to be bridged by a textual encounter in which they occupy the roles of writer and reader, collaborating to fashion an image of the place in which they both grew up that 'merges' elements of their respective memories and experiences: 'Our Clydeside merges home.' This collaborative work of remembering and writing place is crystallised in an image of the brothers as boys crossing the firth together in a rowing boat – 'Exchanged on those waters / Between Gareloch and Greenock' – and absorbed by the sounds and sights of industrial manufacture along the shore: 'Between banks of shipbuilding / The distilled and hurtled out / Industry of mind and heart' (99). Although these images are crucial to the poem's exact and sensuous representation of remembered places, they also illustrate the pervasiveness of its metapoetic dimension. For, the brothers' journey across the firth can be read as a metaphor for the act of communication or correspondence that the poem-letter seeks to perform, an exchange of words that in turn is likened to the productive industry of shipbuilding – Graham's poetry is itself a product of the 'Industry of mind and heart'. This metapoetic dimension recurs in 'To My Mother', where the speaker likens the 'flowing stronghold' of his memories to the 'flowing strongheld Clyde' that 'has ever matchlessly / Changed me towards the sea' (101). Such fluidity is also a characteristic of Graham's conception of language, which is often associated strongly with the restlessness of the sea, so that the act of writing further alters the shape and substance of the speaker's memories of home: 'In words I change them further / Away from the parent fire' (101). The poignant irony articulated in these lines is that, by translating his memories into writing, the speaker both draws closer to his family and childhood home in imagination and sets himself at a distance from them, for he is himself 'changed' towards them and no longer who he was. Hence the speaker's estranged self-depiction in the closing stanzas as 'some man I am', 'stepping away from his / Last home' (101), where the shift from first-person to third-person pronouns underlines the alienation that writing and remembering entail.

Graham's Greenock poems are acutely self-conscious about the process of remembering in which they are engaged, and responsive to the ways in which writing inevitably changes or reshapes what was experienced in the past. On the one hand, his use of the letter form – which recurs in later poems and sequences such as 'Seven Letters' and 'Dear Bryan Wynter' – is motivated by the desire for a direct, personal, and intimate mode of address. On the other hand, it is manifestly a convention of lyric poetry, an instance of what Jonathan Culler calls 'triangulated address', which facilitates an 'address to the reader by means of address to something or someone else'.[46] Perhaps the most distinctive use of triangulated address in lyric poetry is apostrophe, a trope that Graham employs prominently in a late poem, 'Greenock at Night I Find You', in which the speaker addresses his home town directly in the second-person:

> As for you loud Greenock long ropeworking
> Hide and seeking riveting town of my child
> Hood, I know we think of us often mostly
> At night. Have you ever desired me back
> Into the set-in bed at the top of the land
> In One Hope Street? I am myself lying
> Half-asleep hearing the riveting yards
> And smelling the bone-works with no home
> Work done for Cartsburn School in the morning. (219)

What is most arresting about these lines is the way in which they choreograph the shift from the adult speaker's distanced recollection of Greenock, his childhood home, to his imaginative re-inhabiting of his childhood self and the house in which he was born. The weaving of memory in this poem is a nocturnal activity undertaken by a remembering author who claims to be 'Half-asleep', so that the imagined return to his childhood home has the atmosphere of a dream and many of the characteristics of a wish-fulfilment fantasy. Gaston Bachelard associates such dreams of home with a desire to re-experience the security and belonging of the mother's womb: 'When we dream of the house we were born in, in the utmost depths of revery, we participate in this original warmth, in this well-tempered matter of the material paradise'.[47] However, Graham's depiction of the space of home is significantly more ambivalent than Bachelard's account allows. For, while the sounds and smells of industrial manufacture render the surrounding environment with sensuous immediacy, these sensory impressions of the masculine worlds of labour penetrate the maternal sanctuary of the house, rupturing its protective or nurturing enclosure. Furthermore, Graham's deft use of enjambment manages to imply the persistence of a sense of displacement amid the poem's central fantasy of return. Not only does 'childhood' appear fractured or split apart as 'child / Hood', but the speaker's confession that he has not done his homework contains within it the unsettling recognition that, as an adult, he is someone 'with no home'.[48] Although 'Greenock at Night I Find You' articulates its displaced speaker's longing to recover the home place that he has lost to time and writing, then, it also calls the reader's attention to the mechanics of remembering and ironises the fantasy of a return to childhood security.

A strong undertow of nostalgia can be felt in Graham's Greenock poems, particularly those that he published towards the end of his career in the 1970s. Svetlana Boym makes a useful distinction between two kinds of nostalgia, restorative and reflective, both of which are present to differing degrees in Graham's Greenock poems. Restorative nostalgia seeks to bridge the gap between past and present states of being, 'to rebuild the lost home and patch up the memory gaps'; whereas reflective nostalgia entails not the recovery of what once was but rather a 'meditation on history and passage of time' that acknowledges 'the irrevocability of the past and human finitude'.[49] If restorative nostalgia tries to reinstate the past in place of the present, making now and then coincide, then reflective nostalgia underlines the distance between what was and what is, insisting that some spatio-temporal divides simply cannot be bridged. Graham's recurrent fictions of return to Greenock are expressions of restorative nostalgia to the extent that they dissolve the present of the adult writing subject in memories of his childhood. However, his Greenock poems also mobilise reflective nostalgia by calling the reader's attention to the limitations of memory and to the very process of writing that sets his speakers at a distance from their former selves. Often, it is the tension between these two conflicting modes of nostalgic remembering that produces the poems' characteristic effects.

A good example of this multi-layered manifestation of nostalgia can be found in one of Graham's best notebook poems, 'The Greenock Dialogues', which also begins with an apostrophe to his home town:

> O Greenock, Greenock, I never will
> Get back to you. But here I am,
> The boy made good into a ghost
> Which I will send along your streets
> Tonight as the busy nightshifts
> Hammer and spark their welding lights. (319)

These lines simultaneously immerse the reader in a dream of return and unravel the fiction of recovery and restoration that they construct. The initial exclamation emphasises both the speaker's longing for his lost home and his recognition that the past is ultimately irrevocable, apparently establishing the predominance of reflective nostalgia from the outset. However, the split that develops in the speaker's selfhood implies the stubborn persistence of restorative impulses, too. Is the 'I' who sadly affirms 'I never will / Get back' the same as the 'I' who announces 'But here I am'? 'Here' is both Greenock itself – or, rather, the Greenock of his childhood – and the lines of the poem we read, which announces the impossibility of returning to Greenock from the outset. As an adult writer, the poet-speaker is a 'boy made good' whose memory and imagination create a 'ghost' of his childhood self. This 'ghost' is sent out by the speaker along the streets of Greenock as they are reconstructed in the lines of the poem, and the creative work of remembering finds its echo in the unflagging productive energies of Greenock's nocturnal industries. Towards the end of the poem, which recounts a childhood excursion across the Clyde and into the mountains, Graham's speaker seems to address the reader directly, including her through his use of first-person plural pronouns: 'We are here to listen. We are here / to hear the town in the disguise / My memory puts on it' (323). The homophonic pun on 'here' and 'hear' in these lines not only recalls an earlier Greenock poem, 'Listen. Put on Morning', but again emphasises the slippage between the remembered place and the lines of the poem in which it is remembered. Moreover, memory, like writing, alters the past experiences to which it gives form and expression, so that home and childhood only ever appear in the 'disguise' that words give to them.

Cornwall and Modernist Painting

Although Greenock is the most significant affective focus for Graham's poetics of place, his work is distinctive for being bi-located, simultaneously oriented towards and attached to two places – Cornwall and Clydeside – at opposite ends of the island of Britain. Graham spent nearly all his writing life – more than four decades – on or near the West Penwith peninsula, which stretches from St Ives to Land's End and Penzance. Robin Davidson describes West Penwith as a 'mysterious granite world' of bleak uplands with an atmosphere of otherworldliness, 'a sinister land of standing stones, ancient circles and the burial chambers of long-dead chieftains'.[50] After the Second World War, and the terminal decline of Cornwall's fishing and tin-mining industries, this was also a post-industrial landscape scattered with abandoned mine workings and disused harbours.[51] West Penwith's combination of austere natural beauty, the still-evident signs of its industrial histories, and the omnipresence of the sea appear to have been congenial to Graham the poet, and may have reminded him of Greenock. In 1945, Graham wrote from Germoe to the painter John Minton, remarking: 'The more I write here (even with my mind on Scotland) the place around me becomes intimate landscape'; and, in a 1950 letter to Edwin Morgan, he described this intimate landscape in greater detail:

> I sit almost surrounded by "standing stones", cromlechs, and grey piles of rock and grey "drystane dykes" and (I do think I'm the last person to believe in a whimsy way about druid feeling about the landscape) do you know, Edwin, it feels early and Celtic and definitely Unenglish.[52]

Anxious not to fall prey to the Celtic Twilight-isms for which he had rebuked the poets of the Scottish Renaissance, Graham is nonetheless strongly attracted to the 'Celtic', 'Unenglish' character of West Penwith, which he associates with Scotland and describes using a Scots phrase (albeit held within distancing quotation marks). While living at Mevagissey, on the South-east coast of Cornwall, in 1949, Graham also described the 'mystic feeling' of the West Penwith landscape and likened it to that of the Scottish Western Isles.[53] What is more, Graham explicitly links his apprehension of the 'Celtic' character of the part of Cornwall in which he lives and works with the 'definitely Unenglish' sensibility that is given expression in his poetry, which 'tries more and more to break from the oversweet exhibition of sensitivity which is so much the mainstream of English poetry'.[54] Not only does he discover correspondences between the natural and cultural landscapes of Cornwall and Scotland, but Graham also thinks of his own poetry in the English language as manifesting something of their shared 'Unenglish' character as places.

Graham's long residency in Cornwall and imaginative attachment to the landscapes and coastline of West Penwith are not without a degree of ambivalence, however, and he sometimes cultivated the image of the awkward outsider – Denys Val Baker aptly describes him as a 'resident "furriner"'.[55] Moreover, his single-minded dedication to poetry meant that he and Dunsmuir relied heavily on the generosity of friends and patrons for money, fuel, and lodgings, so that their life in Cornwall was often precarious and unsettled. The couple moved frequently and never owned their own home: from 1944–6 they lived in two caravans at Germoe; from 1947–9 they borrowed or rented fishermen's cottages at Mevagissey; in 1956, following a separation of six years when they both lived outside Cornwall, they returned to live in an old coastguard house on the cliff-top at Gurnard's Head; and in 1967 they moved to a small terraced house in Madron owned by their friend, Nancy Wynne-Jones, which would be their home until Graham's death in 1986.[56] Although Graham was attracted to the Romantic image of the heroic, struggling artist, such prolonged experiences of poverty and privation in Cornwall, combined with his heavy drinking and periods of depression, served to deepen his homesickness for Scotland and the lost world of his Greenock childhood. In some respects, Graham the poet resembles the figure of the 'foreigner' as described by Julia Kristeva, the person 'who survives with a tearful face turned towards the lost homeland' but whose very identity is predicated on breaking from his origins and orienting himself towards an '*elsewhere*' upon which 'he has set his hopes' and in which 'his struggles take place'.[57] For Graham, that 'elsewhere' is West Penwith; although it is striking that Cornish places and landscapes only begin to feature explicitly in his collections of the 1970s, *Malcolm Mooney's Land* and *Implements in Their Places*. It was only in the last decade of his life, when he had gained a measure of recognition as a poet and Faber had published his *Collected Poems* (1979) that Graham felt able to acknowledge his attachments to Cornwall and the West Penwith landscape freely. Writing to Tony Lopez in 1981, he claimed that 'in about the last twenty years my poems have contained many rank-Cornish names like – Botallack, Morvah, Lanyon Quoit, Godrevy, Zennor, Gurnard's Head'.[58] And in 1984 he expressed his pleasure that Frank Ruhrmund, a Cornish poet and journalist, had referred to the area around Gurnard's Head as 'Graham country', remarking that: 'In a kind of way there is a great deal of this place in my poems'.[59]

The primary means by which Cornish places and landscapes enter Graham's poems is through his life-long interest in the visual arts, especially painting. Since the 1880s, St Ives and Newlyn were both home to colonies of artists, who had nearly all moved there from elsewhere, attracted by the region's scenic beauty, distinctive light, and inexpensive studio spaces.[60] From the late 1930s, and especially in the two decades following the end of the Second World War, St Ives was the common ground for a loose network of painters, sculptors, and art critics – including Naum Gabo, Barbara Hepworth, Patrick Heron, Roger Hilton, Peter Lanyon, Ben Nicholson, Adrian Stokes, and Bryan Wynter – who were strongly influenced by international modernism but also retained an interest in landscape art. Michael Bird observes that St Ives occupies an almost unique position in the history of modern art as 'a provincial town, not much bigger than a village, that gave its name to an international movement', a convergence of influences and spatial scales that can also be discerned in Graham's poetry.[61] Graham knew many of the St Ives painters personally – his friendships with Hilton, Lanyon, and Wynter were particularly important for his poetry – and he had a good knowledge and understanding of modern art. Nancy Wynne-Jones recalls that he would sometimes drop in to Lanyon's studio in St Ives on the way to or from the pub and, uninvited, give impromptu lectures on abstract art.[62] He produced his own Picasso-esque drawings and paintings, made objects and 'constructions' from wood, glass, and string, and often illustrated his letters with watercolour images and doodles.[63] Consequently, critics of Graham's work have often speculated on the extent to which his poetry can be said to be influenced, directly or indirectly, by the abstract art of the St Ives painters. Lopez argues that Graham can be regarded as 'the poet of the modern St Ives community and what it represents culturally in postwar Britain'; Francis contends that he experiments with words 'in much the same way that modernist painters [...] experimented with paint'; and Ralph Pite observes that Graham shares with Hilton, Lanyon, and Wynter 'a concern with work in which abstract and figurative meet'.[64] In particular, Lanyon's aesthetic of 'landscape taken to the verge of abstraction' is an important point of reference for Graham's poetics of place, which often combines powerfully descriptive evocations of landscapes and seascapes with more abstract, philosophical explorations of the 'spaces' of language, writing, and selfhood.[65]

One of Graham's first and most richly detailed poetic representations of West Penwith occurs in his elegy for Lanyon, 'The Thermal Stair', which he read in a 1968 television documentary on the painter (360). Unlike most of the St Ives painters, Lanyon was a Cornishman whose work combines the techniques of modernist abstraction with a deep personal attachment to the landscapes, people, and history of the region.

As Andrew Causey observes, this attachment to place is given expression in Lanyon's paintings through his rejection of 'the single viewpoint' and exclusion of 'the possibility of landscape as scenic backdrop'.[66] Characteristically, figure and landscape are often merged in Lanyon's paintings, as on a flat plane that nonetheless brings together a range of different perspectives and creates a sense of movement in and through the landscape. In 1959, he began flying a glider in an attempt 'to get to a more complete knowledge of the landscape', and his gliding paintings of the early 1960s – such as *Soaring Flight* (1960), *Thermal* (1960), and *Cloud Base* (1962) – are remarkable for the ways in which they shift attention from the land and coast, which had dominated Lanyon's earlier paintings, to the sea, sky, and weather of South-west Cornwall.[67] In 1964, Lanyon crashed his glider and died suddenly of a blood clot in his leg a few days later; he was forty-six years old.

The opening line of 'The Thermal Stair' is disarmingly conversational, adopting the register of a note to a (temporarily) absent friend: 'I called today, Peter, but you were away' (163). Graham's use of triangulated address here is apparently offhand and natural, but the line depends for its effect upon the reader's awareness that its putative addressee is, in fact, 'away' permanently. Natalie Pollard observes that Graham's frequent use of second-person address creates the illusion that his poems are instances of 'personal correspondence' or 'imagined dialogues between the poet and those closest to him'.[68] This is particularly true of his elegies, including 'The Thermal Stair', which is more concerned to recall and commemorate a friendship than to mourn a dead artist. Importantly, though, that friendship is founded on the two men's shared interests in art and the landscapes of West Penwith. The poem's title phrase refers to the spiral columns of rising air that gliders use to gain altitude, and in its first section the speaker imagines being able to share the artist-pilot's aerial panorama of the whole peninsula:

> Find me a thermal to speak and soar to you from
> Over Lanyon Quoit and the circling stones standing
> High on the moor over Gurnard's Head where some
>
> Time three foxglove summers ago, you came. (164)

In these lines, Lanyon Quoit – the dolmen that shares the painter's name – is brought into apposition with the poet's former home at Gurnard's Head, as though the aerial view of the landscape that flight affords was capable not only of enhancing our understanding of how places and landforms are related to one another spatially, but also of making visible the emotional bonds between the people who inhabit those places. The speaker's desire to take to the sky, to see the landscape as Lanyon once did, modulates into a reflection on the common purposes shared by poetry and painting as art forms. The 'job' of both painter and poet, he claims, 'is Love / Imagined into word or paint'; and 'The Thermal Stair' implies that love of the people and places of Cornwall was the motivating force of Lanyon's art. This love finds its echo both in the intimate, conversational mode of address that Graham's poem employs and in its deliberate acts of naming and remembering. 'The Thermal Stair' is one of Graham's most densely toponymic poems, but in naming the towns, villages, and landmarks of West Penwith – Botallack, Levant, Gurnard's Head, Morvah, St Just, Godrevy and Wolf Rock lighthouses – it is also alluding to the artworks that Lanyon made in response to these places and their histories, many of which bear place-names as titles. For instance, when Graham's speaker recalls Lanyon suggesting they visit 'the old / Tinworkings around / Morvah and St Just' (164–5), he recalls Lanyon's fascination with the region's mining history, which is given expression in paintings such as *Levant Old Mine* (1952), *Botallack* (1952), and *St Just* (1953). In this respect, the way that Graham's speaker apprehends and describes the post-industrial landscapes of Cornwall in 'The Thermal Stair' is indebted to Lanyon's paintings and their distinctive modes of seeing and attention.

One of Graham's best elegies, 'The Thermal Stair' is also his most suggestive exploration of the relationships between poetry and painting, art and landscape. He returns to these themes in 'Dear Bryan Wynter', another elegy for a painter friend, who died of a heart attack in 1975. Like Graham, Wynter was an incomer to Cornwall who stayed for the rest of his life, living from 1945 in a remote stone cottage on Zennor Carn that Graham visited frequently and, after 1964, near the village of St Buryan.[69] Although his later work became increasingly abstract and non-representational, Wynter's paintings of the 1940s and early 1950s – such as *Cornish Landscape* (1947), *Cornish Harbour* (1948), and *Blue Landscape* (1951) – respond to the shapes, textures, and colours of Cornish farms, harbours, and hills, particularly as seen by night. For Wynter, the landscapes of West Penwith were a powerful stimulus to the confluence of inner and outer worlds, encouraging the irruption of images and forms from the artist's unconscious.[70] Moreover, as Peter Maber observes, Graham and Wynter shared an 'openness to experimentation', an interest in Surrealism, and both used drugs – amphetamines and mescaline, respectively – as a stimulus to creativity.[71]

In 'Dear Bryan Wynter', Graham associates his friend closely with his Zennor home in its bleak moorland surroundings of fields and stone walls, but it is the painter's absence from this distinctly uncanny place upon which the poem dwells. As with 'The Thermal Stair', Graham's elegy for Wynter begins in the form of a note regretting a missed meeting: 'This is only a note / To say how sorry I am / You died' (258). Subsequently, this self-reflexive expression of grief is reformulated as: 'This is only a note / To say I am aware / You are not here' (259). 'Here' is where the poet-speaker is speaking from, as he stands (or imagines standing) by the wall of Wynter's empty 'first house' in 'the Zennor wind' (258), and, more importantly, where his friend can no longer be – the world, the land of the living, the lines of the poem itself. The problem of locating the dead man, as though he had merely absconded or gone on a journey from which he might return, becomes a preoccupation for Graham's speaker:

> Are you still somewhere
> With your long legs
> And twitching smile under
> Your blue hat walking
> Across a place? Or am
> I greedy to make you up
> Again out of memory?
> Are you there at all? (258)

The ambiguity of that deictic 'there' in the final line of this passage underlines the speaker's distress and confusion at the fact that Wynter is no longer 'here'. His desire to imagine that, even after death, Wynter might still be 'somewhere', 'walking / Across a place' is clearly an attempt to mitigate the effects of loss. However, he also worries about the ethics of making Wynter up as a fictional character in the poem that we read instead of finding some way of confronting the irrevocability of his death, which ultimately means not being anywhere. Angela Leighton notes that many of Graham's letter-poems and elegies 'make overtures to presence, conceived as human and loved'.[72] What is distinctive about 'Dear Bryan Wynter', however, is the way in which the poem evokes the dead man's presence through the fact of his absence, an absence that in turn seems to dissolve or hollow out the place with which the poet-speaker associates him in his memory: 'The house and the whole moor / Is flying in the mist' (259). Nonetheless, the places where Wynter lived in West Penwith – Zennor and St Buryan – remain the poem's imaginative anchor points as its speaker remembers his absent friend. From his bedroom window in Madron he can see 'St Buryan's church tower', with its encoded pun on 'Bryan' (259); and in the final stanza of the poem, he admits to making 'a symbol' of the foxglove growing on the wall of Wynter's cottage at Zennor, but explains: 'It is because it knows you' (260). People are known by the places and things they live among, Graham suggests, and knowing those things and places is one of the ways in which poetry can remember loved ones after they are gone.

Night and the Sea

In the opening lines of 'The Dark Dialogues', Graham's speaker walks out into a starlit coastal landscape that might be Cornish but subsequently blurs and resolves as the streets and tenements of Greenock by night. Locations and identities are prone to drift or alter suddenly in this poem, while its titular dark dialogues are at once those between the members of a family (both living and dead) and a reference to the communicative possibilities of the poem, or of language itself. Characteristically, 'Language' is granted agency right from the opening lines and 'swings away' before the poet-speaker as he walks out, literally and metaphorically, into the dark:

> Language swings away
> Before me as I go
> With again the night rising
> Up to accompany me
> And that other fond
> Metaphor, the sea.
> Images of night
> And the sea changing
> Should know me well enough. (167)

Besides reinforcing the association between walking and writing that is established in Graham's early poetry, these lines succinctly identify the most important spatio-temporal co-ordinates for the poems of his middle period, as represented by *The White Threshold* and *The Nightfishing*: night and the sea. Denis O'Driscoll has called Graham 'the laureate of the "nightshift"'; and Francis concurs, describing him as 'a poet of the dark, a specialist in nocturnes'.[73] In interview, Graham himself calls attention to the importance of the dark for his writing, remarking that 'when I put my mind to thinking about night I find my words coming easier'.[74] However, Graham's thinking about night is often coupled with images of the sea, which serves in his poetry both as a versatile metaphor for language and the conditions of existence, and as a real space of lived experience. John Mack observes that much writing about the sea 'employs the idea of the sea as metaphor rather than as a lived reality', and this is partly true of Graham's poetry, as his reference to 'that other fond / Metaphor, the sea' knowingly admits.[75] Nonetheless, Graham's poetic representations of the sea are informed not only by a lifetime of living on the coast, but also by his experience of working on fishing boats at Greenock and Mevagissey, and occasional work as an auxiliary coastguard in the lookout post at Gurnard's Head.[76] Given these experiences, the sea is as much a 'lived reality' as it is a 'metaphor' in Graham's poetry, just as the night is at once representational and figurative within the imagined world of the poem.

If the night is creatively enabling for Graham, he is not, however, a poet of sleep and the repose that it brings, but rather one of insomnia and nocturnal restlessness – what Maurice Blanchot calls 'the *other* night', which 'does not let us sleep' and is associated with the 'uninterrupted' or 'incessant' character of both dreams and writing.[77] It is plausible, for instance, to regard the speaker of 'The Dark Dialogues' as a dreamer or sleepwalker who wanders abroad through the half-familiar landscapes of his un-resting imagination. This interpretation goes some way to explaining the uncanny transformations that he undergoes in the poem's central sections, where he takes on the identities of his dead mother and father in turn but retains his own voice and habits of perception. In both cases, the dream narrative of metamorphosis and identification that plays out in the poem is closely associated with the transformative power of words and writing. For instance, in section two the speaker sits awake in a tenement flat watching over children as they sleep, remarking: 'And in this poem I am, / Whoever elsewhere I am / Their mother' (169). Similarly, in the third section the speaker's affirmation of identity with his own father is acknowledged to be a linguistic construction: 'I am made by this word / And this word to occur' (170). Graham's repeated use of the phrase 'I am' – a bold assertion of being – in these lines is at odds with the actual slipperiness of identity that this poem of the night and dreams explores. Blanchot argues that the uncertain identity of the dreamer – the one who dreams as distinct from the one who sleeps – is akin to that of 'the writer when, in a narrative, poetic, or dramatic work, he writes "I", not knowing who says it or what relation he maintains with himself'.[78] This analogy is particularly apt with regard to Graham's speaker in 'The Dark Dialogues', who is both dreamer and writer, creating fictions of identity within language and the space of the poem itself, which is finally 'no other place / Than where I am, between / This word and the next' (174). As these lines indicate, Graham is fascinated by the between-ness of existence, and his poem of the night and the dark unfolds a series of overlapping dialogues between dreaming and writing, self and others, words and the worlds that they seek to describe or create.

Graham's preoccupation with the between-ness of existence also informs his persistent fascination with images of the sea across the whole of his career as a poet. Like the night, the sea is associated with restlessness, movement, and the ever-present possibility of change. Writing to Edwin Morgan in 1949, Graham describes the sea as 'a changing symbol' in his long poem, 'The White Threshold', where it variously signifies language itself, 'the element through which we all move', and 'the urge to really contact and share with the other "inner sea" of other people and break the centre aloneness'.[79] Similarly, Graham explained to Charles Causley in 1955 that he wanted both to depict the real sea as it is known by sailors and fishermen – 'a grey green sea, not a chocolate box sea' – and to use it as a symbol through which to explore 'the essential isolation of man and the difficulty of communication'.[80] This fundamental tension between the existential 'isolation' or 'aloneness' of the human individual and his or her need for community and communication with others in a shared language is explored through the metaphor of the 'white threshold' that marks the boundary between land and sea but also enables one to communicate with the other. One of the characteristic techniques of 'The White Threshold' is to conflate land and sea by intermingling or fusing words that refer to each element, as for example in Graham's striking lines, 'the hailing / Seabraes seabent with swimming crowds' (92), where the Scots word for 'hills' ('braes') is applied to the rearing waves of a stormy sea. A further example occurs when the speaker imagines himself walking on water like Christ in the dark of night:

> O exchanging sea imperilling who
> Walks midnight on your braes, fleetly
> Older stranger by changing stranger
> I approach your causeway-flowing land. (94)

Embarked on a perilous journey across the 'exchanging sea' of language, Graham's speaker is subject to the flux of identity and the estranging force of the very words he uses to approach the 'causeway-flowing land' of human communities, a space that is neither wholly solid nor fluid.

Repeatedly in 'The White Threshold' and other poems related to it, Graham associates the sea with language, writing, and especially with speech. The shoreline, for instance, is a 'welcome-roaring threshold' (92), and the poet-speaker's own voice competes with that of 'the shouting open sea' (98); while the poem itself resounds with 'the human-crowded song / Of the lamenting sea' (96). In 'Men Sign the Sea', Graham's speaker describes waves moving 'over sea-tongued the whole waters' (82), leaving the 'love signed sea / weeded with words' (83); and in 'Three Poems of Drowning' he imagines drowned men arising from 'This morning's wide sea' to 'speak at the white threshold' (85).

Although they often voyage out on it alone, Graham's poet-speakers typically apprehend the sea as an echo chamber of others' voices, and therefore as a potent metaphor for the fundamentally collective, social character of the language in which they move and have their being.

Images of night and the sea changing come together with Graham's guiding themes of language and place particularly memorably in his major long poem, 'The Nightfishing'. As Graham himself remarks, 'The Nightfishing' is 'a sea monster' of a poem that describes a night spent on a herring boat, a return journey from harbour to sea and back again that is also a voyage out into language and a meditation on the paradoxes of selfhood, which is apprehended as simultaneously fluid and consistent.[81] Taking Hopkins's 'The Wreck of the Deutschland', Eliot's *The Waste Land* and *Four Quartets* (1943), and Wallace Stevens's 'Notes Toward a Supreme Fiction' as models, Graham worked hard to shape and fashion his 600-line poem so that it would 'hold together as *one object*' rather than be merely 'a stream of verses'.[82] Like several of his longer poems and sequences – including 'Seven Letters' and 'Clusters Travelling Out' – 'The Nightfishing' is divided into seven uneven sections, written mostly in unrhymed but highly patterned three-stress and five-stress lines. Although the poem's circular voyage narrative and Graham's use of repeated phrases and refrains create a sense of formal cohesion, Leighton rightly observes that the poem's form is not that of 'a box or cage into which to shut meaning' but rather a more open 'lucidity of sound and structure which may not necessarily make lucid sense'.[83] At the most basic level, a loose narrative can be discerned running through the poem's seven sections from beginning to end. In the first section, the speaker (who is both poet and fisherman) is summoned to the quay-side at midnight by the harbour bell; in the second, preparations for departure mingle with reflections on birth and death, dreaming and waking; the third is a long, detailed account of casting nets, then hauling the catch as day breaks over the sea; in the fourth, the crew rest after their long night's work; section five describes the boat's return to harbour; in section six, the speaker sits at his table at home and begins composing the poem we read; and in the final section he returns to the harbour and sets out to sea once more. Cutting across and irrupting within this simple narrative structure, however, is what Graham calls the poem's 'other, more abstract voice', which disrupts its realistic depictions of places and working practices with a series of allegorical reflections on writing, identity, and the meaning of 'home'.[84] As Adam Piette observes, Graham deliberately holds these realist and allegorical elements in tension within the poem, and the overall effect serves 'to ground the metaphysics of writing in the real working world he knew' from direct, personal experience.[85]

From the beginning, the relationship between self and place is established as central to 'The Nightfishing', and yet the identities of both are presented as uncertain and in process of formation, subject to the flux that is the poem's basic ontological condition. Arriving at the quay-side in 'the dead / Of night and the dead / Of my life', the speaker hears his name called and, in that moment of responsive self-awareness, his surroundings suddenly take on definition and meaning: 'Yet this place finds me / And forms itself again' (105). In these lines, and repeatedly throughout the poem, Graham transfers agency from his speaker to the things and places with which he interacts, so that they take on a liveliness and capacity for transformation that is distinctly uncanny. In Edward Casey's terms, 'The Nightfishing' depicts place as 'eventmental', a matter of taking place that foregrounds processes of formation and becoming rather than bounded stability.[86] Moreover, the geography of the poem is deliberately vague and unspecific, making only passing references to the generic, but Scottish-sounding 'Mor Light' (108), 'Black Rosses', and 'Skeer' (115). This relative lack of topographical or toponymic detail facilitates frequent slippages between the representation of actual, physical places – the harbour, the town, the deck of the boat, the sea – and explorations of the textual 'place' of writing in the event of the poem. Hence the speaker's reflexive awareness of 'those words through which I move' (109) as the boat makes its way towards the offshore fishing grounds; or his apprehension of the boat's wake as a 'script of light' 'engraved' upon the 'iron sea' (111). In these lines, the speaking or textual self is constituted in and by language, as a being composed of words, or an agent of becoming whose medium is the material substance of the poem which he narrates.

Throughout, Graham's poem maintains a suggestive but fluid analogy between two very different kinds of work, that of the fisherman and that of the poet, so that the sea figures both as a scene of routine, practical labour and as the 'mingling element' (115) of language from which an identity is always formed in dialogue with otherness. These dual concerns with fishing and writing, the actual and the abstract are given expression through a complex reflection on the meanings of 'place' when the boat returns to harbour with its catch:

So this is the place. This
Is the place fastened still with movement,
Movement as calligraphic and formal as
A music burned on copper.

At this place
The eye reads forward as the memory reads back.
At this last word all words change.

> All words change in acknowledgement of the last.
> Here is their mingling element. (115)

Place, in these lines, is at once the harbour and the text of the poem itself: the one providing a secure anchorage on restless waters, the other wresting pattern and structure from the clamour of language and its 'shifting grounds' (114). Yet, if both the return to port and the act of writing are imagined in terms of resolution and stasis, this is only made possible by the primary flux of movements and minglings that threaten to dissolve the poem's formal fastenings. Although Graham regards writing as a means of arresting change and fixing it in a chosen form of words, his conception of language as inherently fluid – 'All words change in acknowledgement of the last' – ensures that the reader experiences the poem as 'a journey through flux itself'.[87] Flux and stasis, speech and text, self and other, the material and the metaphorical: these conceptual poles are brought into dynamic relation in 'The Nightfishing' through the conceit of a narrative journey that begins and ends where land and water meet.

Constructed Spaces

Although language and place are Graham's most important concerns throughout his oeuvre, his later poetry – gathered in *Malcolm Mooney's Land* and *Implements in Their Places* – is stylistically distinctive, adopting a more direct, conversational mode of address to the reader, simpler diction and more conventional syntax, and giving freer rein to his playful humour. There is also, in these two collections, an intensification of Graham's longstanding interest in the abstract space of communication that is the poem and the material space of the page on which it is written and read. In particular, as Lopez notes, *Malcolm Mooney's Land* is notable for the way in which it creates 'a fictional territory from which the poems speak', a territory that partly resembles aspects of the real world pushed to its extremes, but also a territory of fictions – the terrain of language and the poetic imagination.[88] For instance, 'The Constructed Space' dramatises an encounter between the writer and the reader who communicate across the 'abstract scene' of the poem's language, conceived as 'a public place' (162) in which meanings can be constructed, received, or go astray. The poem itself is construed as a 'space' constructed and shaped for the reader by the poet-speaker, whose identity is itself a function of the 'abstract act' he performs:

> I say this silence or, better, construct this space
> So that somehow something may move across
> The caught habits of language to you and me. (162)

Although the writer actively creates or constructs the poem, these lines imply that he or she is not in full control either of the linguistic materials from which it is made nor the 'lonely meanings' that might be 'read / Into the space we make' (162). In this regard, Graham's poem is a brilliant description of what Timothy Clark calls 'the space of composition', in which the writer's intentions or designs are refracted or 'echoed back' to her 'transformed' by the resistant, alienating force of language.[89] This space of composition is created by and for an event of writing, the outcome of which will always be unpredictable and, to some degree, beyond the writer's conscious control.

'The Beast in the Space' plays a variation on similar themes, but here the writer's relationship to language, which is personified as the titular 'beast', is openly confrontational and antagonistic. Indeed, the speaker threatens to resort to violence – 'I'll give the beast a quick skelp' (157) – to achieve his goals of aesthetic communication, but acknowledges the beast's own violently disruptive potential. The beast of language inhabits the 'curious necessary space' (158) of the poem, which separates writer and reader, but also moves 'across' the gulf between them:

> The beast that lives on silence takes
> Its bite out of either side.
> It pads and sniff between us. Now
> It comes and laps my meaning up. (157)

Semi-feral and prone to fits of destructive behaviour, the beast must be cajoled or threatened by the writer who wishes it to do his bidding, though it may be less refractory towards the reader. In the final lines of the poem, the poet-speaker sends the beast across the void between himself and the reader with a warning – 'Watch. He bites' – that is also simply good advice: 'He means neither / Well nor ill towards you. Above / All, shut up. Give him your love' (158). The reader's role, these lines imply, is to redress the deficiencies of the writer by doing what he has failed to do: namely, to listen instead of speaking, and to love the language despite its disobedient or unruly behaviour. As an allegory of the process of composition, then, 'The Beast in the Space' finds novel metaphors through which to conceptualise the relationship between writer and reader, the constructed space of the poem, and the ways in which it is inhabited by a language that the writer cannot wholly control.

Ian Davidson contends that poems not only represent spaces and places using language as their medium, but the poem itself 'can be usefully conceptualized as a place within the space of language'.⁹⁰ This is precisely what many of Graham's later poems do, although he also conceives of poems as spaces made or constructed out of words, and as abstract scenes inhabited by language. Moreover, Graham conceives of language itself as an agent that exceeds the comprehension and authority of its users, who are in turn used by the language they speak. This is the situation of the speaker in 'What is the Language Using Us For?', who feels manipulated by an inscrutable and irresistible force:

> What is the language using us for?
> It uses us all and in its dark
> Of dark actions selections differ. (200)

Language is essentially social and acts impartially; its 'dark actions' affect 'us' all, though not necessarily in the same ways or for the same purposes. Graham invents a series of spatial metaphors to express this situation, describing the poet-speaker driving endlessly 'through the suburbs' of a language in which he cannot find his way, or trapped 'in a telephoneless, blue / Green crevasse' (199) from which he can neither communicate nor escape. The irony, of course, is that what this poem communicates very powerfully and directly to the reader is the difficulty – but not impossibility – of communication, of using language to speak or write while it simultaneously uses you. Several of Graham's late poems, including 'What is the Language Using Us For?', 'Approaches to How They Behave', and 'Implements in Their Places', might be read as creative elaborations of Martin Heidegger's claim that, in the poem, 'Language speaks': 'For, strictly, it is language that speaks. Man first speaks when, and only when, he responds to language by listening to its appeal'.⁹¹ Heidegger's point is that language is not merely a tool to be used or a system of signs that can be manipulated, but rather the all-pervasive shared environment that makes perceptions, thoughts, and understandings possible in the first place.⁹² Graham similarly conceives of language as a 'space' or world that makes the poet's creative labours possible, but unlike Heidegger he also regards it as a resistant, obstructive, or even manipulative force than can be as disabling as it is generative.

In Graham's parabolic account, the beast of language lives on silence, and many of his later poems are preoccupied by the relationship between the words from which the poem is made and the 'spaces' that 'occur between the words' (178), or with the textual space of the blank page on which the poem takes place. These concerns with silence, blankness, and voids are often explored through Graham's fascination with the ice-bound landscapes of the Arctic, most strikingly in 'Malcolm Mooney's

Land'. A near-silent, frozen world of glaciers and 'grinding bergs' (153), Malcolm Mooney's land is a fictional terrain loosely derived from Graham's reading about actual polar landscapes – Franz Josef Land in the Arctic Ocean and Graham Land on the Antarctic Peninsula are both possible models – and an allegorical depiction of the inhospitable spaces of language and textuality. The speaker is a poet-explorer who keeps a diary, in which he records his impressions of and imaginings about the landscapes of ice and snow across which he moves, and from which he speaks. Suffering from extreme fatigue, loneliness, and hallucinations, he increasingly conflates the external, physical world with the space of the page on which he writes, referring to 'the printed snow' (153) and 'This diary of a place' (156) where unidentified voices mingle with his own. In the poem's final lines, he describes 'Words drifting on words. / The real unabstract snow' (157). There is a strange convergence here, characteristic of Graham's later poetry, between the abstractions of language and the 'unabstract', real world that it represents, as though the poem itself were 'drifting' between the two. In 'Malcolm Mooney's Land', Graham's evocation of the solitude and sublimity of the arctic landscape, its stark, elemental beauty, is powerfully immersive, and yet the reader is always aware of the poem's self-reflexive, allegorical character. As Francis observes, the whiteness of this place of ice and snow 'resembles the whiteness of the page', its coldness is a reminder of the 'impersonality' of writing, and the frozen barrenness of the landscape is 'an appropriate image for the deadness Graham associates with textuality'.[93] Hence, the speaker's self-portrait 'in a white-out in this tent of a place' and his ominous awareness that language 'freezes all around us' (155). In Graham's later poetry, then, polar landscapes provide a distinctive set of images and metaphors through which he explores the poet's relationship to language, dramatising the attempt to communicate in writing as a desperate, but also heroic struggle for survival under extreme conditions.

Graham's modernist aesthetic leads him to affirm that 'every poem should have a kind of strangeness', for: 'The poet does not write what he knows but what he doesn't know'.[94] Through their fictional explorations of polar landscapes and depictions of the constructed spaces of writing, Graham's late poems repeatedly find spatial allegories and analogies for enabling encounters with otherness, giving expression to what their speakers do not know. They amplify the metapoetic tendency that runs through his entire oeuvre but which is also, I have argued, grounded in his engagement with actual, material places. Graham's poetry is recurrently preoccupied with the relationship between language and place, not only figuring language as a place to inhabit or journey across, but also reflecting on the ways in which his attachments to marginal places on the coasts of Scotland and Cornwall condition his self-consciously 'Unenglish' use of the English language. His poetics of place is distinctive for moving fluidly and sometimes disorientatingly between places, particularly his homes in Greenock and West Penwith, finding correspondences between their landscapes and histories without eliding their important differences. In this sense, Graham's poems are fundamentally bi-located, moving restlessly betwixt and between rather than settling in any one place. They are drawn repeatedly to liminal or littoral landscapes, dramatising the processes whereby places and selves are formed, interact, and change one another.

Chapter 4

Lorine Niedecker: Life by Water

Edges are paradoxically central to the poetry of Lorine Niedecker. The defining condition for her geographical imagination is the fact that she spent most of her life by water, and her poems are strongly drawn to the meeting places between terrestrial and aquatic worlds. Aside from a few short periods in New York during the 1930s and in Milwaukee during the 1960s, Niedecker lived and died in the place where she was born (in 1903): Blackhawk Island, a low-lying, flood-prone strip of land on the banks of the Rock River where it enters Lake Koshkonong, in South-east Wisconsin. Her poems attest to a profound, bodily 'implacement' in both the social and the natural communities of her home place, registering its sights and sounds, the change of seasons, and the behaviour of her neighbours – both human and non-human – with a mixture of sympathy and subtle irony.[1]

Niedecker's attachments to people and place are deep but never narrow or exclusive; her poems register the local effects of global political and economic forces, particularly the Depression years, the Atomic age, and the Cold War, bringing world-historical events into focus through her situated perspectives in the Midwest. Her politics were consistently left-wing, and she sympathised with people on the margins of American society; though she became wary of combining poetry and politics in later years.[2] The only daughter of a fisherman, Niedecker was college-educated and her family owned several properties on Blackhawk Island; but she identified with the rural working class, worked as a librarian and hospital cleaner, and lived most of her life in some poverty. Her chosen life as a poet was kept hidden from most of her neighbours, so that she occupied the dual position of long-term inhabitant and artful observer of her native place; at once insider and outsider.[3] This tension between social embeddedness and emotional (or political) distance is crystallised in an untitled poem of 1950, where she writes of working in a print shop 'right down among em / the folk from whom all poetry flows / and dreadfully much else'.⁴ Although she claims that poetry 'flows' from its source 'down among' the 'folk', her poems are often situated at the edges of the community she claims, somewhat ambivalently, as her own. Moreover, as I argue in detail below, Niedecker's texts are drawn repeatedly to the shifting, porous edges of her particular place-world, the boundaries that serve to simultaneously demarcate and connect different domains: land and water; human and non-human habitats; domestic interiors and the outside world.

Niedecker's position within the literary history of modernism remains marginal, despite the increased visibility and critical attention prompted by the publication of her *Collected Works* in 2002. Her commitment to avant-garde poetics began early and remained consistent over her forty-year career as a poet. Indeed, she regularly published her poems in a range of (late) modernist little magazines, including *Poetry, Furioso, The Paris Review, Joglars, Origin*, and *Black Mountain Review*. According to Jenny Penberthy, it was Niedecker's encounter, in Fort Atkinson Public Library, with the 1931 'Objectivist' issue of *Poetry* edited by Louis Zukofsky that 'ignited her career as a poet' and provided 'direction for her restless talent'.[5] She wrote to Zukofsky six months later, beginning a correspondence that would continue until her death in 1970, and which was enormously important to them both as poets.[6] Nonetheless, Niedecker was always more than simply Zukofsky's acolyte or apprentice, and her alignment with the core group of Objectivist poets – George Oppen, Carl Rakosi, Charles Reznikoff, and Zukofsky – all of whom were male, Jewish, and metropolitan, was necessarily equivocal. As Mark Scroggins observes, Niedecker and Basil Bunting are both best understood as 'outriders' of the Objectivist nexus; and Niedecker herself registers this marginality in a letter to Cid Corman, where she notes her position 'on the periphery' of the movement during the 1930s.[7] Niedecker's experience of marginality is double here, for she was conscious of being 'a marginal figure within Objectivism's already marginalized ranks' – a figure on the outer edge of the margins.[8] A significant factor in this metaphorical positioning on the periphery of modernist literary history is Niedecker's decision, following the end of her brief love affair with Zukofsky in 1935, to live and write in Wisconsin at a significant geographical distance from major urban cultural centres such as New York. To borrow Raymond Williams's terms, Niedecker's poetry offers a vantage on literary modernism 'from the deprived hinterlands' rather than from 'within the changing cultural milieu of the metropolis' – though she remained in touch with that milieu through her correspondence with Zukofsky, Corman, and others.[9]

Niedecker always acknowledged the influence of Zukofsky's ideas on poetics for her own poetry. Writing to Kenneth Cox, she claims: 'I literally went to school to William Carlos Williams and Louis Zukofsky and have had the good fortune to call the latter friend and mentor'.[10] In particular, Zukofsky's stress upon the importance of 'economy of presentation' and 'precision of style' in poetry finds its answer in Niedecker's distinctive poetics of condensation, whereby she carefully strips away any unnecessary images or linguistic embellishments.[11] Her poem, 'Poet's Work', is both a product of this strenuous process of composition and a meta-poetic commentary on the process itself. What is distinctive about this meta-poetic statement, however, is the way that Niedecker deliberately re-contextualises Zukofsky's post-Poundian poetics by creating an analogy between the poet's work and Midwestern dairy production:

> I learned
>   to sit at desk
>   and condense
> No layoff
>   from this
>   condensery (194)

As Michelle Niemann explains, condenseries make condensed milk and are a common feature of the landscape around Fort Atkinson; so Niedecker's poem ironically 'figure[s] poetry-writing as agro-industrial labor'.[12] Here is a good example of the way in which Niedecker subtly adapts Objectivist poetic principles to her own local circumstances and non-metropolitan sensibility. Another can be found in her response to Zukofsky's interest in the aural qualities of poetry, particularly in terms of its formal resemblances to music. 'The sound of the words is sometimes 95% of poetic presentation,' writes Zukofsky in *A Test of Poetry* (1948), which Niedecker valued highly as a study of poetic technique.[13] However, where Zukofsky sought to emulate the contrapuntal elegance of Bach's music in his long poem, "A", Niedecker's poems are more often interested in the rhythms of vernacular speech and the distinctive soundscapes of her local environment – what 'Paean to Place' calls Blackhawk Island's 'sublime / slime- / song' (265).[14]

Objectivist poetry is epistemologically realist and anti-transcendental, foregrounding the significance of historical particulars in place of myth and symbolism. As Michael Heller has it, for the Objectivists, 'the world is fact, and the poet is its agency'.[15] However, because the poet mediates between the reader and the world as material reality, Objectivist poetry also calls attention to the acts of perception and intellection through which the world is encountered. In this regard, the poet's agency is informed by an ethics of honesty or sincerity, a responsibility to attend to and render into language the concrete particulars of the world with a minimum of subjective distortion. Burton Hatlen argues that 'the writings of the Objectivists are generally less concerned with the thing seen than with the way we see, a process that becomes in their poetry profoundly problematic'.[16] Although much of her poetry draws upon her own personal experiences, and she believed that poetry was 'depth of emotion condensed', Niedecker often effaces or disguises such autobiographical material.[17] She also tends to displace the centrality of the lyric 'I' through acts of ventriloquism, shifting modes of address, and an emphasis on the sonic and rhythmic qualities of language. As Penberthy observes, 'Niedecker is not easy to find in her poems, and her tendency towards self-dramatization makes the poems doubly misleading'.[18] In a distinctively Objectivist manner, Niedecker's poems also often call attention to the relationship between objects or things and the movements of consciousness by which they are perceived. Consider, for instance, the following short poem from her late sequence, 'Traces of Living Things':

> Mergansers
>   fans
>   on their heads
> Thoughts on things
>   fold unfold
>   above the river beds (246)

Composed of two stepped tercets (a form that Niedecker adapts from William Carlos Williams), this poem initially focuses the reader's attention upon the birds themselves, regular visitors to Lake Koshkonong in summer, and creates a fusion of nature and culture by referring metaphorically to the crests on their heads as 'fans'. However, the second tercet modifies the metaphor by transferring it to the thoughts of an unspecified consciousness (presumably the speaker's), which 'fold' and 'unfold' like a fan on the margins of river and lake. That is, the movement of the poem is from 'things' (mergansers) to the 'thoughts' that are stimulated by the way the birds are seen (through the filters of human culture). In addition, the poem subtly calls our attention to the materiality of language through which the speaker's thoughts are made manifest by its lineation, rhythms, and unobtrusive use of rhyme: not only the full end-rhyme – 'heads' and 'beds' – that links the tercets together, but also the more discordant chiming of 'mergansers' with 'fans', 'fold' and 'unfold', 'above' and 'river'.

However important Zukofsky's ideas and friendship might have been to Niedecker's development as a poet, to consider her work only within the ambit of Objectivism would be misleading. Her poetics is a blend of various influences, and alters significantly in terms of style, subject, and scope over the course of her writing career. Niedecker's oeuvre might be divided roughly into four broad phases, each with its specific formal and thematic features. First, there are her early experiments of the 1930s, where the influence of Surrealism and an interest in tapping the creative resources of the unconscious are apparent.[19] Niedecker's attraction to Surrealism was a cause of tension in her relationship with Zukofsky, but it remained an important, if partly suppressed feature of her poetry throughout her career.[20] Second, from the mid-1930s until the publication of her first collection, *New Goose*, in 1946, Niedecker wrote elliptical, politically-charged poems that fused elements of folk song and ballad traditions with an Objectivist concern for recording concrete, historical particulars. Her aim was to revise the American tradition of Mother Goose rhymes, combining humour and subversive intent. Many of the poems can be read as condensed critiques of the effects of the Depression and the New Deal on ordinary working people, exposing injustice, inequality, and the politics of individualism.[21] However, as Peter Middleton argues, Niedecker did not identify straightforwardly as a folk poet, but rather 'oscillated between immersion and alienation from the local community', behaving as much like an avant-garde folklorist as a member of the 'folk' about whom she writes.[22] This duality can also be found in the language of her poems, where there is a pervading tension between the rhythms of vernacular speech and the syntactical or formal demands of literary sophistication.

Following the publication of *New Goose*, Niedecker moved into a third phase of her writing, working on a series of letter-poems addressed to Zukofsky's son Paul from 1949 to 1953 but also responding more directly to her home place and its riparian ecosystems. Under the influence of Japanese poetry and through her friendship with the poet Cid Corman (beginning in 1960), she further enhanced her poetics of condensation, striving towards a minimalism of utterance in which sound and silence, word and image are intricately counter-balanced. Writing to her neighbours, Gail and Bonnie Roub, Niedecker remarks: 'I like planting poems in deep, silence, each person gets at the poems for *himself*'; and to Corman she observes simply: 'If your ear is acute you sound your poem in silence'.[23] Indeed, in her best work, Niedecker's poetry exemplifies the basic paradox of minimalist art, whereby a process of reduction or concentration achieves an amplification of meaning and effect.[24] One of her most important formal innovations during this period was the creation of a five-line stanza, or 'quintain', loosely based on haiku and tanka, where, Eleanor Berry notes, the combination of very short lines and elliptical syntax makes 'apprehensible the sensuous properties and thingliness of single words, as well as of the poem itself'.[25] Finally, from the mid-1960s to her death in 1970, Niedecker entered a remarkably productive late phase of her career during which her poetry underwent significant transformations in form, subject-matter, and scope. Following her second marriage in 1963, she took several vacation tours in the Midwest and Canada, developed profound interests in geology, botany, and evolutionary biology, and began to write a cluster of serial poems and sequences, beginning with 'Lake Superior' and closing with 'Darwin'. In the last years of her life, she also wrote to friends of a new 'reflective' poetics she felt was emerging in her later work, which would synthesise elements of Imagism, Objectivism, and Surrealism to convey an 'awareness of everything influencing everything'.[26] Rachel Blau DuPlessis aptly describes this manifestation of Niedecker's late style as 'a materialist sublime', a culmination of her imaginative and experiential immersion in the social and natural worlds of Blackhawk Island and the wider North Central region.[27] It is in these later phases of Niedecker's work, from the 1950s to the 1960s, that her distinctive poetics of place is given its fullest expression. Consequently, I offer extended readings of three of her serial or long poems, 'Paean to Place', 'Lake Superior', and 'Wintergreen Ridge', in the second half of this chapter.

Edges and Boundaries

Niedecker's poems repeatedly remind readers of the significance that water – or rather the proximity of land and water – has for her sense of place and subjectivity. What Gaston Bachelard would call her 'material imagination' is closely attuned to the material and metaphorical attributes of water, an intrinsically 'transitory element' associated with change and metamorphosis: 'A being dedicated to water is a being in flux', writes Bachelard, for the being of water is flow.[28] At times, Niedecker's poems give expression to precisely this ontological condition, as when the speaker of her long poem, 'Paean to Place', describes her mother and herself as 'born / in swale and swamp and sworn / to water' (261). To be 'sworn' to water is to align something of one's own being with that element; but this alignment is partially qualified by the fact that Niedecker's speaker claims to have been born 'in swale and swamp' rather than river or lake. What this topographical detail implies is that her being is fundamentally amphibious, compounded of the elements of earth and water, rather than water alone. In this regard, Niedecker's word choices are precise as well as alliteratively consonant: a 'swale' is low-lying, marshy land; and a 'swamp' is forested wetland.[29] Accordingly, the characteristic places of Niedecker's poetry are not aquatic but riparian, the wetland margins of lakeshore and riverbank. As William Howarth observes, wetland environments resist any ascription of an essential identity, for they are characteristically 'hybrid and multivalent: neither land nor water alone, they are water-land; a continuum between terra and aqua'.[30] Niedecker's geographical imagination is crucially shaped by the hybrid water-land in which she spent most of her life, and to which her mature poetry responds in complex ways. Moreover, edges and boundaries are of special significance to her poetics of place, particularly those where land and water, humans and non-humans come into contact, encounter, and recognise one another.

Situated four miles from the city of Fort Atkinson and surrounded by dairy farmland, Niedecker's home place, Blackhawk Island, is not, in fact, an island but a peninsula bounded to the south by the Rock River, to the west by Lake Koshkonong, and to the north by the swamplands of Mud Lake. It takes its name from an episode in the Black Hawk War of 1832, when the Sauk leader Black Hawk and a band of his people took refuge there from the larger forces commanded by General Henry Atkinson.[31] In a letter to Kenneth Cox, Niedecker emphasises the importance of her proximity to the natural world, especially during her formative childhood years:

> Nature is lush here, I feel as tho [sic] I spent my childhood outdoors – redwinged blackbirds, willows, maples, boats, fishing (the smell of tarred nets), tittering and squawking noises from the marsh, a happy, outdoor grandfather who somewhere got hold of nursery and folk rhymes to entrance me [. . .].[32]

Several of the elements of Niedecker's poetics of place are brought together here: a sensory immersion in the sounds and smells of the environment that enables acute observation; an emphasis upon the porosity of boundaries (between indoors and outdoors, land and water, nature and culture); and a fascination with vernacular speech. There is also, however, a hint of nostalgic idealisation in Niedecker's depiction of Blackhawk Island, which was not simply a wetland paradise, even during her childhood, but rather 'summer resort country'.[33] Her maternal grandparents owned a ten-guest hotel on the peninsula, and Lake Koshkonong was popular for hunting and fishing; Niedecker's biographer, Margot Peters, observes that by the 1940s Blackhawk Island had altered 'from a rural paradise to a blue-collar tourist destination'.[34] Readers need to be wary, then, of accepting as authentic Niedecker's occasional tendency to depict her native water-land as an Edenic first place, and to recognise instead both the knowing artifice of such representations and the counter-impulse in many poems to qualify or undermine such myths of origin.

Niedecker was profoundly conscious of, but also somewhat ambivalent about the extent to which her poetry is identified with a particular place and locality. In a letter to Zukofsky, she quipped: 'The Brontes [sic] had their moors, I have my marshes!'[35] However playful or tongue-in-cheek, this remark is an instance of Niedecker laying claim to her own distinctive literary geography whilst also positioning herself in a wider literary history of women writers' engagements with place. More obviously in earnest, Niedecker explained her conception of the relationship between selfhood and place in a letter to her neighbour, Gail Roub: 'Early in life I looked back of our buildings to the lake and said, "I am what I am because of all this – I am what is around me – those woods have made me . . . "'.[36] What Niedecker makes plain here is that she understands the ontological significance of place, its foundational role in grounding and shaping human subjectivity. In this context, J. E. Malpas argues that our identities are 'bound up with particular places or localities', for 'it is only in, and through our grasp of, the places in which we are situated that we can encounter objects, other persons or, indeed, ourselves'.[37]

In her poems, Niedecker repeatedly figures this intimate relationship between place and identity in terms of her origins in, and emergence from, the marshy margins of land and water. For instance, in 'I rose from marsh mud' the speaker dramatises herself rising from the amphibious world of the marsh to attend a friend's wedding:

I rose from marsh mud
algae, equisetum, willows,
sweet green, noisy
birds and frogs (170)

In this first stanza, Niedecker's speaker implies that her identity is composed of the material substance of the marsh – its mud, plants, and animal life – from which she has disembedded herself only reluctantly and with difficulty. It is as though she herself were a willow, a bird, or a frog – a creature that is dependent upon the unique ecosystem that the marsh creates and sustains. Accordingly, a sharp contrast is drawn between the 'sweet', 'noisy' natural life of the marsh and the comparatively sterile 'silence of the church', in which the speaker clearly feels awkward and out-of-place. In part, this sense of being out-of-place is bound up with the speaker's implicitly feminist critique of marriage as a form of 'slavery' in which both bride and groom are 'United for life to serve / silver' (170);

but it also arises because she is literally as well as metaphorically out of her element. The speaker's natural element, the poem implies, is what Niedecker elsewhere calls the 'primordial mud' that forms where land meets and mixes with water.[38] Niedecker's self-portrait in this poem as a kind of swamp-thing temporarily displaced from her native marsh mud is touched with characteristically self-mocking humour. However, it is of a piece with her ecological awareness of 'interconnectedness' as a basic condition of existence, which, Richard Caddell notes, leads her to weave 'her human and natural poetic necessities together'.[39] Most importantly, it succinctly illustrates the way in which her late modernist poetics of place is grounded in her conviction that her wetland environment has made her who and what she is.

Niedecker's strong identification with the riparian zones of her Blackhawk Island home is a pervasive and enabling feature of her poetry. However, she was also wary of being categorised as a provincial or regional writer because of the perceived limitations – in terms of intellectual ambition and formal experiment, as well as content – such designations seemed to imply. Writing to Corman, she complains that a copy of her collected poems, *T&G* (1969), has been placed 'with regional materials' in the University of Wisconsin's library: 'I should ask: What region – London, Wisconsin, New York?'[40] Niedecker's exasperation here is instructive, for it helps both to clarify her self-understanding as a poet and to complicate the relationships between poetry and place in her work. Although her poems are often informed by deep attachments to a specific region and rural locality, they were published by small presses and modernist magazines based in England, Scotland, and Japan, as well as the United States. Accordingly, Ross Hair argues that Niedecker's poetry is at once 'rooted in its environment' and 'far-reaching' because of her participation in an international, but mostly non-metropolitan network of poets, publishers, and readers.[41] That is, the contexts of publication and reception in which Niedecker's poetry needs to be understood necessarily reach far beyond the places to which her geographical imagination responds most intensely. Moreover, whilst Niedecker cultivated anonymity in Blackhawk Island – saying: 'I live among the folk who couldn't understand and it's where I want to live' – she actively and consistently sought publicity among a transnational community of late modernist poets.[42] It is also wrong to assume that Niedecker's imaginative fidelity to her home place sets definite limits on the range and scope of her engagements with history and politics. Arguing that Niedecker's adaptations of 'minor' genres – such as folk verse or haiku – and vernacular idioms constitutes an implicit politics of marginality, Michael Davidson contends that her 'critical regionalism' conjugates local and global forces, 'placing indigenous peoples, local economies, and non-metropolitan spaces within the orbit of capitalist production worldwide'.[43] This technique is perhaps most immediately apparent in Niedecker's folk poems of the 1930s and 1940s, where she illustrates the effects of the global economic Depression – originating in metropolitan New York – upon her local community's modes of living and self-expression: 'A country's economics sick / affects its people's speech' (86). However, I want to argue that Niedecker's critical regionalism finds its fullest expression in her attention to the edges of places where land and water, human and natural habitats meet. For it is here that metaphors of marginality are grounded in the geographical, historical, and existential particulars that her poetry is so assiduous to record.

Although the geographical bounds of Blackhawk Island can be described and mapped without much difficulty, the edges of Niedecker's place-world are more difficult to define with confidence. On the one hand, her home place might be said to begin and end at the water's edge, where riverbank, lakeshore, and swamp serve as natural borders. However, as I have argued above, this definition overlooks the inherently hybrid character of wetland environments and fails to recognise the fluctuating character of such boundaries between land and water over time – for instance, during the spring floods that regularly affected Blackhawk Island during Niedecker's lifetime. Niedecker typically regards water as an integral part of her poetics of place; her speakers' modes of inhabiting place involve crossing back and forth between land and water, human settlements and non-human habitats (those of birds, frogs, and trees in particular). In this regard, the distinction that Edward Casey makes between 'borders' and 'boundaries' in his phenomenological study of edges is illuminating. Borders, Casey argues, are 'clearly demarcated edges' that are geometrically linear and ideally impermeable, dividing one thing, place, or event clearly from others. By contrast, boundaries are 'inherently indeterminate, porous, and often change configuration', serving at once to enclose and to open out towards what lies beyond them.[44] Although places typically possess a multiplicity of edges, Casey contends that 'the edges of places are more like boundaries than borders', for places themselves characteristically exhibit 'an inherent openness and vagueness of spatial extent'.[45] Moreover, because places are fundamentally historical entities that change over time, their edges will necessarily fluctuate or change in the manner that is distinctive of boundaries. Appositely, Casey refers to 'the permeability of natural entities like riverbanks and marshlands' as a concrete instance of the qualities of boundaries as edges of place.[46] Adopting Casey's distinctions and definitions, I contend that Niedecker's poetry is particularly drawn to the porous and shifting character of various kinds of boundaries – between interior and exterior spaces, land and water, nature and human culture – in its representations of place. Indeed, it is precisely at the margins of Blackhawk Island, where it bleeds or blends into the lake, river, and swamps that surround it, that Niedecker's sense of place is most highly charged.

Overflows

Perhaps the most immediately striking way in which Niedecker explores the unstable, permeable edges of place in her poetry is through her responses to the seasonal cycle of spring floods that she, her family, and her neighbours endured as a regular feature of life on Blackhawk Island. Floods typically occurred in March or April following the break-up of winter ice in the Rock River basin, and Mary Pinard observes that there were twenty-six floods recorded in or near Blackhawk Island between 1935 and 1956, averaging six feet above ordinary levels.[47] Niedecker's ambivalent feelings about these flood events are apparent in several of her letters. Describing the summer flood of 1950 to Zukofsky, she seems exhilarated by the river's redrawing of its boundary with the land because of the new relationships it makes possible between her and the local wildlife: 'The flood is subsiding and maybe the monsoon has passed. The birds and animals came close, practically inside the house because on two sides I had only a couple of feet of land'.[48] On this occasion, the boundary between indoors and outdoors was threatened, but not breached; in April 1959, however, Niedecker had to leave her river-side cabin because of rising water levels. 'I was evacuated!' she wrote to Zukofsky:

> Wind very high, grey high waves, I was glad to get out. [. . .] Disorder and leaving home – but I was thinking too with no time to write it down. Intense emotion generates thought like a coiled spring. And my thought: some day I'll leave this place for good.[49]

Two things are worth noting here. Firstly, that Niedecker is understandably disturbed by the 'disorder' caused by the flood and its capacity to displace her from her 'home', to the extent that she seriously considers leaving Blackhawk Island; and secondly, that she also experiences the flood as a powerful stimulus for both 'thought' and writing, although there is no opportunity to write during the flood event itself. In this regard, Niedecker recognises the dual character of floods as natural phenomena, their simultaneous capacity for destruction and creation.⁵⁰ Floods are at once a threat to her home place, causing temporary or perhaps permanent displacement, and an inherent feature of the kind of place that Blackhawk Island is.

Several of Niedecker's flood poems focus on the unhappy figure of her mother, Daisy, associating the disorder of the flood with her deafness (which began after Lorine's birth) and her dysfunctional marriage.⁵¹ For example, an untitled poem published in *New Goose* alternates between an apparently neutral, third-person voice and what are presented as the first-person reflections of Daisy Niedecker:

> Well spring overflows the land,
> floods floor, pump, wash machine
> of the woman moored to this low shore by deafness.
> [. . .]
> I've wasted my whole life in water.
> My man's got nothing but leaky boats.
> My daughter, writer, sits and floats. (107)

The initial opposition of 'woman' and floodwaters modulates in the final stanza, through Daisy's frank, first-person assessment of her 'wasted' life, to a statement of grievance that takes in both husband and daughter, where the dominant opposition is internal to the family group itself. Strikingly, Niedecker employs internal rhyme to identify the 'daughter' figure – who is pointedly identified as a 'writer' – with the 'water' that has wrought destruction on her mother's life, as though the creative force of poetry were somehow allied with the 'overflows' of the river. The fluidity of boundaries between land and water, domestic interior and riverbank is further emphasised in the first stanza through the full-rhyming of 'floor' with 'shore', as well as the pattern of consonance that links '*fl*oods', '*fl*oor', and 'over*fl*ows'.

Observing that Niedecker 'lived in an environment in which the natural world always seemed about to overwhelm the human one', Rae Armantrout argues that such boundary-breaching serves in the poems as a metaphor for depressive states, particularly as manifest in the 'tall, tormented / darkinfested' (287) figure of her mother, with whom she identifies.⁵² Up to a point, this is a plausible way of reading Niedecker's flood poems; except that she also tends to depict mother and daughter as antagonists and sometimes represents her mother as a stoic survivor of the metaphorical and actual floods that threaten her. A later poem, written after her mother's death in 1951, ends by quoting Daisy's defiant words: 'I didn't sink, I sewed and saved / and now I'm on the second floor' (167). However, this poem further reinforces the link between Daisy's daughter and the river's floodwaters by describing Daisy giving birth during a spring flood and locating 'Henry's daughter' in a natal 'boat' floating 'on the stream' (166). So, whilst Daisy is closely associated with the home on dry land that is threatened annually by spring floods, her daughter is repeatedly linked to the very waters that would inundate and overwhelm it.

This antagonism is absent from Niedecker's most important flood poem, 'My Life by Water', the title of which foregrounds her existential situation on the boundary that defines her wetland place-world. The poem itself is a collage of images and perceptions that collectively sketch out a compressed, elliptical autobiography in which the relation of self to place is primary, but where subjectivity is progressively merged with the sensory qualities of the environment. It is written in nine stepped tercets using very short lines (between one and four syllables) and heavily enjambed, its form tightly controlled but also sinuous and flowing. It begins at a moment of seasonal transition as the speaker moves deliberately from one element to another:

My life
   by water—
      Hear
spring's
   first frog
   or board
out on the cold
   ground
      giving (237)

As the injunction 'Hear' implies, sound and the sense of hearing are crucial in these lines, both thematically and formally. For the speaker, the sound of the 'first frog' of spring marks a moment of re-awakening, implying on her part a heightened state of 'ecological consciousness', or sensitivity to the non-human signs of seasonal change (including annual flood cycles).[53] Moreover, the frog's croaking is interpreted as an invitation to leave dry land for the more amphibious 'ground' of the adjacent swamp. At a formal level, the patterns of assonance, alliteration, and internal rhyme create an impression of fluid inter-mingling; and the initial rhyme of 'My' and 'by' serves to cement the association of 'life' with 'water' from the outset. As in 'I rose from marsh mud', Niedecker creates a strong impression that her speaker is not only born in, but born *of* the wetland habitat that she describes, and that her 'board[ing] / out' on its unstable terrain is a kind of return to origins. The lines that follow shift position from the edge of the swamp to the interior of the speaker's cabin, but only deepen the reader's sense that the boundaries between inside and outside, human and non-human forms of life are eroding:

'Muskrats / gnawing / doors // to wild green / arts and letters' (237). This image derives from a 1962 letter to Corman, following another late spring flood: 'Another flood come and gone. This time not in my house. Muskrats grinding their catch just outside my door in the middle of the night'.[54] So, whilst the poem itself does not explicitly mention floodwaters, it is the land's inundation by the river that not only implicates the speaker's life with those of frogs, muskrats, and rabbits, but provides an illustration of the porousness of several kinds of boundary: land/water, interior/exterior, human/non-human, self/other.

The final lines of 'My Life by Water' shift perspective again, relocating the speaker's implied position to the riverbank and prioritising movements from water to land:

>   One boat
> two—
>   pointed toward
>   my shore
> thru birdstart
>   wingdrip
>   weed-drift
> of the soft
>   and serious—
>   Water (237–8)

Where the speaker had previously contemplated 'board[ing] out' on the waterlogged ground of the swamp's edge, making the transition from land to water, now both boats are 'pointed toward / my shore', enacting a circular return from one element to the other. Interestingly, as Pinard observes, the speaker's use of the first-person possessive pronoun here – '*my* shore' rather than 'the shore' – implies that 'this boundary or surrounding land is a part of the speaker – as if she were a river or some body of water itself'.[55] This idea is reinforced by Niedecker's use of unusual spondaic compounds – 'birdstart', 'wingdrip', 'weed-drift' – in the penultimate tercet, where the clustering of stresses along with alliterative and assonantal patterning formally conveys a sense of being immersed in the sonic world of the wetland environment itself: an ambient soundscape of bird calls, dripping trees, and the bass swell of the river's current. At the same time, the very strangeness of these neologisms draws the reader's attention to the thickened textures of the poem's linguistic surface. This is followed by the looser, iambic-anapestic rhythm and sibilance of the final tercet, which suggests a release of tension that is associated with the flowing properties of water, an element (capitalised in the final line as 'Water') that is acknowledged to be both 'soft' and 'serious'. The boats' unhurried journey through the water to the speaker's 'shore' can be read as an autobiographical allegory, then, for her present self appears to be formed by the event of their arrival at the boundary between the two elements of earth and water.[56] In this way, Niedecker's poem not only illustrates Casey's point that the edges of a place are 'an integral part of its being'.[57] It also suggests that the divide between self and place becomes permeable or subject to overflows at the boundary where land and water intermix.

The Place was Water

'My Life by Water' might be regarded as a prelude to Niedecker's long autobiographical poem, 'Paean to Place', which is her most sustained and multi-faceted exploration of the relationships between self, others, and place. Writing to Corman in 1968, Niedecker described it punningly as her 'life long poem': both a long poem about her life on Blackhawk Island and the poem that she has spent her life preparing to write.[58] It is clear from her letters that, in common with her other late long poems, Niedecker undertook significant research on natural history – a subject that fascinated her – prior to writing 'Paean to Place'; though she told Zukofsky that, in the end, she used 'what [she] had always known anyhow!'[59] The title suggests a primary focus on place itself, and Niedecker explicitly referred to it as her 'marsh poem'; but the poem's celebration of her wetland place-world is also a meditation on family relationships, subjectivity, and an exploration of what the poem calls 'the unknown' (267).[60] In this regard, its title is curiously inapt: in modern usage, a 'paean' is 'any song of joy or triumph'; but Niedecker also seems to have regarded 'Paean to Place' as an elegy for her parents, and for the water-land of her childhood years.[61] In a letter to Florence Dollase, she describes it as a 'longish poem which is a kind of *In Memoriam* of my father and mother and the place I've never seemed really to get away from'.[62] There is a certain dissonance in the generic affiliations of 'Paean to Place', then, whereby the impetus to praise or rejoice is tempered by a stronger undertow of memories, in which mourning and loss are the prevalent modes of relating to place and the past. DuPlessis describes Niedecker's poem as 'a selective autobiography of the growth of a poet's mind, an American mini-*Prelude*, very keen on watery spots of time'.[63] The analogy is apposite given that, as a young woman, Niedecker read Wordsworth's poetry while 'rowing a boat or walking the woods' at Blackhawk Island, so that his poetry was intricately bound up with her personal experiences of place at a formative stage.[64] Indeed, the speaker of 'Paean to Place' compounds this association between water, reading, and Romantic poetry further when she compares herself to Percy Shelley, who 'could steer / as he read' (265). What is also characteristic about the poem is the way in which it correlates the growth of the poet's mind with fluid movements between land and water, emphasising the permeable edges of the places that it remembers and describes.

The form of 'Paean to Place' is paradoxical in several ways. Firstly, at 205 lines it manifests a length and scope that is unusual in Niedecker's oeuvre; but, at the same time, it is written in forty-one quintains, the five-line stanza form that she often used for her haiku-like miniatures. So 'Paean to Place' combines amplitude and imaginative ambition with the poetics of condensation that is her distinctive signature. Moreover, as Eleanor Berry observes, Niedecker employs four different versions of her quintain stanza, varying their patterns of indentation but mostly linking the third and fourth lines through rhyme or assonance. This creates a consistent but flexible structure within which there is significant room for improvisation, so that the shape of the poem on the page resembles the meandering course of a river or stream flowing down the left-hand margin.[65] Secondly, although 'Paean to Place' is autobiographical, its narrative impulse is interrupted by its fragmentary form and use of montage techniques to weld different images, materials, and perspectives together. Indeed, DuPlessis contends that its 'organizational strategy' is 'essentially nonnarrative, a discrete series, although it is generally chronological'.[66] Thirdly, the poem is divided into twelve uneven sections or groups of between two and seven stanzas, each of which functions as a verse paragraph. Within the groups, however, there is often significant use of enjambment, so that sentences flow across line endings and stanza breaks. Moreover, Niedecker deliberately suppresses punctuation marks throughout her poem, including full stops, so that the divisions between sections are signalled chiefly by gaps and the white space of the page. 'In every punctuation mark thoughtfully avoided,' notes Theodor Adorno, 'writing pays homage to the sound it suppresses'.[67] Niedecker's thoughtful avoidance of punctuation makes the gaps or silences in 'Paean to Place' resonant; and while the poem incorporates a series of internal edges or divides within itself, these are porous boundaries rather than hard borders.

'Paean to Place' begins with an epigraph, apparently of Niedecker's own invention but with an Old Testament cadence: 'And the place / was water'.[68] Place itself is granted elemental significance here through its equation with water, the element regarded by Presocratic philosophers as 'the primordial stuff of life' and 'the source of material change'.[69] From the outset, Niedecker conceives of place in terms of fluidity, process, and the dynamic character of matter, rather than as a fixed and demarcated site. Similarly, she describes the experience of being-in-place through aquatic metaphors: 'the rise and sink / of life' (264); 'O my floating life' (268). The opening lines of the poem immerse the reader in the wetland environment of Blackhawk Island through a cascade of proper nouns, alliteration, and clusters of stressed monosyllables:

Fish
    fowl
        flood
            Water lily mud
My life

in the leaves and on water (261)

This initial burst of concrete particulars serves both as an elliptical description of Niedecker's natal water-land and as a verbal-visual illustration of the downwards movement, from surface to depth, that recurs over the course of the poem. For instance, the speaker recalls her father's knowledge of the natural ecosystem in which he lived and worked: 'He knew duckweed // fall-migrates / toward Mud Lake bottom' (263). Subsequently, she remarks that all living things 'move towards / the light', but immediately qualifies this generalisation: 'except those / that freely work down / to ocean's black depths' (267). Given Niedecker's longstanding interest in the unconscious, the drift (and direction) of this metaphor is fairly clear; though it can also be read, as DuPlessis argues, as part of a pervasive anti-transcendent materialism whereby 'immersion or saturation' is the proper condition of existence.[70] It is also worth noting that Niedecker's recasting and elaboration of the phrase 'My life by water' as 'My life // in the leaves and on water' implies an intrinsic duality (emphasised by the way the phrase straddles the stanza break), for her speaker's life is stretched between terrestrial and aquatic worlds, leaves and water.

Having established this complex relationship between self and place, the poem segues to a compressed origin myth, and then opens out into a composite portrait of familial and marital relationships:

My mother and I
            born
in swale and swamp and sworn
to water

My father
thru marsh fog
    sculled down
        from high ground (261)

A psychodrama of belonging is enacted in these lines, where mother and daughter are figured as literal 'natives' – born in a swamp and sworn to water – whereas the father is presented as an outsider or interloper who makes his way 'down' to Blackhawk Island from elsewhere, and specifically from 'high ground'.[71] Moreover, whilst he settles and comes to be closely identified with swamp, lake, and river through his work as a fisherman and masculine provider – 'He kept us afloat' (262) – the father's belonging there is described in terms of suffering and endurance: he 'bore the weight of water' (261). Indeed, the father's social ambitions for his daughter associate education with displacement, for he hopes that, unlike him, she 'might go high / on land / to learn' (261). At least initially, then, the poem's speaker associates her mother with water and native belonging and her father with land and the threat of displacement. However, as the poem unfolds, Niedecker complicates and undercuts this simple binary schema, chiefly by tracing her mother's progressive alienation from her husband, daughter, and her home place.

It is her deafness, and her knowledge of her husband's infidelity, which cause the speaker's mother to turn inwards, becoming estranged from her family and from the place-world of Blackhawk Island itself. An account of this process forms the elegiac core of 'Paean to Place'. Strikingly, it is in terms of her insensibility to the distinctive soundscape of Blackhawk Island, and her corresponding detachment from its non-human habitats, that the speaker mourns her mother's condition:

> I mourn her not hearing canvasbacks
> their blast-off rise
>   from the water
>   Not hearing sora
> rails's sweet
>
> spoon-tapped waterglass—
> descending scale—
>   tear-drop-tittle (263)

Birdsong – in this case, the 'spoon-tapped waterglass' call of the reclusive sora rail – is a crucial component of the 'acoustic signature' that is distinctive of Niedecker's Blackhawk Island.[72] Subsequently, her speaker vividly recalls 'Pewee glissando / sublime / slime- / song' (265), and the aural effects of her poem often seek to recreate the distinctive soundscape of the non-human environment in human language. As Anne Waldman remarks, Niedecker's poetry 'listen[s] acutely to the particulars of her natural world (e.g. birdsong)' and, in so doing, encourages readers to pay close attention to the sonic qualities of place.[73] Niedecker's eyesight was poor throughout most of her life, and she told Zukofsky that she knew birds primarily 'by their sound'.[74] Moreover, her attitude towards the non-human world was at once reverential and determinedly realist: 'For me, when it comes to birds, animals and plants, I'd like the facts because the facts are wonderful in themselves'.[75] For the speaker of 'Paean to Place', the songs of the sora rail and the wood pewee are not only facts that she seeks to record, through sibilance, assonance, and onomatopoeia, as exactly as possible. They are also intrinsic features of the sensory experience of being-in-place, so that her mother's deafness is conceived as a condition of placelessness in which the world has shrunk to the dimensions of the human body. Yet, as the speaker's mother is progressively estranged from the place of her birth by disability and bitterness, her father is depicted as a figure who has become 'Anchored here' over time. This anchorage is not entirely happy, for the speaker observes sympathetically that 'He netted / loneliness' (264) along with carp.

At the centre of 'Paean to Place' is a series of fragmentary self-portraits in which Niedecker's speaker stresses her close affinities both with the natural world and with the paraphernalia of reading and writing. In the first of three central sections, she writes: 'I grew in green / slide and slant / of shore and shade' (264). What is interesting about these lines is not just the parallel they create between human and natural processes of growth, but also the emphasis they place on movements ('slide and slant') at the water's edge. This association between physical or psychological growth and riparian boundaries is further compounded in the following elliptical lines: 'Grew riding the river / Books / at home-pier' (265). Books and boats are intimately connected here, so that reading and riding the river are simultaneous experiences, equally formative of the speaker's youthful sense of being-in-place. Moreover, Niedecker depicts 'home' itself as a 'pier', a structure built out from land over water, facilitating movements between the two domains.

The next section of the poem continues this focus upon the riverbank as a place associated with literary creativity by depicting the poet-speaker as a wading bird:

> I was the solitary plover
> a pencil
>   for a wing-bone
> From the secret notes
> I must tilt
>
> upon the pressure
> execute and adjust (265)

Where she had previously recalled the songs of the sora rail and the wood peewee, in these lines Niedecker's speaker figuratively crosses the species barrier in an act of remembering that enables a zoomorphic transformation. As Peters observes, throughout much of her life Niedecker 'identified intimately with birds', and many friends described her as bird-like: diminutive, fine-boned, unobtrusive, but possessed of a distinctive song. Niedecker herself occasionally encouraged such comparisons, describing herself to Edward Dahlberg as 'just a sandpiper in a marshy region'.[76] It is very likely that the 'solitary plover' Niedecker has in mind in these lines is a killdeer, an early spring migrant to the Midwest that usually lives near water – mudflats, marshes, riverbanks – and which Niedecker observed nesting on the shore at Blackhawk Island.[77] However, at the same moment that she identifies *with* the bird, Niedecker's speaker also self-consciously identifies *as* a poet. The 'secret notes' are at once the eponymous song of the killdeer itself and the beginnings of a poem, just as the bird's wing-bone is also a pencil with which the poet will 'tilt' her words' flight across the page. The bird's tilting, uncertain flight also serves as a metaphor for Niedecker's career as a poet, describing her own adjustments to 'pressures' that are by turns personal, poetic, and political.

In the later sections of 'Paean to Place', the river becomes a particularly powerful symbolic presence, initially through memories of spring floods, where the boundaries between interior and exterior are disturbingly breached: 'Water endows us / with buckled floors' (268). However, as in Niedecker's other flood poems, the flood event itself is experienced ambivalently as both violently destructive and a source of regenerative energies. While she mourns her parents' absence, Niedecker's speaker, facing the flood alone, turns to the natural world for signs of new life: 'Expect the long-stemmed blue / speedwell to renew / itself' (268). This tentative anticipation of renewal, as well as the sense of imaginative communion with her dead forebears, is extended into the final section of the poem, where the river becomes a metaphor for the form of the poem itself, with its intermingling streams of memory and consciousness:

On this stream
my moonnight memory
    washed of hardships
        maneuvers barges
thru the mouth

of the river (269)

In these lines, Niedecker figuratively immerses her speaker's consciousness in the wetland environment she inhabits, so that the processes of perception and recollection are entangled with the things remembered and perceived. The mouth of the river is conflated with the mouth of the poet, for it is on the 'stream' of language that the speaker's 'moonnight memory' manoeuvres thoughts, images, and fragmentary recollections into a fluent whole. However, Niedecker's punning coinage 'moonnight memory' implies that acts of remembering are simultaneously illuminating (moonlight) and obscure (midnight). This reflexive, self-referential aspect of the poem is melded with an apparently realistic depiction of people fishing by the moonlit river, in which stars and planets are reflected:

>   In Fishes
> red Mars
>
> rising
> rides the sloughs and sluices
>   of my mind
>   with the persons
> on the edge (269)

The astrological significance of Mars rising in the constellation Pisces is probably less important in these lines than the correspondence they suggest between astronomical and earthly 'fishes' in the same river. This river is at once literal and figurative: it is the Rock River 'on the edge' of which Niedecker and her family lived for generations, and it is also the 'mind' of the speaker, whose thought-stream is characterised by 'sloughs and sluices'. In American English, 'slough' (pronounced 'sloo' or 'slew') refers to a side channel or backwater, and a 'sluice' is a drain or small stream that carries off surplus water; so Niedecker depicts the mind's activity in terms of the irregular currents, flows, and overflows of a river. The speaker's sometimes painful acts of remembering have left her 'washed of hardships' and, crucially, reaffirmed her identification with those others who, like her, survive 'on the edge'.

North Central

If 'Paean to Place' is Niedecker's most extensive and accomplished poetic meditation on her native place, Blackhawk Island, then two other long poems of the late 1960s – 'Lake Superior' and 'Wintergreen Ridge' – significantly expand the scope of her attention, both geographically and historically. For a variety of reasons, including gender stereotyping and metropolitan preconceptions, Niedecker's work has often been regarded as characteristically modest in scope and scale – dealing chiefly with domestic subjects and the natural world – and profoundly rooted in its immediate, marginal locality. For instance, one of her earliest champions, the poet and publisher Jonathan Williams, describes her as 'the most absolute poetess since Emily Dickinson' and continues: 'She shuns the public world, lives, reads, and writes, very quietly, near the town of Fort Atkinson, Wisconsin'.[78] As Gilbert Sorrentino observes, such characterisations of Niedecker as a 'bumpkin-savant', however well-meant, risk sentimentalising and over-simplifying her achievements.[79] They also overlook an important parallel development in her poetics during the last five years of her life, whereby an expanded conception of place coincides with her experiments in longer forms. In 'Lake Superior' and 'Wintergreen Ridge', Niedecker moves decisively beyond the bounds of her home place to explore the meanings of place in contexts that are at once regional, geological, and transnational. Here, her concern is with what she variously calls 'the North', 'Northland' (249), or 'North Central': by which she means the whole region bordering Lake Superior and Lake Michigan, and straddling the US-Canadian border.[80] Both poems seek not only to record this region's human history, including interactions between European explorers or settlers and indigenous peoples, but also to situate human actions and endeavours in the much longer perspectives of geological time. In their different ways, 'Lake Superior' and 'Wintergreen Ridge' are manifestations of what Jonathan Skinner calls Niedecker's 'poetics of flow', in which a Lucretian preoccupation with the mutability of all things demonstrates the interdependence of the organic and the inorganic, human and natural history.[81]

On 26 July 1966, as the US war in Vietnam intensified, Niedecker and her husband Al Millen set off by car for a week's vacation in the Great Lakes region. From their home in Blackhawk Island, Wisconsin they travelled north along the shores of Lake Michigan to Sault Saint Marie. There, they crossed the border into Canada and followed the north shore of Lake Superior, passing through Heron Bay, Nipigon, and Port Arthur, then crossed the border again at Pigeon River. Before heading home through Minnesota, they made a visit to Lake Itasca, believed to be the source of the Mississippi River, and to Al's childhood home at Swan River. Niedecker planned for this trip thoroughly and meticulously. She read books on the history and geography of the region, the memoirs of French and British explorers, and made extensive notes on geology, a subject that fascinated her.[82] Indeed, geology provided her with a new vocabulary for describing her poetics of condensation and the slow process of composition itself. Writing to Corman following her circle tour of Lake Superior, she explained: 'I need time, like an eon of limestone or gneiss, time like I used to have, with no *thought* of publishing'.[83] During the vacation, she kept a journal and, on her return, composed a prose travel narrative, 'Lake Superior Country'. She made lists of evocative place-names – Michilimackinac, Scalp Lake, Laughing Fish, the River of the Dead – pasted images in a scrapbook, and ordered geological maps from the US government office in Washington D.C.[84] All of this research and writing was directed towards a single purpose: the composition of a long poem, 'Lake Superior', which Niedecker described as her '*magma* opus' – pun intended.[85] Originally entitled 'Circle Tour', the poem was first published as 'TRAVELERS / Lake Superior Region' in a 1967 issue of *Arts in Society*, then revised as 'Lake Superior' for publication in her 1968 collection, *North Central*. In its final version, the poem occupies five pages, 101 lines, and comprises just 395 words; whereas the prose notes that informed its composition run to some 260 typed, single-spaced pages.[86] This is a good illustration of Niedecker's mature creative practice, which often begins with extensive, wide-ranging research followed by a secondary process of strenuous compression and elision to fashion her diverse factual materials into poetry.

By comparison with other late modernist texts – Zukofsky's *"A"*, for instance, or even Williams's *Paterson* – 'Lake Superior' is not a long poem; nor does it neatly fit the definition of the modernist long poem proposed by Margaret Dickie: 'Long in the time of composition, in the initial intention, and in the final form, the Modernist poem is concerned first and last with its own length'.[87] However, for a poet who was primarily known and valued for her haiku-like miniatures, it marks a significant formal development in her oeuvre; the first of six longer serial poems or sequences that Niedecker began to write in her mid-sixties.[88] Considered together, these long poems – 'Lake Superior', 'Wintergreen Ridge', 'Paean to Place', 'Thomas Jefferson', 'His Carpets Flowered', and 'Darwin' – are instances of what Edward Said calls 'late style': they introduce 'a new idiom' into Niedecker's work, one marked less by 'harmony and resolution' than by 'intransigence, difficulty, and unresolved contradiction'.[89] These longer poems can be divided roughly into two groups: 'Lake Superior', 'Wintergreen Ridge', and 'Paean to Place' are each extended responses to particular places or regions; while 'Thomas Jefferson', 'His Carpets Flowered', and 'Darwin' are all semi-biographical meditations on the lives and works of men Niedecker admired.

There is evidence in her correspondence from the 1960s that Niedecker was beginning to chafe against the limitations of the shorter forms that she had mastered, but also reluctant to forsake them altogether. To Corman she confides: 'I've been going through a bad time – in one moment (winter) I'd have thrown over all my [. . .] years of clean-cut, concise short poem manner for "something else" (still don't know what to call it)'.[90] And to her editor, Morgan Gibson, she writes: 'Oh the terrors of the long poem (altho [sic] I maintain a long poem is made up of short ones).'[91] This last, parenthetical remark that a long poem is made up of short poems encapsulates the solution that Niedecker hit upon. As Joseph Conte observes, the thirteen sections from which 'Lake Superior' is composed are both 'discontinuous' – resisting arrangement as parts of a sequential narrative – and inter-related, for they each 'participate in the ongoing process of the whole'.[92] This is why 'Lake Superior' is best described as a 'serial' poem rather than a 'sequence' or simply a long poem. The poem is at once fragmentary and expansive, a collage of field notes, historical vignettes, and quotations that nonetheless cohere around a set of recurrent ideas or themes and a consistent – though varied – geography.

The poem begins with a pair of rather abstract statements that give succinct expression to Niedecker's mature materialism, contending that 'rocks' are fundamental to the very possibility of life on earth:

> In every part of every living thing
> is stuff that once was rock
>
> In blood the minerals
> of the rock (232)

The geological tenor of Niedecker's imagination is immediately apparent in these lines, but her interest in 'rocks' is part of a much broader inquiry into the 'stuff' of life, the material substance of 'living things'. 'Lake Superior' recognises the 'creative' potential of non-living matter, 'because it is non-living matter that produced living matter in the first place'.[93] Moreover, Niedecker understands that geology is fundamentally a science of change and metamorphosis. In her prose journal, 'Lake Superior Country', she remarks: 'A rock is made of minerals constantly on the move and changing from heat, cold and pressure'.[94] The poem develops this idea by noting that minerals are constantly on the move within human (and animal) bodies through the circulation of our 'iron-ore-red' blood and also on the waters of Lake Superior, where freighters made of iron are observed transporting loads of iron ore to smelting plants in the East:

> Iron the common element of earth
> in rocks and freighters
>
> Sault Sainte Marie—big boats
> coal-black and iron-ore-red
> topped with what white castlework

> The waters working together
>   internationally
> Gulls playing both sides (232)

Iron is 'the common element of earth', the primary substance from which our planet is made; and, in her journal, Niedecker notes that 'three-fourths of the iron ore in the US is found in the Lake Superior region', much of it passing through the port city of Sault Sainte Marie following extraction.[95] In the condensed image networks of these lines, then, iron is the common denominator linking organic and inorganic beings, natural elements and the products of human labour. In this way, 'Lake Superior' is informed by precisely the kind of ecological ethics that Jane Bennett describes, where the aim is 'to cultivate the ability to discern nonhuman vitality, to become perceptually open to it'.[96] Niedecker's poem makes its readers newly aware of the extent to which they are implicated in a world of vibrant matter, sharing their substance with rocks and minerals, plants and animals, and always on the way to becoming something else.

Sault Sainte Marie is located on the St Marys River, which flows from Lake Superior into Lake Huron and marks the political border between the US and Canada. Indeed, there are two cities called Sault Sainte Marie, one on the Michigan shore and another on the Ontario bank of the river. Taken together, these twin cities and their hinterlands comprise what Casey calls a 'borderland', a place that combines 'an exactly determined existing border' with 'the informality and imprecision of a natural boundary'.[97] Characteristically, Niedecker's poem emphasises fluid movements between and across – 'The waters working together / internationally / Gulls playing both sides' – rather than static divisions and demarcations, depicting water as an element that connects or brings together rather than separates. In 'Lake Superior', movements and metamorphoses are fundamental conditions of life and of the material world itself, as is manifest in the behaviour of rocks, boats, and gulls, as well as latter-day *voyageurs*. Nonetheless, Niedecker's distinctive mode of ecological materialism does not lead her to posit placelessness – the absence of attachments to specific places – as a basic existential condition. Rather, her poem conceives of place as, in Doreen Massey's words, 'a constellation of processes rather than a thing' – as open and unfinished rather than fixed or strictly demarcated.[98] Hence, the organising metaphor of the journey that recurs throughout the poem, whether it be colonial voyages of exploration and plunder, the motoring vacation that stimulated the poem itself, or the much slower and more protracted journeys of mineral elements through aeons of geological time.

Several of these journeys come together in a later section of 'Lake Superior', where Niedecker describes the 1832 voyage of the geographer and ethnologist Henry Rowe Schoolcraft in search of the source of the Mississippi. Tellingly, the poem chooses not to linger on Schoolcraft's achievements, directing the reader's attention instead to the effects of time that are visible in the landscape through which he and his Ojibwe attendants travelled by canoe:

> Passed peaks of volcanic thrust
> Hornblende in massed granite
> Wave-cut Cambrian rock
> painted by soluble mineral oxides
> wave-washed and the rains
> did their work and a green
> running as from copper (235)

In these lines, the physical landscape of Lake Superior's southern shore is shown to be subject to the ongoing processes of erosion by wind, waves, and weather. The rocks themselves have been created by vast geological upheavals ('volcanic thrust') and their beautiful colours are a consequence of chemical reactions between their minerals and oxygen in the air. 'Beauty: impurities in the rock' (233), writes Niedecker in an earlier section; and in her journal, she elaborates:

> The North is one vast, massive, glorious corruption of rock and language – granite is underlaid with limestone or sandstone, gneiss is made-over granite, shale, or sandstone and so forth and so on [. . .]. And look what's been done to language! – People of all nationalities and color have changed the language like weather and pressure have changed the rocks.[99]

Rocks and language, earth processes and human interactions have combined to make the Lake Superior region what it is today and will continue to refashion and 'corrupt' it further in years to come. Niedecker is implicitly critical of some of the human processes of change that her poem describes, such as the role of missionaries in the colonial history of North America: 'Through all this granite land / the sign of the cross' (233). On the whole, though, both 'impurity' and 'corruption' are regarded positively in 'Lake Superior' as conditions of encounter, intermixture, and change. Throughout, Niedecker's geological imagination leads her to express a materialist conception of being-in-place in which all that is solid melts and is re-formed, becoming something else in the long perspectives of geological time.

One way of reading 'Lake Superior' is as a particularly intricate and oblique example of what Robert Tally calls 'literary cartography'. Tally explains that:

> The act of writing might be considered a form of mapping or cartographic activity. Like the mapmaker, the writer must survey territory, determining which features of a given landscape to include, to emphasize, or to diminish [. . .]. The writer must establish the scale and the shape, no less of the narrative than of the places within it.[100]

Simile and metaphor predominate in Tally's account of 'literary cartography'; but we know that Niedecker made use of actual maps of the Lake Superior region while she was working on her poem, and she researched its geography, geology, and toponymy in detail. Her title establishes the scale of her poem's attention from the outset, and its geographical focus also conditions its engagement with historical and scientific sources. Several of the French and American explorers to whom the poem refers – Jacques Marquette, Louis Joliet, and Schoolcraft – made maps of Lake Superior, as well as journeys that prefigured Niedecker's own circle tour in 1966.[101] However, if 'Lake Superior' can be read as a kind of poetic 'map', it is one that consciously evades the tendency of cartographic images to freeze time and empty places of their histories. As Massey observes, maps can be a valuable stimulus for the geographical imagination; but they also need to be understood as a 'technology of power' that is not ideologically neutral, and which tends to resolve the complex openness of space as 'a flat surface' and 'a coherent closed system'.[102] Such resolution and fixity is clearly at odds with Niedecker's affirmation in 'Lake Superior' of movements and metamorphoses as the truth of being-in-place. Moreover, because 'Lake Superior' is, at least in part, an elliptical account of a circular journey that crosses a series of state and national borders, the poem tends to emphasise movements in, through, and across places rather than any static mode of apprehending or inhabiting space.

Donald Davie has remarked that, for all her evident research into the history of the Lake Superior region, Niedecker 'shows no interest in heroic exploits' and tends to give precedence to geological time-scales rather than those of human history. Ultimately, argues Davie, it is rocks and minerals that are 'the only true "heroes" of the poem first and last'.[103] The risk that 'Lake Superior' consequently runs is not just that of modernist impersonality, but of failing to give due weight to the human experiences of colonisation and expropriation upon which Niedecker touches only in passing. Certainly, it is true that many of the details of Niedecker's own journey are elided from the poem itself – though most can be reconstructed by cross-referencing with her prose journal – and the first-person pronoun is absent until its penultimate section. In this regard, 'Lake Superior' stubbornly displaces the anthropocentric perspective that Davie expects and regards as necessary. Consequently,

Niedecker's poem is best understood not as a failed historical poem but rather as what Lawrence Buell calls 'an environmentally oriented work' in that it treats the non-human environment as a significant, active presence and shows 'that human history is implicated in natural history'.[104] This implication of human and natural histories is fundamental to the poem's conception of life as a material continuum or cycle of organic and inorganic forms. Consider, for instance, the speaker's wry account of her visit to Lake Itasca, the 'true source' of the Mississippi River:

> The smooth black stone
> I picked up in true source park
>   the leaf beside it
> once was stone (236)

Because of its emphasis on movements and metamorphoses, Niedecker's poem is sceptical about the possibility of any return to origins. Yet, on the other hand, these lines counsel readers to slow down and look more carefully, so that the temporality of human existence can be grasped in terms of fundamental geological processes. It is only when we think with geology, Niedecker implies, that the common substance of stone and leaf, inorganic matter and living plant becomes available to perception, and we begin to understand our deeper implication in the non-human world of vibrant matter that is our own 'true source' and ultimate destination.

Personal experience and references to contemporary historical events are a more prominent feature of Niedecker's next major poem, 'Wintergreen Ridge', although here again the longer perspectives of geological and evolutionary time play an important, defamiliarising role. As Penberthy observes, 'Wintergreen Ridge' can be read as 'a companion poem' to 'Lake Superior': both are Great Lakes poems in which the scope of Niedecker's geographical imagination expands along with the texts' formal parameters.[105] As with 'Lake Superior', 'Wintergreen Ridge' has its origins in a vacation trip by car, this time to the Ridges Sanctuary in Door County, a peninsula on the north-western shore of Lake Michigan, in September 1967.[106] The Ridges is a wetland ecosystem, a series of curved ridges and hollows formed over millennia by fluctuations in the lake's shore, and is home to unique collection of boreal plants, including thirty varieties of orchid. In her book, *Journeys in Green Places* (1963) – which Niedecker read – Virginia Eifert describes the Ridges Sanctuary as 'a living museum of plant life' that preserves in one place an unparalleled record of the 'plant changes and successions from the Ice Age to the present'.[107] On the one hand, it is a place in which time seems to have stood still; on the other, it provides a window onto the vast material processes of change that have produced the conditions of life in the present. Clearly, this is one of the chief attractions of the Ridges Sanctuary for Niedecker: 'Wintergreen Ridge' is centrally concerned with documenting 'the evolution / of matter' (247). However, Niedecker never loses sight of the human histories of struggle and endurance that are bound up with this grander narrative. For example, her poem pays homage to the actions of local people in resisting commercial development in the area and ultimately having it declared a nature preserve in 1937:

> Who saved it?—
>   Women
>   of good wild stock
> stood stolid
>   before machines
>   They stopped bulldozers
> cold
>   We want it for all time
>   they said (249–50)

By describing the women of Bailey's Harbor as 'of good wild stock', Niedecker deftly creates an identification between them and the ecosystem they are seeking to protect. Their victory over the bulldozers is not only an act of local resistance to capitalism's destruction of the natural environment but is also framed as an (ultimately futile) attempt to arrest the effects of time itself: 'We want it for all time'. Throughout 'Wintergreen Ridge', Niedecker balances this ecological ethics of preservation against an awareness that change is nonetheless a fundamental condition of all life: 'continuous life // through change / from Time Began' (249).

At 282 lines, 'Wintergreen Ridge' is Niedecker's longest poem, and she told Corman it was 'the best thing I've ever done'.[108] Formally, it is also distinctive: where 'Lake Superior' and 'Paean to Place' are both composed of a number of shorter sections, 'Wintergreen Ridge' is written as an uninterrupted sequence of stepped tercets in which enjambment and lineation create a sense of onward momentum while also placing particular emphasis upon individual words or sounds. As Michael Heller notes, the 'ground bass of the poem is the sentence with the tercet acting as counterpoint'.[109] 'Wintergreen Ridge' is also tonally diverse, combining chatty familiarity – 'We are gawks / lusting // after wild orchids' (248–9) – with a more meditative, philosophical voice: 'Man / lives hard / on this stone perch' (247). Niedecker draws upon the work of naturalists such as Eifert, Linnaeus, and Darwin; and her own personal impressions of the Ridges Sanctuary are interwoven with allusions to, or quotations from the work of other writers, including Basil Bunting, T. S. Eliot, Henry

James, D. H. Lawrence, and Henry David Thoreau. At times, the poem resembles a set of botanical field notes, lists of flowers spotted and observations on their habitat or modes of life, especially those of the insectivorous drosera with which Darwin was fascinated in later life. At others, particularly towards the end of the poem, Niedecker's speaker responds to local news stories – 'human parts found / wrapped in newspaper' (256), the suicide of a 'second shift steamfitter' (257) in Milwaukee – and reflects on contemporary historical events: the Cold War space race, protestors pelting police with flowers, the war in Vietnam 'which "cannot be stopped"' (256). Consequently, the reader of 'Wintergreen Ridge' must negotiate a series of rapid shifts in scale and perspective, from botanical explorations in the Ridges Sanctuary to the ramifications of international wars and the evolution of matter from time's beginning.

Like 'Lake Superior', but more explicitly, 'Wintergreen Ridge' describes a circular journey. It begins with an act of orientation and arrival – 'Where the arrows / of the road signs / lead us' (247) – and ends with a return home to Blackhawk Island, where a storm has just passed and the poet-speaker apostrophises an unbowed 'Old sunflower' (257). The resilience of plants, their capacity to survive in even the most hostile or unforgiving of conditions, is a recurrent preoccupation of the poem and a source of inspiration for the speaker. She marvels at horsetails and club mosses that have 'stayed alive / after dinosaurs / died' (250) and describes 'thin to nothing lichens' that grind 'granite to sand': 'These may survive / the grand blow-up // the bomb' (253–4), she thinks. Davidson remarks that 'Wintergreen Ridge' celebrates the North Central region by 'linking two forms of resilience, social and natural'; but Niedecker also implies that the natural world will survive humankind's self-destruction.[110] The poet-speaker's attitude occasionally verges on the misanthropic despair of Henry James Sr, who 'long ago / pronounced human affairs // gone to hell' (256). However, she also eschews sentimental idealisations of nature for a materialist world-view in which change is the only constant, and where there is no absolute distinction between organic life and inorganic things:

> Life is natural
>   in the evolution
>   of matter
> Nothing supra-rock
>   about it
>   simply
> butterflies
>   are quicker
>   than rock (247)

These lines adapt and compress an idea that Niedecker must have encountered while reading Eifert's book on Door Peninsula: 'The stone is really no more permanent than the spring flower or the butterfly; yet the latter are geared to coming and going quickly, while the former knows the long, slow change which in the world of nature knows no hurry'.[111] This interlacing of different temporalities – different rates of change – is a key feature of 'Wintergreen Ridge', but Niedecker goes further than Eifert by insisting that both 'rock' and 'butterfly' share the same essential substance. Life itself is no more or less than the evolution of matter, the circulation of minerals in blood or leaf-plasma and their eventual return to the soil from which new rocks will be formed. In this respect, the writer's impulse to create 'durable works' might seem futile; but the work of artistic creation is itself also a manifestation of the evolution of matter and a way of surviving 'on this stone perch'.

'Wintergreen Ridge' and 'Lake Superior' mark a new departure in Niedecker's poetics of place, expanding the scope of her geographical imagination from her home place of Blackhawk Island to the wider bioregion of North Central, which spans the US/Canada border. Deriving from experiences of travel, they each give expression to new interests in geology, botany, and evolutionary biology, drawing upon extensive and enthusiastic research. With 'Paean to Place', these three poems also mark a decisive shift towards longer, more complex serial forms. Nonetheless, as poems of wetlands ecosystems, lakeshores, and riverbanks, they each amplify the fundamental condition for all Niedecker's writing: her sensuous implacement at the edges where land and water meet. Whether responding to seasonal floods, listening to birdsong in the swamps behind her cabin, or recalling her amphibious childhood, the edges of riparian landscapes are Niedecker's most characteristic places. Her poems reveal such edges to be porous, shifting boundaries rather than hard borders, liable to inundation or displacement over time. Moreover, the edges of lakes, rivers, and peninsula are places where humans and non-humans, nature and culture, organic and inorganic beings interact as part of the larger, and ongoing metamorphosis of all material things.

Chapter 5

Charles Olson's Mappemunde

If the poetic method of Charles Olson's sprawling late modernist epic, *The Maximus Poems*, is fundamentally historical in character, then it is also informed by a profound, but less-remarked preoccupation with geography. Famously, Olson derives his conception of history from Herodotus, translating *'istorin* as a verb rather than a noun; history means '"finding out for oneself," instead of depending on hearsay'.[1] It is significant, however, that much of what Olson seeks to find out for himself in the more than 600 pages of *The Maximus Poems* concerns a particular place – the port city of Gloucester, Massachusetts, and the neighbouring peninsula of Cape Ann. Of course, the scope of Olson's omnivorous imagination is such that his text is about many other things besides – from pre-Homeric cultures and Jungian psychology to theories of continental drift. Nonetheless, most of these interests are loosely connected to the poem's core geographical themes of westward voyages and migrations, which tend to converge on the North Atlantic coast of New England. The deep history of place that Olson undertakes in the first volume of *The Maximus Poems* (1960), focusing upon the origins of Gloucester as a colonial settlement in the early seventeenth century, is a necessary prelude to the much more expansive and fragmentary mytho-historical parallels that he draws between places in the Eastern Mediterranean and the North Atlantic in *Maximus IV, V, VI* (1968), and *The Maximus Poems: Volume Three* (1975). Moreover, among the multifarious documents and sources that Olson's epic plunders for material or inspiration, the maps drawn by sixteenth- and seventeenth-century navigators have an important, even central place. In this chapter, I argue that Olson's recurrent fascination with these (and other) maps of Gloucester, New England, and the wider Atlantic world has far-reaching effects not only on the content of *The Maximus Poems* but also on its form. For, one of the ways in which the poet encourages us to read his text is as a map of the world – a late modernist mappamundi – that has been made and remade by the 'restless' wanderings of 'Western man'.[2]

Given the monumental scale and 'textual depth' of *The Maximus Poems*, which evolved over the course of twenty years and remained unfinished at the time of Olson's death in 1970, it is no surprise that the text's poetics of place is complex and at times deeply contradictory.[3] Part of that complexity arises from the biographical circumstances in which the poem was written. Born and raised in industrial Worcester, Olson spent his boyhood summers at Gloucester (beginning in 1915) and later pounded its streets during shifts as a temporary mail carrier.[4] From 1957 until his death in 1970, he rented an apartment at Fort Square, in the heart of the city's busy harbour, but much of *The Maximus Poems* (which was begun in 1950) was written elsewhere – in Washington D.C., and while Olson was teaching at Black Mountain College, North Carolina, Buffalo, New York, and the University of Connecticut.[5] Writing to Ezra Pound from Gloucester in 1946, during a brief stay with his mother, Olson affirmed 'This is home'; and in 1950, while in Washington D.C., he instructed the Gloucester poet, Vincent Ferrini, to: 'write to me, and tell me how / my streets / are, what / gulls are up your way'.[6] However, Olson's sense of belonging to Gloucester (and of Gloucester belonging to him) is willed rather than natal, and it coexists with a sense of distance and estrangement that is given voice early in *The Maximus Poems*: 'I was not born there, came, as so many of the people came, / from elsewhere'.[7] Crucially, as I argue below, this situation of identifying strongly with a particular place but of coming 'from elsewhere' aligns Olson's poetics of place with the experiences of immigrants – such as his Swedish father and his Irish grandfather – who seek to make a home for themselves in America.

Appropriately, *The Maximus Poems* is initially framed as a series of letters in which a poet-voyager, Maximus – modelled partly on the ancient Greek philosopher Maximus of Tyre and partly on Olson himself – addresses the people of his home city from afar.[8] In this way, the basic rhetorical form of the text mediates its central thematic concern with the dialectic of belonging and displacement. William Carlos Williams thought that Olson should have called the poem *Gloucester*, following the logic of his own *Paterson*, one of its most important poetic models.[9] However, where Williams's Mr Paterson is presented both as a citizen and as an embodiment of the city in human form ('one man – like a city'), Olson's Maximus is more ambiguously identified with Gloucester, hailing its citizens from across distances of space and time.[10] Indeed, the opening line of the poem places him not in the city's streets but 'Off-shore, by islands hidden in the blood' (5), addressing Gloucester's citizens from a mobile position somewhere out to sea. Olson's title accommodates such mobility and suggests a mode of attention that transcends any one place ('Maximus' means 'the greatest' in Latin). The question of Maximus's relationship to Gloucester also opens onto the ambivalent relationship between Gloucester and the American nation. On the one hand, Olson seems to present the city as a 'microcosm' for the United States, a founding site for the nation that epitomises both its enormous promise and its many failures.[11] On the other, his poem frequently depicts Gloucester as a place apart, an 'island' or 'rare place' (15) that has somehow retained its utopian potential despite the 'pejorocracy' (7, 77) – the rule of the worst – into which contemporary America has sunk. Hence Maximus's solemn prayer for Gloucester in 'Letter 3': 'o tansy city, root city / let them not make you / as the nation is' (15); and Olson's conceit of Gloucester 'sail[ing] away' from the North Atlantic continent in *Volume Three* (499).

A similarly radical ambiguity inhabits Olson's attitude towards the idea of the 'local' or 'localism'. For instance, Olson acknowledged parallel debts to Pound and Williams, his two most significant modernist precursors, as follows: 'if i think EP gave any of us the methodological clue: THE RAG-BAG; bill gave us the lead on the LOCAL'.[12] As Don Byrd explains, Olson learned from Williams's *Paterson* that 'the local is the place of immediacy' and therefore 'what must be engaged first, before the light from any more distant place appears'.[13] However, while Olson certainly finds the history and geography of Gloucester to be creatively enabling, he also sometimes bristles at the limitations of 'localism', associating it with the debased features of American consumer capitalism – 'the trick / of corporations, newspapers, slick magazines, movie houses' (14). In addition, he claimed that Williams restricted the scope of *Paterson* unduly by 'making his substance historical of one city'.[14] Consequently, if the kinetic motion of *The Maximus Poems* is initially centripetal, zeroing in ever more tightly upon the historical and material particulars of an intimately known place, it also becomes increasingly centrifugal as it goes on, radically expanding the focus of the poem's attention to take in all manner of speculative connections between the New World and the Old World, the North Atlantic and the Mediterranean, post-war America and the earliest phases of human civilisation. At its most ambitious, Olson's poem aspires to 'Take the earth in under a single review' (586) and therefore to practice a writing or description of the Earth that is one of the root meanings of 'geography'.

Geography Lessons

Olson's enthusiasm for geography spans the whole of his career as a poet and his interests are characteristically wide-ranging, if idiosyncratic. In 1955, when they were both at Black Mountain College, Olson counselled the younger poet Ed Dorn to study 'the geology & geography' of North America 'as a whole' and suggested that he get hold of a copy of A. K. Lobeck's physiographic map of the United States, in order 'to get that topographic sense in the mind as you have it in the feet'.[15] He also repeatedly recommended the work of the historical geographer, Carl O. Sauer, whom he had met in Berkeley in 1947 and with whom he kept up a fitful correspondence until 1960.[16] Olson called Sauer his 'great master in geography', regarding him as one of the 'new scientists of man' whose contributions to human knowledge far surpassed, in his view, those of the major modernist artists and writers ('Peek-gas-so, Prrrroost, JJJJoys').[17] There is a degree of posturing involved in this judgement, but Olson's respect for Sauer's formidable knowledge, and for the wider discipline of historical geography was sincere. One of the reasons that Olson felt drawn to Sauer's work was likely their shared fascination with origins and beginnings. Sauer's work on pre-Columbian and prehistoric cultures in North America gave shape and substance to Olson's more nebulous conviction that the post-war American writer needed 'to get back, in order to get on'.[18] Another was Sauer's emphasis on process and change, particularly through his geographical conception of 'culture' as 'the impress of the works of man on the area', whereby the 'natural landscape' is transformed over time into a 'cultural landscape'.[19] Olson likely had Sauer in mind when he remarked to Robin Blaser that 'Geography is landscape' – that is, geography traces the processes through which natural landscapes become cultural landscapes.[20] In any case, *The Maximus Poems* is chiefly concerned with documenting and exploring the 'cultural landscapes' of New England, with Gloucester as its principal focus.

It is remarkable how frequently Olson's poetry and prose adapts or appropriates terms from the conceptual vocabulary of geography: 'place', 'landscape', 'topography', 'local', and – most strikingly – 'space'. As Tom Clark observes, the key concepts of 'projective or OPEN verse' and 'COMPOSITION BY FIELD' that Olson introduces in his manifesto-essay, 'Projective Verse', derive from his eclectic reading in modern geometry and mathematics.[21] By comparison, Olson typically gives 'space' – which is 'a fundamental term in his prose' – a more explicitly geographical inflection.[22] For instance, near the beginning of his study of Herman Melville, *Call Me Ishmael* (1947), Olson declares:

'I take SPACE to be the central fact to man born in America, from Folsom cave to now. I spell it large because it comes large here. [. . .] It is geography at bottom, a hell of a wide land from the beginning.'[23] Here, 'SPACE' is spelled large to convey the vastness of North America's 'wide land', its daunting but also exhilarating geographical scale, as pictured on Lobeck's physiographic map. Crucially, the 'central fact' of space refers to the cultural landscapes of the continent as they have been shaped and re-shaped by 'man born in America', from its earliest human inhabitants – alluded to metonymically via the Folsom archaeological site – to the present.[24] In Olson's post-Einsteinian poetics, space is never divorced from time, and history is a necessary complement to geography. As Olson told Dorn, 'the locus is now both place & time (topology)'; while, in his lectures on *The Special View of History* (1970), he argues that: 'History is the practice of space in time'.[25] Olson is consistently engaged with 'the practice of space' in *The Maximus Poems*, particularly via his recurrent excavations of Gloucester's founding and development through time, the patterns of migration and settlement through which the city emerges and persists as a place. In this regard, however, the orientation of Olson's epic is towards the vast spaces of the North Atlantic and the New England coast rather than the 'wide land' of the continent's unfenced interior.

Geography, like history, is one of the enabling conditions of *The Maximus Poems*, a fundamental component of its poetic methodology (*'meta hodos*, the way after') that is occasionally thematised explicitly.[26] For instance, in *Volume Three* Olson offers his own working definition of 'geography' while alluding to several of the most influential ancient Greek geographers:

> Take the earth in under a single review
> as Eratosthenes as
> Ptolemy as had Ptolemy's Tyrian teacher who had the name <u>marine</u> in
> history
> as there was John Gallop   John Tilley   Osman Dutch   Ralph Green
>   Gloucester
> at various times with staging rights Fisherman's Field (586)

As is characteristic of the final volume of Olson's epic, these lines are profoundly paratactic, placing unlike things – classical geographers and the early settlers of Gloucester, the city's first encampment at Fisherman's Field and the earth perceived as a whole – in apposition and leaving the reader to puzzle out their possible connections. What links these topics in Olson's imagination is seafaring, navigation, and westward voyages, as his pointed allusion to 'Ptolemy's Tyrian teacher', Marinus of Tyre, 'who had the name <u>marine</u> in / history' suggests. Marinus's appellation also activates the recurrent parallel that Olson's text employs between Gloucester and Tyre, the ancient city of the seafaring Phoenicians. The connection between geography and sea voyages is further underlined subsequently, when Olson describes 'the lines Eratosthenes ran before Pytheas', which 'were as good as all the distances of the globe then turned out to / be' (586). Eratosthenes made the first attempt to scientifically calculate the circumference of the earth – 'all the distances of the globe' – and he was also 'the first Greek geographer to have delineated a system of lines of latitude and meridians of longitude' (which was later adapted and refined by Ptolemy).[27] Importantly, Eratosthenes based some of his calculations on the voyage narrative of the fourth-century BCE Greek explorer, Pytheas of Massalia, who sailed through the Strait of Gibraltar and circumnavigated the Atlantic coast of North-west Europe, perhaps travelling as far as Shetland, Norway, or Iceland – a frozen land he called Thule.[28]

Pytheas is a significant figure who recurs repeatedly across all three volumes of *The Maximus Poems*, taking on an emblematic role as one of the many avatars of Olson's hero-voyager Maximus. As Byrd observes, Pytheas's voyage exemplifies 'the migration of the center of culture away from the eastern Mediterranean, toward western Europe' and beyond in the direction of North America, a large-scale historical process that *The Maximus Poems* repeatedly seeks to describe and map.[29] Moreover, by dramatically extending the bounds of the Greek *oikoumene*, the inhabited or habitable world, Pytheas is an ancient precursor of those early modern navigators and explorers of the New World who, Peter Sloterdijk argues, radically revised the existing world picture. In the period following Columbus's first crossing of the Atlantic (1492) and Magellan's circumnavigation of the earth (1519–22), seafarers and geographers began to fashion a 'new image of the world' that replaced 'the notion of a largely terran earth' with that of 'the oceanic planet' and marked a decisive 'westward turn' in the direction of human history and the spatial imagination of the age.[30] Accordingly, Olson depicts Pytheas as a pioneer of the Atlantic world with which he is chiefly concerned:

>   the 1st to navigate
>   those waters
>   thus to define
>   the limits
>   of the land
> [. . .] there was Pytheas
> out into the Atlantic
>
>   far enough up into the North
>   for the Atlantic to be known (251)

Pytheas's key achievement, these lines suggest, was that he sailed out beyond the enclosed world of the Mediterranean and 'into the Atlantic'. In doing so, Olson notes that he was probably preceded by 'Phoenicians / Semite sailors' (251), who founded a settlement at 'Gades' (Cadiz) on the Atlantic coast of Iberia as early as the eighth century BCE.[31] However, it was the geographer-explorer Pytheas who, by writing a narrative of his voyages, first made it possible 'for the Atlantic to be known', thereby enabling further journeys westwards and northwards. Moreover, by defining 'the limits / of the land' he not only began the process of displacing the Mediterranean from the centre of the European world picture but also anticipated the modern conception of the earth as an oceanic planet.

Olson's allusions to Pytheas, Eratosthenes, Ptolemy, and Marinus of Tyre indicate the profundity of his interest in the origins and practice of geography as a science, but readers of his poem are likely to require the assistance of commentaries and glosses to grasp their full significance. A more directly personal, at times openly autobiographical reflection on the significance of geography occurs in 'Maximus to Gloucester, Letter 27 [withheld]', which begins with a memory of Olson's childhood summers at Stage Fort Park, Gloucester:

> I come back to the geography of it,
> the land falling off to the left
> where my father shot his scabby golf
> and the rest of us played baseball [. . .]
>
> To the left the land fell to the city,
> To the right, it fell to the sea (184)

In these opening lines, the recollection of past experience is figured in terms of a return to 'the geography of it', where 'it' appears to refer equally to the city of Gloucester and to the poet-speaker's life-course. Moreover, as Peter Middleton remarks, Olson is not simply describing the remembered landscapes of his boyhood but also affirming that 'geography is fundamental'.[32] Probing the relationship between self and place through anecdotes featuring his parents and playmates, the poem enacts a process of orientation, taking up a position near the shoreline between 'the city' and 'the sea'. By comparison, its middle sections are more abstract, drawing upon the process philosophy of A. N. Whitehead to reflect on the way in which personal experience is informed by manifold historical forces and circumstances – 'all those antecedent predecessions, the precessions // of me' (184) – that necessarily exceed the individual in the present moment.[33] Notably, Olson seeks to grasp this expansive historical 'inheritance' in terms of a voyage through time: 'the slow westward motion of // more than I am' (184). In this way, Olson's personal and family history is situated in the much wider context of the 'westward' migrations of European peoples to the Americas, which is a crucial geographical frame for making sense of *The Maximus Poems* in its fragmentary and sometimes wildly diffuse whole.

In the final section of the poem, Olson reflects on the role of the body in mediating our perceptions of and relations to the spaces we inhabit or move through. Importantly, he renders this rather abstract idea dramatic and particular by suggesting that his speaker (clearly a version of himself) has been shaped by the 'geography' of Gloucester, the places and landscapes of his childhood memories, but also seeks to shape it in his turn through writing and his titanic persona, Maximus:

> that forever the geography
> which leans in
> on me I compell
> backwards I compell Gloucester
> to yield, to
> change
>   Polis
> is this (185)

These lines not only attest to the continuing force of place, which 'forever' 'leans in' on the speaker, conditioning his very being, but also present the heroic struggle of the citizen-poet to 'change' and remake his home place, to compel it 'backwards', a direction that Olson associates with origins and creative power.[34] The poem's final, deictic 'this' is ambiguous, referring either to Gloucester or to the poem we read and the process of creative transformation that it depicts. 'Polis', as Michael Davidson observes, is 'Olson's word for community' conceived as a gathering of individuals rather than 'an idealized collectivity'.[35] Moreover, Gloucester's utopian role as 'polis' – a New World version of the autonomous Greek city-state – is oriented towards the past ('backwards') as well as the future. Earlier in the poem, Olson has Maximus 'hark back to an older polis' (24) by contrast with the debased contemporary city that is celebrated by his interlocutor, the poet Vincent Ferrini. At the same time, he declares that 'Polis' is 'a coherence not even yet new' (15). Olson's exhaustive, obsessive research into the history of Gloucester from the early seventeenth century to the present is in part driven by the utopian bent of his geographical imagination, which seeks to recover the city's lost possibilities as a means to renewal and change in a projected future that his poem will delineate.

Reading Maps

Like his literary hero, Melville, Olson 'read to write' and 'knew how to appropriate the work of others'.[36] However, among the hundreds of sources upon which he draws, Olson grants particular importance to maps, as is evident from the fact that he chose cartographic images for the covers of the first two volumes of *The Maximus Poems*. The first volume bears a detail from a U.S. Coast and Geodetic Survey of Gloucester, showing a close-up of the harbour and Fort Point; whereas *Maximus IV, V, VI* features a map of Pangaea, the super-continent hypothesised by Alfred Wegener, which 'started to come apart at the seams, some 125 million years ago' (168).[37] The posthumously-published third volume of Olson's text also bears a map image, this time showing an early seventeenth-century sketch of the Massachusetts coastline from 'Cape Ann to / Boston' (457) that Olson attributes to John Winthrop.[38] In this way, the three constituent volumes of *The Maximus Poems* foreground the symbolic significance of local, global, and regional maps, respectively, through their paratextual framing.[39] Biographers and scholars have noted Olson's fascination with maps and their ubiquity in the places where he chose to live and write. Clark records that the walls of his Fort Square apartment in Gloucester were covered with 'Charles's annotated maps' and his wife Betty's 'large "petroglyphic" canvases'; while Ralph Maud notes that for many years Olson displayed a physiographic map of the Atlantic sea-floor in his kitchen.[40] Late in life, he extolled the importance of maps to students at the University of Connecticut, telling them: 'we are all cartographic instances'.[41] Critics have had surprisingly little to say, however, about the ways in which Olson makes use of maps as part of his creative practice, often generating poems through attempts to read and re-read particular maps by sixteenth- and seventeenth-century navigators and explorers, particularly those by Juan de la Cosa, John Smith, and Samuel de Champlain. The distinctively modernist spatial self-consciousness of *The Maximus Poems* is manifest in multiple instances of what Jon Hegglund calls 'metatopographia', descriptions of representations of places, such as maps, landscape paintings, journals, or guidebooks. Such reflections, argues Hegglund, 'often draw attention to the constructed nature of space and place, thus denaturalizing a static, hierarchical geographical order'.[42] In Olson's case, his metatopographical engagements with maps and mapmakers in *The Maximus Poems* prompt readers to reflect on the complicity of early modern cartography with the nascent ideologies of European imperialism as well as its practical role in the discovery, settlement, and colonisation of North America.

Before turning to consider some examples of metatopographia in Olson's text, it is worth noting that as well as referring to actual maps and charts, he also repeatedly makes use of maps and mapmaking as metaphors for describing the epic poem that he is attempting to write. For instance, in one of the many metapoetic fragments that punctuate *Maximus IV, V, VI*, Olson records the following note to himself: 'you drew the space in / reticule / now spread the iron net, / Enyalion' (354). The mythic figure of Enyalion, loosely based on a Cretan war god, is another of the poem's versions of Maximus; but more important is the process of mapmaking that is described here – a 'reticule' or 'graticule' is a grid of fine lines used by cartographers – which implies that the representational space of the map is a figure for the space of the poem-in-progress. Olson revisits this metaphor later in the text via an aside to the reader, casting himself as a historian-cartographer: '17th Century within my eyes & on my skin as / in my mind [. . .] I / write and map for you each lot' (518). Absorbed in his research on early Gloucester, Olson's poet-speaker seeks to translate what is in his mind and on his skin into words on the pages we read. The implication here is that writing and mapping are closely related, interdependent practices bound together in the text of the poem.

This idea, that writing is a kind of mapping, receives its most resonant, memorable articulation when Olson tells the reader: 'I am making a mappemunde. It is to include my being' (257). A 'mappemunde' or mappamundi is a late medieval world map, informed more by religious or metaphysical principles than by modern concerns for geographical accuracy, and deliberately encyclopaedic in scope, composing an image of 'the entire history and philosophy of the human race organized within a geographical framework'.[43] *The Maximus Poems* resembles a mappamundi in terms of its sheer syncretic comprehensiveness, as a vast 'compendium of ideas' and information, but also in terms of its efforts to integrate space and time, geography and history, for mappaemundi often incorporated Biblical stories and scenes from secular historical events of various periods.[44] Moreover, during the 1960s Olson increasingly aligned his ambitions for the poem with the attempt to conceive of the Earth as 'a knowable, a seizable, a single, and *your* thing'.[45] This shift of focus from Gloucester to the Earth as a whole is signalled clearly near the beginning of *Volume Three*, where Olson writes: 'but the city / is only the beginning of the earth   the earth / is the world' (406–7). Indeed, by the end of *The Maximus Poems*, 'place' has become co-extensive with the planet itself: 'And the Place of it All? / Mother   Earth   Alone' (634). Based on this evidence, Olson's claim to be 'making a mappemunde' makes sense, but we should also note some important differences between his poem and the late medieval world maps he invokes. Until the fourteenth century, mappaemundi were oriented towards the East, the direction of sunrise and beginnings as well as the location of the Garden of Eden, whereas the orientation of Olson's epic poem is decisively towards the West and the New World of the Americas.[46] Furthermore, whereas most late medieval mappaemundi focus on the Mediterranean but are essentially 'terracentric', foregrounding land masses over the oceans, which are pushed to the periphery of their images, *The Maximus Poems* depicts the Earth as a post-Columbian 'waterworld', a terraqueous globe in which the North Atlantic and its seaboards are given prime importance.[47]

The many voyages of exploration and discovery undertaken by European navigators during the fifteenth and sixteenth centuries generated a huge amount of new geographical knowledge, which in turn drove the development of modern cartography and made possible new maps of the world.[48] As Sloterdijk observes, such cartographic representations also became essential to the emergence of a colonial world system, particularly in the Americas, for maps and globes 'were a manner of land register, documents of appropriative acts and archives of locating knowledge that accumulated over centuries, as well as route maps for seafaring'.[49] Olson reflects on this complicity between cartography, seafaring, and colonial expansion in 'On first Looking out through Juan de la Cosa's Eyes', which alludes to De la Cosa's 1500 mappamundi, the first world map to depict the Americas. For Olson, De la Cosa is a pioneer, and his map marks an important advance on other cartographical representations of the period, such as Martin Behaim's 1492 globe, which features 'nothing' where North America should be and only 'one floating island' in the Atlantic Ocean, the legendary isle of St Brendan:

> But before La Cosa, nobody
> could have
> a mappemunde (81)

De la Cosa's world map is a model for Olson's poetic 'mappemunde', chiefly because it brings together the Old World of Europe and the New World of the Americas in a single image for the first time. As James Smith notes, De la Cosa's map is a hybrid text, 'neither medieval nor early modern, but transitional', that combines elements of the 'world-map' and 'navigational sea-chart' genres.[50] Importantly, while Olson acknowledges De la Cosa's seminal achievement, he does not offer a detailed description of the map itself, directing the reader's attention instead to the practical geographical knowledge possessed by those fishermen who sailed out of 'St Malo', 'Biscay', or 'Bristol' (81) to the North

Atlantic fishing grounds known to Portuguese and Spanish sailors as 'Tierra, / de bacalaos' (83). Indeed, just prior to the lines praising De la Cosa's cartographical achievements, Olson's Maximus tells an anecdote about fishermen from his 'two towns' (Gloucester and Tyre), who:

talk, talked of Gades, talk
of Cash's

drew, on a table, in spelt,
with a finger, in beer, a
portulans' (81).

A 'portulans' or portolan chart is a topographic map of coastlines and shoals – such as Cashes Ledge, eighty miles east of Cape Ann – originally developed by early Greek sailors in the Mediterranean.[51] The effect of Maximus's anecdote is to subtly undermine the authority of such prestigious cartographical representations as De la Cosa's by setting it in apposition with other more demotic forms of mapmaking that are grounded in the practical knowledge of ordinary fishermen and sailors.

If De la Cosa's mappamundi is significant for Olson because it is the first representation of the North American continent on a world map, then the seventeenth-century explorer and cartographer John Smith is a crucial figure in the colonial history of New England with which *The Maximus Poems* is so frequently absorbed. Although he made no new discoveries himself, Smith was the first Englishman to survey the whole coast of the Gulf of Maine and to represent it in his highly influential 1616 map of New England, while also promoting the region's rich natural resources – fish, timber, furs – to audiences in England.[52] Indeed, J. B. Harley describes Smith's map as 'the founding document of European colonization' in the region, not least because of its bold substitution of English place names – it was the first map to use the name 'New England' – for the Indigenous toponyms that Smith collected but suppressed.[53] This process of re-naming had an important ideological function, for the English names on Smith's map 'made the unbelievable seem more familiar, the unknown more knowable, and the wilderness less wild'.[54] Olson is clearly aware of these circumstances, noting that Smith had a keen 'eye' 'for what New England offered' (54) while praising him as the man 'who sounded / her bays, ran her coast, and wrote down / Algonquin so scrupulously' (53). The poem is curiously silent, however, about Smith's erasure of New England's (or Norumbega's) Algonquin place names in favour of English alternatives, and this silence makes Olson's association of Smith with 'the truth of the place' (28) ring hollow. Jim Cocola argues that while *The Maximus Poems* 'appears to cut across the grain of Americanization in some ways, it reinforces the project of settler colonialism in other respects', and this is evident in Olson's relatively uncritical view of Smith's activities as 'heroic'.[55] 'Why I sing Smith is this,' writes Olson, 'that the *geographic*, the sudden *land* of the place, is in there' in his prose, and he goes on to praise Smith's map of New England for rendering that 'land' so 'known' that 'the states still stand their boundaries by it'.[56] This sense that Smith's writing and maps have had a lasting effect upon the ways in which New England is understood and experienced as a place also finds expression in the poem:

> Smith
> changed
> everything: he pointed
> out
> Cape Ann,
>
> named her
> so it's stuck (128)

What *The Maximus Poems* remains strangely blind to, however, despite its acknowledgement of the decimation of Algonquin tribes due to European diseases (53, 107), is the process of displacement and dispossession that such acts of 'discovery' and re-naming entail for the region's Indigenous peoples.[57]

The third cartographer-explorer with whom Olson engages creatively is the Frenchman Samuel de Champlain, whose 1606 map of what would become Gloucester harbour is a recurrent touchstone across all three volumes of *The Maximus Poems*. Douglas McManis notes that Champlain undertook three voyages along the New England seaboard between 1604 and 1607, keeping 'journals that may be considered the first comprehensive geography of the coast', and drawing upon the knowledge of native guides to create his detailed maps of the region.[58] In fact, as Harley remarks, one of the deep ironies of the exclusion of Indigenous peoples and place names from European maps of North America is that they often rely upon 'a hidden stratum of Indian geographical knowledge'.[59] Olson is fascinated by Champlain's map chiefly because it is a partial exception to this general pattern of cartographical exclusion, showing Algonquin villages on Cape Ann and around Gloucester harbour almost two decades before the first attempt by English fishermen to establish a settlement there. In 'proem', for instance, he writes:

> the Algonquins had cleared the land there, Champlain
> shows Stage Fort as containing five wigwams with
> crops, it was the first place the English as fishermen
> Westcountry men used to settle on [. . .] (306)

These lines offer a perfect example of metatopographia, a 'narrative instance of what is clearly marked as a *representation* of place – a description of a description'; in this case, a description of Champlain's map of Gloucester.[60] They also compose a layered figuration of Stage Fort Park, on the western shore of Gloucester harbour, as a 'first place', for it is simultaneously the site of an Algonquin village, the place where Dorset fishermen over-wintered in 1623, and the scene of Olson's most formative childhood experiences during summer holidays there with his parents. Champlain's map refers to Gloucester as 'le beau port', and Olson self-consciously borrows the epithet in a letter to Ferrini soon after moving back to the city in 1957: 'She is still a place to go fishing from. She is still le beauport. She is a form of mind'.[61] It is through reading maps such as Champlain's that Olson begins to perceive Gloucester as 'a form of mind' as well as a material place overlaid with the traces of multiple human histories. The city and its harbour constitute a first place not only for him personally, but for generations of European migrants and settlers before him, and first of all for the Indigenous inhabitants to whose presence Champlain's map insistently directs his attention.

Olson's creative and keenly self-conscious engagements with these and other maps in *The Maximus Poems* have an important bearing not only on the content of his text, but also upon its experiments with form. In his manifesto-essay, 'Projective Verse', he places particular emphasis upon the 'relations' and 'tensions' between the various textual, sonic, and semantic 'elements' of the poem within its larger 'field', referring to these as 'the space-tensions of a poem'.[62] Moreover, as Tim Woods observes, for Olson: 'The materiality and typography of the writing is as important as the content'.[63] Olson made exacting demands of his publishers and typesetters, insisting that they reproduce precisely the shapes and 'spacing' he gave to his poems; while his habit of rotating the page to produce cross-poems and vortical forms – most famously in 'The Rose of the World' (479) – created particular challenges for the editors of *Volume Three*.[64] Given his pervasive 'use of the page as a very literal spatial field' in *The Maximus Poems*, it should not be surprising – though it is little remarked by critics – that Olson writes poems that often look and behave like maps.[65] For instance, in 'Letter, May 2, 1959', he distributes words and place names on the page in such a way as to create a visual image of Gloucester's spatial layout during the late seventeenth and eighteenth centuries, including a vertical line of 'o's to represent a land boundary or stone wall (150).[66] Even more strikingly, on the final page of this poem Olson composes a spatialised text-image that approximates many of the details of Champlain's map of Gloucester harbour, including 'the depths of the channel' – marked with numerals denoting fathoms – and showing the respective positions of 'Ten / Pound Island', 'Rocky / Neck', and 'Eastern Point' (156). A further example of such cartographic verse form is 'The River Map and we're done', the penultimate text of *Maximus IV, V, VI*, where Olson's intricate patterns of lineation, spacing, and indentation sketch a visual image of islands and peninsulas of words between and around which run channels or streams of white space, the form of the poem mimicking the image from William Saville's 1822 *Plan of Squam River from the Cut to the Light House* to which it responds.[67] In this way, the material configurations of words on the space of the page in *The Maximus Poems* effect what Tim Cresswell calls 'a poetic topological correspondence' between the text and the place it represents.[68] More precisely, several of the poem-images that Olson creates deliberately echo the forms of the maps that he reads and writes about in the course of his unfolding investigation into Gloucester's evolution as a place in time.

Sea City

The Maximus Poems is not much concerned with maps and descriptions of North America's vast continental interior, focusing instead on its 'serrated, indented, and ragged' (345) Atlantic coast. John Mack observes that coasts are 'places of transaction, of negotiation between the realms of the sea and the land'.[69] Accordingly, Olson characterises Gloucester from the outset as an ambiguous 'sea city' (6), situated at the interface between terrestrial and maritime worlds, while belonging wholly to neither. A large part of his purpose in the first volume of the poem is to examine the city's origins as a deep-sea fishing port, not only to contrast its early modern promise with the contemporary decline of mid-twentieth-century Gloucester but also to problematise the dominant historical narrative of New England's founding by Puritan colonists. In this regard, as Woods remarks, *The Maximus Poems* 'stresses that it is the marginalia of history which is central to historical understanding'.[70] We should add, however, that the text's historical revaluations are bound up with its attention to the human settlements and cultural landscapes that flourish along the geographical margins of seacoasts and shorelines. Chief among these, of course, is Gloucester; but, as Olson's epic gradually expands its spatio-temporal scope, the fishing communities of Cape Ann are increasingly situated in relation to the much longer historical development of what John Gillis calls 'seaboard civilizations', such as the ancient Phoenicians and Greeks, the sea-faring

Norse who landed at 'l'Anse aux Meadow', Newfoundland around '1006 / AD' (444), and 'the early modern naval powers of northwestern Europe'.[71] Gillis observes that such amphibious coastal societies 'are best described by their routes rather than their roots', for they established extensive 'thalassocracies' by moving from one island or peninsula to the next, establishing ports, enclaves, and trading posts alongshore.[72] When Olson repeatedly depicts the primal scene of fourteen Dorchester fishermen 'huddled / above Half Moon beach' (106), over-wintering for the first time at '"fisherman's Field"' (110) in 1623, he is seeking to memorialise a particular instance of this larger historical process as it played out at Gloucester and Cape Ann, 'where fishing continues / and my heart lies' (112).

In 'December, 1960', Olson underlines the ambiguous, liminal character of the geography that most concerns him in *The Maximus Poems*: 'a coast / is not the same / as land / a coast / is not the main' (194). Neither land nor sea, the coast is a hybrid, in-between place that marks the zone where maritime and terrestrial systems interact. One of the more radical effects of Olson's focus upon coastal landscapes in the poem is to undermine the idea that Gloucester can be understood as a quintessentially American place, a 'microcosm' for the whole nation.[73] If, as Paul Giles argues, twentieth-century American modernism 'tended to be wrapped into a rhetoric of nativist utopia' that sought to reconcile local particularities with 'a larger national matrix', then *The Maximus Poems* is written against the grain of this tendency.[74] Repeatedly, Olson depicts Gloucester as an 'island' city (15, 432) that is only ambiguously linked with the larger continent of North America:

> These
> are the chronicles
> of an imaginary
> town
>
> placed as an island
> close to the shore (273)

Significantly, the 'imaginary / town' of Gloucester is also conceived as a peripheral 'sea city', oriented towards the Atlantic Ocean and its fishing grounds to the east. Olson describes Cape Ann as 'this stuck-out / 10 miles Europe-pointing / cape' (153), a peninsula that is situated 'between the old // North Atlantic [. . .] / and the new' (124). Rather than seeking to integrate Gloucester with the nation, then, Olson's text more often presents the city and its harbour as radically eccentric, part of a North Atlantic 'rim' established during the early modern period, whereby 'the northern latitudes of Europe and America were attached to one another by their coasts'.⁷⁵ This is evident in the pervasively transatlantic character of Olson's geographical imagination in *The Maximus Poems*, which recurrently looks east towards Europe from the shores of New England while also tracing the various permutations of that irrepressible 'Westward motion' that brings people, with their ideas and languages and cultures, 'to land' at Gloucester over the centuries (125).

With his characteristic yen for origins, in 'Letter 10' Olson poses a key question concerning Gloucester's history: 'on founding: was it puritanism, / or was it fish?' (49). Much of the remainder of the first volume of *The Maximus Poems* tries to work out a satisfactory answer by delving into a plethora of printed and archival documents, many of which are quoted or otherwise incorporated into the text. Indeed, as Michael André Bernstein notes, Olson's use of his historical materials 'itself constitutes an important thematic element in the epic', while a conflict over control of fishing rights at Cape Ann in the 1620s, between the Plymouth Puritans and a group of commercial fishermen, is presented as 'a microcosm of America's entire history'.⁷⁶ Olson makes no secret of where his sympathies lie, depicting the fishermen's cause as a struggle against 'mercantilism' and 'nascent capitalism except as it stays the individual adventurer / and the worker on share' (105). Puritan theocracy and colonialism are regarded as establishing the basis for modern America's capitalist economy and banking system – 'a nation fizzing itself / on city managers, / mutual losing banks' (118) – whereas the Dorchester Company's men represent a spirit of resistance and independent enterprise that Olson wishes to commemorate, in words if not in stone:

> They should raise a monument
> to a fisherman crouched down
> behind a hogshead, protecting
> his dried fish. (118)

This 'monument', which exists only in the 'imaginary / town' of the poem, is dedicated to a lost cause, for the Dorchester Company ultimately failed to establish a permanent settlement at Cape Ann, and by the time of Gloucester's incorporation as a city in 1642 it was wholly under the control of the Puritan-led Massachusetts Bay Colony.⁷⁷ Part of Olson's purpose in *The Maximus Poems* is to recover the utopian promise of that missed opportunity, figuring Gloucester as a place 'where polis / still thrives' (26) because it was originally founded upon 'fish fish fish' (108) rather than Puritan religion. Indeed, Olson's poetics resembles Walter Benjamin's version of historical materialism to the extent that it seeks to grasp 'the constellation which his own era has formed with a definite earlier one' – in this case, the constellation that links post-war Gloucester to its abortive first settlement by Europeans.[78]

Although colonial settlements in New England were scarce and temporary until the early seventeenth century, 'tens of thousands of European mariners had firsthand experience in the northwest Atlantic before 1600', including Basque, French, Portuguese, and Spanish fishermen drawn to the abundant marine ecosystems of Newfoundland and the Gulf of Maine.[79] The discovery of fishing grounds in the North Atlantic – 'Georges // the Channel, Middle Ground / Browns, Pollock Rip' (131) – is of equal consequence to Columbus's landfall in the Bahamas for Olson's tale of 'GLOUCESTER Queen of the fishtowns' (113). Reflecting on De la Cosa's mappamundi, he notes that 'The New Land was, / from the start, even by name was / Bacalhaos' (82) – the Portuguese and Basque word for 'cod' – and later describes how the English navigators Bartholomew Gosnold and Martin Pring encountered 'fish so thick the waters you could put no prow'd / go through' (113) in the Gulf of Maine. This early modern abundance contrasts sharply, however, with the contemporary decline of the fishing industry in Gloucester, which is bound up with what Olson regards as the wider ills of American consumer capitalism. As Jeffrey Bolster observes, the future of the New England fisheries 'looked bleak' by the time that Olson began to write *The Maximus Poems* in 1950, because of chronic overfishing, corruption, and labour disputes.[80] The poem's most powerful depiction of this crisis occurs when Olson describes the 'industrial fish' now caught and processed at Gloucester's Gordon-Pew plant, where a 'cornucopia' is unloaded from boats and taken by truck 'to the De-Hy / to be turned into catfood, / and fertilizer' (131). Bernstein observes that Olson's text repeatedly attacks 'wage-slavery' and corporate 'ownership' (18), particularly in the fishing industry, but it 'fails to suggest any actions that could challenge the power of the monopolies'.[81] In part, this is because Olson sees the process of corruption and decline as beginning very early, soon after Gloucester's incorporation as a city in the mid-seventeenth century. For instance, reflecting on the early settlement of the New England coast, he claims that 'the newness // the first men knew was almost / from the start dirtied / by second comers':

    About seven years
and you can carry cinders
in your hand for what

America was worth. (138–9)

As these lines illustrate, if Gloucester is often figured in *The Maximus Poems* as an Edenic 'first place' (110) that retains some of its unrealised utopian potential, then Olson is also engaged in writing a version of the Fall set on the coast of Cape Ann.

Olson knew something about fishing, and not just from the books that he read. He spent three weeks as a deckhand on a swordfishing schooner, *Doris M. Hawes*, in July 1936, during which time he kept a detailed journal and recorded the talk of his shipmates.[82] Although he has Maximus ruefully admit that 'The sea was not, finally, my trade' (56), Olson certainly regarded the mariner as 'a hero of practical reason' and sought to learn as much as he could through talk and close observation.[83] In his letters, he presents himself as a kind of honorary seaman, 'listening to wharves & men' or roaming 'the bars with my friends the fishermen'.[84] As much as the navigators and cartographers of the New World, Gloucester's fishermen – 'The men of the matter of this city' (38) – are the heroes of *The Maximus Poems*, exemplifying both physical courage and pride in their work. Early in the first volume, Olson describes how his father's namesake, Captain Carl Olsen 'could set his dories out / as a landsman sows his fields // and reap such halibut / it was to walk the streets of Gloucester different' (23). Returning to the legendary figure of Olsen in *Volume Three*, the poem reflects on how such men 'tie Gloucester / to her earliest life' (475) and so embody something of its as-yet unrealised possibility. Indeed, Gloucester's fishermen are occasionally transfigured via Olson's mythic method as 'gods' washed in 'the Basin of Morning' (558) – figures of miraculous resurrection – or even as living 'principles of the universe'.[85] At times, this tendency towards mythologisation has the effect of undermining the text's otherwise scrupulous attention to historical and material particulars, and also contributes to the 'phallic mysticism' of its more overtly mythopoeic passages.[86] As Rachel Blau DuPlessis observes, the world of *The Maximus Poems* is emphatically masculine, focusing almost exclusively on 'the gendered relations among men' while effectively 'erasing [women] as workers and members of the polis'.[87] In this regard, the image of Gloucester that the poem constructs as a harmonious and independent coastal community of working people is wildly unbalanced and at best incomplete.

Migrations

Notwithstanding its marked gender imbalance, Olson's Gloucester is consistently figured as a multi-ethnic, polyglot city, a seaport enriched by the presence of Portuguese, Italian, English, Irish, and Scandinavian immigrants over the centuries. As Mack observes, 'sea ports were amongst the first urban centres to develop cosmopolitan populations' because of the multi-ethnic character of most ships' crews, and some even have their own distinctive 'maritime languages'.[88] In 'Letter 3', Olson has Maximus reflect upon the cosmopolitan character of his city and on his own status as an internal immigrant:

> I was not born there, came, as so many of the people came,
> from elsewhere. That is, my father did. And not from the Provinces
> not from Newfoundland. But we came early enough. [. . .]
>
> As the people of the earth are now, Gloucester
> is heterogeneous, and so can know polis (14)

In these lines, Maximus emphatically aligns his own experience and perspective with those migrants who came to Gloucester (and, by extension, the United States) 'from elsewhere', seeking work and a better life for themselves and their children, as Olson's father and grandfather did. Importantly, though, Olson's conception of Gloucester as fundamentally 'heterogeneous', a microcosm of 'the people of the earth', is at odds with the ideology of social assimilation that was implicit in 'the myth of America as a land of immigrants' during the first decades of the twentieth century.[89] Rather, it is the stubborn heterogeneity of Gloucester and its status as a place apart from contemporary America, both its nativist 'localism' and the homogenising 'mu-sick' of its popular culture (14), that means that the city 'can know polis'. David Herd argues that a profound contradiction arises here between the apparent 'localism' of Olson's intense focus upon Gloucester, which is driven by the conviction that 'we cannot grasp our limitations unless we grasp our contingency upon place', and the more general preoccupation of *The Maximus Poems* with various forms of 'movement across space'.[90] Hence, Maximus's warning to the cosmopolitan peoples of Gloucester that corporate wage slavery 'would keep you off the sea, would keep you local, / my Nova Scotians, / Newfoundlanders, / Sicilianos / Isolatos' (16). One way of making sense of this contradiction, I suggest, is to read *The Maximus Poems* as a world map of migrations tracing the westward movements of peoples and their cultures over the course of several millennia, from the Old World of the Mediterranean to the New World of the North Atlantic, with Gloucester as their destination. In this way, the text offers a deep history – albeit profoundly fractured and riddled with mythopoeic interludes – of the origins of Gloucester's social and cultural heterogeneity.

Olson was acutely conscious of being the son and grandson of European immigrants, and this consciousness permeates *The Maximus Poems* in a variety of ways. His father, Karl Olson, was born in Örebro, Sweden in 1882 but emigrated with his mother the following year and became a U.S. citizen in 1890, later developing a fascination with American history that he passed on to his son.[91] Olson remarks that his father 'valued America, as immigrants do, more than the native' and comments: 'I'm not sure it's a good thing'.[92] His mother's father, Jack Hines, was an Irishman from Galway who crossed the Atlantic to work as a furnace stoker and nightwatchman for U.S. Steel in Worcester.[93] Noting his parents' immigrant backgrounds in 'The Present is Prologue', Olson seems to regard his forebears' experiences of movement and translocation as fundamental to his writing, for he affirms that 'the work of each of us is to find out the true lineaments of ourselves by facing up to the primal features of those founders who lie buried in us'.[94] Such 'founders' may be literary or historical as well as familial, of course, and Olson's search for the 'primal features' of himself reaches much farther back than one or two generations. Also significant is the fact that during the Second World War, Olson worked as a publicist for the Common Council for American Unity, which advocated on behalf of immigrant citizens in a context of rising xenophobia.[95] Finally, a seminal event in confirming Olson's self-identification as an immigrant American was his break with Pound in 1948 over the elder poet's aggressive nativism and racist slurs.[96] In a combative letter, Olson sides decisively with 'immigrant Amurrika', telling Pound that he will 'have to deal with us Olsons, Leite-Rosenstock-Huessys; your damn ancestors let us in'.[97]

These personal circumstances and experiences combined to ensure that, when Olson began to write *The Maximus Poems* in the early 1950s, he was sympathetically drawn to Gloucester's multi-layered histories of migration and settlement over the course of more than three centuries. Recent historical and political events also likely played a role, for, as Herd argues, Olson's conception of the 'polis' in his epic poem is motivated by 'the question of how political belonging should be formulated and re-thought' in the post-war period, especially in light of 'the fact of the concentration camps'.[98] Olson's interest in questions of belonging and migration broadened considerably as his epic evolved, so that in a late interview he would claim that: 'I regard Gloucester as the final movement of the earth's people, the great migratory thing [. . .]. The migratory act of man ended in Gloucester'.[99] Although it bears little scrutiny as a statement of fact, this claim is revealing as a description of the underlying narrative logic informing *The Maximus Poems*, especially its second and third volumes. Indeed, Olson presents the reader with a condensed summary of the text's ramifying voyage narratives when he casts Maximus as a migrant traveller through space and time:

> He sent flowers on the waves from the mole
> of Tyre. He went to Malta. From Malta
> to Marseilles. From Marseilles to Iceland.
> From Iceland to Promontorium Vinlandiae.
> Flowers go out on the sea. On the left
> Of the Promontorium. On the left of the
> Promontorium, Settlement Cove. (257)

'Settlement Cove' is the name that Olson gives to the area of shore on Stage Head where fourteen Dorchester fishermen first overwintered; so these lines describe a sea voyage from ancient Tyre, on the coast of Lebanon, to Gloucester in the 1620s.[100] In doing so, they also conflate several other westward journeys represented elsewhere in the poem, including those of Phoenician sailors between Tyre and Malta; Pytheas's voyage from Marseille to Iceland (or Thule) in the fourth century BCE; and the course navigated by Norse settlers from Iceland to Vinland, on the coast of Newfoundland, in the eleventh century. Moreover, the practice of laying 'flowers on the waves' in memory of dead sailors and fishermen is first described as a custom of Gloucester's citizens (84); while 'the mole / of Tyre' has its double in highway route 128, which crosses the Annisquam River, linking the 'island' of Gloucester to the mainland: '128 a mole / to get at Tyre' (250).

Over the course of its three volumes, Olson's poem not only brings distant places and different human cultures into conjunction with one another; it also repeatedly underlines the significance of migration as a motive force in world history. Thomas Nail argues that most human societies view migration and movement as disruptive activities that must be subjected to control because their core ideologies presuppose 'social illusions of stasis'.[101] In fact, movement is ontologically primary, for sedentary societies maintain themselves by redirecting social flows (of people, goods, ideas) rather than via their grounding in a given, inviolable territory: 'Before there is anything like a territory, there is movement. Movement creates a territory; the social territory does not come ready-made. Before there is the territory, there is a process of *territorialization*'.[102] Moreover, because the movement of migrants plays such a crucial role in this process of territorialisation, it can best be understood as 'the constitutive condition for the qualitative transformation of society as a whole'.[103] Olson comes close to articulating this very argument in the third volume of *The Maximus Poems* when he describes migration as a paradoxically constant impetus for change in the long durée of human history:

> Migration in fact (which is probably
> as constant in history as any <u>one</u> thing: migration

is the pursuit by animals, plants & men of a suitable
—and gods as well—& preferable

environment; and leads always to a new center. (565)

To the extent that they conceive of migration as 'constant in history', these lines also figure migration as a primary force in driving its character and direction. Moreover, the changing relationship between beings – animals, plants, 'men', and gods – and their environments over time is central to migration, which entails moving in search of a more 'suitable' or 'preferable' place in which to live. Finally, this search for a mutually beneficial relationship between living organisms and their places entails a process of displacement and re-centring, the iterative process of territorialisation. If, as Olson argues in 'Human Universe', such re-centring in the post-war period requires renewing humankind's relationship with 'nature', 'the most powerful agent of all', then *The Maximus Poems* suggests that migration is the most powerful historical process whereby this end might be achieved.[104]

Olson makes a point of alluding to the migrations of the 'gods' in the course of human history; though, as a self-described 'euhemerist', he assumes that 'gods are men first' and that myths are chiefly of interest for what they can tell us about the prehistory of ancient human civilisations.[105] Consequently, as Miriam Nichols observes, myth and history are interwoven in the map of migrations that *The Maximus Poems* elaborates: 'Historical journey segues into myth; myth leads back to history'.[106] For instance, in 'MAXIMUS, FROM DOGTOWN – I' Olson tells and retells the tale of a Gloucester folk-hero, the 'Handsome Sailor' (172) James Merry, who was killed fighting a bull, but then conflates this historical figure with the mythical Manes or Menes, the traditional founder figure of Ancient Egypt. The compound voyager-hero that results is punningly called 'Many' – Olson's epigraph to *The Maximus Poems* is '*All my life I've heard / one makes many*' (3) – and is depicted as having first migrated to 'Ireland', where he 'died of a bee'; though subsequently he crossed the Atlantic and 'built a castle / at Norman's woe' (177), a few miles west of Gloucester. In this way, Egyptian myths of origins are interwoven with fragments of the history and folklore of Cape Ann, all of which share some connection to the master tropes of sea journeys and westward migrations.

As an enthusiastic student of pre-Homeric mythology, with its 'primordial & phallic energies', Olson was keenly aware that 'the earliest surviving human writing recounts migrations as well as tensions or exchanges with nomads or other settled communities'.[107] His reworking of the figure of Typhon, from Hesiod's *Theogony*, is a powerful example of his engagements with such narratives in *The Maximus Poems*. In Hesiod's text, Typhon (or Typhoeus) is a fearsome monster with 'a hundred snaky heads' who battles Zeus, king of the Olympian gods, near the River Orontes in Northern Syria, but is defeated and hurled down to Tartarus, a prison deep below the earth.[108] In Olson's version of this tale, however, 'the blue monster' Typhon escapes and travels by boat to Malta, passing Rhodes and Crete, then out of the Mediterranean 'to arrive at Ireland' and thence 'into the Atlantic', ultimately making landfall 'in a / grapevine corner' – Wingaersheek Beach on the north shore of Cape Ann – 'to shake off his cave-life / and open an opening / big enough for himself' (264).[109] That is, Typhon becomes a migrant or refugee who travels from the Eastern Mediterranean to the coast of Northern Massachusetts in search of a more suitable environment in which to live freely. His journey conflates those of Tyre's Phoenician sailors, Pytheas of Massalia, Manes or Many, and the Dorchester Company fishermen, as well as Olson's migrant hero Maximus, in a single mytho-historical account of European settlement on Cape Ann.

Continental Drift

Shortly after the end of the Second World War, Olson began to develop plans for an ambitious new writing project, which he sometimes called *West*, that would comprise 'an epic fable of the myths and history of the Americas' or, in another version, 'cover the history of Western man for the past 2,500 years, beginning with Ulysses'.[110] These are the misty origins of *The Maximus Poems*, which would retain the decisive theme of westward movement but anchor its epic scope in the material and historical 'particulars' of Gloucester (101). Yet, while methodologically crucial, the poem ultimately reveals such anchorage to be necessarily provisional. Olson's text does not only illustrate the ontological priority of movement over stasis or territory through its manifold representations of human migrations over several millennia, from the Mediterranean to Western Europe and then across the Atlantic to New England. In its later stages, *The Maximus Poems* also seeks to map those more fundamental movements that occur in the long perspectives of geological time, particularly the formation and migration of continents as described in the new theories of continental drift that emerged during the 1960s. Considered within this extended time-frame of hundreds of millions of years, Gloucester itself is rendered a mobile object shifting its position on the face of the Earth and crossing the Atlantic Ocean – like most of its latter-day citizens – from what is now the coast of West Africa:

> In mid-Mesozoic
> time, 150,000,000 years ago—and Gloucester still moves
> <u>away</u> from the Canaries—she was Terceira
> "lightest" of those Islands and where Cape Juby
> is now on the run-off of the Atlas Mountains (548)

These lines radicalise the figuration of Gloucester as an island introduced much earlier in the poem by imagining Cape Ann migrating away from the Canary Islands, which lie off Cape Juby in South-west Morocco, due to tectonic forces over the course of 150 million years. Indeed, Olson notes that 'Gloucester still moves / <u>away</u> from the Canaries' in the present, as the geological processes underlying continental drift are continuous. In the Mesozoic Era, Cape Ann and Cape Juby were twins, whereas now an Ocean separates them; and the island of Gloucester is now an American city, but also a place-in-motion drifting slowly north-westward, its destination uncertain. Considered in this way, Olson's Maximus observes, 'migrations / turn out to be / as large as / bodies of earth' (524).

The theory of continental drift was first developed by Alfred Wegener in the 1910s, immediately generating controversy and debate among geologists, though it was not widely accepted (with important modifications) until the early 1960s, when Olson was writing *Maximus IV, V, VI*. That volume bears on its cover an image of Pangaea, the supercontinent hypothesised by Wegener, who argued that 'continents were joined together at a certain time in the past; thereafter, they drifted like rafts over the ocean floor, finally reaching their present position'.[111] Olson gleaned most of his knowledge of continental drift not from Wegener himself but from a 1963 article by Tuzo Wilson, which is the source of many of the factual details and images that he works into poems in the final volume of *The Maximus Poems*.[112] Indeed, *Maximus IV, V, VI* includes the following acknowledgement: 'I owe to Alfred Wegener, and Tuzo Wilson, the basis of the cover – which is of course the Earth (and Ocean) before Earth started to come apart at the seams, some 125 million years awhile back – and India took off from Africa & migrated to Asia' (168). It seems likely that the British poet, Jeremy Prynne, who shared and stimulated many of Olson's geological interests, supplied an image of Wegener's 'Map of the Earth', at Olson's request.[113] Wilson's article is important for the way in which it links a lucid exposition of Wegener's theory to recent research on mid-oceanic ridge systems and convection currents in the Earth's mantle, which supply a more plausible explanation for the capacity of continents to 'drift' for thousands of miles.[114] Olson leans particularly heavily on Wilson in 'ESSAY ON QUEEN TIY', a poem that disorientingly conflates prehistoric human migrations with the migrations of continents in the geological past.

Describing the disintegration of Pangaea in lines that are themselves broken and grammatically incomplete, he abruptly shifts into a more prosaic, factual aside: '150,000,000 years ago to the t, / definitely now established by / J. Tuzo Wilson as well as other / oceanographers & geographers' (523). The many maps and illustrations in Wilson's article clearly stimulated Olson's imagination as much as his words, and the poet also made use of Bruce Heezen and Marie Tharp's physiographic map of the North Atlantic seafloor, a copy of which adorned the wall of his Fort Square kitchen in the late 1960s.[115] For instance, in a late poem he describes the seamounts 'Cruiser & Flato', between which 'Gloucester / tore her way West North West' from the coast of Africa 'to arrive / where she is' (601).

Olson's fascination with Wegener's map of Pangaea, the supercontinent in which all the planet's 'bodies of earth' are made one, might be regarded as another manifestation of what Anthony Mellors calls his mythic 'will to coherence', an impulse to totalise or unify that is ultimately 'at odds with poetry that gets its energy from the symbolic irresolution of violently contrasting elements'.[116] To the extent that he conceives of *The Maximus Poems* as a world map or mappamundi, the cover image of *Maximus IV, V, VI* can be read as a visual analogue for the text's repeated attempts to discover some underlying principle of order in the deep past. This is certainly how Byrd interprets the image, as 'the sign of the earth's primal coherence'.[117] However, Olson would have learned from Wilson's article that Pangaea was not, in fact, a 'primeval' reality but rather 'assembled from still older fragments'. Indeed, the theory of plate tectonics, which emerged from Wegener's continental drift, postulates 'a long history of periodic assembly and disassembly of continents and fracturing and spreading of ocean floors, as convection cells in the mantle proceeded to turn over in different configurations'.[118] That is, the supercontinent of Pangaea was only a temporary instance of convergence within a longer and ongoing geological process. Rather than figuring the disintegration of some primal unity, argues Brendan Gillott, continental drift offered Olson 'the idea that over a long enough timespan all landscape, and so all maps, are only local expressions of a work in progress'.[119] In this regard, the ongoing formation and fragmentation of the Earth's land masses and oceans suggests an apt analogy for the evolving form and vast scale of Olson's epic poem. For instance, when Maximus reports his vision of a 'form' that 'is sewn / in all parts, under / and over' (343) he is simultaneously describing the faulted surface of the Earth and the mosaic form of the poem we read, a 'weave / of interlocking / pieces' (194–5) like the joined and sundered fragments of continents.

It is certainly true, as DuPlessis has it, that *The Maximus Poems* is 'ORBsessive': 'Taking the whole world, the whole earth, even the whole universe in and correlating it, co-real-relating it'.[120] Similarly, Jeremy Prynne argues that Olson's poem is uniquely powerful for the way in which it conveys 'the notion that the planet, the whole globe, the earth upon which we live, is home to us'.[121] Olson's Maximus is at once a citizen of Gloucester, acutely interested in the mundane particulars of its history and social life, and a restless voyager who is at home everywhere on the face of the Earth. One of his roles, it seems, is 'to perambulate the bounds' of 'a cosmos' (516); while in another poem he sails 'On the Earth's Edge' as though the 'Spinning Globe' were a 'Little Spun Boat or Beetle of Her Places / In the Great Heaven of Ocean' (487). Notice, however, that the extended metaphor in these lines implies that not only Maximus but also the (feminised) Earth herself is in constant motion, 'Going at 11,000 Miles / Per Twenty Four Hours Always' (487). Part of the imaginative stimulus that Olson finds in the idea of continental drift clearly derives from its sheer spatio-temporal scale, evoking vast creative and destructive forces that affect the entire planet and its capacity to support life. However, just as important is the fact that continental drift discloses a conception of the earth and its geological processes as intrinsically dynamic and kinetic, a profound manifestation of what Olson calls 'The Animate', or matter in motion.[122] In *The Maximus Poems*, the process of 'place formation', which entails 'carving out "permanences" from the flow of processes creating spatio-temporality' is dramatised on a planetary scale.[123]

These elements – scale and dynamism – come together memorably in a poem on the Cabot Fault, which Olson describes as 'a split in the Atlantic Ocean, a fault which runs just where my own attention has been, northeast [. . .] straight through Gloucester'.[124] Named after the fifteenth-century explorer, John Cabot, the fault extends 'from Boston to northern Newfoundland' and may, according to Wilson, have been linked to the Great Glen Fault system in Scotland in the deep past.[125] Consequently, Olson tends to regard it as a synecdoche for that greater rift, the Atlantic Ocean itself. In the opening lines of the poem, he depicts Maximus as a version of Shakespeare's Anthony, bestriding an ocean and seeking to bridge an ever-widening divide:

> Astride
> the Cabot
> fault,
>
> one leg upon the Ocean one leg
> upon the Westward drifting continent (404)

Linking sea and land, like Gloucester itself, Olson's monumental poet-protagonist is nonetheless engaged in an impossible task: to suture the sundered continents and stabilise a planet whose material surface is in constant motion. The key image here is of 'the Westward drifting continent', the migrating land mass of North America, which is inexorably 'rushing westward 2' / each 100 / years' (404) as the Atlantic Ocean widens on both sides of its mid-oceanic ridge. This image recurs repeatedly in the third volume of *The Maximus Poems*; for instance, when Olson describes 'the / full American continent going / North by the Pole and // West' (504), and again when he conflates the drifting of continents with 'The / northwest course of shifting man' (512). Importantly, the text of the Cabot Fault poem is tilted on the page, so that its left-hand margin mimics the angle of the fault itself and also suggests the kinetic energy of 'the earth // going NNW' (404) through the long durée of geological time. In this way, the form of Olson's poetry as well as its manifest content is deeply affected by his interest in the theory of continental drift.

In 1955, when he had begun to publish the first sections of *The Maximus Poems*, Olson advised his friend and former student, the poet Ed Dorn, to '*dig one thing or place or man* until you know more abt that than is possible to any other man'.[126] This is what he did himself with Gloucester, immersing himself in the minutiae of its history, economy, and geography until he began to fear that his poem was becoming overburdened with 'local research' and that he was becoming little more than 'a tireless [. . .] crawler of my own / ground' (556).[127] By the end of his text, however, the spatio-temporal frames within which his poetics of place unfolds have radically expanded, taking in everything from the North Atlantic fishing grounds and the routes of westward migrations from Europe and the Near East to contemporary theories of continental drift. Nonetheless, Olson consistently figures Gloucester as his 'first place' (110), the primary focus for his geographical imagination and a vantage from which to grasp 'that unit, Earth' as a composite whole, even as the city is itself rendered mobile, a place in process of displacement as continents drift and oceans are born.[128] Across the whole of *The Maximus Poems*, as I have argued, maps and mapping play a crucial if under-appreciated role in Olson's creative practice. Not only is his text studded with complex examples of metatopographia, as he generates poems by reading and re-reading the maps produced by navigators and cartographers of the New World, but Olson also explicitly encourages his readers to think of *The Maximus Poems* as a multi-dimensional world map, 'a mappemunde' (257). His experiments with form, typography, and the space of the page often result in poem-images that look and behave like maps or create topological correspondences with the places they represent. At a thematic level, the text's preoccupation with movement and displacements, of land masses as well as peoples, means that it is best understood as a map of migrations, one that elaborates a deep history both of Gloucester's heterogeneous, multi-ethnic population and of its geological formation over hundreds of millions of years.

Chapter 6

Gwendolyn Brooks: From Bronzeville to the Warpland

During the mid-1940s, the poet Gwendolyn Brooks lived with her husband and young son in a one-room kitchenette apartment at 623 East 63rd Street, on the southern edge of Bronzeville, Chicago. Situated at an intersection and overlooking a stretch of the L-train line, Brooks's flat was also, for a short time, one of the meeting places of African American late modernism, a venue for parties attended by many of the writers, artists, musicians, and photographers associated with the Chicago Black Renaissance. When Brooks threw a party for her friend Langston Hughes, the Harlem Renaissance poet, perhaps 100 people squeezed into her tiny kitchenette.[1] Moreover, the apartment was also a 'scene of writing' for Brooks, the place where 'the everyday practices, encounters, and networks' of her social life were worked into poetry.[2] Brooks remarks in her autobiography, *Report from Part One* (1972): 'If you wanted a poem, you only had to look out of a window. There was material always, walking or running, fighting or screaming or singing'.[3] That is, Brooks's apartment window offered a panorama of the everyday lives of her fellow Bronzeville citizens, whose activities provide the raw 'material' from which her poems are fashioned or 'distilled'.[4]

In this chapter, I examine the centrality of Bronzeville and its people to Brooks's late modernist poetry in detail, with particular attention to her representations of living spaces and the public spaces of the city's streets. I also argue that Brooks's work, when considered as a whole, reveals Bronzeville to be a mutable and transient phenomenon, a place-in-process that is shaped and reshaped by Chicago's histories of migration, racial segregation, and urban redevelopment in the period from the end of the First World War until the 1960s. Brooks was born at the beginning of this period, in 1917, began to publish her poetry during the 1930s, when Bronzeville acquired its name, and underwent a profound aesthetic and political realignment in the late 1960s, when Bronzeville's identity as a black urban community and cultural hub had dwindled to little more than a memory. Thereafter, her geographical imagination is largely decoupled from the streets and kitchenette buildings of Bronzeville, turning instead to the allegorical landscapes of the American Warpland in the post-Civil Rights era and to the wider solidarities of the African diaspora. My purpose, then, is to show that a historicised understanding of Bronzeville's social and cultural geographies can both illuminate individual poems and help to account for some of the major shifts in Brooks' career, particularly during her most productive phase as a poet from 1940 to 1970.

Late Modernism in Chicago

Brooks, as both an African American poet and a late modernist, might be regarded as doubly marginal to the main currents of modernism. However, she is also a pivotal mediating figure within African American literature of the twentieth century: a leading writer of the Chicago Black Renaissance with links to both the Harlem Renaissance of the 1920s and the Black Arts Movement of the 1960s, as well as a major influence on younger neo-modernist poets such as Harryette Mullen, Erica Hunt, and Evie Shockley.[5] Brooks's work exhibits the 'doubleness' that Paul Gilroy regards as characteristic of black artistic practice, which, because of the shared histories and legacies of slavery in the black Atlantic world, is 'inescapably both inside and outside the dubious protection modernity offers'.[6] For African American late modernists such as Brooks and Melvin Tolson, this doubleness manifests itself in attempts to overcome the 'cultural dichotomy' between 'modernist artifice and African-American speech'. The result, argues Matthew Hart, is a mode of poetic expression that 'can be hyperallusive, fragmentary, unmusical, and still lay claim to the category of blackness'.[7] Brooks's poetry is typically less hyperallusive and fragmentary than is Tolson's, though her use of compressed syntax, varied and often recondite diction, ventriloquism and shifting perspectives, and mastery of many different forms or genres (sonnet sequences, ballads, mock-epics, long narrative poems, elegies, and dramatic monologues) clearly aligns her work with modernist strategies of artifice and linguistic experiment.

Nonetheless, the ways in which Brooks engaged with such modernist influences, and the representational dilemmas that they raise for African American writers, varies across her career because of important shifts in her aesthetic priorities and political commitments. Her 'reconstruction of the epic subject' and adaptation of high modernist style to the life-story of a working-class black girl in *Annie Allen* (1949) garnered acclaim from white liberal readers and led to her becoming the first African American winner of the Pulitzer Prize in 1950.[8] However, following her 1967 encounter at Fisk University with a younger generation of militant black poets led by Amiri Baraka, Brooks laid claim more emphatically to the category of blackness and in part foreswore the elaborate forms and complex diction of her earlier work, affirming her commitment to writing for and about 'black people'.[9] This new sensibility finds its first expression in two key volumes from the late 1960s, *In The Mecca* (1968) and *Riot* (1969). Nonetheless, it should be noted that Brooks's abiding concern with the ordinary lives of black people is evident from her first collection, *Along the Streets of Bronzeville* (1945), and is bound up with her sophisticated poetics of place. Moreover, while Brooks observed in 1973 that 'this does not seem to me to be a sonnet time', apparently rejecting inherited poetic forms, she continued to stress the poet's fundamental 'duty to words' and suggested that younger poets would, in time, need to hone their 'technique' so that their present 'rawness' might 'come to some maturation'.[10] In 'The Chicago Picasso' her speaker affirms: 'we must cook ourselves and style ourselves for Art'.[11]

The major phase of Brooks's career as a poet, from the early 1940s to about 1970, is therefore best understood in terms of her sliding positions on a spectrum defined by the 'interplay of integrationism and radicalism, of high modernism and social realism'.[12] The characteristic doubleness of Brooks's poetry is also conditioned by the nature and sequence of her encounters with the work of older modernist writers. Importantly, Brooks's first exposure to modernist innovation occurred via the poets of the Harlem Renaissance, particularly through reading (in the mid-1930s) Countee Cullen's anthology *Caroling Dusk* (1927), which included work by Cullen, Claude McKay, Sterling Brown, and Fenton Johnson.[13] As an aspiring teenage poet, Brooks also corresponded with James Weldon Johnson and Langston Hughes; the latter became an important friend and mentor as her career took off in the 1940s.[14] Consequently, as Karen Jackson Ford argues, Brooks's formative engagements with modernism and early affinity with traditional forms such as the sonnet were mediated as much by African American precursors as by European or Anglo-American influences.[15] At Johnson's suggestion, Brooks began to read the work of American modernist poets, including T. S. Eliot, Ezra Pound, and e. e. cummings; but it was only in the early 1940s, as a member of the Chicago Poetry Group led by Inez Cunningham Stark, that Brooks gained what she called 'an education in modern poetry' and modernist technique in particular.[16] On the one hand, this literary apprenticeship led Brooks to internalise the aesthetic values of what she came to regard as 'white writing'; on the other, as Lubna Najar observes, it encouraged her to explore 'the relationship between high modernism and the construction of racial identity' in ways that would eschew Anglo-American primitivism.[17] As a consequence of this course of development, African American and Anglo-American modernist influences converge but also sometimes come into conflict within Brooks's poetry.

Brooks's late modernist poetics also need to be understood in terms of her self-conscious role as the poet of Bronzeville, the heart of African American life and culture in Chicago's South Side. James Smethurst argues that the distinctive African American experience of modernity, and modernism, in the early twentieth century was contingent upon the emergence of a 'new geography of race', which was characterised by mass migration to industrial cities in the North, such as Chicago, and the creation of black ghettos through the 'territorial racialization of the city'.[18] As I argue below, Brooks's poetic representations of Bronzeville are at once products of this new geography of race and attempts to document its effects, even when migration and racial segregation are not taken up as explicit themes. Smethurst also notes that African American modernists depict the urban ghetto as a profoundly ambiguous space, 'simultaneously new home, refuge, trap, and exile'; at once 'black metropolis and destroyer of black culture'.[19] This multiplicity is certainly a feature of Brooks's Bronzeville, a black metropolis characterised by overcrowding and racial injustice but also a vital social and cultural nexus, the focus for a second wave of African American modernist achievement beyond Harlem, the Chicago Black Renaissance.

Where the Harlem Renaissance occurred during the Jazz Age in metropolitan New York and bore the imprint of its cultural exuberance, the Chicago Black Renaissance emerged in the industrial Midwest under the very different social and economic conditions of the Depression. Grounded in the streets of Bronzeville, where most of its key institutions (libraries, galleries, theatres, and newspaper offices) were located, it was a multi-disciplinary 'cultural flowering' that created a 'distinct generational milieu' in which collaboration and cultural exchange was often central.[20] As Liesl Olson observes, the literary texts of Chicago's African American writers are often embedded in 'a distinct neighbourhood' and 'distinguished by a desire to write for the black working classes' but share the aesthetic sensibility of the wider Chicago Renaissance, in which 'a documentary impulse to narrate' is combined with 'a modernist birthright that revels in stylistic experiment'.[21] This fusion of precepts drawn from modernism and social realism is exemplified in the 1937 manifesto essay, 'Blueprint for Negro Writing', which was written by

Richard Wright in collaboration with other members of the South Side Writers Group. In it, Wright espouses writing that has 'a *complex simplicity*' and a strong social consciousness, focusing upon 'Negro life' but 'with no limit to technical and stylistic freedom.'²² Whilst these basic principles accord closely with the priorities of Brooks's poetry, her position within the Chicago Black Renaissance is rather ambiguous, appearing at once central and curiously marginal. For instance, while Robert Bone and Richard Courage commend the 'documentary, realist core' of Brooks's first collection, *A Street in Bronzeville*, they regard her 'shift towards modernist poetics' in *Annie Allen* as emblematic of the 'waning' and decline of the cultural renaissance in Bronzeville around 1950.²³ Elizabeth Schroeder Schlabach regards Brooks's poetry as more consistently central to the Chicago Black Renaissance, chiefly because of its focus on the people of Bronzeville and 'great feeling of place', but she also tends to emphasise its 'poetic realism' over its modernist innovations.²⁴ By contrast, in what follows I argue that it is the late modernist character of Brooks's poetics of place that makes her representations of Bronzeville so distinctive and significant.

Throwntogetherness

The close, mutually enriching relationship between Brooks's poetry and Chicago's South Side is widely acknowledged by critics of her work. Her biographer, Angela Jackson, casts this relationship as 'a love affair with black Chicago' and suggests that Brooks's poems are so deeply rooted in her home ground that they 'grow up organically out of the experience of the Black Metropolis'.²⁵ More circumspectly, Schlabach notes that Brooks's life and work reflect 'a profound commitment to Chicago – most importantly Bronzeville'; and Courtney Thorsson describes her poetry as 'radically local' because of its tendency to move 'in ever smaller concentric circles from Bronzeville to its individual backyards'.²⁶ However, it is rarely noticed how thoroughly interwoven is the arc of Brooks's career as a poet, from her apprenticeship during the Depression years to her political and aesthetic radicalisation in the late 1960s, with the story of Bronzeville's genesis and dissolution as a distinct place and close-knit African American community. As St Clair Drake and Horace Clayton observe in their landmark sociological study, *Black Metropolis* (1945), the name 'Bronzeville' has its origins in an unofficial mayoral competition run first by the *Chicago Bee* newspaper and subsequently the *Chicago Defender* (where Brooks published her first poems) during the early 1930s.²⁷ In this way, the area formerly known pejoratively as the 'Black Belt' was renamed by its residents in an 'act of self-determination' that is echoed in the title of Brooks's first collection, *A Street in Bronzeville*, and also in many individual poems, including 'Bronzeville Man with a Belt in the Back', 'Bronzeville Woman with a Red Hat', and 'A Bronzeville Mother Loiters in Mississippi. Meanwhile, a Mississippi Mother Burns Bacon'.[28] In an important sense, Brooks participates in the collective invention of Bronzeville as a place at the same time as she records and represents its distinctive forms of social life in her poems. However, following the publication of *The Bean Eaters* (1960) – which had the working title, 'Bronzeville Men and Women' – the name 'Bronzeville' drops out of the vocabulary of Brooks's writing.[29] Indeed, by the time that she was appointed poet laureate of Illinois in 1968, Brooks had stopped being the poet of Bronzeville, for Bronzeville itself had effectively ceased to exist. 'I started out talking about Bronzeville,' recalls Brooks in a 1970 interview, 'but "Bronzeville's" almost meaningless by now, I suppose, since Bronzeville has spread and spread and spread all over.'[30]

Bronzeville came into being during the 1930s because of two interlocking socio-geographical processes: migration and racial segregation. During the Great Migration, millions of African Americans left the Southern states for cities in the North and Midwest to escape the Jim Crow system of domestic apartheid and rising racist violence. Manning Marable notes that 'in 1940, 22 percent of all blacks lived in the North, compared to 10 percent in 1910'.[31] Hundreds of thousands came to industrial Chicago, seeking work and a better standard of life. Accordingly, the black population of the city increased rapidly from 44,000 in 1910 to 337,000 in 1945; by the end of the Second World War, 80 per cent of African Americans were born in the South and over 90 per cent were crowded into a narrow Black Belt – 'a city within a city' – extending south of the city centre.[32] One of these migrants was the novelist Richard Wright, who moved to Chicago's South Side from rural Mississippi in 1927. Wright describes the experience of the newly-arrived migrant as 'the beginning of living on a new and terrifying plane of consciousness', bewildered by the new sights, sounds, and customs of the big city. He also notes the poor-quality housing in 'crowded, barn-like rooms' and 'old rotting buildings' that African American families typically endured.[33] The scale and rapidity of black migration to Chicago in the early twentieth century sparked racial tensions that occasionally erupted in riots, and segregation was a basic fact of life for the inhabitants of Bronzeville. Widespread use of restrictive covenants prevented African American families from moving into adjacent, majority-white neighbourhoods, while unscrupulous landlords charged exploitative rents for sub-standard rooms and kitchenette apartments.[34] However, this dense concentration of African American migrants in a well-defined urban area of streets and cabarets, dance halls and storefront churches provided the basis for a remarkably rich cultural scene, making Bronzeville a vital hub for African American artists, jazz and blues musicians, journalists, and writers.[35] Indeed, Bone and Courage speak of a 'Bronzeville Renaissance', noting that from about 1935 to 1950 'Chicago rather than New York was the focal point of African American writing and a major center of visual arts'.[36] In this regard, the twin processes of migration and segregation that shaped Bronzeville as a distinctive place produced cultural goods as well as social ills.

In her 1951 magazine essay, 'They Call it Bronzeville', Brooks foregrounds the injustice of racial segregation at the same time as she stresses the ordinariness and basic humanity of Bronzeville's residents to her white readers. She characterises Bronzeville as 'a place that should not exist – an area set aside for the halting use of a single race'. However, in this city within a city there 'resides essentially only what is ordinary: human struggle, human whimsicality, and human reach towards soul-settlement'.[37] This contradiction lies at the heart of Brooks's poetics of place: for, if the lives of Bronzeville's citizens are fundamentally 'ordinary', the social and spatial conditions in which they are lived are not. A keen awareness of the geographical boundaries of Bronzeville's black community is implicit in much of Brooks's writing and repeatedly comes to the surface. For instance, in her novel *Maud Martha* (1953), the protagonist is described taking night walks 'east of Cottage Grove' with her family and is puzzled by the ubiquity of strange 'white faces' (151) beyond her Bronzeville neighbourhood.[38] Similarly, in 'Gang Girls' a female Blackstone Ranger day-dreams about the world that lies 'beyond her Ranger rim of Cottage Grove' (449) but doesn't dare leave her gang's sharply demarcated turf to discover it. Many of Brooks's female characters chafe against the socio-spatial constraints that are imposed upon their lives, though their rebelliousness is also curbed by an understanding of the violence – both structural and physical – that underpins racial segregation. This understanding is given explicit expression in 'The Ballad of Rudolph Reed', which depicts a black family's 'hunger' for a better 'home of their own' and the murderous consequences of their attempts to settle in a white neighbourhood – 'a street of bitter white' (377). Part tragic cautionary tale and part celebration of resistance to the racist logic of spatial segregation, Brooks's poem dramatises the conflict between African American mobility and the socio-geographical fixity that is central to the maintenance of white power in Chicago.

Although she lived in Chicago nearly all of her life and affirmed that the city 'nourishes' her as a writer, it is worth recalling that Brooks was born in Topeka, Kansas, her mother's home town.[39] Her father, David, migrated to Chicago from Oklahoma in the early years of the twentieth century and met her mother, Keziah Wims, there in 1914.[40] In common with most other citizens of Bronzeville, then, migration was an important part of Brooks's family history and a necessary condition for her relationship with the city, though it rarely figures as an explicit theme in her work. An important exception to this general rule is 'of De Witt Williams on his way to Lincoln Cemetery', which opens with the following lines:

> He was born in Alabama.
> He was bred in Illinois.
> He was nothing but a
> Plain black boy.
>
> Swing low swing low sweet sweet chariot
> Nothing but a plain black boy. (39)

Besides foregrounding the deceased man's Southern origins, Brooks's poem self-consciously combines a blues ballad verse with a modified Spiritual refrain, thereby adapting distinctively African American musical forms that have their origins in the rural South but were transplanted to urban Chicago during the 1920s and 1930s by musicians such as Bill Broonzy, Memphis Minnie, and Tampa Red.[41] In one sense, De Witt Williams's final journey to Lincoln Cemetery on the southern outskirts of the city replays, in miniature and in reverse, his migration to Chicago as a boy. However, the poem also stresses the strong emotional and social bonds that the dead man had to Bronzeville's streets, bars, and dance halls while alive: 'Down through Forty-seventh Street: / Underneath the L, / And—Northeast Corner, Prairie, / That he loved so well' (39). Naming the streets and venues in which De Witt Williams spent his time and money, the poem elegises its subject by recalling his participation in the dense social networks of his home place, foregrounding his status as an inhabitant as well as a migrant. As Thomas Nail observes, 'migratory figures function as mobile social positions and not fixed identities'.[42] That is, De Witt Williams was not born a migrant but became one; and, following his journey north from Alabama to Illinois, he became a citizen of Bronzeville. Moreover, he is not exceptional but rather a kind of representative figure in Brooks's poetry, for the Bronzeville that her work takes as its central concern is a community of African American migrants and their children, a place founded upon mobility and the interweaving of thousands of individual life stories.

Given the role that migration and racial segregation play in making Bronzeville the kind of place that it is, I want to suggest that Brooks's poetics of place can usefully be understood in terms of what Doreen Massey calls 'throwntogetherness'. For Massey, place is neither fixed or self-contained but rather open and permeable, 'an ever-shifting constellation of trajectories' that brings people and objects into temporary configurations, thereby posing 'the question of our living together'. Such configurations make strangers neighbours and give rise to antagonisms as well as creative fusions, so that place is experienced by, and changes its inhabitants not through 'some visceral belonging' but rather 'through the *practising* of place, the negotiation of intersecting trajectories'.[43] Throwntogetherness manifests itself in Brooks's work both in terms of the histories of African American migration that define Bronzeville's distinctive social life and in her recurrent depictions of overcrowded, semi-public domestic spaces and apartment buildings, particularly in her long poem 'In the Mecca', where she seeks 'to present a variety of personalities against a mosaic of daily affairs'.[44] It is also evident in the characteristically urban subject-matter and sensibility of her poetry. Indeed, Brooks remarks that '[t]he kind of work that I am doing needs a busy city as a background', for: 'The city is the place to observe man *en masse* and in his infinite variety'.[45] Notice Brooks's conception of the city as a 'background' here, a means rather than the end of her poetry, which is primarily concerned with people and the question of their living together rather than with place per se. Tellingly, when asked in interview whether she seeks 'to evoke place' in her work, Brooks replies: 'No, I start with the people'.[46]

The particular constellation of trajectories that is Brooks's Bronzeville was a temporary, mutable phenomenon, contingent upon the living together of hundreds of thousands of African American migrants and the forces of racial segregation that (temporarily) confined the vast majority within one area of the city. In this regard, Brooks's poetry can best be grasped in terms of what Peter Merriman calls 'the practising or becoming of place', which 'shifts our attention from place as a noun – a thing, a finished entity – to place as a verb', a process that unfolds or works itself out over time.[47] What was formerly known as the Black Belt became Bronzeville in the early 1930s, when the teenage Brooks was beginning to publish her first poems in local newspapers and magazines. During the Depression years, the Second World War, and well into the 1950s, it was a vital matrix for African American literature and art. Initially located around 35th Street and South State during the Jazz Age, Bronzeville's social and cultural centre moved southwards to 47th Street and South Parkway by the 1930s, while the neighbourhood itself stretched as far as 63rd Street, where Brooks lived during the 1940s.[48] By the 1960s, however, Bronzeville had begun to lose its identity as a distinct urban community as a result of post-war redevelopment, large-scale public housing projects, and industrial decline, which led to an 'exodus of the black middle and working class'.[49] This is a phenomenon that Brooks noted as early as 1961, when she remarked that: 'If Bronzeville keeps spreading [. . .] I may run out of material. It won't be Bronzeville anymore'.[50] There is a note of incipient nostalgia in this wry observation, but more important is Brooks's keen awareness of Bronzeville's volatile, metamorphic character. Indeed, Liesl Olson aptly describes Bronzeville as 'a fluctuating ecosystem, a nexus of people and places that was constantly changing': 'Bronzeville was a circulation of people and ideas – in Chicago, certainly, but held together only tenuously by bricks and mortar'.[51] Brooks experienced this circulation and impermanence herself – she recalls living in five different rented rooms and kitchenettes during the early years of her marriage – and the fluctuations of Bronzeville's social and cultural ecosystem are the 'material' from which her poems are made.[52] This is clear from the opening lines of her early poem, 'the vacant lot': 'Mrs Coley's three-flat brick / isn't here any more' (41). From the beginning of her career as a poet, Brooks emphasises the shifting, unsettled character of the urban environments and human communities that coalesce as Bronzeville, which is itself recurrently subject to change.

Everyday Life in Bronzeville

Brooks's fascination with the low-key human dramas of everyday life is also evident from the 1940s and persists after her catalytic encounter with the Black Arts Movement at Fisk University in 1967. As early as 1942, Brooks advised herself and her fellow poets to 'Scrape the stuff of your everyday living into the poetry you write'; while in 1969 she was planning a return to the poetry of ordinary experience – 'pictures of black life as I see it today' – that she had pioneered in *A Street in Bronzeville*.[53] The most important influence on this aspect of Brooks's poetry was Langston Hughes, whose work she first encountered in the mid-1930s and whom she deeply admired both for his 'clear pride in his race' and his persistent concern with 'the ordinary aspects of black life'.[54] In his 1926 essay, 'The Negro Artist and the Racial Mountain,' Hughes celebrates the vitality and creativity of working-class African Americans – 'the low-down folks, the so-called common element' – arguing that their lives and cultural expressions 'furnish a wealth of colorful, distinctive material for any artist because they still hold their own individuality in the face of American standardizations'.⁵⁵ Brooks took this creative principle to heart and adapted it to her own Bronzeville milieu. Moreover, although she had a respectable lower-middle-class upbringing, Brooks's ambiguous class position and first-hand experience of poverty in Bronzeville's decaying kitchenette buildings as an adult makes her a kind of organic intellectual, a bona fide member of 'the black community' about which she writes in her poems.⁵⁶ Certainly, she insists that, as a writer, she does not 'feel *apart* from other people', affirming: 'I am an ordinary human being who is impelled to write poetry'.⁵⁷ That is, Brooks is an ordinary person who happens to write poetry about ordinary people.

A good illustration of Brooks's conception of the everyday and its importance for her aesthetic politics can be found in the opening chapter of her autobiographical novel, *Maud Martha*, which depicts the protagonist as a girl, day-dreaming on her back porch and looking for flowers in her yard:

> But dandelions were what she chiefly saw. Yellow jewels for everyday, studding the patched green dress of her back yard. She liked their demure prettiness second to their everydayness; for in that latter quality she thought she saw a picture of herself, and it was comforting to find that what was common could also be a flower. (144)

The first impulse of Maud Martha's romantic imagination is to transform the humble dandelions that she sees into 'yellow jewels', thereby lifting them out of the milieu of everyday life and projecting her naïve fantasies of beauty and wealth onto the 'patched green dress' of her family's lawn. In this sense, Brooks supplies a miniature allegory of literature's tendency to aestheticise everyday life by calling readers' attention to it, exhibiting a 'heightened sensitivity' to its details that contrasts with the 'casual inattentiveness' that 'defines the everyday experience of everyday life', according to Rita Felski.⁵⁸ However, Maud Martha also qualifies this tendency by preferring the 'everydayness' of the dandelions to their 'demure prettiness', seeing 'a picture of herself' in them because they are both 'common' and 'a flower'. As a dark-skinned girl living in working-class Bronzeville, Maud Martha is attracted to the dandelions because their combination of ordinariness and beauty seems to undermine the hierarchies of race, skin colour, gender, and class that have already begun to place limits on her life's potential. This intersection of social and political inequalities is characteristic of Brooks's interest in the everyday, and her poems frequently depict the lives and experiences of black women in Bronzeville in such a way as to bring out both what is ordinary and what is extraordinary in them.

It is important, however, to distinguish between two interwoven but conflicting aspects of the representation of everyday life in Brooks's poetry. The first, which comes to the fore with the publication of *Annie Allen* and Brooks's Pulitzer Prize in 1950, is characterised by a conception of everyday life as a shared condition that encompasses and transcends the differences that fracture human societies, including the divisions and inequalities of race. As Henri Lefebvre argues, everyday life can be thought of as a 'meeting place' or 'common ground', in which 'the sum total of relations which make the human – and every human being – a whole takes its shape and its form'.[59] Accordingly, by depicting the sheer ordinariness of black lives as they are lived in Bronzeville, Brooks's poems make them seem familiar and fundamentally 'human' to her (implicitly white) readers. Hence her characterisation of Bronzeville not as a Black Metropolis but merely as 'a place where People live'.[60] This conception of everyday life is consistent with a broadly integrationist or 'inclusionist' political vision, which 'assumes that African-Americans are basically "Americans who happen to be black"' and 'calls for the eradication of all sites of racial particularity and social isolation' – such as Bronzeville itself, a place that Brooks claimed should not exist.[61]

Running alongside this impulse in Brooks's poetry, however, is a different, deeper awareness that, as Audre Lorde observes, the 'fabric' of black women's daily lives 'is stitched with violence and with hatred'.[62] In this context, everyday life reveals itself less as a common ground of shared human experiences than through those conditions of life that are ordinary for some (black) people but extraordinary for others (white people). Consequently, when her poetry foregrounds the insidious effects of racial prejudice and colorism, or the overcrowded and unhomely domestic spaces that are one consequence of racial segregation, or the drudgery of black women's domestic labour in white people's homes, Brooks highlights the violence and hatred that is woven into the fabric of black lives rather than its putatively universal qualities. This second conception of everyday life, which is present from *A Street in Bronzeville* through to *In the Mecca*, is more closely aligned with the 'black nationalist' political vision that Brooks would consciously espouse after 1967, which regards African Americans as 'African people who happen to speak English and live in America' and 'suggests that blacks must define themselves within their own autonomous cultural context'.[63] Crucially, Brooks insists that her explicit concern with 'black life' in her later work is implicit or unconscious in much of her earlier poetry, too, affirming that she has 'been talking about blackness and black people all along'.[64] These two conceptions of everyday life, as the ground of a common humanity and as the set of conditions particular to black lives in a racist society, are co-present and intertwined in much of Brooks's work of the 1940s and 1950s. They increasingly come into conflict during the 1960s until the former is abandoned in favour of the latter.

Living Spaces

Brooks's fascination with the everyday lives of African American city-dwellers, and the throwntogetherness that is characteristic of their experiences of place, finds expression through her recurrent representations of living spaces, domestic interiors, and apartment buildings. Felski observes that 'home' might be regarded as the 'privileged symbol' of everyday life, for it 'constitutes a base, a taken-for-granted grounding, which allows us to make forays into other worlds'.[65] However, it is worth noting that the meanings of 'home' are complicated for African American women writers by issues related to race as well as gender. On the one hand, bell hooks argues that the 'homeplace' has long served black women as both a refuge from 'white racist aggression' and 'a site of resistance' to the forces of domination.[66] Home offers safety as well as a kind of grounded authenticity; it is 'the place – any place – where growth is nurtured, where there is constancy'.[67] On the other hand, Toni Morrison contends that the African American sense of 'home' is fundamentally unsettled because of the long histories of slavery and racism in the United States, which have bequeathed profound 'feelings of foreignness' to its black citizens: 'Of not being at home in one's homeland; of being exiled in the place one belongs'.[68] Where hooks conceives of the private, woman-centred space of the home as a place of renewal and self-recovery that is effectively cut off from a deeply racist society, Morrison suggests that the racial oppressions that were fundamental to Western modernity have deformed the very concepts of home and belonging. Indeed, Morrison contends that the challenge facing African American writers is that of living in the 'racial house' of American society and transforming it 'into a race-specific yet nonracist home'.[69]

In Brooks's poetry, home places are closely associated with the ordinary experiences of women and children but depicted both as refuges from an unforgiving world and as unsettled living spaces that expose their inhabitants to material and mental privations. This fundamental ambivalence is due in part to the peculiar character of the kitchenette buildings that were a key feature of working-class life in Bronzeville during the first half of the twentieth century. A typical kitchenette consisted of a one-room apartment equipped with a bed, a gas stove, and a refrigerator; the communal bathroom would be shared between six or more families living on the same floor. As Drake and Clayton explain, kitchenettes were usually created by white landlords sub-dividing large buildings in declining middle-class neighbourhoods; they were 'crowded and inconvenient' but had the advantage of being 'near the center of Bronzeville's activities'.[70] Besides their cramped dimensions and the lack of privacy, Brooks often highlights the psychological effects of frustration, boredom, and depression that afflict their occupants. In this regard, Thorrsson's claim that in Brooks's work 'environment does not create individuals' rings somewhat hollow, though she is right to note that domestic space is (also) defined by its inhabitants.[71] For instance, in *Maud Martha* Brooks's protagonist makes plans to decorate and thereby personalise the tiny kitchenette that she has recently moved to with her husband Paul, but is increasingly oppressed by the 'gray' colours, smells, and sounds that threaten to envelop her: 'There was a whole lot of grayness here' (205–6). This surfeit of 'grayness' is also connected to the kitchenette building's role as a place of throwntogetherness, for as Wright observes, such living spaces throw 'desperate and unhappy people into an unbearable closeness of association, thereby increasing latent friction, giving birth to never-ending quarrels of recrimination, accusation, and vindictiveness'.[72] Brooks's kitchenette buildings are rarely quite as turbulent as Wright describes, though she does emphasise their social frictions, and part of Maud Martha's problem is certainly the unbearable proximity of other people, their smells and love-making and 'bodily functions' (206).

The life of the mind and, by implication, the poetic imagination come into conflict with the material conditions of everyday life in Brooks's poem, 'kitchenette building', which develops a set of contrasts between a fragile but tenacious 'dream' and the ordinary cares of Bronzeville's apartment-dwellers:

> We are things of dry hours and the involuntary plan,
> Grayed in, and gray. 'Dream' makes a giddy sound, not strong
> Like 'rent', 'feeding a wife,' 'satisfying a man.' (20)

The phrase 'things of dry hours' half-echoes Eliot's 'Gerontion' – 'Thoughts of a dry brain in a dry season' – except that it is the 'hours' of the day that are 'dry' rather than the speaker's mind.[73] Moreover, the first-person plural voice of Brooks's speaker suggests a mode of collective experience and consciousness that contrasts with the solipsism of Eliot's old man, something further underlined by the fragments of quoted speech in the third line. The 'involuntary plan' that rules the 'gray' lives of this kitchenette building's occupants may allude, as Maria Balshaw argues, to the 'modernist language of city planning, rationalisation, and organisation'; though it clearly also refers to the ordinary needs of money, food, and sex that sustain daily existence and tend to drown out the 'giddy sound' of the speaker's 'dream'.[74] Nonetheless, this dream is maintained as a possibility, figuring as an 'aria' sung among 'onion fumes' and 'yesterday's garbage ripening in the hall', until the final tercet, where the speaker is distracted by the thought of 'lukewarm water' in the shared bathroom and hopes 'to get in' (20). If the speaker's dream is also a kind of song (an 'aria'), then Brooks's poem might be said to be reflecting on its own conditions of possibility within the domestic but not-quite-private living spaces of working-class Bronzeville. Moreover, while the sound made by the dream is 'not strong' and tends to get interrupted by the demands and practices of everyday life, it is nonetheless persistent as thought, image, and idea. In this sense, Brooks's poem dissents from Gaston Bachelard's view that the urban apartment building lacks the oneiric and 'poetic depth' of the true house, for: 'Everything about it is mechanical and, on every side, intimate living flees'.[75] Even in the absence of 'intimate living' and the 'cosmicity' that Bachelard regards as essential to the poet's practice of day-dreaming, Brooks shows that dreams and songs remain possibilities in the odoriferous hallways and gray rooms of the kitchenette building, and that they are worth recording.

Brooks returns repeatedly to the 'semi-public' living spaces of the kitchenette building in her later poetry.[76] For example, the final lines of 'The Anniad' (from *Annie Allen*) depict its heartbroken heroine 'Kissing in her kitchenette / The minuets of memory' (109); and 'The Explorer' (from *The Bean Eaters*) describes a man in mental crisis, seeking 'a still spot in the noise' but discovering that in his apartment building there are 'no quiet rooms' (327). For the most part, Brooks's speakers are sympathetically aligned with the kitchenette-dwellers they depict. The main exception to this rule is 'The Lovers of the Poor', in which Brooks employs cool and cutting irony to depict a Bronzeville kitchenette building from the perspective of a group of philanthropic, upper-middle-class white ladies, 'the Ladies' Betterment League' (349). These intrepid, middle-aged women leave their North Shore enclaves of Lake Forest and Glencoe to patronise 'The worthy poor' (350) with their 'loathe-love largesse' (352) but recoil in horror at the black lives and working-class living spaces they encounter:

Oh Squalor! This sick four-story hulk, this fibre
With fissures everywhere! [...]
Tin can, blocked fire escape and chitterling
And swaggering seeking youth and the puzzled wreckage
Of the middle passage, and urine and stale shames

And, again, the porridges of the underslung
And children children children. Heavens! (351–2)

Although Brooks's speaker usually maintains a measured distance from the Ladies, referring to them repeatedly in the third-person, here she voices their exclamations and rising sense of panic through a nauseous crescendo of sensory perceptions. Among these, the mingled smells of chitterling, porridge, and urine imply a strong undertow of abjection, which is occasionally given overt expression: 'Oh Squalor!'; 'Heavens!'. The building itself is perceived as 'sick', a 'hulk' riven with 'fissures' and strewn with 'wreckage', while its inhabitants are either threatening – the 'swaggering seeking youth' – or excessively numerous: 'children children children'. The racial and class character of the Ladies' aversions is readily apparent in these lines, and Brooks recalls that this is one of the poems that prompted reviewers to accuse her of 'forsaking lyricism for polemics'.[77] However, what 'The Lovers of the Poor' also depicts is the violent reaction of an elite group against the very condition of thrown-togetherness that is central to Bronzeville's social life, and to the lives of 'the underslung' – with whom Brooks strongly identifies – in particular.

As Jackson observes, Brooks's personal experience of 'living in kitchenette apartments' and 'trying to find a suitable place to settle in a segregated city' informs her preoccupation with 'the crucial issue of housing' in her poetry and fiction.[78] Nowhere is this theme given more extended and accomplished treatment than in her 800-line long poem, 'In the Mecca', an 'African American epic' that is self-consciously modernist in style and wholly set in the Mecca apartment building.[79] Occupying a whole block on 34th Street, between South State and Dearborn, the four-story Mecca building was built in 1891–2 as a luxury complex of ninety-six flats four miles south of Chicago's city centre. Although architecturally striking, it never succeeded in attracting the white middle-class professionals for whom it was designed, and by the end of the 1910s most of the Mecca's tenants were working-class African Americans drawn to the city's Black Belt from the Southern states.[80] By the 1940s, the building was chronically overcrowded, home to over 1,000 residents crammed into 176 subdivided apartments. It was ultimately demolished in 1952, after a ten-year fight led by black tenants facing eviction, in order to make way for the Illinois Institute of Technology's new campus, designed by the modernist architect Ludwig Mies van der Rohe.[81] John Lowney notes that, during the early 1950s, the Mecca building became one focus for a wider 'discourse of urban decline' that was strongly inflected by racial and class prejudices, notably in John Bartlow Martin's *Harper's* essay, 'The Strangest Place in Chicago', which supplies one of the epigraphs for Brooks's poem.[82] Importantly, though, Brooks brings Martin's white outsider's perspective on the Mecca's 'great gray hulk' (404) into constellation with the voices of three black residents of the local neighbourhood – an anonymous 'Meccan', a Blackstone Ranger (Richard 'Peanut' Washington), and a Bronzeville activist (Russell Meek) – who each contest the authority of Martin's perspective on the building and the lives of its residents. Indeed, while the poem's central plotline concerns the abduction and murder of a young girl, Pepita Smith, Brooks's poem displaces the journalistic narrative of urban and moral decline in favour of creating a fragmentary, polyvocal panorama of the building's complex human geography, a 'reconstructive report of the Mecca's interior life'.[33]

Brooks's reconstructive report is a work of memory that, in the words of Walter Benjamin, 'brings about the convergence of imagination and thought'.[84] Brooks herself never lived in the Mecca building, though she did work there for four months in the late 1930s as assistant to a 'spiritual advisor', whose fictional counterpart in her poem is the wife-beating charlatan, Prophet Williams (425–7).[85] It was not, however, until 1957 – five years after the apartment building was demolished – that she began to work seriously on a novel about the Mecca; and another decade passed before the novel metamorphosed into 'In the Mecca'.[86] This belatedness is crucial to the elegiac character of Brooks's poem, which reconstructs a day in the life of a vanished building and depicts the throwntogetherness of a diverse black community that has since been evicted and dispersed. That is, 'In the Mecca' is engaged in an act of 're-membering', which Homi Bhabha describes as 'a putting together of the dismembered past to make sense of the trauma of the present'.[87] Crucially, it is the dismembered past of a Bronzeville that has all but ceased to exist that Brooks's poem seeks to recover imaginatively. As Olson observes, by the time that *In the Mecca* was published in 1968 much of Bronzeville's material fabric had been 'torn down' by successive waves of 'urban redevelopment'. Consequently, her long poem elaborates a central paradox: 'that place is extremely important even if place no longer exists'.[88] The increasingly desperate search for Pepita Smith in the Mecca's human labyrinth gives Brooks's poem its central narrative thread, and her murder underlines the dangers that women and children often faced in kitchenette buildings. However, Pepita's death is also implicitly linked with the decline of the whole building and the death of Bronzeville itself. This parallel is given cryptic expression in the poem's climax, where the would-be poet Alfred curses the Mecca but also intuits some new and vital force calling from within it, 'an essential sanity, black and electric' that promises 'a reportage and redemption':

'A material collapse / that is Construction' (433). This is a distinctively modernist vision of creative destruction, where the material collapse of the building is the necessary condition for some new social order to emerge. At the same time, this work of 'Construction' is the very poem we read, which, through acts of memory and imagination, seeks to redeem the material and moral collapse that it reports.

Focusing initially on the figure of Mrs Sallie Smith, a 'low-brown butterball' (407) who works as a maid and is a single mother to nine children, Brooks emphasises her conflicted feelings towards her home place. Weary after a day's toil in the grander home of a white family, Mrs Sallie 'hies to marvellous rest' but is already oppressed by her surroundings as she 'ascends the sick and influential stair' (407) and despairs at the state of her 'sick kitchen' (410). Her children are undernourished – 'skin wiped over bones' (414) – and resentful of more privileged children in the 'sewn suburbs' (412). Yet, while she carefully renders their shared conditions of hunger, poverty, and subordination, Brooks is scrupulous to individualise each child, giving expression to their experiences and personalities: Melodie Mary's sympathy for roaches and rats; Briggs's longing to join a street gang; Thomas Earl's obsession with tales of Johnny Appleseed. Moreover, as the poem develops, so its social vision becomes progressively broader, expanding from Mrs Sallie and her family to their neighbours and then to the whole apartment building with its thousand residents. Knocking on doors in search of their missing sister, the Smith children unlock the stories and memories of the building's eccentric inhabitants, whose fragmentary narratives confront the reader with a kaleidoscopic panorama of the Mecca's social life – its dense 'mosaic of daily affairs'.[89] As Lowney observes, Brooks's narrative technique is conspicuously 'dialogic', mixing different registers, styles, and forms, combining 'the synoptic, lofty vision of the epic poet with the more provisional, vernacular voice of the oral storyteller'.[90] Crucially, this digressive, polyvocal narrative form allows Brooks to incorporate into her reconstructive report memories drawn from the annals of the African American past, such as Great Gram's recollections of her girlhood as a slave (417) or Way-out Morgan's searing accounts of 'his Sister / mob-raped in Mississippi' (430). In this way, Brooks's poem is at once grounded in a particular time and place – the Mecca building in Bronzeville around 1950 – and serves as a kind of meeting place for stories and memories about other places and times that are significant to the collective experience of African Americans but often absent from the official record of history.

In her notes for 'In the Mecca', Brooks remarks that: 'To touch every note in the life of this block-long block-wide building would be to capsulize the gist of black humanity in general'.[91] That is, she conceives of the Mecca as a microcosm not just of black Chicago but of the wider collective of black humanity with which she has lately begun to identify explicitly. In a striking anachronism, Brooks has her friend and fellow poet, Don Lee (Haki Madhubuti), speak in the poem of 'a new nation / under nothing' rather than the 'various America' (423) of integrationist utopias. In this sense, 'In the Mecca' is certainly a 'transitional poem', one charged with Brooks's new enthusiasms for black nationalist and Afrocentric cultural politics but still deeply informed by the modernist 'mastery of form' that distinguished her earlier work.[92] Composed for the most part in 'long-swinging free verse' but also incorporating elements of more traditional forms – blank verse, couplets, the sonnet, the ballad – 'In the Mecca' consists of fifty-eight irregular stanzas, which range from one to forty-two lines in length.[93] Like many other late modernist long poems, Brooks's text is a heterogeneous assemblage of different poetic forms and techniques, some of which are in tension or conflict with each other. However, this formal variety is congruent with the human diversity of the black community that the poem seeks to represent and render articulate. Moreover, Daniela Kukrechtová argues that there is a correspondence between the form of 'In the Mecca' and the interior spaces of the Mecca building itself, for its 'disconnected free-verse stanzas' resemble 'long dark corridors punctuated by numerous doors'.[94] Indeed, in the second half of the poem, stanza breaks frequently coincide with the shift to a new apartment doorway, where another Mecca resident will respond to Pepita's disappearance with concern, indifference, or (more often) their own self-absorbed narratives. What this congruence between poetic form and spatial design also illustrates is the extent to which private interiors and public spaces are thoroughly imbricated in the semi-public world of the Mecca.

The Streets of Bronzeville

A person walking down the street, remarks Henri Lefebvre, 'is immersed in the multiplicity of noises, murmurs, rhythms' that make up everyday life in the city, but pays little attention to them. However, for the person watching and listening at her window, 'the noises distinguish themselves, the flows separate out, rhythms respond to one another'.[95] That is, the urban rhythms of street life become comprehensible and available to reflection only from without, and ideally from an interior space that opens onto the public realm beyond. Brooks makes a strikingly similar point in an interview while describing her relationship as a writer with the streets of Bronzeville:

> In my twenties when I wrote a good deal of my better-known poetry I lived on 63rd Street – at 623 East 63rd Street – and there was a good deal of life in the raw all about me. [. . .] I wrote about what I saw and heard in the street. I lived in a small second-floor apartment at the corner, and I could look first on one side and then on the other. There was my material.[96]

Notice that Brooks regards the 'raw' life of the street as essential 'material' for her poetry and emphasises her own proximity to the streets, not only through the finicky precision with which she gives her former address but also when she claims that her poetry records 'what [she] saw and heard in the street'. However, just as the 'raw' life of Bronzeville's streets must be cooked or styled into art, Brooks observes that life from behind the windowpanes of her second-floor corner apartment rather than from the sidewalk itself. For Brooks, the act of writing is at once intimately bound up with the public space of the street and curiously alienated or distanced from it.

I have argued above that Brooks's poetry is frequently drawn to the semi-public living spaces of the kitchenette apartment and the apartment building, the characteristic home places of most of Bronzeville's African American residents. Nonetheless, it is also true that the city street features as a crucial element in the literary geography of Brooks's poetry from her first collection, the aptly titled *A Street in Bronzeville*. Describing the title sequence of that volume, Brooks explains: 'My idea was to take my own street and write about a person or incident associated with each of the houses on the block'.[97] Moreover, her abiding interest in depicting the everyday lives of black people makes the city street, as a 'place of passage, of interaction, of movement and communication', an important, if not essential representational space.[98] Indeed, one of the things that Brooks admires in Langston Hughes's poetry is his ability to convey in poetry the street's 'multiple heart, its tastes, smells, alarms, formulas, flowers, garbage and convulsions'.[99] This awareness of the multiplicity and miscellaneity of the street as a social space is certainly a feature of Brooks's poetry, though it is rarely experienced directly by her female characters. Superficially at least, her work echoes the normative gendering of public and private spaces that Patricia Hill Collins describes: 'Male space included the streets, barber shops, and pool halls; female arenas consisted of households and churches'.[100] Think, for instance, of the late De Witt Williams haunting the 'Warwick and Savoy' dance halls, 'Where he picked his women, where / He drank his liquid joy' (39); or the seven young men playing pool at The Golden

Shovel in 'We Real Cool' (331). These men are at home and at ease in the streets and public spaces of Bronzeville in ways that Brooks's female characters rarely are. Even Mame, 'Queen of the Blues', complains of the way she is sexualised and disrespected by men in the Midnight Club, where she performs: 'Men don't tip their / Hats to me. / They pinch my arms / And they slap my thighs' (58–9).

As Mame's complaint illustrates, Brooks's female characters are often acutely conscious of the ways in which places are gendered, designated as female or male spaces, and of their exclusion from or objectification within the latter. This is true even for the speaker of 'a song in the front yard', a young girl whose censorious mother warns her against playing with 'the charity children' 'down the alley', but who rebels against the moral and spatial limitations imposed upon her life:

> And I'd like to be a bad woman, too,
> And wear the brave stockings of night-black lace
> And strut down the streets with paint on my face. (28)

Brooks maintains a delicate balance in these lines between childish naivety and the deeper stirrings of transgressive desire, which entails crossing the police bounds set by both class hierarchies and conventional gender roles. Although the girl's romantic image of herself as a 'bad woman' strutting down in the public streets of the city is lightly ironised, it nonetheless serves as one possible model of freedom from the constraints she feels when confined to her family's over-cultivated front yard. Tellingly, her hankering for wildness – the back yard, 'Where it's rough and untended and hungry weed grows' (28) – is transposed in the final stanza to the male space of the street, where women are inevitably sexualised if not stigmatised.

Brooks's most thorough depiction of the street as a place of passage, encounter, and interaction is 'The Sundays of Satin-Legs Smith', which emphasises the spatial (and sexual) freedoms that men enjoy in the streets of Bronzeville while also exploring the performative character of masculine identity. Adapting the mock-heroic registers of Pope and Eliot to the vernacular ballad, this poem builds an ironic portrait of a zoot suit-wearing African American man who prefers bar-room blues to Grieg or Saint-Saëns and seeks his pleasures in the movie theatres, diners, and 'sore avenues' (45) of the city. Brooks underlines the element of 'performance' (42) in Satin-Legs Smith's self-presentation from the outset, first through his studied rituals of washing and dressing, then by informing readers of his Southern origins, 'His heritage of cabbage and pigtails, / Old intimacy with alleys, garbage pails' (43). Smith is, like most inhabitants of Bronzeville, a migrant rather than a Chicago native and his air of urban sophistication is hard-won, a cultivated style that dissembles both the 'shabby days' (42) of his weekday life and the rural poverty of his childhood. As Schlabach notes, the heart of Brooks's poem depicts Smith's performance of 'the Sunday stroll', walking the sidewalks of 47th and State in order 'to socialize, to fraternize, to strut his stuff'[101]. However, Smith's flamboyant pedestrianism is also curiously self-absorbed, for he barely registers the sounds and sights that Brooks's more keenly observant narrator relays to the reader:

> Sounds about him smear,
> Become a unit. He hears and does not hear
> The alarm clock meddling in somebody's sleep;
> Children's governed Sunday happiness;
> The dry tone of a plane; a woman's oath;
> Consumption's spiritless expectoration (45)

The sounds of illness and ill-temper, modern transportation and time-keeping gadgets mingle in these lines with the 'governed' noise of children playing, a range of overlapping rhythms and timbres that are neatly distinguished from one another by Brooks's scrupulous punctuation but 'smear' together in the half-hearing ears of the ambulant protagonist. In this way, the reader is simultaneously given access to Smith's street-level perceptions and granted a measure of enabling distance from them, as though viewing the street from an apartment window.

Although he makes himself conspicuous on the streets of Bronzeville and takes a different girl out every weekend, Satin-Legs Smith is a somewhat solitary figure, a version of the lonely modern individual in the crowd. This sense of the street as a milieu of urban alienation is replaced in Brooks's later work by an awareness of its potential as a site of collective identifications and cultural politics. In her trio of poems on the Blackstone Rangers gang, for instance, she depicts 'Thirty at the corner / Black, raw, and ready' (446), a new generation impatient with the icons of their elders – 'Belafonte, King, / Black Jesus, Stokely, Malcolm X' – and mutely staking their claim to a territory of their own: 'Their country is a Nation on no map' (447). The black nationalist overtones of these poems are given further emphasis in 'The Wall', a poem that commemorates a community arts mural – the Wall of Respect – which was painted on the side of a former slum building on 43rd and Langley in 1967.[102] Bearing the images of black writers, intellectuals, musicians, and politicians as well as the words of Amiri Baraka's poem, 'S.O.S.', the Wall of Respect was at once a collective work by local amateur artists and an emblem of black solidarity for a community in transition. Moreover, as Margo Natalie Crawford explains, its creation entailed a profoundly symbolic 'revision of the old script of African American dispossession': 'The "slum" building that becomes the site of the mural is simply a sign of the larger dispossession that African Americans have suffered'.[103] This act of revision and appropriation has particular resonance with Brooks's work as a poet, given her preoccupation with the living spaces of Bronzeville's kitchenettes and apartment buildings in her earlier writing.

'The Wall' is the second of 'Two Dedications' written for public artworks that opened in Chicago in 1967. In the first, 'The Chicago Picasso', Brooks's narrator attempts to mediate between the modernist internationalism of Pablo Picasso's monumental abstract sculpture – which the artist gifted to the people of the city – and the interests of ordinary, African American citizens.[104] 'Art hurts,' she writes: 'Art urges voyages— / and it is easier to stay at home' (442). By contrast, in 'The Wall', Brooks depicts herself as a full participant in a much more inclusive cultural event, one located in the scruffier streets of Bronzeville – 'South of success and east of gloss and glass' (444) – rather than among the grand plazas and skyscrapers of the city centre. Beginning with ceremonial African drums – 'A drumdrumdrum. / Humbly we come' (444) – the poem depicts its multi-racial audience metonymically via their earrings, 'flowercloth' dresses, and raised fists ("Black Power!"), emphasising both a celebratory sense of coming-together and of politicised resistance to racism and injustice:

On Forty-third and Langley
black furnaces resent ancient
legislatures
of ploy and scruple and practical gelatin. (445)

Anger is an important component of the 'ferment-festival' (445) that 'The Wall' describes, and Brooks gives it relatively straightforward expression through the metaphor of 'black furnaces' burning on the streets of Bronzeville. More cryptic, however, is the reference to 'practical gelatin', an estranging allusion to recent legislation, such as the 1964 Civil Rights Act, which sought to gel together conflicting groups within the American body politic but exacerbated violence against blacks across the South, illustrating the limitations of reform.[105] Brooks describes the mural itself via a series of highly suggestive but opaque metaphors as 'this Appointment / this still Wing / this Scald this Flute this heavy Light this Hinge' (445). Suggesting temporal novelty and the possibilities of change ('Appointment', 'Hinge'), Brooks also mobilises figures for illumination ('Light') and flight ('Wing') as well as musical ('Flute') and literary metaphors ('Scald' refers to the ancient poet as well as a burn).

The excess of signification in these lines contrasts sharply with the lilting vernacular chants that Brooks employs elsewhere in the poem – 'All / worship the Wall' (445) – and demonstrates that even in her most Black Arts-influenced poems, she retains a fascination for the polysemy and figurative complexity of modernist style.

The Warpland

Brooks repeatedly described her encounter with the Black Arts Movement at Fisk University in April 1967 as revelatory and transformative, remarking that: 'Until 1967 my own blackness did not confront me with a shrill spelling of itself.'[106] Besides giving her a new vocabulary for self-expression and leading her to embrace a more radical mode of Afrocentric black nationalism, this event caused Brooks to re-think some of the aesthetic foundations of her poetry. In particular, she sought to fashion a 'newish voice' that would have wide popular appeal, reaching out and 'calling' to ordinary 'black people in taverns, black people in alleys, black people in gutters, schools, offices, factories, prisons, the consulate'.[107] However, as Evie Shockley notes, a different kind of 'black aesthetics' was already implicit in Brooks's work from the 1940s, derived largely from the New Negro Renaissance.[108] It would also be misleading to suggest that Brooks abandons her late modernist poetics of place altogether in the late 1960s. For one thing, she affirms her determination to produce 'an extending adaptation of today's G.B. voice' rather than an 'imitation' of the work of the younger poets she admired.[109] Moreover, several astute critics of Brooks's work have noted the extent of the formal and stylistic continuities between her poems before and after 1967.[110] It might be argued that the most consequential change that Brooks made in the late 1960s was her decision to publish her work exclusively with small black presses, such as Broadside Press and Third World Press, and to self-publish from 1980.[111]

It is also worth noting that Brooks's political radicalisation had begun around a decade before her appearance at Fisk, during the Civil Rights struggles of the late 1950s, and that this was manifest in her poetry from the early 1960s. Brooks told Haki Madhubuti that her 'integration stage' came to an end in 1957, the year of the desegregation conflict in Little Rock, Arkansas and not long after the Montgomery bus boycott of 1956.[112] Brooks wrote poems about both of these events – 'The Chicago *Defender* Sends a Man to Little Rock' and 'In Montgomery', respectively – as well as two poems on the lynching of 14-year-old Emmett

Till in Money, Mississippi in 1955, 'A Bronzeville Mother Loiters in Mississippi' and 'The Last Quatrain of the Ballad of Emmett Till'.[113] The Little Rock and Emmett Till poems appeared in *The Bean Eaters*, which, Brooks noted, was criticised by reviewers for being 'too social' and the book seemed, in hindsight, to mark 'a turning point, "politically"' in her career as a writer.[114] That is, Brooks's political awakening had already begun many years prior to the 1967 Fisk conference and the publication of *In the Mecca* in 1968. Indeed, her *Selected Poems*, which appeared in 1963 – the pivotal year in what Martin Luther King called 'the Negro Revolution' – featured a new poem, 'Riders to the Blood-red Wrath', which was inspired by the Freedom Rides and sit-in protests in Southern cities during the early 1960s.[115]

Although none of these Civil Rights poems feature the distinctive language and separatist politics of black nationalism that Brooks would adopt later in the decade, they are nonetheless powerful aesthetic expressions of the 'rage' against injustice that is an important component of Brooks's poetry at least since 'Negro Hero', a poem dating from the mid-1940s.[116] What is also striking about these poems, however, is the way in which they make connections between Bronzeville and the cities and towns of the South that were the epicentres of protest and racist violence during the struggle for Civil Rights. The *Chicago Defender* newspaper had its premises in the heart of Bronzeville, on South Parkway, and often reported on racist violence in the South for its urban, African American readership – hence its reporter's assignment in Little Rock; while Emmett Till was born and raised in Chicago's South Side but was visiting relatives in the Mississippi Delta when he was murdered.[117] These Northern origins are recalled somewhat obliquely in 'The Last Quatrain', where Brooks depicts Mamie Till grieving for her 'killed boy' in a 'red room' that looks out on a desolate Midwestern landscape: 'Chaos in windy grays / through a red prairie' (340). Besides the obvious use of pathetic fallacy in these lines, their image of a 'red prairie' swirling with chaotic winds is perhaps the first instance of a major shift in the geographical imagination animating Brooks's later poetry, her transition from predominantly realist descriptions of the people and material environments of Bronzeville to more abstract and symbolic evocations of African American spatial histories. Another important instance of this shift can be found in 'Riders to the Blood-red Wrath', where the speaker 'remembers' six centuries of African American history, from pre-colonial Africa through the Middle Passage and American Slavery to the present moment of struggle, which is figured in terms of headlong journey through time and space: 'And I ride ride I ride on to the end— / Where glowers my continuing Calvary' (392).

While the Hill of Calvary is an apt image for a Civil Rights poem, given the movement's strongly 'religious character', this Christian iconography is replaced in Brooks's subsequent work by the secular figure of the 'Warpland', a vernacular recasting of Eliot's Waste Land that foregrounds the 'warped' character of a stubbornly racist society but also suggests the 'war plan' that was being implemented contemporaneously in Vietnam.[118] As Jeni Rinner observes, with the publication of *In the Mecca* in 1968, Brooks's characteristically 'geographical' preoccupation with 'people bound together in a place' is progressively displaced by a new interest in the 'conceptual' space of 'people called to a black nationalist identity'.[119] Consequently, from the late 1960s Brooks's poetry tends to evoke Bronzeville through the prism of cultural memory or shifts its attention from the streets and buildings of black Chicago to the allegorical and apocalyptic terrain of the 'Warpland', her figure for the United States during the post-Civil Rights era, within which it becomes possible to discern the shape of a new black 'commonwealth' (454). Thereafter, during the 1970s and 1980s, Brooks's work expands its geographical and historical focus still further to take in the wider African diaspora and the contemporary struggle against Apartheid in South Africa, informed by her self-identification as 'an essential African' rather than an American 'Negro'.[120]

Between the passage of the Civil Rights Act in 1964 and the assassination of Martin Luther King in 1968, 'massive black rebellions swept across almost every major U.S. city in the Northeast, Middle West and California', leading to 250 deaths, 60,000 arrests, and billions of dollars of damage.[121] The NAACP leader, Medgar Evers, was murdered in 1963 and Malcolm X was shot dead in 1965; Brooks included elegies for both men in *In the Mecca*. These events, marking the end of the reformist phase of the Civil Rights movement and the emergence of new forms of black rebellion, are essential contexts for understanding Brooks's three 'Sermons' on the Warpland, which she described modestly as 'little addresses to black people'.[122] In 'The Sermon on the Warpland' and 'The Second Sermon on the Warpland' (both published in *In the Mecca*), Brooks's speaker marries the rolling cadences of the Old Testament to the oratorical energy of African American evangelism, exhorting her audience/readers to build a new 'Church' with 'love like black, our black' (451, 452); to 'Live and go out' (455), breaking the bounds of racial and social limitations on the scope of their lives. Accordingly, Rinner argues that these Warpland poems issue 'a call to survive together in this place that is no place'.[123] In both poems, the social and political crisis of contemporary American society is figured in Shakespearean terms as a mighty storm that creates as it destroys, the 'brash and terrible weather'

(451) that must be met and the 'whirlwind' that carries within it the seeds of 'our commonwealth' (454). Indeed, the revolutionary tenor of 'The Second Sermon' inheres less in its self-conscious adoption of the rhetoric of blackness than its affirmation of the generative potential of the violence it describes: 'Conduct your blooming in the noise and whip of the whirlwind' (456). The poem also celebrates human resilience during Bronzeville's terminal decline, describing 'the cold places' of Chicago's South Side ravaged by 'pushmen and jeopardy, theft' (455) before shifting the reader's attention to the undaunted figure of Big Bessie, who stands alone in a patch of waste ground: 'In the wild weed / she is a citizen, / and is a moment of highest quality; admirable' (456). Big Bessie, who appears in *The Bean Eaters* as 'Bessie of Bronzeville' (373), is here presented at once as the last survivor of a ruined city neighbourhood and as a true citizen of the black commonwealth of the future.

By comparison with its precursors, 'The Third Sermon on the Warpland' (which appeared in *Riot*) is more fragmentary and polyvocal, weaving together the voices of Chicago youths and gang members with those of a Black Philosopher and Brooks's roving narrator, who reports on the riots that followed King's assassination in 1968. Debo argues that the 'complex structure' of the poem, with its montage of disparate images and abrupt shifts of tone and perspective, 'mirrors the chaotic form of a riot'.[12] However, the Warpland that is described in 'The Third Sermon' is more geographically specific than the allegorical weather-worlds of the earlier poems and is clearly entangled with the actual cityscape of Chicago. Besides allusions to the *Chicago Sun-Times* newspaper, the theatre director Val Gray Ward, and the Disciples and Blackstone Rangers gangs, the poem depicts the burning of a restaurant on West Madison Street in the downtown area – 'Crazy flowers / cry up across the sky' (473) – and young men looting records from stores nearby. Brooks explicitly mocks white liberal conceptions of 'a clean riot' (474) and focuses instead upon the restless energy of the groups of young men and women who affirm their presence in the city streets, whether advancing or retreating:

> The young men run.
> The children in ritual chatter
> scatter upon
> their Own and old geography.
>
> The Law comes sirening across the town. (475)

Although the police sirens of the Law seek to reimpose order upon riot-wracked streets, these lines also imply that the 'old geography' of the city is giving way to new trajectories and conjunctures, other ways of responding to the problem of our living together. Scattering and reforming in the streets of downtown Chicago, Brooks's 'little rioters' (474) evade the surveillance powers of the city authorities and open up 'a space for maneuvers of unequal forces'.[125] Interestingly, where Brooks's previous 'Sermons' figured the modernist concept of creative destruction in terms of a storm or whirlwind, here she associates the subversive movements and actions of the Chicago rioters with the metaphor of the phoenix, which – like the city itself – is consumed by flames only to be reborn anew. As Sullivan observes, 'this mythic framework has an African provenance' that is apposite given the poem's rejection both of white liberal moralising and the structures of authority through which the city is governed.[126] It also points towards the diasporic, Afrocentric direction that Brooks's poetry would take in the 1970s and 1980s, while the poem retains something of the geographical specificity that characterises her earlier Bronzeville period.

Brooks's poetic figurations of the Warpland radicalise the black aesthetic of her earlier Civil Rights poems and mark a definite shift from documentary realism towards a more allegorical and, at times, apocalyptic register. In several important ways, they also grow out of her personal and political engagements with Bronzeville, which is the focus for her late modernist poetics of place. Crucially, Brooks depicts Chicago's black metropolis as a place-in-process rather than simply a place apart, which comes into being through a collective act of self-definition on the part of its African American citizens and is reconfigured by the socio-spatial forces of migration, racial segregation, and urban redevelopment. From her first collection in 1945, she reveals a fascination with the everyday lives of black people, writing as a member of the community she observes and records, while stressing both the common humanity of African Americans and the violence that is woven into their daily existence. Brooks is recurrently concerned with the semi-public spaces of apartment buildings, kitchenettes, and shared living spaces, developing a polyphonic portrait of life in a long-demolished block of flats that is also a fragmentary history of African American experiences of dispossession in her long poem, 'In the Mecca'. At the same time, her poems are keenly attuned to the politics of race and gender as they are played out in the performative spaces of Bronzeville's streets, bars, and pool halls.

Conclusion: After Late Modernism

One of the core arguments of this book is that late modernism in Anglophone poetry is best understood not as a phase of decline or obsolescence, nor of assimilation to mainstream cultural values, but as the stubborn living on of modernist aesthetic energies in the post-war period and well into the second half of the twentieth century. Nonetheless, as Peter Howarth remarks, the term 'late modernism' seems to imply a condition of 'belatedness – as if living and breathing poets were just survivals from another age, rather than ahead of their time'.[1] As the foregoing chapters make clear, my view of such 'survivals' in the work of Gwendolyn Brooks, Basil Bunting, W. S. Graham, David Jones, Lorine Niedecker, and Charles Olson is that they are more often heroic than pathetic, and always interesting. In this conclusion I want to consider the significance of such survivals, particularly the role that late modernist poets play as mediating figures, key influences for a range of younger poets from Britain, the United States, and the Caribbean for whom, in Marjorie Perloff's words, the 'modernist challenge [. . .] remains open'.[2] In doing so, I also hazard some answers to the question of what comes after late modernism.

Lines of influence from the first generation of modernist writers run through the work of late modernist poets in a variety of ways. The examples of Ezra Pound and William Carlos Williams are especially important for Bunting and Olson, who each met and corresponded with the elder poets for many years. For Niedecker, aspects of Pound's and Williams's poetics were crucial for the development of her own style, though their influence was largely indirect, mediated by her friend Louis Zukofsky. More important for the poetry of Jones and Graham were the linguistic and formal experiments of T. S. Eliot and James Joyce, particularly *The Waste Land* and *Finnegans Wake*. Brooks also acknowledged the powerful influence of Eliot on her own work, though her formative encounters with modernist poetics came via the poets of the Harlem Renaissance, especially Langston Hughes. There are some important differences between modernist and late modernist poets, however, not least in terms of their political alignments. As Anthony Mellors observes, those late modernist poets who began their careers in the Depression years, lived through the aftermath of the Second World War, and reached aesthetic maturity during the counter-cultural ferment of the 1960s, typically eschew 'the reactionary politics of high modernists such as Yeats, Eliot, and Pound'.[3] A partial exception ought to be made for Jones, who was ambivalently attracted to fascism in the late 1930s; but both Bunting and Olson broke with Pound over his racism and antisemitism, while Brooks, Graham, and Niedecker each occupied varying positions on the political left. Furthermore, I have sought to show that the work of these late modernists is distinctive for their multi-layered poetics of place, which often entail immersion in the histories and geographies of particular localities or regions as well as tracking the movements of humans and non-humans between places. While the city retains an important place in several of these texts, the geographical imaginations that are most characteristic of late modernist poetry are non-metropolitan, more often drawn to margins and peripheries than to cultural and political centres.

If late modernism is best understood as a mode of persistence and survival, carrying over modernism's aesthetic of formal experiment into the changed conditions of the post-war period, then late modernist poets played an important role as influences and exemplars for a wide range of younger poets who began to publish in the 1950s and 1960s. In North America, these included the Black Mountain poets (Robert Creeley, Edward Dorn, Denise Levertov), the poets of the San Francisco Renaissance (Robin Blaser, Robert Duncan, Jack Spicer), and the New York poets (John Ashbery, Barbara Guest, Frank O'Hara). The Beat poets (Allen Ginsberg, Lawrence Ferlinghetti, Diane di Prima) and Black Arts poets (Amiri Baraka, Nikki Giovanni, Haki Madhubuti, Sonia Sanchez) were less obviously modernist in style, though they were 'clearly part of the politicised avant-garde legacy in the United States'.[4] Moreover, Perloff traces an avant-garde lineage from early modernism through the Objectivists, Black Mountaineers, and New Yorkers to the work of the Language poets (Charles Bernstein, Lyn Hejinian, Susan Howe, Steve McCaffery) in the 1970s and 1980s.[5] These developments in post-war American poetry were, in turn, a key influence on the British Poetry Revival of the 1960s and 1970s, a phenomenon that brought together poets as various as Allen Fisher, Lee Harwood, Barry MacSweeney, Wendy Mulford, J. H. Prynne, and Denise Riley.[6] The Revival can be understood as a deliberate 'counter-movement', opposing a range of modernist and avant-gardist styles to the anti-modernist orthodoxy epitomised by Philip Larkin and the Movement poets.[7] Its lively networks of little magazines and ethos of self-publication were informed by a conception of poems as 'anti-commodities', circulating outside of the economic circuits of the capitalist marketplace. Nonetheless, British small presses such as Fulcrum and Goliard published key texts by late modernists, including Bunting, Jones, Niedecker, and Olson, as well as high-quality books and pamphlets by younger poets on both sides of the Atlantic.[8]

Drew Milne argues cogently that such manifestations of post-war modernism in Britain are best understood as instances of 'neo-modernism', observing that: 'Where modernists might once have sought to break with preceding traditions, above all with Romanticism, postwar continuations of modernism involve renewals'.[9] Neo-modernist poets are those who seek to renew, reconfigure, or recycle the techniques and ethos of earlier generations of modernist writers in a period characterised both by anti-modernist reaction and the ascendancy of postmodernist paradigms. However, where Milne subsumes the work of late modernist poets, such as Bunting, Jones, and Hugh MacDiarmid, under the category of neo-modernism I want to distinguish between the two. For, if the late modernist poets upon whose work I have focused in this book were senior figures by the 1960s, when many of them published their major works – Olson's *The Maximus Poems*, Bunting's *Briggflatts*, Niedecker's *North Central*, Brooks's *In the Mecca* – then a younger generation of neo-modernists, most of whom were born in the 1920s or 1930s, were just beginning their careers in that decade. The distinction is intended to be heuristic rather than dogmatic, but it has the merit of differentiating between those late modernist poets whose continuation of modernism entails straddling the decisive historical break of the Second World War and those neo-modernists whose renewal of modernist styles begins in the altered conditions of the Cold War. Given Milne's view of modernism as 'an experimental orientation developed through cosmopolitan networks', it seems reasonable to extend the reach of 'neo-modernism' beyond the bounds of Britain to include post-war modernist poetics in North America and the Caribbean.[10] In addition, as Redell Olsen remarks, the terms 'neo-modernist' and 'late modernist' both imply a self-conscious differentiation on the part of various post-war poets from 'postmodernism', understood as 'the latest dominant cultural whim of the fashion market in ideas'.[11]

The influence of late modernists on neo-modernist poets is clear enough in several cases. As the major theorist and exponent of projective poetics, Olson not only shaped the work of younger Black Mountain poets, such as Creeley and Dorn, but also served as antagonist-exemplar for several San Francisco and Beat poets, particularly Duncan, who briefly worked at Black Mountain College.[12] Furthermore, Olson was an enabling figure for several British neo-modernists, including Allen Fisher, Prynne, and Iain Sinclair. In particular, these poets sought to adapt Olson's treatment of the space of the page as a 'compositional open field' and his dense collages of documentary sources concerning geography and history.[13] Bunting was a key late modernist figure for younger British poets, including Roy Fisher, Maggie O'Sullivan, Tom Pickard, and MacSweeney; though he also impressed Americans such as Jonathan Williams and Dorn, who called *Briggflatts* 'the great love poem of the twentieth century'.[14] O'Sullivan names Niedecker alongside Gertrude Stein, Mina Loy, and H. D. as 'pioneering poets' for younger generations of linguistically innovative women writers in Britain and North America.[15] Similarly, Graham and Jones feature (along with David Gascoyne, J. F. Hendry, and Nicholas Moore) in Sinclair's controversial anthology, *Conductors of Chaos* (1996) as 'significant figures from previous generations' selected and introduced by their neo-modernist heirs.[16] Besides serving as a mentor for several poets associated with the Black Arts Movement (including Madhubuti and Sanchez), Brooks is a key influence on younger African American neo-modernists such as Harryette Mullen.[17] Particularly during the 1960s and 1970s, late modernists and neo-modernist poets often published their work with the same small presses and little magazines, or appeared together at readings, conferences, and other performance venues. For instance, Olson headlined the Berkeley Poetry Conference in 1965, reading alongside Creeley, Dorn, Duncan, and Ginsberg; while Bunting was elected President of the Poetry Society in 1971 during its brief neo-modernist take-over.[18]

Late modernist poets played a crucial role in stimulating neo-modernist poets' interests in place, space, and landscape. At the same time, of course, these poets are responding to larger socio-spatial forces, particularly the 'intense phase of space-time compression' that characterises the post-war period, as the combined effects of economic globalisation, decolonisation and neo-imperialism, new transport and communications technologies, and an accelerating climate crisis continue to reshape conceptions and experiences of place.[19] Given these conditions, argues Eric Falci, British and Irish poets are apt to depict experiences of disorientation and displacement, emphasising the dynamic qualities of 'dissolving landscapes, places that open underfoot into murky indeterminacies, and spaces made and unmade by modernity's alterations, accidents, and disasters'.[20] A good example is Wendy Mulford's *The East Anglia*

Sequence (1998), which excavates the history, economy, and social life of the flood-prone coastlines of Eastern England, 'where settlement and sea contend', through an assemblage of lyric verse, discursive prose, and borrowings from a range of documentary sources.[21] Mulford's text is an instance of what Harriet Tarlo calls contemporary radical landscape poetry, a sub-genre that takes inspiration from late modernists such as Bunting, Niedecker, and Olson, fascinated by place but often conceiving of it as 'inassimilable to human understanding'.[22] Tarlo's account of neo-modernist poets' engagements with place and landscape – including work by Elisabeth Bletsoe, Thomas A. Clark, Frances Presley, and Peter Riley, as well as Mulford – tends to privilege rural or natural landscapes over urban or industrial locations, places over non-places. Another kind of urban or ex-urban radical landscape poetry can be found in long poems such as Allen Fisher's multi-volume project *Place* (1971–85) or Roy Fisher's *City* (1961) and *A Furnace* (1986). Roy Fisher's poetry is particularly striking for the way it depicts the inter-digitations of city and country, upland pastures and post-industrial edgelands in texts that attend scrupulously to the creative role of consciousness and perception in experiences of place.[23]

Post-war American poets also display a range of interests in the shifting character of spaces and places that are substantially inherited from their late modernist forebears. Lytle Shaw identifies a significant 'turn to place, and later site' in the work of poets such as Baraka and Creeley, Gary Snyder and Joanne Kyger, which was catalysed by the examples of Olson and William Carlos Williams. Developing a mode of 'site-specific poetics' that is attentive to the fluidity and entanglements of particular places, these American neo-modernists 'became experimental historiographers and ethnographers of place'.[24] Shaw's characterisation might also be extended to the case of Susan Howe, whose associative, archival poets frequently interrogates the repressed or forgotten histories of colonial New England. In 'Thorow', from *Singularities* (1990), Howe focuses her attention on Lake George in upstate New York, the site of battles between the English, French, and local Algonquin tribes in the mid-eighteenth century, in a disjunctive meditation on history and geography, violence and language. 'Pathfinding believers in God and grammar spelled the lake into *place*,' writes Howe, underlining both the creative power of names and the complicity between acts of language and colonial conquest.[25] In this regard, Howe's text continues and deepens the focus upon 'the processes of production of places' that Ian Davidson regards as characteristic of American poetry from the 1950s to the 1970s, giving Frank O'Hara, Olson, and Dorn as prime examples.[26] For instance, Dorn's early poetry characteristically examines the cultural landscapes of the American West, exposing the layers of human settlement and use that undermine its mythic incarnations as wilderness or frontier. In 'Idaho Out', from his collection *Geography* (1965), Dorn describes crossing the mountains from Idaho to Montana: 'there seems at the border a change / but it is only because man has / built a tavern there'.[27] The built structure of the tavern not only demarcates the (artificial) border between two states but also effects a more profound 'change' in the space it occupies and produces, because of the wider structures of social and economic exchange in which it is implicated. In Dorn's poetry, any engagement with place or landscape is necessarily mediated by the commercial interests and cultural logic of American capitalism, the global reach of which is memorably crystallised in the titular image of a subsequent collection, *The North Atlantic Turbine* (1967).

One response on the part of post-war poets to the time-space compression that results from economic globalisation is to seek what Jim Cocola calls 'a condition of ubeity – an understanding of whereness connected at once to a particular place and a planetary location'. Such a 'translocal' poetics is particularly evident in the work of several Anglophone Caribbean poets, including Kamau Brathwaite, Lorna Goodison, M. NourbeSe Philip, and Derek Walcott, whose work renews aspects of Euro-American modernism in their attempts to depict the histories and imaginative geographies of the Black Atlantic.[28] Born in the 1930s and 1940s, and initially educated under British colonial rule, these poets began to publish their work following the gradual break-up of the Empire that occurred in the two decades after the end of the Second World War. As Simon Gikandi argues, the relation of Caribbean writers to a modernist heritage that derives from the imperial metropoles of Europe is deeply ambivalent, entailing historical anxiety as well as cultural invigoration. Consequently, Caribbean modernism is 'opposed to, though not necessarily independent of European notions of modernism', adopting 'highly revisionary' strategies of creolisation that fuse aspects of Western modernity with elements of those 'other' discourses and cultures that colonialism sought to repress.[29] Developing a similar thesis, Jahan Ramazani argues that the 'intercultural poetic forms of modernism' have been adapted by a range of postcolonial poets from Africa, the Caribbean, and India in the post-war period to 'break through monologic lyricism, to express their cross-cultural experience, despite vast differences in ethnicity, geography, politics, and history from the Euromodernists'.[30] Like Gikandi, Ramazani emphasises the processes of 'adaptation' and 'indigenisation' through which postcolonial poets effect renewals of modernist forms and styles in their texts.[31] For Caribbean modernist poets, the themes of history, language, and colonial subjectivity are common preoccupations, though the complexities of diasporic experience are often explored via the spatial tropes of journeys, voyages, and migrations.

The poetry of Kamau Brathwaite, who was born in Barbados in 1930, is recurrently concerned with geographical and cultural crossings as part of its ramifying enquiry into the relationships between people, place, and history in the Caribbean archipelago. For instance, his New World trilogy, *The Arrivants* (1973) – comprising the volumes *Rights of Passage* (1967), *Masks* (1968), and *Islands* (1969) – seeks to answer a fundamental question of belonging and origins: 'How did we get into the Caribbean? Our people, the black people of the Caribbean – what was the origin of their presence in the Caribbean?'[32] It does so through a series of fractured, non-linear narratives in a variety of voices and registers that reconstruct the pre-colonial societies of West Africa, imagine Columbus's 'discovery' of the Bahamas in 1492, give oblique expression to the African experience of the Middle Passage and plantation slavery, and depict the Caribbean diaspora in the cities of North America and Western Europe. On the one hand, Brathwaite's work is engaged in 'the recuperation of African survivals in the Caribbean', especially as manifest in language, music, and religious customs.[33] On the other, he foregrounds migrancy, exile, and uprooting as intrinsic to the Caribbean experience of modernity. For instance, in his portrait of a migrant labourer whose life-course links Castries, Kingston, and Port of Spain to Brixton, Chicago, and Tiger Bay:

Never seen
a man
travel more
seen more
lands
than this poor
path-
less harbour-
less spade.[34]

Brathwaite's characteristically short, syncopated lines, which frequently break words into their constituent syllables via enjambement, create a dense aural weave of assonance, anaphora, and internal rhyme that adapts rhythms from jazz, calypso, and dub music. Famously, he identifies T. S. Eliot as a major influence on the vernacular 'nation language' and polyphonic qualities of his own poetry, though Brathwaite's debt to Eliot is best understood in terms of 'competitive fusion', as 'an instance of cross-cultural literary adaptation' that is 'staged along an index of opposition'.³⁵ That is, Brathwaite's anti-colonial vernacular poetics seeks to renew and recontextualise aspects of Eliot's high modernism while rejecting his reactionary cultural politics and xenophobia.

Brathwaite's 'nation language' is one solution to the problem that many postcolonial poets face: of finding a way to use the coloniser's language – in this case, English – as a means of expression while acknowledging its complicity in colonial violence and slavery. For the Tobago-born Canadian poet M. NourbeSe Philip, this dilemma is especially acute for, where the conditions of slavery stripped New World Africans of their names and native languages, the English language that was forced upon them 'served to articulate the non-being of the African'.³⁶ Hence the lament of Philip's speaker in 'Discourse on the Logic of Language', from *She Tries Her Tongue, Her Silence Softly Breaks* (1989), who can only speak of her lost (African) 'mother tongue' in the colonial 'father tongue' of English:

> language
> l/anguish
>   anguish
> english
> is a foreign anguish³⁷

The slippage in these lines that equates 'language' with 'anguish' is symptomatic of historical trauma, while the 'foreign' character of 'english' (rendered deliberately in the lower-case) implies that acts of speaking and writing compound the Caribbean writer's experience of dislocation even as they make its expression possible. Philip has said that she writes 'from place' rather than 'about place', adding that 'the place I write from is Tobago, even though I only spent the first eight years of my life there'.³⁸ Personal experiences of exile and migration inform her poetry's acute sensitivity to the various forms of displacement, both literal and metaphorical, endured by the descendants of African slaves in the Caribbean. Her most recent long poem, *Zong!* (2008), revisits a massacre of African slaves who were thrown overboard from a slave ship bound for Jamaica in 1781 by dismembering and radically reconfiguring the language of a legal decision, *Gregson v. Gilbert*, the only surviving public document relating to the incident. The progressive fragmentation of Philip's text, which intercuts different voices and languages while also scattering individual words and phonemes across its pages in visual or sculptural patterns, formally echoes 'the displacements of those captured and sold into slavery'.³⁹ In this way, *Zong!* foregrounds the impossibility (and ethical necessity) of telling the story of the massacre from the perspectives of the drowned slaves, 'lying dead / under seas', while also illustrating the enduring significance of the sea as a site for Caribbean modernist poets' engagements with history and its haunting silences.[40]

Philip's artful dispersals of words and phrases on the material space of the page clearly owe something to Olson's open field poetics; while Brathwaite describes Bunting's *Briggflatts* as a 'nation language (*jordie*) long poem', suggesting affinities with his own mode of vernacular poetics.[41] He has also acknowledged the formative influence of 'Mother Brooks' on his work.[42] Other lineages and traditions are, of course, also important to these writers; but my larger point is that late modernist poets have played a significant, though under-recognised, role as enabling influences for several generations of younger poets from Britain, North America, and the Caribbean, who have sought to renew modernist aesthetics in the late twentieth and early twenty-first centuries. Poets such as Brooks, Bunting, Graham, Jones, Niedecker, and Olson did not only provide their neo-modernist heirs with a living link to the formal experiments and iconoclastic energies of high modernism. They also demonstrated how modernist aesthetics could persist in altered or reconfigured forms well into the post-war period, albeit in the margins of cultural milieux characterised by anti-modernist reaction and the emergence of a hostile postmodernism.

Moreover, as I have argued in detail over the course of this book, the work of these late modernists is distinctive for its compelling poetics of place. In Brooks's Bronzeville, Graham's Clydeside, Jones's Black Mountains, and Niedecker's Rock River, readers encounter acts of placemaking that are acutely responsive to specific landscapes, environments, and ecosystems, the majority of which are non-metropolitan. At the same time, these places are apprehended in terms of the historical forces that mould them and the socio-economic relationships that link them to other places at a range of different spatial scales. Late modernist poets trace various kinds of mobility in, through, and between places – the sea voyages of Bunting's *Briggflatts*, for instance, or Olson's world map of westward migrations in *The Maximus Poems*. They also engage reflexively with the contemporaneous work of geographers and geologists, adapting key terms and concepts – place, space, landscape, site, map – to fit the varieties of embodied and emplaced experience they seek to depict. Late modernist poems are worth reading not only as literary-historical curiosities, instances of the living on of modernism after its well-publicised death in the Second World War. They deserve to be read for their historically attuned geographical imaginations, their subtle explorations of how the world comes to be known, and for the eloquence with which they attest to the continuing significance of place.

Notes

Introduction

1. For some variations on this account of modernism's literary history, see: Malcolm Bradbury and James Macfarlane, eds, *Modernism 1890–1930* (Harmondsworth: Penguin, 1991); Christopher Butler, *Early Modernism: Literature, Music, and Painting in Europe 1900–1916* (Oxford: Clarendon Press, 1994); Michael North, *Reading 1922: A Return to the Scene of the Modern* (Oxford: Oxford University Press, 1999); Keith Williams and Steven Matthews, *Rewriting the Thirties: Modernism and After* (London: Longman, 1997).
2. Ezra Pound, *The Cantos of Ezra Pound* (New York: New Directions, 1970); A. David Moody, *Ezra Pound: Poet: Volume One: The Young Genius 1885–1920* (Oxford: Oxford University Press, 2007), pp. 306–7.
3. Raymond Williams, *Politics of Modernism: Against the New Conformists* (London: Verso, 2007), p. 32.
4. Williams, *Politics of Modernism*, pp. 33, 35.
5. Williams, *Politics of Modernism*, p. 35.
6. Douglas Mao and Rebecca Walkowitz, 'The New Modernist Studies', *PMLA* 123.3 (2008), 737–48 (pp. 738, 739).
7. Andreas Huyssen, 'Geographies of modernism in a globalizing world', in Peter Brooker and Andrew Thacker, eds, *Geographies of Modernism: Literatures, Cultures, Spaces* (Abingdon: Routledge, 2005), pp. 6–18 (p. 9).
8. Susan Stanford Friedman, *Planetary Modernisms: Provocations on Modernity Across Time* (New York: Columbia University Press, 2015), p. 91.
9. Tyrus Miller, *Late Modernism: Politics, Fiction, and the Arts Between the World Wars* (Berkeley: University of California Press, 1999), p. 7.
10. Miller, *Late Modernism*, pp. 19, 20, 45, 64.
11. Cheryl Hindrichs, 'Late Modernism, 1928–1945: Criticism and Theory', *Literature Compass* 8.11 (2011), 840–55 (p. 850).
12. John Whittier-Ferguson, *Mortality and Form in Late Modernist Literature* (Cambridge: Cambridge University Press, 2014), pp. 4, 3, 9, 78.
13. Edward W. Said, *On Late Style: Music and Literature Against the Grain* (London: Bloomsbury, 2006), pp. 7, 12.

14. Jed Esty, *A Shrinking Island: Modernism and National Culture in England* (Princeton: Princeton University Press, 2004), pp. 3, 43.
15. Esty, *A Shrinking Island*, p. 30.
16. Esty, *A Shrinking Island*, 46.
17. Marina MacKay, *Modernism and World War II* (Cambridge: Cambridge University Press, 2007), pp. 2, 10.
18. A qualification needs to be made for Esty here, for he identifies late modernism with a longer period of 'imperial contraction' from 1930 to 1960. However, the majority of his literary examples of late modernist texts date from the 1930s and early 1940s. Esty, *A Shrinking Island*, p. 4.
19. Charles Jencks, *Late-Modern Architecture and Other Essays* (London: Academy Editions, 1980), pp. 6, 8. See also Charles Jencks, *Modern Movements in Architecture*, 2nd edn (Harmondsworth: Penguin, 1985), pp. 371–89.
20. Fredric Jameson, *Postmodernism, or, The Cultural Logic of Late Capitalism* (London: Verso, 1991), p. 305.
21. Perry Anderson, *The Origins of Postmodernity* (London: Verso, 1998), p. 84. The argument here significantly modifies Anderson's earlier account of the end of modernism. See Perry Anderson, 'Modernity and Revolution', *New Left Review* 1.144 (1984), 96–113 (pp. 106–9).
22. Fredric Jameson, *A Singular Modernity: Essay on the Ontology of the Present* (London: Verso, 2002), pp. 161, 169.
23. Jameson, *A Singular Modernity*, p. 166.
24. Jameson, *A Singular Modernity*, pp. 168, 198. On Stevens's poetry and the ideology of modernism, see also Fredric Jameson, *The Modernist Papers* (London: Verso, 2007), pp. 207–22.
25. Tim Armstrong, *Modernism: A Cultural History* (Cambridge: Polity Press, 2005), p. 40.
26. Rachel Blau DuPlessis, 'Lyric and Experimental Long Poems: Intersections', in *Time in Time: Short Poems, Long Poems, and the Rhetoric of North American Avant-Gardism, 1963–2008*, ed. by J. Mark Smith (Montreal: McGill-Queens University Press, 2013), pp. 22–50 (p. 38).
27. David James and Urmila Seshagiri, 'Metamodernism: Narratives of Continuity and Revolution', *PMLA* 129.1 (2014), 87–100 (pp. 88, 97, n. 1).
28. Matthew Hart, *Nations of Nothing But Poetry: Modernism, Transnationalism, and Synthetic Vernacular Writing* (New York: Oxford University Press, 2010), p. 15.
29. Anthony Mellors, *Late Modernist Poetics: From Pound to Prynne* (Manchester: Manchester University Press, 2005), pp. 2–3.
30. Mellors, *Late Modernist Poetics*, p. 19.
31. Mellors, *Late Modernist Poetics*, p. 23.
32. Hart, *Nations of Nothing But Poetry*, p. 16.
33. Richard Burton, *A Strong Song Tows Us: The Life of Basil Bunting* (Oxford: Infinite Ideas, 2013), pp. 170–83; 162–7; 359–60; 7–8; 423–5.
34. On *Poetry* as a modernist magazine, see Helen Carr, '*Poetry: A Magazine of Verse* (1912–36), "Biggest of the Little Magazines"', in Peter Brooker and Andrew Thacker, eds, *The Oxford Critical and Cultural History of Modernist Magazines: Volume II: North America 1894–1960* (Oxford: Oxford University Press, 2012), pp. 40–60.

35. On Fulcrum Press, see Robert Sheppard, *The Poetry of Saying: British Poetry and its Discontents 1950–2000* (Liverpool: Liverpool University Press, 2005), p. 39.
36. Alex Latter, *Late Modernism and the English Intelligencer: On the Poetics of Community* (London: Bloomsbury, 2015), pp. 3–6; Eric Falci, *The Cambridge Introduction to British Poetry, 1945–2010* (Cambridge: Cambridge University Press, 2015), pp. 91–125.
37. Robert Hampson and Will Montgomery, 'Innovations in Poetry', in Peter Brooker, Andrzej Gąsiorek, Deborah Longworth and Andrew Thacker, eds, *The Oxford Handbook of Modernisms* (Oxford: Oxford University Press, 2010), pp. 63–84 (p. 76).
38. C. D. Blanton, *Epic Negation: The Dialectical Poetics of Late Modernism* (New York: Oxford University Press, 2015), p. 76.
39. DuPlessis, 'Lyric and Experimental Long Poems', p. 39.
40. Jim Cocola, *Places in the Making: A Cultural Geography of American Poetry* (Iowa City: University of Iowa Press, 2016), p. 4.
41. Edward S. Casey, *Getting Back into Place: Toward a Renewed Understanding of the Place-World* (Bloomington: Indiana University Press, 1993), p. 13. See also Edward S. Casey, *The Fate of Place: A Philosophical History* (Berkeley: University of California Press, 1997), p. ix.
42. Tim Cresswell, *Place: An Introduction*, 2nd edn (Chichester: Wiley-Blackwell, 2015), p. 19.
43. Henri Lefebvre, *The Production of Space*, trans. Donald Nicholson-Smith (Oxford: Blackwell, 1991), p. 26.
44. Lorine Niedecker, *Collected Works*, ed. Jenny Penberthy (Berkeley: University of California Press, 2002), p. 261; W. S. Graham, *New Collected Poems*, ed. Matthew Francis (London: Faber, 2004), p. 105.
45. David Jones, *Epoch and Artist: Selected Writings*, ed. Harman Grisewood (London: Faber and Faber, 1959), p. 304.
46. William Carlos Williams, *Paterson*, ed. Christopher MacGowan (New York: New Directions, 1992), p. 2; William Carlos Williams, *I Wanted to Write a Poem: The Autobiography of the Works of a Poet*, ed. Edith Heal (New York: New Directions, 1978), p. 72.
47. Charles Olson, *Collected Prose*, ed. Donald Allen and Benjamin Friedlander (Berkeley: University of California Press, 1997), p. 17; Charles Olson, *The Maximus Poems*, ed. George F. Butterick (Berkeley: University of California Press, 1983), p. 184.
48. Tom Clark, *Charles Olson: The Allegory of a Poet's Life* (New York: W. W. Norton, 1991), p. 126.
49. Jonathan Miles, *Backgrounds to David Jones: A Study in Sources and Drafts* (Cardiff: University of Wales Press, 1990), pp. 97–109; Jenny Penberthy, 'Writing Lake Superior', in *Radical Vernacular: Lorine Niedecker and the Poetics of Place*, ed. Elizabeth Willis (Iowa City: University of Iowa Press, 2008), pp. 61–79.
50. Jon Hegglund, *World Views: Metageographies of Modernist Fiction* (New York: Oxford University Press, 2012), p. 25.
51. Jürgen Habermas, 'Modernity versus Postmodernity', trans. Seyla Ben-Habib *New German Critique* 22 (1981), 3–14 (p. 4). On literary modernism and geography, see Alex Davis and Lee M. Jenkins, eds, *Locations*

of *Literary Modernism: Region and Nation in British and American Modernist Poetry* (Cambridge: Cambridge University Press, 2000); Andrew Thacker, *Moving Through Modernity: Space and Geography in Modernism* (Manchester: Manchester University Press, 2003); Peter Brooker and Andrew Thacker, eds, *Geographies of Modernism: Literature, Cultures, Spaces* (Abingdon: Routledge, 2005); Neal Alexander and James Moran, eds, *Regional Modernisms* (Edinburgh: Edinburgh University Press, 2013).

52. Malcolm Bradbury, 'The Cities of Modernism', in *Modernism, 1890–1930*, pp. 96–104 (p. 96).
53. Andrew Thacker, *Modernism, Space and the City: Outsiders and Affect in Paris, Vienna, Berlin and London* (Edinburgh: Edinburgh University Press, 2019), pp. 2–3.
54. Williams, *Paterson*, p. xiii.
55. Jameson, *The Modernist Papers*, pp. 39, 10.
56. Williams, *Paterson*, p. 100.
57. David Harvey, *The Condition of Postmodernity: An Enquiry into the Origins of Cultural Change* (Oxford: Basil Blackwell, 1989), p. 25.
58. Thacker, *Moving Through Modernity*, pp. 7, 8.
59. Rebecca Walsh, *The Geopoetics of Modernism* (Gainesville: University Press of Florida, 2015), p. 4.
60. Doreen Massey, *For Space* (London: Sage, 2005), p. 130.
61. Doreen Massey, *Space, Place and Gender* (Cambridge: Polity Press, 1994), p. 154.
62. Giovanni Arrighi, *The Long Twentieth Century: Money, Power and the Origins of our Times* (London: Verso, 2010), pp. 66–70; David Harvey, *The Enigma of Capital and the Crises of Capitalism* (London: Profile, 2010), pp. 31–2.
63. Arrighi, *The Long Twentieth Century*, p. 82.
64. Cresswell, *Place*, pp. 75, 82.
65. Jahan Ramazani, *A Transnational Poetics* (Chicago: The University of Chicago Press, 2009), p. 35.
66. Thacker, *Moving Through Modernity*, p. 5.
67. For a brief outline of literary geography as a field of research, see Neal Alexander, 'On Literary Geography', *Literary Geographies* 1.1 (2015), 3–6.
68. William Sharp, *Literary Geography* (London: Pall Mall, 1904); Virginia Woolf, 'Literary Geography', *The Essays of Virginia Woolf: Volume 1*, ed Andrew McNeillie (Oxford: Oxford University Press, 1986), pp. 32–5.
69. See, for example, D. C. D. Pocock, ed., *Humanistic Geography and Literature: Essays on the Experience of Place* (London: Croom Helm, 1981); J. Douglas Porteous, 'Literature and Humanist Geography', *Area* 17.2 (1985), 117–22; Raymond Williams, *The Country and the City* (London: Hogarth Press, 1973); Leonard Lutwack, *The Role of Place in Literature* (Syracuse, NY: Syracuse University Press, 1984).
70. Marc Brousseau, 'In, Of, Out, With, and Through: New Perspectives in Literary Geography', in Robert T. Tally Jr, *The Routledge Handbook of Literature and Space* (Abingdon: Routledge, 2017), pp. 9–27 (p. 10).
71. Sheila Hones, *Literary Geographies: Narrative Space in* Let the Great World Spin (Basingstoke: Palgrave Macmillan, 2014), pp. 171, 163.

72. Franco Moretti, *Atlas of the European Novel 1800–1900* (London: Verso, 1998), p. 5.
73. Sara Luchetta, 'Literary Mapping: At the Intersection of Complexity and Reduction', *Literary Geographies* 4.1 (2018), 6–9 (pp. 7–8).
74. Andrew Thacker, 'The Idea of a Critical Literary Geography', *New Formations* 57 (2005), 56–73 (p. 63).
75. Thacker, 'The Idea of a Critical Literary Geography', p. 60.
76. Brosseau, 'In, Of, Out, With, and Through', p. 11.
77. Sheila Hones, 'Text as It Happens: Literary Geography', *Geography Compass* 2.5 (2008), 1301–17 (p. 1307); Hones, *Literary Geographies*, p. 171.
78. Hones, 'Text as It Happens', 1302.
79. Hones, 'Text as it Happens', 1301; Jon Anderson, 'Towards an Assemblage Approach to Literary Geography', *Literary Geographies* 1.2 (2015), 120–37 (pp. 124–5).
80. Hones, *Literary Geographies*, p. 16.
81. Theodor W. Adorno, *Aesthetic Theory*, eds Gretel Adorno and Rolf Tiedemann, trans. Robert Hullot-Kentor (London: Continuum, 2004), p. 232.
82. Bertrand Westphal, *Geocriticism: Real and Fictional Spaces*, trans. Robert T. Tally Jr (New York: Palgrave Macmillan, 2011), p. 112.
83. Westphal, *Geocriticism*, p. 126.
84. Robert T. Tally Jr, *Spatiality* (Abingdon: Routledge, 2013), p. 144.
85. Tim Cresswell, *Geographical Thought: A Critical Introduction* (Chichester: Wiley-Blackwell, 2013), pp. 16, 108. See also Derek Gregory, *Geographical Imaginations* (Oxford: Blackwell, 1994).
86. Jessica Berman, 'Modernism's Possible Geographies', in Laura Doyle and Laura Winkiel, eds, *Geomodernisms: Race, Modernism, Modernity* (Bloomington: Indiana University Press, 2005), 281–96 (pp. 285–6).
87. Marc Brosseau, 'Geography's Literature', *Progress in Human Geography* 18.3 (1994), 333–53 (p. 349).
88. Burton, *A Strong Song Tows Us*, pp. 258–9, 263–4, 318.
89. Jenny Penberthy, *Niedecker and the Correspondence with Zukofsky 1931–1970* (Cambridge: Cambridge University Press, 1993), pp. 172, 174, n. 4.
90. Margot Peters, *Lorine Niedecker: A Poet's Life* (Madison, WN: The University of Wisconsin Press, 2011), pp. 234–5, 247; Burton, *A Strong Song Tows Us*, p. 428.
91. Tony Lopez, 'Graham and the 1940s', in Ralph Pite and Hester Jones, eds, *W. S. Graham: Speaking Towards You* (Liverpool: Liverpool University Press, 2004), pp. 26–43 (p. 37); Clark, *Charles Olson*, pp. 332–5.
92. Angela Jackson, *A Surprised Queenhood in the New Black Sun: The Life and Legacy of Gwendolyn Brooks* (Boston: Beacon Press, 2017), pp. 122–6, 143–6.

1. David Jones: The Sites of History

1. T. S. Eliot, *Selected Prose*, ed. Frank Kermode (London: Faber and Faber, 1975), p. 38.

2. David Jones, *Epoch and Artist: Selected Writings*, ed. Harman Grisewood (London: Faber and Faber, 1959), pp. 141, 167.
3. David Jones, *The Anathémata: Fragments of an Attempted Writing* (London: Faber, 1972), p. 34.
4. Neil Corcoran, *The Song of Deeds: A Study of* The Anathémata *of David Jones* (Cardiff: University of Wales Press, 1982), p. 108.
5. 'I've no scholarship – I've just nosed about as best I can to find out the things I wanted to know or check up on things I half knew': David Jones, *Letters to Vernon Watkins*, ed. Ruth Pryor (Cardiff: University of Wales Press, 1976), p. 20.
6. Huw Ceiriog Jones, *The Library of David Jones: A Catalogue* (Aberystwyth: The National Library of Wales, 1995), pp. 118, 186, 276, 292.
7. Jones, *The Library of David Jones*, pp. 1, 11, 16–17, 104, 126, 150–1, 215–17, 241, 275.
8. Robert T. Tally Jr, *Spatiality* (Abingdon: Routledge, 2013), p. 45.
9. See Thomas Dilworth, *David Jones in the Great War* (London: Enitharmon Press, 2012).
10. David Jones, *The Dying Gaul and Other Writings*, ed. Harman Grisewood (London: Faber and Faber, 1978), p. 23.
11. Jones, *Epoch and Artist*, p. 28; Thomas Dilworth, *David Jones: Engraver, Soldier, Painter, Poet* (London: Jonathan Cape, 2017), pp. 35–104.
12. Jones, *The Dying Gaul*, pp. 35, 30.
13. Peter Nicholls, *Modernisms: A Literary Guide* (Basingstoke: Macmillan, 1995), p. 167; Jones, *Epoch and Artist*, p. 82.
14. Eliot, *Selected Prose*, p. 177.
15. Paul Robichaud, *Making the Past Present: David Jones, the Middle Ages, & Modernism* (Washington, D.C.: The Catholic University of America Press, 2007), p. 123.
16. Elizabeth Ward, *David Jones: Mythmaker* (Manchester: Manchester University Press, 1983), pp. 6, 3, 10.
17. Theodor W. Adorno, *Aesthetic Theory*, ed. Gretel Adorno and Rolf Tiedemann, trans. Robert Hullot-Kentor (London: Continuum, 2004), pp. 382, 373.
18. David Jones, *In Parenthesis* (London: Faber and Faber, 1963), p. 30. Thomas Dilworth claims that *In Parenthesis* is 'certainly the greatest literary treatment of war in English': Thomas Dilworth, *The Shape of Meaning in the Poetry of David Jones* (Toronto: The University of Toronto Press, 1988), p. 368.
19. David Jones, *The Sleeping Lord and Other Fragments* (London: Faber and Faber, 1995), pp. 18, 52.
20. Andrew Thacker, *Moving Through Modernity: Space and Geography in Modernism* (Manchester: Manchester University Press, 2003), p. 7.
21. Kathleen Henderson Staudt, *At the Turn of a Civilization: David Jones and Modern Poetics* (Ann Arbor: The University of Michigan Press, 1994), pp. 31, 29.
22. See Robichaud, *Making the Past Present*, p. 64.
23. Jones, *The Anathémata*, p. 235.
24. Jones, *In Parenthesis*, pp. x–xi.
25. Jones, *In Parenthesis*, p. 79.

26. Vincent B. Sherry Jr, 'A New Boast for *In Parenthesis*: The Dramatic Monologue of David Jones', *Notre Dame English Journal* 14.2 (1982), 113–28 (p. 113).
27. Jones, *In Parenthesis*, 70.
28. Jones, *The Anathémata*, pp. 15–16; Jones, *The Dying Gaul*, p. 156; Jones, *Epoch and Artist*, p. 139.
29. Jones, *Epoch and Artist*, pp. 150, 181–2; Jones, *The Dying Gaul*, p. 174.
30. Dilworth, *David Jones*, p. 221. For a thorough critical account of Spengler's influence on Jones, see Jonathan Miles, *Backgrounds to David Jones: A Study in Sources and Drafts* (Cardiff: University of Wales Press, 1990), pp. 36–64.
31. David Jones, *Dai Greatcoat: A Self-portrait of David Jones in his Letters*, ed. René Hague (London: Faber and Faber, 1980), p. 115.
32. Jones, *The Anathémata*, p. 21.
33. Jones, *Epoch and Artist*, p. 242.
34. Dilworth, *David Jones*, p. 129.
35. Dilworth, *The Shape of Meaning*, p. 63.
36. Jones, *The Anathémata*, p. 50.
37. Jones, *The Anathémata*, pp. 50, 28–9.
38. Staudt, *At the Turn of a Civilization*, p. 69.
39. Jones, *The Anathémata*, p. 50.
40. Jones, *The Sleeping Lord*, pp. 89–90.
41. Jones, *In Parenthesis*, pp. 185, 155.
42. Jones, *The Sleeping Lord*, p. 88.
43. See W. Linnard, *Welsh Woods and Forests: A History* (Llandysul: Gomer, 2000), pp. 81–94.
44. Thomas Dilworth, *Reading David Jones* (Cardiff: University of Wales Press, 2008), p. 218.
45. Lawrence Buell, *The Environmental Imagination: Thoreau, Nature Writing, and the Formation of American Culture* (Cambridge, MA: Harvard University Press, 1995), p. 7.
46. Jones, *Epoch and Artist*, pp. 16, 220.
47. Jones, *The Dying Gaul*, p. 59.
48. Jones, *Epoch and Artist*, p. 48.
49. Neil Corcoran, *English Poetry Since 1940* (London: Longman, 1993), pp. 26–7.
50. Jones, *In Parenthesis*, p. x.
51. Jones, *The Anathémata*, p. 11.
52. Jed Esty, *A Shrinking Island: Modernism and National Culture in England* (Princeton: Princeton University Press, 2004), pp. 2–3.
53. Esty, *A Shrinking Island*, pp. 7, 10, 19.
54. Jones, *The Dying Gaul*, pp. 38–9; Esty, *A Shrinking Island*, pp. 17–18, 49.
55. René Hague in Jones, *Dai Greatcoat*, p. 23.
56. Jones, *The Anathémata*, p. 19.
57. Jones, *In Parenthesis*, p. xiii. In a letter of December 1952 to Jim Ede, Jones affirms that 'the Welsh mythological element is an *integral* part of our tradition': Jones, *Dai Greatcoat*, p. 156.
58. Corcoran, *The Song of Deeds*, p. 91.
59. Jones, *The Anathémata*, p. 112.

60. David Jones, cited in René Hague, *A Commentary on* The Anathémata *of David Jones* (Wellingborough: Christopher Skelton, 1977), p. 138.
61. Jones, *In Parenthesis*, p. xi.
62. Jones, *Epoch and Artist*, p. 204.
63. Jones, *Epoch and Artist*, pp. 232, 216.
64. Jones, *The Sleeping Lord*, p. 68.
65. Gerard Manley Hopkins, *Selected Poetry*, ed. Catherine Phillips (Oxford: Oxford University Press, 1996), p. 117.
66. Jones, *In Parenthesis*, p. 82; Jones, *The Anathémata*, p. 196; Jones, *The Sleeping Lord*, p. 76; Jones, *Epoch and Artist*, p. 233; David Jones, *The Roman Quarry and Other Sequences*, ed. Harman Grisewood and René Hague (London: Agenda Editions, 1981), pp. 66, 71, 74.
67. Pete Hay, 'A Phenomenology of Islands', *Island Studies Journal* 1.1 (2006), 19–42 (pp. 22, 23).
68. Jones, *The Anathémata*, p. 17; Jones, *Dai Greatcoat*, p. 156.
69. Jones, *Epoch and Artist*, pp. 238–9.
70. John Brannigan, *Archipelagic Modernism: Literature in the Irish and British Isles, 1890–1970* (Edinburgh: Edinburgh University Press, 2015), p. 13.
71. Brannigan, *Archipelagic Modernism*, p. 17.
72. Jones, *The Anathemata*, p. 85; Dilworth, *The Shape of Meaning*, pp. 161–2.
73. Jones, *The Anathémata*, p. 97.
74. Jones, *The Anathémata*, p. 99.
75. Jones, *The Anathémata*, pp. 107, 108.
76. René Hague, *David Jones* (Cardiff: University of Wales Press, 1975), p. 43; Dilworth, *The Shape of Meaning*, p. 234.
77. Jones, *The Anathémata*, pp. 97, 182.
78. Jones, *The Anathémata*, pp. 110, 111.
79. Jones, *The Anathémata*, p. 111.
80. Jon Hegglund, *World Views: Metageographies of Modernist Fiction* (New York: Oxford University Press, 2012), pp. 16, 8.
81. Jones, *The Anathémata*, pp. 114–15.
82. Jones, *The Anathémata*, p. 115; John Mack, *The Sea: A Cultural History* (London: Reaktion Books, 2011), p. 21.
83. Jones, *The Anathémata*, p. 115.
84. Robichaud, *Making the Past Present*, p. 107. For contrasting critical accounts of Jones's political alignments, see Ward, *David Jones: Mythmaker*, pp. 51–7, and Thomas Dilworth, 'David Jones and Fascism,' *Journal of Modern Literature* 13.1 (1986), 49–62.
85. David Jones, *Letters to a Friend*, ed. Aneurin Talfan Davies (Swansea: Triskele Books, 1980), p. 76; Jones, *The Anathémata*, p. 25.
86. Adorno, *Aesthetic Theory*, pp. 267, 264.
87. Dilworth, *David Jones*, p. 124.
88. Jones, *Epoch and Artist*, p. 304.
89. Jones, *The Dying Gaul*, p. 46.
90. Jones, *The Dying Gaul*, p. 31.
91. Martin Heidegger, *Poetry, Language, Thought*, trans. Albert Hofstadter (New York: Harper Collins, 2001), pp. 114, 115.

92. Martin Heidegger, *The Question Concerning Technology and Other Essays*, trans. William Lovitt (New York: Harper Perennial, 1977), pp. 4, 17.
93. Martin Heidegger, *Discourse on Thinking*, trans. John M. Anderson and E. Hans Freund (New York: Harper & Row, 1966), pp. 47, 48–9.
94. Jeremy Hooker, 'David Jones and the Matter of Wales', in Belinda Humfrey and Anne Price-Owen, eds, *David Jones: Diversity in Unity: Studies of his Literary and Visual Art* (Cardiff: University of Wales Press, 2000), pp. 11–25 (p. 17). On the relationships between Heidegger's thought and Nazi ideology, see Charles Bambach, *Heidegger's Roots: Nietzsche, National Socialism, and the Greeks* (Ithaca, NY: Cornell University Press, 2003).
95. Heidegger, *Poetry, Language, Thought*, pp. 145, 144, 155.
96. Jonathan Miles, *Eric Gill & David Jones at Capel-y-Ffin* (Bridgend: Seren, 1992), p. 91; Hooker, 'David Jones and the Matter of Wales', p. 22.
97. Edward S. Casey, *Getting Back into Place: Toward a Renewed Understanding of the Place-World* (Bloomington: Indiana University Press, 1993), p. 65.
98. 'The world-city means cosmopolitanism in place of "home", cold matter-of-fact in place of reverence for tradition and age, scientific irreligion as a fossil representative of the older religion of the heart, "society" in place of the state, natural instead of hard-earned rights.' Oswald Spengler, *The Decline of the West: Vol. I: Form and Actuality*, trans. Charles Francis Atkinson (London: George Allen & Unwin, 1926), p. 33.
99. Jones, *The Sleeping Lord*, pp. 13–14.
100. Ward, *David Jones: Mythmaker*, p. 10; Thomas Dilworth, 'Antithesis of place in the poetry and life of David Jones', in Alex Davis and Lee M. Jenkins, eds, *Locations of Literary Modernism: Region and Nation in British and American Modernist Poetry* (Cambridge: Cambridge University Press, 2000), pp. 67–88 (p. 67).
101. Jones, *The Sleeping Lord*, pp. 46, 45.
102. Jones, *The Sleeping Lord*, p. 55.
103. Jones, *The Sleeping Lord*, pp. 50–1.
104. Jones, *The Sleeping Lord*, p. 50.
105. J. E. Malpas, *Place and Experience: A Philosophical Topography* (Cambridge: Cambridge University Press, 1999), p. 35.
106. Jones, *The Sleeping Lord*, pp. 52–3.
107. Jones, *The Sleeping Lord*, p. 62.
108. Jones, *The Sleeping Lord*, p. 59.
109. Jones, *The Sleeping Lord*, pp. 59, 60.
110. Jones, *The Sleeping Lord*, p. 62.
111. Jones, *The Sleeping Lord*, p. 63.
112. Jones, *The Sleeping Lord*, p. 62.
113. Jones, *The Sleeping Lord*, p. 63.
114. Jones, *Letters to a Friend*, p. 37.
115. Jones, *The Sleeping Lord*, pp. 61–2. The gammer's prayer in Jones's poem resembles ALP's prayer for her children at the end of Book II, Chapter 1 of Joyce's *Finnegans Wake*; though the 'gammer' herself is adapted from

Book I, Chapter 8. See James Joyce, *Finnegans Wake*, 3rd edn (London: Faber and Faber, 1975), pp. 258–9, 215.
116. Dilworth, *The Shape of Meaning*, p. 311.
117. Anne Price-Owen, 'Feminist Principles in David Jones's Art', in *David Jones: Diversity in Unity*, pp. 91–106 (p. 91).
118. Jones, *The Sleeping Lord*, p. 63.
119. Jones, *The Sleeping Lord*, pp. 63–4.
120. Corcoran, *English Poetry since 1940*, p. 28.
121. Jones, *The Anathémata*, pp. 19, 20.
122. Jones, *The Sleeping Lord*, p. 61.
123. Jones, *Letters to a Friend*, p. 120.
124. Ward, *David Jones: Mythmaker*, pp. 188, 190.
125. Fredric Jameson, 'Notes on Globalization as a Philosophical Issue', in Fredric Jameson and Masao Miyoshi, eds, *The Cultures of Globalization* (Durham, NC: Duke University Press, 1998), pp. 54–77 (pp. 56, 57).
126. Michael Hardt and Antonio Negri, *Empire* (Cambridge, MA: Harvard University Press, 2000), p. 44.
127. Jones, *The Library of David Jones*, pp. 100, 102, 305, 234, 270, 229, 234, 265.
128. Jones, *Epoch and Artist*, p. 30; Jones, *The Dying Gaul*, p. 30.
129. Jones, *Epoch and Artist*, pp. 52.
130. John Challinor, *A Dictionary of Geology*, 5th edn (Cardiff: University of Wales Press, 1978), p. 81.
131. Jones, *The Dying Gaul*, pp. 46, 181.
132. On early nineteenth-century attempts to define geology as a science, see Roy Porter, *The Making of Geology: Earth Science in Britain 1660–1815* (Cambridge: Cambridge University Press, 1977), pp. 202–4.
133. Jones, *The Anathémata*, p. 82.
134. Jones, *The Anathémata*, p. 90.
135. Corcoran, *The Song of Deeds*, p. 77.
136. Doreen Massey, *for space* (London: Sage, 2005), p. 130.
137. Jacques Rancière, *The Aesthetic Unconscious*, trans. Debra Keates and James Swenson (Cambridge: Polity, 2009), p. 36.
138. Corcoran, *The Song of Deeds*, p. 46.
139. Miles, *Backgrounds to David Jones*, p. 109.
140. Jones, *The Anathémata*, p. 63.
141. Jones, *The Anathémata*, p. 70.
142. Jones, *The Anathémata*, p. 74.
143. Dilworth, *David Jones*, pp. 338–9.
144. Jones, *In Parenthesis*, p. 51.
145. Jones, *In Parenthesis*, p. 198, n. 36.
146. Jones, *The Sleeping Lord*, p. 70.
147. Joyce, *Finnegans Wake*, p. 7. Joyce 'conceived of his book as the dream of old Finn, lying in death beside the river Liffey and watching the history of Ireland and the world – past and future – flow through his mind like flotsam on the river of life.' Richard Ellmann, *James Joyce* (Oxford: Oxford University Press, 1982), p. 544.
148. Jones, *The Sleeping Lord*, pp. 71–2.

149. Jones, *The Sleeping Lord*, p. 86.
150. J. Pringle and T. Neville George, *British Regional Geology: South Wales*, 3rd edn (London: Her Majesty's Stationery Office, 1970), pp. 83–100; John Davies, *A History of Wales* (London: Penguin, 1994), pp. 400–4.
151. Jones, *The Sleeping Lord*, pp. 91–2.
152. Dilworth, *David Jones*, p. 338. On the Aberfan disaster and its consequences, see Martin Johnes, *Wales Since 1939* (Manchester: Manchester University Press, 2012), pp. 245–7.
153. Jones, *The Sleeping Lord*, p. 93. See Miles, *Backgrounds to David Jones*, p. 108.
154. Adorno, *Aesthetic Theory*, p. 85.

2. Basil Bunting's Regional Modernism

1. Bunting was born in Scotswood-on-Tyne on 1 March 1900. His biographer, Richard Burton, observes that Bunting 'spent only around six months in his beloved Northumbria' during the 1920s and 1930s; and he served with the RAF in Scotland, the Eastern Mediterranean, and Iran during the Second World War. Richard Burton, *A Strong Song Tows Us: The Life of Basil Bunting* (Oxford: Infinite Ideas, 2013), pp. 21, 4, 271–95.
2. Georg Lukács, *The Theory of the Novel: A Historico-philosophical Essay on the Forms of Great Epic Literature*, trans. Anna Bostock (London: The Merlin Press, 1978), p. 41.
3. Malcolm Bradbury, 'The Cities of Modernism', in Malcolm Bradbury and James McFarlane, eds, *Modernism 1890–1930* (Harmondsworth: Penguin, 1991), pp. 96–104 (p. 96).
4. Marshall Berman, *All That is Solid Melts into Air: The Experience of Modernity* (London: Verso, 1983), p. 316.
5. See Neal Alexander and James Moran, 'Introduction: Regional Modernisms', in Neal Alexander and James Moran, eds, *Regional Modernisms* (Edinburgh: Edinburgh University Press, 2013), pp. 1–21.
6. James Joyce, *Ulysses: The 1922 Text*, ed. Jeri Johnson (Oxford: Oxford University Press, 2008), p. 112. On Joyce, Lawrence, and MacDiarmid see, respectively: Gerry Kearns, 'The Spatial Poetics of James Joyce', *New Formations* 57 (2006), 107–25; Andrew Harrison, 'The Regional Modernism of D. H. Lawrence and James Joyce,' in *Regional Modernisms*, pp. 44–64; Robert Crawford, 'MacDiarmid in Montrose', in Alex Davis and Lee M. Jenkins, eds, *Locations of Literary Modernism: Region and Nation in British and American Modernist Poetry* (Cambridge: Cambridge University Press, 2000), pp. 33–56; John Brannigan, *Archipelagic Modernism: Literature in the Irish and British Isles, 1890–1970* (Edinburgh; Edinburgh University Press, 2015), pp. 160–72.
7. Drew Milne, 'Modernist Poetry in the British Isles', in Alex Davis and Lee M. Jenkins, eds, *The Cambridge Companion to Modernist Poetry* (Cambridge: Cambridge University Press, 2008), pp. 151–3; Neil Corcoran, *English Poetry Since 1940* (London: Longman, 1994), pp. 82–3.
8. Peter Howarth, *British Poetry in the Age of Modernism* (Cambridge: Cambridge University Press, 2005), p. 3.

9. Corcoran, *English Poetry Since 1940*, p. 27.
10. Crawford, 'MacDiarmid in Montrose', p. 33.
11. William Wooten, 'Basil Bunting, British Modernism and the Time of the Nation', in James McGonigal and Richard Price, eds, *The Star You Steer By: Basil Bunting and British Modernism* (Amsterdam: Rodopi, 2000), pp. 17–34 (p. 18).
12. Burton, *A Strong Song Tows Us*, pp. 298, 486–9.
13. Donald Davie, *Under Briggflatts: A History of Poetry in Great Britain 1960–1988* (Manchester: Carcanet, 1989), p. 41.
14. Milne, 'Modernist Poetry in the British Isles', p. 153.
15. Basil Bunting, *The Poems of Basil Bunting*, ed. Don Share (London: Faber, 2016), pp. 544–5. Further references to this volume will be given parenthetically.
16. Ezra Pound, *Literary Essays of Ezra Pound*, ed. T. S. Eliot (London: Faber and Faber, 1985), pp. 24, 7.
17. Burton, *A Strong Song Tows Us*, pp. 183–4.
18. See Parvin Loloi and Glyn Purslove, 'Basil Bunting's Persian Overdrafts: A Commentary', in Carroll F. Terrell, ed., *Basil Bunting: Man and Poet* (Orono, ME: The National Poetry Foundation, 1981), pp. 343–53; and Basil Bunting, *Bunting's Persia*, ed. Don Share (Chicago, IL: Flood Editions, 2012).
19. Dennis Brown, 'Basil Bunting: *Briggflatts*', in Gary Day and Brian Docherty, eds, *British Poetry from the 1950s to the 1990s: Politics and Art* (Basingstoke: Macmillan, 1997), pp. 23–32 (p. 30).
20. Milne, 'Modernist Poetry in the British Isles', p. 149.
21. Basil Bunting, cited in Richard Caddel, 'Bunting and Welsh', in *Locations of Literary Modernism*, pp. 57–66 (p. 60).
22. Theodor Adorno, *The Jargon of Authenticity*, trans. Knut Tarnowski and Frederic Will (London: Routledge, 2003), pp. 4–7.
23. Eric Falci, 'Place, Space, and Landscape', in Nigel Alderman and C. D. Blanton, eds, *A Concise Companion to Postwar British and Irish Poetry* (Oxford: Wiley-Blackwell, 2009), pp. 200–20 (p. 208); Richard Caddel and Anthony Flowers, *Basil Bunting: A Northern Life* (Newcastle upon Tyne: Newcastle Libraries & Information Centre, 1997), p. 48.
24. Samuel Rogers, '"Local Site and Historical Depth": *Briggflatts*, *A Drunk Man*, and British Modernist Poetics of Place', *English* 65.251 (2016), 332–62 (pp. 333, 335).
25. Tim Cresswell, *On the Move: Mobility in the Modern Western World* (Abingdon: Routledge, 2006), p. 3.
26. Thomas Nail, *The Figure of the Migrant* (Stanford: Stanford University Press, 2015), p. 145.
27. Tim Cresswell, *The Tramp in America* (London: Reaktion Books, 2001), p. 15. See also Cresswell, *On the Move*, pp. 12–13.
28. Burton, *A Strong Song Tows Us*, pp. 107, 119–20; Peter Makin, *Bunting: The Shaping of His Verse* (Oxford: Clarendon Press, 1992), pp. 26–7.
29. Burton, *A Strong Song Tows Us*, pp. 109, 256–8.
30. Keith Tuma, *Fishing by Obstinate Isles: Modern and Postmodern British Poetry and American Readers* (Evanston: Northwestern University Press, 1998), pp. 167, 168.

31. John Tomaney, 'Keeping a Beat in the Dark: Narratives of Regional Identity in Basil Bunting's *Briggflatts*', *Environment and Planning D: Society and Space* 25 (2007), 355–75 (p. 369).
32. Tomaney, 'Keeping a Beat in the Dark', 370, 371.
33. Martin Heidegger, *Poetry, Language, Thought*, trans. Albert Hofstadter (New York: Perennial, 2001), p. 144. On sedentarist metaphysics, see Cresswell, *On the Move*, pp. 26–43.
34. Basil Bunting, cited in Don Share, 'Annotations', *The Poems of Basil Bunting*, p. 365; Burton, *A Strong Song Tows Us*, p. 194.
35. Victoria Forde, *The Poetry of Basil Bunting* (Newcastle-upon-Tyne: Bloodaxe Books, 1991), p. 135.
36. Edward S. Casey, *The Fate of Place: A Philosophical History* (Berkeley: University of California Press, 1998), p. 337.
37. Tomaney, 'Keeping a Beat in the Dark', p. 370.
38. John Allen, Doreen Massey, and Allan Cochrane, *Rethinking the Region: Spaces of Neo-Liberalism* (London: Routledge, 1998), p. 5.
39. Doreen Massey, *Space, Place and Gender* (Cambridge: Polity, 1994), p. 154–5; Doreen Massey, *For Space* (London: Sage, 2005), p. 130.
40. Henri Lefebvre, *The Production of Space*, trans. Donald Nicholson-Smith (Oxford: Blackwell, 1991), p. 88.
41. Peter Davidson, *The Idea of North* (London: Reaktion Books, 2005), p. 20.
42. Katharine Cockin, 'Introducing the Literary North', in Katharine Cockin, ed., *The Literary North* (Basingstoke: Palgrave Macmillan, 2012), p. 3.
43. Rob Shields, *Places on the Margin: Alternative Geographies of Modernity* (London: Routledge, 1991), pp. 208–15.
44. Dave Russell, *Looking North: Northern England and the National Imagination* (Manchester: Manchester University Press, 2004), pp. 14–44.
45. Basil Bunting, *Basil Bunting on Poetry*, ed. Peter Makin (Baltimore: The Johns Hopkins Press, 1999), p. 16.
46. Frank Musgrove, *The North of England: A History from Roman Times to the Present* (Oxford: Basil Blackwell, 1990), p. 45.
47. Pound, *Literary Essays* p. 5; Basil Bunting, cited in Dale Reagan, 'Basil Bunting obiter dicta', in *Basil Bunting: Man and Poet*, pp. 229–74 (p. 242).
48. Basil Bunting, cited in Andrew Lawson, 'Basil Bunting and English Modernism', *Sagetrieb* 9.1/2 (1990), 95–121 (p. 108).
49. Bunting, *Basil Bunting on Poetry*, pp. 5, 10.
50. Bunting, *Basil Bunting on Poetry*, p. 137.
51. Makin, *Bunting*, p. 149.
52. Julian Stannard, *Basil Bunting* (Tavistock: Northcote House, 2014), p. 5.
53. See Bunting's gloss on this passage in Peter Quartermain and Warren Tallman, 'Basil Bunting Talks about *Briggflatts*', *Agenda* 16.1 (1978), 8–19 (pp. 9–10).
54. Basil Bunting, 'A Note on *Briggflatts*', in *Briggflatts* (Tarset: Bloodaxe Books, 2009), p. 40.
55. Basil Bunting, cited in Forde, *The Poetry of Basil Bunting*, p. 121.
56. Burton, *A Strong Song Tows Us*, pp. 275–8.
57. Burton, *A Strong Song Tows Us*, p. 283.

58. Keith Aldritt, *The Poet as Spy: The Life and Wild Times of Basil Bunting* (London: Aurum Press, 1998), p. 107.
59. Burton, *A Strong Song Tows Us*, pp. 300–1.
60. Burton, *A Strong Song Tows Us*, pp. 309, 332.
61. Burton, *A Strong Song Tows Us*, p. 351.
62. Alex Niven, 'Towards a New Architecture: Basil Bunting's Postwar Reconstruction,' *ELH* 81.1 (2014), 351–79 (p. 355).
63. See Forde, *The Poetry of Basil Bunting*, pp. 205–6.
64. Burton, *A Strong Song Tows Us*, p. 339.
65. Stannard, *Basil Bunting*, p. 66.
66. Burton, *A Strong Song Tows Us*, pp. 278–9.
67. Forde, *The Poetry of Basil Bunting*, p. 179.
68. Alex Niven, 'The Formal Genesis of Basil Bunting's *Briggflatts*', *Cambridge Quarterly* 42 3 (2013), 203–24 (pp. 203–5).
69. Burton, *A Strong Song Tows Us*, pp. 358, 356.
70. Quartermain and Tallman, 'Basil Bunting Talks about *Briggflatts*', 17–18.
71. Ezra Pound, *ABC of Reading* (London: George Routledge & Sons, 1934), pp. 20, 77; Basil Bunting, cited in Reagan, 'Basil Bunting obiter dicta', p. 237.
72. C. D. Blanton, *Epic Negation: The Dialectical Poetics of Late Modernism* (New York: Oxford University Press, 2015), p. 29.
73. Matthew Hart, *Nations of Nothing But Poetry: Modernism, Transnationalism, and Synthetic Vernacular Writing* (Oxford: Oxford University Press, 2010), p. 83.
74. For a thorough discussion of musical influences on Bunting's poetry, see Makin, *Bunting*, pp. 239–65.
75. Theodor W. Adorno, *Aesthetic Theory*, eds Gretel Adorno and Rolf Tiedemann, trans. Robert Hullot-Kentor (London: Continuum, 2004), p. 163.
76. Ian Gregson, '"Adult Male of a Merciless Species": Basil Bunting's Rueful Masculinity', in *The Star You Steer By*, pp. 109–22 (p. 115).
77. R. Murray Schafer, *The Soundscape: Our Sonic Environment and the Tuning of the World* (Rochester, VT: Destiny Books, 1994), p. 7.
78. Josh Epstein, *Sublime Noise: Musical Culture and the Modernist Writer* (Baltimore: Johns Hopkins University Press, 2014), p. xxvii.
79. Basil Bunting, 'The Poet's Point of View', in *Briggflatts*, p. 42; Bunting, *Basil Bunting on Poetry*, p. 20.
80. On Bunting's adaptations of techniques derived from Old English and Welsh poetry, see Makin, *Bunting*, pp. 160–89; Caddel, 'Bunting and Welsh', pp. 57–66; and Niven, 'The Formal Genesis of Basil Bunting's *Briggflatts*', pp. 219–22.
81. Peter Quartermain, *Basil Bunting: Poet of the North* (Durham: Basil Bunting Poetry Archive, 1990), p. 16.
82. Forde, *The Poetry of Basil Bunting*, p. 79–80; Pound, *Literary Essays*, p. 25.
83. Jacques Derrida, *Of Grammatology*, trans. Gayatri Chakravorty Spivak (Baltimore: The Johns Hopkins University Press, 1978), pp. 11–12.
84. Basil Bunting, 'Three Other Comments', in *Briggflatts*, p. 44.
85. Basil Bunting, cited in Reagan, 'Basil Bunting obiter dicta', p. 240.

86. Hart, *Nations of Nothing But Poetry*, p. 96.
87. Derrida, *Of Grammatology*, p. 35.
88. Andrew Duncan, *Origins of the Underground: British Poetry between Apocryphon and Incident Light, 1933–79* (Cambridge: Salt, 2008), p. 53.
89. Bunting, 'A Note on Briggflatts', in *Briggflatts*, p. 40.
90. Tony Lopez, *Meaning Performance: Essays on Poetry* (Cambridge: Salt, 2006), p. 154.
91. Raphael Samuel, *Island Stories: Unravelling Britain: Theatres of Memory*, vol. 2 (London: Verso, 1998), p. 49.
92. Tom Nairn, *The Break-up of Britain: Crisis and Neo-Nationalism*, 2nd edn (London: Verso, 1981), p. 71.
93. Basil Bunting, cited in Jonathan Williams, 'Some Jazz from the Baz: The Bunting-Williams Letters', in *The Star You Steer By*, pp. 253–88 (p. 282).
94. Fiona Stafford, *Local Attachments: The Province of Poetry* (Oxford: Oxford University Press, 2010), p. 5.
95. Burton Hatlen, 'Regionalism and Internationalism in Basil Bunting's *Briggflatts*', *The Yale Journal of Criticism* 13.1 (2000), 49–66 (p. 61).
96. See Burton, *A Strong Song Tows Us*, pp. 31–3.
97. Bunting, 'A Note on *Briggflatts*', p. 41.
98. Burton, *A Strong Song Tows Us*, pp. 28, 64–75.
99. Basil Bunting, cited in Reagan, 'Basil Bunting obiter dicta', p. 271.
100. See A. D. Mills, *A Dictionary of British Place Names*, rev. ed. (Oxford: Oxford University Press, 2011), pp. 520, 521. The place-name is usually spelled 'Brigflatts', though the Quaker Meeting House there is 'Briggflatts' and Bunting always adopts the latter, older form of the name.
101. Makin, *Bunting*, p. 134.
102. Tim Armstrong, *Modernism: A Cultural History* (Cambridge: Polity, 2005), p. 9.
103. Edward Said, *Late Style: Music and Literature Against the Grain* (London: Bloomsbury, 2006), p. 17.
104. Wooten, 'Basil Bunting, British Modernism and the Time of the Nation', p. 28.
105. Lawson, 'Basil Bunting and English Modernism', p. 117.
106. Hatlen, 'Regionalism and Internationalism in Basil Bunting's *Briggflatts*', p. 52.
107. Walter Benjamin, *Illuminations*, ed. Hannah Arendt, trans. Harry Zohn (London: Pimlico, 1999), p. 198.
108. Peter Middleton and Tim Woods, *Literatures of Memory: History, Time and Space in Postwar Writing* (Manchester: Manchester University Press, 2000), p. 277.
109. Burton, *A Strong Song Tows Us*, pp. 252–5, 258.
110. Forde, *The Poetry of Basil Bunting*, p. 239.
111. Michel Serres with Bruno Latour, *Conversations on Science, Culture, and Time*, trans. Roxanne Lapidus (Ann Arbor: The University of Michigan Press, 1995), p. 60.

3. W. S. Graham: Between Places

1. Tony Lopez, *The Poetry of W. S. Graham* (Edinburgh University Press, 1989), pp. 24, 126.
2. Matthew Francis, *Where the People Are: Language and Community in the Poetry of W. S. Graham* (Cambridge: Salt, 2004), p. 8.
3. Fredric Jameson, *The Modernist Papers* (London: Verso, 2007), pp. 6–7.
4. Raymond Williams, *Politics of Modernism*, ed. Tony Pinkney (London: Verso, 2007), pp. 45–6.
5. For succinct accounts of Graham's periods in Glasgow, London, and New York during the 1940s, see Tony Lopez, 'Graham and the 1940s', in Ralph Pite and Hester Jones, eds, *W. S. Graham: Speaking Towards You* (Liverpool: Liverpool University Press, 2004), pp. 26–42 (pp. 26–30, 37).
6. W. S. Graham, *The Nightfisherman: Selected Letters*, eds Michael Snow and Margaret Snow (Manchester: Carcanet, 1999), pp. 118, 119.
7. Graham, *The Nightfisherman*, pp. 141, 227, 163.
8. W. S. Graham, 'Notes on a Poetry of Release', in Graham, *The Nightfisherman*, pp. 379, 379–80.
9. Alain Badiou, *Theoretical Writings*, ed. and trans. Ray Brassier and Alberto Toscano (London: Bloomsbury, 2015), p. 243.
10. Graham, 'Notes on a Poetry of Release', p. 380.
11. 'One cannot step twice in the same river, nor can one grasp any mortal substance in a stable condition, but it scatters and again gathers; it forms and dissolves, and approaches and departs.' Charles H. Kahn, *The Art and Thought of Heraclitus* (Cambridge: Cambridge University Press, 1979), p. 53. On the influence of Heraclitus upon Graham, see Lopez, *The Poetry of W. S. Graham*, pp. 62, 101; and Francis, *Where the People Are*, pp. 71–2, 94–5.
12. Graham, 'Notes on a Poetry of Release', p. 383.
13. Theodor Adorno, *Notes to Literature: Volume One*, ed. Rolf Tiedemann, trans. Shierry Weber Nicholsen (New York: Columbia University Press, 1991), p. 43.
14. Graham, 'Notes on a Poetry of Release', p. 379.
15. Graham, *The Nightfisherman*, p. 86.
16. John Haffenden, '"I Would Say I Was a Happy Man"': W. S. Graham interviewed by John Haffenden', *Poetry Review* 76.1/2 (1986), 67–74 (p. 70).
17. Graham, 'Notes on a Poetry of Release', p. 382.
18. Roland Barthes, *S/Z*, trans. Richard Miller (New York: Hill and Wang, 1974), p. 4; Graham, 'Notes on a Poetry of Release', p. 382
19. W. S. Graham, 'from Poetry Society Bulletins', *Edinburgh Review* 75 (1987), 37.
20. W. S. Graham, *New Collected Poems*, ed. Matthew Francis (London: Faber and Faber, 2004), pp. 154, 178. All further references to this volume will be given parenthetically.
21. Graham, 'Notes for a Poetry of Release', p. 382.
22. Graham, *The Nightfisherman*, p. 17.
23. Michael and Margaret Snow, 'To Set the Scene', in Graham, *The*

Nightfisherman, p. 5. On the importance of walking in Graham's early poetry, see Francis, *Where the People Are*, p. 63.
24. Lopez, *The Poetry of W. S. Graham*, p. 34; Francis, *Where the People Are*, p. 22.
25. David Wright, 'W. S. Graham in the Forties: Memories and conversations', *Edinburgh Review* 75 (1987), 49–56 (p. 51); Edwin Morgan, 'The Poetry of W. S. Graham', in *W. S. Graham: Speaking Towards You*, pp. 186–94 (p. 187).
26. Paul de Man, *Blindness and Insight: Essays in the Rhetoric of Contemporary Criticism*, 2nd edn (London: Methuen, 1983), p. 185.
27. David Munro and Bruce Gittings, *Scotland: An Encyclopedia of Places & Landscape* (Glasgow: Collins, 2006), p. 237; T. M. Devine, *The Scottish Nation 1700–2000* (London: Penguin, 1999), p. 156.
28. Lopez, *The Poetry of W. S. Graham*, p. 126. On Graham's 'unusual mechanical form of pastoral', see Francis, *Where the People Are*, pp. 74–80.
29. Christopher Harvie, *No Gods and Precious Few Heroes: Twentieth-Century Scotland*, 3rd edn (Edinburgh: Edinburgh University Press, 1998), p. 47.
30. Michael and Margaret Snow, 'To Set the Scene', pp. 5–6; Lopez, *The Poetry of W. S. Graham*, pp. 1–2.
31. George Barker, 'Tribute', in Ronnie Duncan and Jonathan Davidson, eds, *The Constructed Space: A Celebration of W. S. Graham* (Lincoln: Jackson's Arm, 1994), p. 98.
32. Graham, *The Nightfisherman*, p. 349.
33. Michael and Margaret Snow, '"I am a Poet": The First Seven Years', in *The Nightfisherman*, p. 10; David Whittaker, *Give Me Your Painting Hand: W. S. Graham & Cornwall* (Charlbury: Wavestone Press, 2015), pp. 9–11.
34. Graham, *The Nightfisherman*, pp. 137, 353.
35. Graham, *The Nightfisherman*, pp. 97, 240.
36. On Graham's status as a 'Scottish' poet and his ambivalent relations to English literary culture, see Lopez, *The Poetry of W. S. Graham*, pp. 10–11; and Alan Riach, 'W. S. Graham and his Scottish Contemporaries', *Journal of British and Irish Innovative Poetry* 4.1 (2012), 65–75.
37. Jacques Derrida, *Monolingualism of the Other; or, The Prosthesis of Origin*, trans. Patrick Mensah (Stanford: Stanford University Press, 1998), pp. 17, 24, 25.
38. Graham also plays variations on this idea in his letters – for instance: 'Yes I speak English fairly well. I very / Am not an Englishman. My life is spent / Translating Scotch into the English language.' Graham, *The Nightfisherman*, p. 293.
39. Margery Palmer McCulloch, *Scottish Modernism and its Contexts 1918–1959: Literature, National Identity and Cultural Exchange* (Edinburgh: Edinburgh University Press, 2009), pp. 1, 6, 29.
40. Graham, *The Nightfisherman*, pp. 80, 22.
41. Graham, *The Nightfisherman*, p. 80.
42. Francis, *Where the People Are*, p. 43.
43. Francis, *Where the People Are*, p. 49.
44. Graham, *The Nightfisherman*, p. 210.
45. Paul Ricoeur, *Memory, History, Forgetting*, trans. Kathleen Blamey and David Pellauer (Chicago: The University of Chicago Press, 2004), p. 41.

46. Jonathan Culler, *Theory of the Lyric* (Cambridge, MA: Harvard University Press, 2015), p. 186.
47. Gaston Bachelard, *The Poetics of Space*, trans. Maria Jolas (Boston: Beacon Press, 1994), p. 7.
48. On the significance of Graham's use of line-breaks more generally, see Adam Piette, '"Roaring between the lines": W. S. Graham and the White Threshold of Line-Breaks', in *W. S. Graham: Speaking Towards You*, pp. 44–62.
49. Svetlana Boym, *The Future of Nostalgia* (New York: Basic Books, 2001), pp. 41, 49.
50. Robin Davidson, *Cornwall* (London: B. T. Batsford, 1978), p. 15.
51. F. E. Halliday, *A History of Cornwall*, 2nd edn (London: Duckworth, 1975), p. 308; Andrew Causey, *Peter Lanyon: Modernism and the Land* (London: Reaktion Books, 2006), pp. 113–14.
52. Graham, *The Nightfisherman*, pp. 40, 116.
53. Graham, *The Nightfisherman*, p. 83.
54. Graham, *The Nightfisherman*, p. 116.
55. Denys Val Baker, *The Timeless Land: The Creative Spirit in Cornwall* (Bath: Adams & Dart, 1973), p. 28.
56. Whittaker, *Give Me Your Painting Hand*, pp. 11, 14, 18, 32.
57. Julia Kristeva, *Strangers to Ourselves*, trans. Leon S. Roudiez (New York: Columbia University Press, 1991), pp. 9, 29.
58. Graham, *The Nightfisherman*, p. 366.
59. Graham, *The Nightfisherman*, p. 374.
60. Michael Bird, *The St Ives Artists: A Biography of Place and Time* (Aldershot: Lund Humphries, 2008), pp. 22–4.
61. Bird, *The St Ives Artists*, p. 12.
62. Nancy Wynne-Jones, 'W. S. Graham in Cornwall,' *Edinburgh Review* 75 (1987), 66–9 (p. 66).
63. Peter Maber, '"The poet or painter steers his life to maim": W. S. Graham and the St Ives Modernist School', *Word & Image* 25.3 (2009), 258–71 (pp. 261, 266); Whittaker, *Give Me Your Painting Hand*, pp. 18, 24–5.
64. Lopez, *The Poetry of W. S. Graham*, p. 9; Francis, *Where the People Are*, p. 54; Ralph Pite, 'Abstract, Real and Particular: Graham and Painting', in *W. S. Graham: Speaking Towards You*, pp. 65–84 (p. 67).
65. Causey, *Peter Lanyon*, p. 176.
66. Causey, *Peter Lanyon*, p. 20.
67. Peter Lanyon, cited in Chris Stephens, *Peter Lanyon: At the Edge of Landscape* (London: 21 Publishing, 2000), p. 155; Causey, *Peter Lanyon*, p. 177.
68. Natalie Pollard, *Speaking to You: Contemporary Poetry and Public Address* (Oxford: Oxford University Press, 2012), p. 49.
69. Michael Bird, *Bryan Wynter* (Farnham: Lund Humphries, 2010), pp. 17, 154.
70. Bird, *Bryan Wynter*, p. 48.
71. Peter Maber, '"Strange to language": W. S. Graham's Bryan Wynter and the Problematics of Verbal-Visual Communication', *Journal of British and Irish Innovative Poetry* 4.1 (2012), 33–49 (p. 35).

72. Angela Leighton, *On Form: Poetry, Aestheticism, and the Legacy of a Word* (Oxford: Oxford University Press, 2007), p. 215.
73. Denis O'Driscoll, 'W. S. Graham: Professor of Silence', in *The Constructed Space*, pp. 51–65 (p. 61); Francis, *Where the People Are*, p. 18.
74. Haffenden, '"I Would Say I Was a Happy Man"', p. 74.
75. John Mack, *The Sea: A Cultural History* (London: Reaktion Books, 2011), p. 25.
76. Lopez, 'Graham and the 1940s', p. 36; Whittaker, *Give Me Your Painting Hand*, p. 19; Graham, *The Nightfisherman*, pp. 150, 167.
77. Maurice Blanchot, *The Space of Literature*, trans. Ann Smock (Lincoln, NE: University of Nebraska Press, 1982), pp. 168–9, 266–7.
78. Maurice Blanchot, *Friendship*, trans. Elizabeth Rottenberg (Stanford: Stanford University Press, 1997), p. 142.
79. Graham, *The Nightfisherman*, p. 92.
80. Graham, *The Nightfisherman*, p. 144.
81. Graham, *The Nightfisherman*, p. 89.
82. Graham, *The Nightfisherman*, p. 113.
83. Leighton, *On Form*, p. 205.
84. Graham, *The Nightfisherman*, p. 171.
85. Piette, '"Roaring between the lines"', p. 51.
86. Edward S. Casey, *The Fate of Place: A Philosophical History* (Berkeley: University of California Press, 1997), p. 337.
87. Francis, *Where the People Are*, p. 101.
88. Lopez, *The Poetry of W. S. Graham*, p. 80.
89. Timothy Clark, *The Theory of Inspiration: Composition as a Crisis of Subjectivity in Romantic and Post-Romantic Writing* (Manchester: Manchester University Press, 1997), p. 22.
90. Ian Davidson, *Ideas of Space in Contemporary Poetry* (Houndmills: Palgrave Macmillan, 2007), p. 37.
91. Martin Heidegger, *Poetry, Language, Thought*, trans. Albert Hofstadter (New York: Harper Collins, 2001), pp. 194, 214. On the likely influence of Heidegger's thought on Graham's poetry and poetics, see Lopez, *The Poetry of W. S. Graham*, pp. 106–7, 109; and Piette, '"Roaring Between the Lines"', pp. 47–9, 60, n. 11.
92. Timothy Clark, *Martin Heidegger* (London: Routledge, 2002), p. 73.
93. Francis, *Where the People Are*, pp. 110–11.
94. Graham, *The Nightfisherman*, pp. 200, 14.

4. Lorine Niedecker: Life by Water

1. Edward S. Casey, *The Fate of Place: A Philosophical History* (Berkeley: University of California Press, 1998), p. 233.
2. Michael Davidson, *On the Outskirts of Form: Practicing Cultural Poetics* (Middletown, CT: Wesleyan University Press, 2011), p. 80; Margot Peters, *Lorine Niedecker: A Poet's Life* (Madison: The University of Wisconsin Press, 2011), pp. 46, 64, 187, 203.
3. Rachel Blau DuPlessis, *Blue Studios: Poetry and its Cultural Work* (Tuscaloosa: University of Alabama Press, 2006), p. 145.

4. Lorine Niedecker, *Collected Works*, ed. Jenny Penberthy (Berkeley: University of California Press, 2002), p. 142. Subsequent references to this volume will be given parenthetically.
5. Jenny Penberthy, *Niedecker and the Correspondence with Zukofsky 1931–70* (Cambridge: Cambridge University Press, 1993), pp. 17, 18.
6. Peters, *Lorine Niedecker*, p. 36; Penberthy, *Niedecker and the Correspondence with Zukofsky*, pp. 7–8.
7. Mark Scroggins, 'Objectivist Poets', in Alex Davis and Lee M. Jenkins, eds, *A History of Modernist Poetry* (Cambridge: Cambridge University Press, 2015), pp. 381–97 (p. 383); Lorine Niedecker, *'Between Your House and Mine': The Letters of Lorine Niedecker to Cid Corman, 1960–1970*, ed. Lisa Pater Faranda (Durham, NC: Duke University Press, 1986), p. 193.
8. Elizabeth Willis, 'Introduction', in Elizabeth Willis, ed., *Radical Vernacular: Lorine Niedecker and the Poetics of Place* (Iowa City: University of Iowa Press, 2008), pp. xiii–xxiii (p. xv).
9. Raymond Williams, *Politics of Modernism* (London: Verso, 2007), pp. 47, 44.
10. Lorine Niedecker, 'Extracts from Letters to Kenneth Cox', in Peter Dent, ed., *The Full Note: Lorine Niedecker* (Budleigh Salterton: Interim Press, 1983), pp. 36–42 (p. 36).
11. Louis Zukofsky, *Prepositions: The Collected Critical Essays* (London: Rapp & Carroll, 1967), pp. 22, 23.
12. Michelle Niemann, 'Towards an Ecopoetics of Food: Plants, Agricultural Politics, and Colonized Landscapes in Lorine Niedecker's Condensery', *Modernism/modernity* 25.1 (2018), 135–60 (p.135).
13. Louis Zukofsky, *A Test of Poetry* (New York: Jargon/Corinth Books, 1964), p. 58; Penberthy, *Niedecker and the Correspondence with Zukofsky*, pp. 155, 246.
14. On Zukofsky's adaptations of Bach's fugues in *"A"*, see Mark Scroggins, *Louis Zukofsky and the Poetry of Knowledge* (Tuscaloosa: University of Alabama Press, 1998), pp. 193–200.
15. Michael Heller, *Conviction's Net of Branches: Essays on the Objectivist Poets and Poetry* (New York: Spuyten Duyvil, 1985), p. 10.
16. Burton Hatlen, 'A Poetics of Marginality and Resistance: The Objectivist Poets in Context', in Rachel Blau DuPlessis and Peter Quartermain, eds, *The Objectivist Nexus: Essays in Cultural Poetics* (Tuscaloosa: University of Alabama Press, 1999), pp. 37–55 (p. 49).
17. Niedecker, *'Between Your House and Mine'*, p. 64.
18. Penberthy, *Niedecker and the Correspondence with Zukofsky*, p. 35.
19. Penberthy, *Niedecker and the Correspondence with Zukofsky*, pp. 4–5, 21–5.
20. Peter Nichols, 'Lorine Niedecker: Rural Surreal', in Jenny Penberthy, ed., *Lorine Niedecker: Woman and Poet* (Orono, ME: National Poetry Foundation, University of Maine, 1996), pp. 193–217 (p. 197); Peters, *Lorine Niedecker*, pp. 32, 42–3, 47.
21. Penberthy, *Niedecker and the Correspondence with Zukofsky*, p. 39; Peters, *Lorine Niedecker*, pp. 54–5.
22. Peter Middleton, 'Lorine Niedecker's "Folk Base" and Her Challenge to the American Avant-Garde', in *The Objectivist Nexus*, pp. 160–88

(pp. 175, 181). On Niedecker's folk poetry, see also Ross Hair, *Avant-Folk: Small Press Poetry Networks from 1950 to the Present* (Liverpool: Liverpool University Press, 2016), pp. 35–65.
23. Niedecker, *'Between Your House and Mine'*, pp. 241, 121.
24. Warren Motte, *Small Worlds: Minimalism in Contemporary French Literature* (Lincoln: University of Nebraska Press, 1999), p. 4.
25. Eleanor Berry, 'Paradoxes of Form in the Poetry of Lorine Niedecker', in Eric Haralson, ed., *Reading the Middle Generation Anew: Culture, Community, and Form in Twentieth-Century American Poetry* (Iowa City: University of Iowa Press, 2006), pp. 203–32 (pp. 206, 212).
26. Lorine Niedecker, cited in Gail Roub, 'Getting to Know Lorine Niedecker', in *Lorine Niedecker: Woman and Poet*, pp. 79–86 (p. 86). See also Niedecker, *'Between Your House and Mine'*, p. 149.
27. Rachel Blau DuPlessis, 'Lorine Niedecker's "Paean to Place" and Its Fusion Poetics', *Contemporary Literature* 46.3 (2005), 393–421 (p. 411).
28. Gaston Bachelard, *Water and Dreams: An Essay on the Imagination of Matter*, trans. Edith Farrell (Dallas: The Dallas Institute of Humanities and Culture, 1999), pp. 3, 6.
29. These definitions are adapted from the OED and William J. Mitsch and James G. Gosselink, *Wetlands*, 5th edn (Hoboken, NJ: Wiley, 2015), pp. 33–5.
30. William Howarth, 'Imagined Territory: The Writing of Wetlands', *New Literary History* 30.3 (1999), 509–39 (p. 520).
31. Peters, *Lorine Niedecker*, pp. 8–9. Niedecker remarked to Louis Zukofsky: 'After I read about the Black Hawk War I don't think much of white people'. Penberthy, *Niedecker and the Correspondence with Zukofsky*, p. 128.
32. Niedecker, 'Extracts from Letters to Kenneth Cox', p. 36.
33. Cid Corman, 'A Footnote to *With Lorine*', in *The Full Note*, pp. 54–5 (p. 54).
34. Peters, *Lorine Niedecker*, pp. 9, 70.
35. Penberthy, *Niedecker and the Correspondence with Zukofsky*, p. 146.
36. Niedecker, cited in Roub, 'Getting to Know Lorine Niedecker', p. 86.
37. J. E. Malpas, *Place and Experience: A Philosophical Topography* (Cambridge: Cambridge University Press, 1999), p. 177.
38. Penberthy, *Niedecker and the Correspondence with Zukofsky*, p. 151. On the tendency of water to combine with other elements, especially earth, see Bachelard, *Water and Dreams*, pp. 13, 93–114.
39. Richard Caddell, 'Consider: Lorine Niedecker and her Environment', in *Lorine Niedecker: Woman and Poet*, pp. 281–6 (p. 282).
40. Niedecker, *'Between Your House and Mine'*, p. 208.
41. Hair, *Avant-Folk*, p. 7.
42. Lorine Niedecker, 'Local Letters', in *Lorine Niedecker: Woman and Poet*, pp. 88–99 (p. 94). For a thorough critical assessment of Niedecker's principled anonymity, see DuPlessis, *Blue Studios*, pp. 139–61.
43. Davidson, *On the Outskirts of Form*, pp. 76, 87.
44. Edward S. Casey, *The World on Edge* (Bloomington: Indiana University Press, 2017), pp. 7–8, 15.
45. Casey, *The World on Edge*, pp. 77, 78.

46. Casey, *The World on Edge*, pp. 9, 146–50.
47. Mary Pinard, 'Niedecker's Grammar of Flooding', in *Radical Vernacular*, pp. 21–30 (pp. 22–3).
48. Penberthy, *Niedecker and the Correspondence with Zukofsky*, p. 170.
49. Penberthy, *Niedecker and the Correspondence with Zukofsky*, pp. 249, 250.
50. See John Withington, *Flood: Nature and Culture* (London: Reaktion Books, 2013), pp. 55–6.
51. For the relevant biographical details, see Peters, *Lorine Niedecker*, pp. 10–11, 17.
52. Rae Armantrout, 'Darkinfested', in *Radical Vernacular*, pp. 103–12 (pp. 103, 107).
53. Lawrence Buell, *The Environmental Imagination: Thoreau, Nature Writing, and the Formation of American Culture* (Cambridge, MA: The Belknap Press of Harvard University Press, 1995), p. 221.
54. Niedecker, 'Between Your House and Mine', p. 33.
55. Pinard, 'Niedecker's Grammar of Flooding,' p. 29.
56. DuPlessis suggests that the two boats might be interpreted as metaphors for the speaker's parents. DuPlessis, *Blue Studios*, p. 153.
57. Casey, *The World on Edge*, p. 79.
58. Niedecker, 'Between Your House and Mine', p. 140.
59. Jonathan Skinner, 'Particular Attention: Lorine Niedecker's Natural Histories', in *Radical Vernacular*, pp. 41–60 (p. 45); Penberthy, *Niedecker and the Correspondence with Zukofsky*, p. 354.
60. Niedecker cited in Peters, *Lorine Niedecker*, p. 232.
61. *The Princeton Encyclopedia of Poetry and Poetics*, 4th edn, eds Stephen Cushman, Clare Cavanagh, Jahan Ramazani, and Paul Rouzer (Princeton: Princeton University Press, 2012), p. 990.
62. Niedecker, cited in Jane Shaw Knox, *Lorine Niedecker: An Original Biography* (Fort Atkinson, WI: Dwight Foster Public Library, 1987), p. 14.
63. DuPlessis, 'Lorine Niedecker's "Paean to Place"', p. 403.
64. Penberthy, *Niedecker and the Correspondence with Zukofsky*, pp. 238, 239, n. 1.
65. Berry, 'Paradoxes of Form', p. 215.
66. Duplessis, 'Lorine Niedecker's "Paean to Place"', p. 404.
67. Theodor W. Adorno, *Notes to Literature: Volume One*, ed. Rolf Tiedemann, trans. Shierry Weber Nicholsen (New York: Columbia University Press, 1991), p. 97.
68. Compare Genesis 1.2: 'And the Spirit of God moved upon the face of the waters.'
69. David Macauley, *Elemental Philosophy: Earth, Air, Fire, and Water as Elemental Ideas* (Albany: State University of New York Press, 2010), p. 45.
70. Peters, *Lorine Niedecker*, p. 32; DuPlessis, 'Lorine Niedecker's "Paean to Place"', p. 407.
71. Niedecker's father, Henry, was born in Sutter, California, and moved with his family to Wisconsin when he was a boy. See Peters, *Lorine Niedecker*, p. 10.

72. David Hendy, *Noise: A Human History of Sound and Listening* (London: Profile Books, 2013), p. 22. On the sora rail as an archetypal bird of Midwestern marshlands, see Paul L. Errington, *Of Men and Marshes* (Iowa City: University of Iowa Press, 2012), p. 17.
73. Anne Waldman, 'Who Is Sounding? Awakened View, Gaps, Silence, Cage, Niedecker', in *Radical Vernacular*, pp. 207–22 (p. 218).
74. Peters, *Lorine Niedecker*, pp. 10, 66, 100; Penberthy, *Niedecker and the Correspondence with Zukofsky*, p. 140.
75. Penberthy, *Niedecker and the Correspondence with Zukofsky*, p. 243.
76. Peters, *Lorine Niedecker*, p. 66.
77. Dana Gardner and Nancy Overcott, *Fifty Common Birds of the Upper Midwest* (Iowa City: University of Iowa Press, 2006), p. 19; Penberthy, *Niedecker and the Correspondence with Zukofsky*, pp. 148–9, 151.
78. Jonathan Williams, cited in Knox, *Lorine Niedecker*, pp. 27–8.
79. Gilbert Sorrentino, 'Misconstruing Lorine Niedecker', in *Lorine Niedecker: Woman and Poet*, pp. 287–92 (p. 289).
80. Lorine Niedecker, 'Lake Superior Country', in *Lorine Niedecker: Woman and Poet*, pp. 311–26 (p. 313); Lorine Niedecker, *North Central* (London: Fulcrum, 1968).
81. Skinner, 'Particular Attention', pp. 42, 48.
82. Peters, *Lorine Niedecker*, p. 205; Penberthy, *Niedecker and the Correspondence with Zukofsky*, p. 90.
83. Niedecker, *'Between Your House and Mine'*, p. 91.
84. Peters, *Lorine Niedecker*, pp. 205, 207.
85. Niedecker, *'Between Your House and Mine'*, p. 94.
86. Jenny Penberthy, 'Writing Lake Superior', in *Radical Vernacular*, pp. 61–79 (p. 61).
87. Margaret Dickie, *On the Modernist Long Poem* (Iowa City: University of Iowa Press, 1986), p. 6.
88. Kenneth Cox, 'The Longer Poems', in *Lorine Niedecker: Woman and Poet*, pp. 303–10 (p. 303).
89. Edward W. Said, *On Late Style: Music and Literature Against the Grain* (London: Bloomsbury, 2006), pp. 6, 7.
90. Niedecker, *'Between Your House and Mine'*, p. 153.
91. Niedecker, 'Local Letters', p. 90.
92. Joseph Conte, 'Natural Histories: Serial Form in the Later Poetry of Lorine Niedecker', in *Lorine Niedecker: Woman and Poet*, pp. 347–60 (p. 347).
93. Thomas Nail, *Theory of the Earth* (Stanford: Stanford University Press, 2021), p. 137.
94. Niedecker, 'Lake Superior Country', p. 311.
95. Niedecker, 'Lake Superior Country', p. 315.
96. Jane Bennett, *Vibrant Matter: A Political Ecology of Things* (Durham, NC: Duke University Press, 2010), p. 14.
97. Casey, *The World on Edge*, p. 14.
98. Doreen Massey, *for space* (London: Sage, 2005), p. 141.
99. Niedecker, 'Lake Superior Country', pp. 313–4.
100. Robert T. Tally Jr., *Spatiality* (Abingdon: Routledge, 2013), p. 45.

101. Douglas Crase, 'Niedecker and the Evolutional Sublime', in *Lorine Niedecker: Woman and Poet*, pp. 327–46 (pp. 330–1); Niedecker, 'Lake Superior Country', p. 316.
102. Massey, *for space*, pp. 107, 106.
103. Donald Davie, 'Lorine Niedecker: Lyric Minimum & Epic Scope', in *The Full Note*, pp. 64–73 (pp. 69, 72, 73).
104. Buell, *The Environmental Imagination*, p. 7.
105. Penberthy, *Niedecker and the Correspondence with Zukofsky*, p. 92.
106. Peters, *Lorine Niedecker*, p. 222.
107. Virginia S. Eifert, *Journeys in Green Places: The Shores and Woods of Wisconsin's Door Peninsula*, rev edn (Sister Bay, WI: Wm. Caxton Ltd., 1989), p. 31.
108. Niedecker, 'Between Your House and Mine', p. 136.
109. Michael Heller, *Uncertain Poetries: Selected Essays on Poets, Poetry and Poetics* (Cambridge: Salt, 2005), p. 102.
110. Davidson, *On the Outskirts of Form*, p. 87.
111. Eifert, *Journeys in Green Places*, p. 21.

5. Charles Olson's Mappemunde

1. Charles Olson, *The Special View of History*, ed. by Ann Charters (Berkeley: Oyez, 1970), p. 20.
2. Charles Olson, *Collected Prose*, eds Donald Allen and Benjamin Friedlander (Berkeley: University of California Press, 1997), p. 17.
3. Brendan C. Gillott, 'The Depth of Charles Olson's *Maximus Poems*', *English* 66.255 (2017), 351–71 (p. 353).
4. Tom Clark, *Charles Olson: The Allegory of a Poet's Life* (New York: W. W. Norton, 1991), pp. 4, 8–9, 19.
5. Clark, *Charles Olson*, pp. 267–8, 166–8; Jim Cocola, *Places in the Making: A Cultural Geography of American Poetry* (Iowa City: University of Iowa Press, 2016), p. 61.
6. Charles Olson, *Selected Letters*, ed. Ralph Maud (Berkeley: University of California Press, 2000), pp. 54, 106–7.
7. Charles Olson, *The Maximus Poems*, ed. George F. Butterick (Berkeley: University of California Press, 1983), p. 14. Further references to this volume will be given parenthetically in the text.
8. Charles Olson, *Muthologos: Lectures and Interviews*, ed. Ralph Maud (Vancouver: Talonbooks, 2010), p. 15; George F. Butterick, *A Guide to the Maximus Poems of Charles Olson* (Berkeley: University of California Press, 1980), pp. xxvii–xxviii, 5–8.
9. Walter Sutton, 'A Visit with William Carlos Williams', in Linda Welshimer Wagner, ed., *Interviews with William Carlos Williams: Speaking Straight Ahead* (New York: New Directions 1976), pp. 38–47 (p. 41).
10. William Carlos Williams, *Paterson*, ed. Christopher MacGowan (New York: New Directions, 2000), p. 7.
11. Michael Davidson, *On the Outskirts of Form: Practicing Cultural Poetics* (Middletown, CT: Wesleyan University Press, 2011), p. 121; Rachel Blau DuPlessis, 'Olson and his *Maximus Poems*', in David Herd, ed.,

      Contemporary Olson (Manchester: Manchester University Press, 2015), pp. 135–48 (p. 137).
12. Olson, cited in Don Byrd, *Charles Olson's* Maximus (Urbana: University of Illinois Press, 1980), p. 7.
13. Byrd, *Charles Olson's* Maximus, pp. 6–7.
14. Olson, cited in *Thomas F. Merrill, The Poetry of Charles Olson: A Primer* (East Brunswick, NJ: Associated University Presses, 1982), p. 163.
15. Olson, *Collected Prose*, pp. 306, 300.
16. Clark, *Charles Olson*, p. 126; James J. Parsons, '"Mr Sauer" and the Writers', *Geographical Review* 86.1 (1996), 22–41 (pp. 30–1, 32).
17. Olson, *Muthologos*, p. 427; Olson, *Collected Prose*, 301.
18. Olson, *Collected Prose*, p. 168; Parsons, '"Mr Sauer and the Writers', 34.
19. Carl Ortwin Sauer, *Land and Life*, ed. John Leighly (Berkeley: University of California Press, 1963), pp. 326, 333.
20. Olson, *Selected Letters*, p. 245.
21. Olson, *Collected Prose*, p. 239; Clark, *Charles Olson*, pp. 114–15.
22. Reitha Pattison, '"Empty Air": Charles Olson's cosmology', in *Contemporary Olson*, pp. 52–63 (p. 55).
23. Olson, *Collected Prose*, p. 17.
24. In 1927, the excavation of a site near Folsom, New Mexico, unearthed artifacts which indicated that humans had been in North America for at least 10,000 years. See Olson, *Collected Prose*, p. 381. Sauer discusses the significance of the finds at Folsom in his 1944 article, 'A Geographic Sketch of Early Man in America', which Olson likely read, noting that they conclusively undermined the widespread 'dogma of the recent peopling of the New World'. Sauer, *Land and Life*, pp. 199–200.
25. Olson, *Collected Prose*, p. 308; Olson, *The Special View of History*, p. 27.
26. Olson, *Collected Prose*, p. 302.
27. Butterick, *A Guide to the Maximus Poems*, pp. 713–4; Cameron McPhail, 'Pytheas of Massalia's Route of Travel', *Phoenix* 68.3/4 (2014), 247–57 (p. 250).
28. McPhail, 'Pytheas of Massalia's Route of Travel', 250–1, 252–4; Daniela Dueck and Kai Brodersen, *Geography in Classical Antiquity* (Cambridge: Cambridge University Press, 2012), pp. 56–7.
29. Byrd, *Charles Olson's* Maximus, p. 91.
30. Peter Sloterdijk, *In the World Interior of Capital: For a Philosophical Theory of Globalization*, trans. Wieland Hoban (Cambridge: Polity, 2013), pp. 21, 40, 34–5.
31. Butterick, *A Guide to the Maximus Poems*, p. 361. See also Duane W. Roller, *Through the Pillars of Herakles: Greco-Roman Exploration of the Atlantic* (New York: Routledge, 2006), pp. 5, 22.
32. Peter Middleton, 'Discoverable Unknowns: Olson's Lifelong Preoccupation with the Sciences', in *Contemporary Olson*, pp. 38–51 (p. 44).
33. Butterick, *A Guide to the Maximus Poems*, pp. 263–4; Middleton, 'Discoverable Unknowns', pp. 45–6.
34. For instance, in his 1951 essay 'The Gate and the Center', Olson argues that: 'We are only just beginning to gauge the backward of literature, breaking through the notion that Greece began it, to the writings farther back'. Olson, *Collected Prose*, p. 171.

35. Davidson, *On the Outskirts of Form*, p. 129.
36. Olson, *Collected Prose*, p. 39.
37. Butterick, *A Guide to the Maximus Poems*, p. xl.
38. See Butterick, *A Guide to the Maximus Poems*, pp. 590–1, 592.
39. On the paratextual significance of book covers, see Gérard Genette, *Paratexts: Thresholds of Interpretation*, trans. by Jane E. Lewin (Cambridge: Cambridge University Press, 1997), pp. 23–32.
40. Clark, *Charles Olson*, p. 269; Ralph Maud, *Charles Olson's Reading: A Biography* (Carbondale: Southern Illinois University Press, 1996), pp. 178–9.
41. Maud, *Charles Olson's Reading*, p. 203.
42. Jon Hegglund, *World Views: Metageographies of Modernist Fiction* (New York: Oxford University Press, 2012), p. 15.
43. Evelyn Edson, *The World Map, 1300–1492: The Persistence of Tradition and Transformation* (Baltimore: Johns Hopkins University Press, 2007), pp. 14–15.
44. Naomi Reed Kline, *Maps of Medieval Thought: The Hereford Paradigm* (Woodbridge: The Boydell Press, 2001), p. 12; Edson, *The World Map*, pp. 22–3.
45. Olson, *Muthologos*, p. 118.
46. Edson, *The World Map*, p. 20; Alessandro Scafi, 'Mapping Eden: Cartographies of the Earthly Paradise', in Denis Cosgrove, ed., *Mappings* (London: Reaktion Books, 1999), pp. 50–70 (pp. 63–5).
47. Sloterdijk, *In the World Interior of Capital*, pp. 40–2.
48. David N. Livingstone, *The Geographical Tradition: Episodes in the History of a Contested Enterprise* (Oxford: Blackwell, 1992), pp. 49–51.
49. Sloterdijk, *In the World Interior of Capital*, pp. 106–7.
50. James L. Smith, 'Europe's Confused Transmutation: the Realignment of Moral Cartography in Juan de la Cosa's *Mappa Mundi* (1500)', *European Review of History – Revue européene d'histoire* 21.6 (2014), 799–816 (pp. 802, 810–11).
51. Edward S. Casey, *Representing Place: Landscape Painting and Maps* (Minneapolis: University of Minnesota Press, 2002), pp. 181–2; Butterick, *A Guide to the Maximus Poems*, pp. 117–18.
52. Douglas R. McManis, *Colonial New England: A Historical Geography* (New York: Oxford University Press, 1975), pp. 20–1.
53. J. B. Harley, *The New Nature of Maps: Essays in the History of Cartography*, ed. Paul Laxton (Baltimore: Johns Hopkins University Press, 2001), pp. 179, 180.
54. Harley, *The New Nature of Maps*, p. 181. On the importance of names and the practice of re-naming in the history of European colonialism generally, see Sloterdijk, *In the World Interior of Capital*, pp. 104–6.
55. Cocola, *Places in the Making*, p. 69. During a 1962 lecture at Godard College, Olson declared: 'Smith is one of my heroes'. Olson, *Muthologos*, p. 15.
56. Olson, *Collected Prose*, pp. 319, 320.
57. Olson briefly comments on the absence of 'Indian names' on Cape Ann in a late interview with Herb Kenny. Olson, *Muthologos*, p. 441.
58. McManis, *Colonial New England*, pp. 15–17.

59. Harley, *The New Nature of Maps*, p. 171.
60. Hegglund, *World Views*, p. 15.
61. Olson, *Selected Letters*, p. 252. See the photograph of Olson's heavily annotated copy of Champlain's map in Butterick, *A Guide to the Maximus Poems*, between pp. xxxii and xxxiii.
62. Olson, *Collected Prose*, pp. 243, 244.
63. Tim Woods, '"Moving Among my Particulars": the "Negative Dialectics" of *The Maximus Poems*', in *Contemporary Olson*, pp. 233–51 (p. 235).
64. Olson, *Selected Letters*, pp. 187–90; Butterick, *A Guide to the Maximus Poems*, pp. xxxix, lii–liii; George F. Butterick, *Editing The Maximus Poems: Supplementary Notes* (Storrs: The University of Connecticut Library, 1983), p. vii and Appendix 1: Difficult manuscripts.
65. Mandy Bloomfield, *Archaeopoetics: Word, Image, History* (Tuscaloosa: The University of Alabama Press, 2016), p. 3.
66. Butterick, *A Guide to the Maximus Poems*, p. 207.
67. Butterick, *A Guide to the Maximus Poems*, p. 498.
68. Tim Cresswell, 'Towards *Topopoetics*: Space, Place and the Poem', in Bruce B. Janz, ed., *Place, Space and Hermeneutics* (Cham: Springer, 2017), pp. 319–31 (p. 326).
69. John Mack, *The Sea: A Cultural History* (London: Reaktion Books, 2011), p. 169.
70. Woods, '"Moving among my particulars"', p. 237.
71. John R. Gillis, *The Human Shore: Seacoasts in History* (Chicago: The University of Chicago Press, 2012), p. 40.
72. Gillis, *The Human Shore*, p. 55.
73. Olson, *Muthologos*, p. 419.
74. Paul Giles, *The Global Remapping of American Literature* (Princeton: Princeton University Press, 2011), pp. 10, 11.
75. Gillis, *The Human Shore*, p. 94.
76. Michael André Bernstein, *The Tale of the Tribe: Ezra Pound and the Modern Verse Epic* (Princeton: Princeton University Press, 1980), p. 249.
77. Bernstein, *The Tale of the Tribe*, p. 285.
78. Walter Benjamin, *Illuminations*, ed. Hannah Arendt, trans. Harry Zohn (London: Pimlico, 1999), p. 265.
79. W. Jeffrey Bolster, *The Mortal Sea: Fishing the Atlantic in the Age of Sail* (Cambridge, MA: The Belknap Press of Harvard University Press, 2012), p. 43.
80. Bolster, *The Mortal Sea*, p. 271.
81. Bernstein, *The Tale of the Tribe*, pp. 260–1.
82. Clark, *Charles Olson*, pp. 30–3; Ralph Maud, *Charles Olson at the Harbor* (Vancouver: Talonbooks, 2008), pp. 39–40.
83. Margaret Cohen, 'Literary Studies on the Terraqueous Globe', *PMLA* 125.3 (2010), 657–62 (p. 660).
84. Olson, *Selected Letters*, pp. 69, 29.
85. Olson, *Muthologos*, p. 226.
86. Anthony Mellors, *Late Modernist Poetics: From Pound to Prynne* (Manchester: Manchester University Press, 2005), p. 110.
87. DuPlessis, 'Olson and his *Maximus Poems*', pp. 137, 138.
88. Mack, *The Sea*, pp. 29, 175.

89. Giles, *The Global Remapping of American Literature*, p. 10.
90. David Herd, 'The View from Gloucester: Open Field Poetics and the Politics of Movement', in David Herd, ed., *Contemporary Olson*, pp. 278, 282.
91. Clark, *Charles Olson*, pp. 4, 10.
92. Olson, *Collected Prose*, p. 219.
93. Clark, *Charles Olson*, p. 4.
94. Olson, *Collected Prose*, pp. 205, 206.
95. Clark, *Charles Olson*, pp. 73–4.
96. Clark, *Charles Olson*, pp. 132–3; Maud, *Charles Olson at the Harbor*, pp. 68–9.
97. Olson, *Selected Letters*, pp. 75, 77.
98. Herd, 'The View from Gloucester', pp. 275, 273.
99. Olson, *Muthologos*, p. 439.
100. Butterick, *A Guide to the Maximus Poems*, p. 368.
101. Thomas Nail, *The Figure of the Migrant* (Stanford: Stanford University Press, 2015), p. 13.
102. Nail, *The Figure of the Migrant*, pp. 39, 42.
103. Nail, *The Figure of the Migrant*, p. 13.
104. Olson, *Collected Prose*, p. 160.
105. Olson, *Collected Prose*, p. 168.
106. Miriam Nichols, 'Myth and Document in Charles Olson's *Maximus Poems*', in *Contemporary Olson*, pp. 25–37 (p. 31).
107. Olson, *Collected Prose*, p. 173; Michael H. Fisher, *Migration: A World History* (New York: Oxford University Press, 2014), p. 13.
108. Hesiod, *Theogony; Works and Days* / Theognis, *Elegies*, trans. Dorothea Wender (London: Penguin, 1973), pp. 50–1; Butterick, *A Guide to the Maximus Poems*, pp. 217–18.
109. Butterick, *A Guide to the Maximus Poems*, pp. 378–9; Olson, *Muthologos*, pp. 440–1.
110. Clark, *Charles Olson*, p. 119; Butterick, *A Guide to the Maximus Poems*, p. xxi.
111. Gabriel Gohau, *A History of Geology*, trans. Albert V. Carozzi and Marguerite Carozzi (New Brunswick: Rutgers University Press, 1990), pp. 187, 188.
112. Maud, *Charles Olson's Reading*, p. 179; Butterick, *A Guide to the Maximus Poems*, pp. 652–3.
113. *The Collected Letters of Charles Olson and J. H. Prynne*, ed. Ryan Dobran (Albuquerque: University of New Mexico Press, 2017), pp. 155, 137–8.
114. J. Tuzo Wilson, 'Continental Drift', *Scientific American* 208.4 (1963), 86–103 (pp. 89–90, 93–6).
115. Maud, *Charles Olson's Reading*, pp. 178–9, 197; Butterick, *A Guide to the Maximus Poems*, p. 731.
116. Mellors, *Late Modernist Poetics*, p. 33.
117. Byrd, *Charles Olson's Maximus*, p. 114.
118. Wilson, 'Continental Drift,' 99; Gohau, *A History of Geology*, pp. 212–13.
119. Gillott, 'The Depth of Charles Olson's *Maximus Poems*', 366.

120. DuPlessis, 'Olson and his *Maximus Poems*', p. 136.
121. J. H. Prynne, 'On *Maximus IV, V, VI*', *Minutes of the Charles Olson Society* 28 (1999), 3–13 (p. 6).
122. Olson, *Collected Prose*, p. 369.
123. David Harvey, *Justice, Nature and the Geography of Difference* (Oxford: Blackwell, 1996), p. 294.
124. Olson, *Muthologos*, p. 122.
125. Wilson, 'Continental Drift', 90.
126. Olson, *Collected Prose*, pp. 306–7.
127. Olson cited in Clark, *Charles Olson*, p. 272.
128. Olson, *Muthologos*, p. 121.

6. Gwendolyn Brooks: From Bronzeville to the Warpland

1. Gwendolyn Brooks, *Report from Part One* (Detroit: Broadside Press, 1972), p. 70; Rebekah Presson, 'Interviews with Gwendolyn Brooks', in Gloria Wade Gayles, ed., *Conversations with Gwendolyn Brooks* (Jackson: University Press of Mississippi, 2003), pp. 133–9 (p. 137).
2. Angharad Saunders, *Place and the Scene of Literary Practice* (Abingdon: Routledge, 2018), p. xii.
3. Brooks, *Report from Part One*, p. 69.
4. 'I always say that poetry is life distilled.' Kevin Bezner, 'A Life Distilled: An Interview with Gwendolyn Brooks', in *Conversations with Gwendolyn Brooks*, pp. 117–24 (p. 124).
5. See Alison Cummings, 'Public Subjects: Race and the Critical Reception of Gwendolyn Brooks, Erica Hunt, and Harryette Mullen', *Frontiers: A Journal of Women's Studies* 26.2 (2005), 3–36; Courtney Thorsson, 'Gwendolyn Brooks's Black Aesthetic of the Domestic', *MELUS* 40.1 (2015), 149–76 (pp. 149–50).
6. Paul Gilroy, *The Black Atlantic: Modernity and Double Consciousness* (London: Verso, 1993), p. 58.
7. Matthew Hart, *Nations of Nothing But Poetry: Modernism, Transnationalism, and Synthetic Vernacular Writing* (New York: Oxford University Press, 2010), pp. 144, 146.
8. Evie Shockley, *Renegade Poetics: Black Aesthetics and Formal Innovation in African American Poetry* (Iowa City: University of Iowa Press, 2011), p. 28; George Kent, *A Life of Gwendolyn Brooks* (Lexington: The University Press of Kentucky, 1990), pp. 76, 88–90.
9. Kent, *A Life of Gwendolyn Brooks*, pp. 196–202; Brooks, *Report from Part One*, p. 177.
10. Hoyt Fuller, Eugenia Collier, George Kent, and Dudley Randall, 'Interview with Gwendolyn Brooks', in *Conversations with Gwendolyn Brooks*, pp. 67–73 (p. 68); Brooks, *Report from Part One*, pp. 149–50.
11. Gwendolyn Brooks, *Blacks* (Chicago: Third World Press, 1987), p. 442. Further references to this volume will be given parenthetically.
12. Timo Müller, 'The Vernacular Sonnet and the Resurgence of Afro-Modernism in the 1940s', *American Literature* 87.2 (2015), 253–73 (p. 262).

13. Brooks, *Report from Part One*, pp. 170, 173; Presson, 'Interviews with Gwendolyn Brooks', p. 137.
14. Kent, *A Life of Gwendolyn Brooks*, pp. 26–7; Angela Jackson, *A Surprised Queenhood in the New Black Sun: The Life and Legacy of Gwendolyn Brooks* (Boston: Beacon Press, 2017), pp. 12–14.
15. Karen Jackson Ford, 'The Sonnets of Satin-Legs Brooks', *Contemporary Literature* 48.3 (2007), 345–73 (pp. 354–5).
16. Brooks, *Report from Part One*, p. 174; Roy Newquist, 'Gwendolyn Brooks', in *Conversations with Gwendolyn Brooks*, pp. 26–36 (p. 30).
17. Brooks, *Report from Part One*, p. 177; Lubna Najar, 'The Chicago Poetry Group: African American Art and High Modernism at Midcentury', *Women's Studies Quarterly* 33.3/4 (2005), 314–23 (p. 317).
18. James Smethurst, *The African American Roots of Modernism: From Reconstruction to the Harlem Renaissance* (Chapel Hill: The University of North Carolina Press, 2011), p. 13.
19. Smethurst, *The African American Roots of Modernism*, p. 121.
20. Robert Bone and Richard A. Courage, *The Muse in Bronzeville: African American Creative Expression in Chicago, 1932–1950* (New Brunswick: Rutgers University Press, 2011), pp. 6–7, 2.
21. Liesl Olson, *Chicago Renaissance: Literature and Art in the Midwest Metropolis* (New Haven, CT: Yale University Press, 2017), pp. 13, 243.
22. Richard Wright, 'Blueprint for Negro Writing', in Angelyn Mitchell, ed., *Within the Circle: An Anthology of African American Literary Criticism from the Harlem Renaissance to the Present* (Durham, NC: Duke University Press, 1994), pp. 97–106 (pp. 103, 104).
23. Bone and Courage, *The Muse in Bronzeville*, pp. 224, 225.
24. Elizabeth Schroeder Schlabach, *Along the Streets of Bronzeville: Black Chicago's Literary Landscape* (Urbana: University of Illinois Press, 2013), pp. 75, 89.
25. Jackson, *A Surprised Queenhood in the New Black Sun*, pp. 50, 51.
26. Schlabach, *Along the Streets of Bronzeville*, p. 93; Thorsson, 'Gwendolyn Brooks's Black Aesthetic', 150.
27. St Clair Drake and Horace R. Clayton, *Black Metropolis: A Study of Negro Life in a Northern City: Volume II* (New York: Harper & Row, 1967), p. 383; Kent, *A Life of Gwendolyn Brooks*, p. 24.
28. Olson, *Chicago Renaissance*, p. 16; Schlabach, *Along the Streets of Bronzeville*, pp. 20–1.
29. Kent, *A Life of Gwendolyn Brooks*, p. 129.
30. Brooks, *Report from Part One*, p. 160.
31. Manning Marable, *Race, Reform, and Rebellion: The Second Reconstruction in Black America, 1945–1990* (Jackson: University Press of Mississippi, 1991), p. 10.
32. Bone and Courage, *The Muse in Bronzeville*, p. 4; Drake and Clayton, *Black Metropolis: Volume I*, pp. 99, 174, 12.
33. Richard Wright and Edwin Rosskam, *12 Million Black Voices* (New York: Thunder's Mouth Press, 1988), pp. 99, 103.
34. Preston H. Smith, *Racial Democracy and the Black Metropolis: Housing Policy in Postwar Chicago* (Minneapolis: University of Minnesota Press,

2012), pp. 23–4; Drake and Clayton, *Black Metropolis: Volume I*, pp. 179, 184.
35. Schlabach, *Along the Streets of Bronzeville*, p. 24.
36. Bone and Courage, *The Muse in Bronzeville*, pp. 7, 8.
37. Gwendolyn Brooks, 'They Call it Bronzeville', *Holiday* (October 1951), 61–7, 112–16 (p. 61).
38. Brooks recalls taking similar walks 'east of Cottage Grove Avenue' with her young son in the 1940s and remarks, 'we counted ourselves lucky when we weren't thrown at'. Newquist, 'Gwendolyn Brooks', p. 32.
39. Brooks, *Report from Part One*, pp. 135, 47. Brooks said that she 'resented' the fact that she was born in Topeka, for she felt she was 'really a native Chicagoan'. Newquist, 'Gwendolyn Brooks', p. 26.
40. Kent, *A Life of Gwendolyn Brooks*, p. 2.
41. Bone and Courage, *The Muse in Bronzeville*, pp. 97–102; Amy Absher, *The Black Musician in the White City: Race and Music in Chicago, 1900–1967* (Ann Arbor: The University of Michigan Press, 2014), pp. 48–81.
42. Thomas Nail, *The Figure of the Migrant* (Stanford: Stanford University Press, 2015), p. 3.
43. Doreen Massey, *for space* (London: Sage, 2005), pp. 151, 154.
44. Brooks, *Report from Part One*, p. 189.
45. Brooks, *Report from Part One*, pp. 140, 135.
46. Brooks, *Report from Part One*, p. 161.
47. Peter Merriman, *Mobility, Space and Culture* (Abingdon: Routledge, 2012), p. 58.
48. Schlabach, *Along the Streets of Bronzeville*, pp. 9–10, 12.
49. Schlabach, *Along the Streets of Bronzeville*, p. 119.
50. Brooks, cited in Kent, *A Life of Gwendolyn Brooks*, p. 153.
51. Olson, *Chicago Renaissance*, p. 281.
52. Brooks, *Report from Part One*, p. 59.
53. Brooks, cited in Bone and Courage, *The Muse in Bronzeville*, p. 218; Brooks, *Report from Part One*, pp. 159–60.
54. Kent, *A Life of Gwendolyn Brooks*, pp. 26, 40; Brooks, *Report from Part One*, pp. 70, 170.
55. Langston Hughes, 'The Negro Artist and the Racial Mountain', in *Within the Circle*, pp. 55–9 (p. 56).
56. Kent, *A Life of Gwendolyn Brooks*, pp. 4–5, 32–3, 56–9; Jackson, *A Surprised Queenhood*, pp. 19–21, 24, 66; Brooks, *Report from Part One*, pp. 58–9, 160.
57. Brooks, *Report from Part One*, p. 135.
58. Rita Felski, *Doing Time: Feminist Theory and Postmodern Culture* (New York: New York University Press, 2000), p. 90.
59. Henri Lefebvre, *Critique of Everyday Life: Volume I: Introduction*, trans. John Moore (London: Verso, 2008), p. 97.
60. Brooks, 'They Call it Bronzeville', p. 116.
61. Manning Marable, *Beyond Black and White: From Civil Rights to Barack Obama* (London: Verso, 2016), pp. 209–10.
62. Audre Lorde, *Your Silence Will Not Protect You* (London: Silver Press, 2017), p. 100.
63. Marable, *Beyond Black and White*, pp. 211, 210.

64. Claudia Tate, 'Interview with Gwendolyn Brooks', in *Conversations with Gwendolyn Brooks*, pp. 104–10 (p. 108).
65. Felski, *Doing Time*, p. 85.
66. bell hooks, *Yearning: Race, Gender, and Cultural Politics* (London: Turnaround, 1991), p. 47.
67. bell hooks, *Belonging: A Culture of Place* (Abingdon: Routledge, 2008), p. 203.
68. Toni Morrison, *Mouth Full of Blood: Essays, Speeches, Meditations* (London: Vintage, 2020), p. 8.
69. Morrison, *Mouth Full of Blood*, pp. 132, 133.
70. Drake and Clayton, *Black Metropolis: Volume II*, pp. 576–7.
71. Thorsson, 'Gwendolyn Brooks's Black Aesthetic of the Domestic', p. 158.
72. Wright and Rosskam, *12 Million Black Voices*, p. 108.
73. T. S. Eliot, *Collected Poems 1909–1962* (London: Faber, 1974), p. 40.
74. Maria Balshaw, *Looking for Harlem: Urban Aesthetics in African American Literature* (London: Pluto Press, 2000), p. 103.
75. Gaston Bachelard, *The Poetics of Space*, trans. Maria Jolas (Boston: Beacon Press, 1994), pp. 6, 27.
76. Smethurst, *The African American Roots of Modernism*, p. 111.
77. Brooks, *Report from Part One*, p. 165.
78. Jackson, *A Surprised Queenhood in the New Black Sun*, p. 24.
79. Thorsson, 'Gwendolyn Brooks's Black Aesthetic of the Domestic', p. 168.
80. Daniel Bluestone, 'Chicago's Mecca Flat Blues', *Journal of the Society of Architectural Historians* 57.4 (1998), 382–403 (pp. 383, 391).
81. Bluestone, 'Chicago's Mecca Flat Blues', 394, 396, 399–400.
82. John Lowney, *History, Memory, and the Literary Left: Modern American Poetry, 1935–1968* (Iowa City: University of Iowa Press, 2006), pp. 130, 138–40.
83. C. K. Doreski, *Writing America Black: Race Rhetoric in the Public Sphere* (Cambridge: Cambridge University Press, 1998), p. 128.
84. Walter Benjamin, *The Writer of Modern Life: Essays on Charles Baudelaire*, ed. Michael W. Jennings, trans. Howard Eiland (Cambridge, MA: The Belknap Press of Harvard University Press, 2006), p. 146.
85. Kent, *A Life of Gwendolyn Brooks*, p. 42; Jackson, *A Surprised Queenhood in the New Black Sun*, pp. 15–16; Newquist, 'Gwendolyn Brooks', p. 28.
86. Kent, *A Life of Gwendolyn Brooks*, p. 124.
87. Homi K. Bhabha, *The Location of Culture* (Abingdon: Routledge, 2004), p. 90.
88. Olson, *Chicago Renaissance*, p. 281.
89. Brooks, *Report from Part One*, p. 189.
90. Lowney, *History, Memory, and the Literary Left*, p. 141.
91. Brooks, *Report from Part One*, p. 190.
92. Fuller et al., 'Interview with Gwendolyn Brooks', p. 69; Houston A. Baker, Jr., *Modernism and the Harlem Renaissance* (Chicago: The University of Chicago Press, 1989), p. 86.
93. Brooks, *Report from Part One*, p. 190.
94. Daniela Kukrechtová, 'The Death and Life of a Chicago Edifice: Gwendolyn Brooks's "In the Mecca"', *African American Review* 43.2/3 (2009), 457–72 (p. 460).

95. Henri Lefebvre, *Rhythmanalysis: Space, Time and Everyday Life*, trans. Stuart Elden and Gerald Moore (London: Bloomsbury, 2013), p. 38.
96. Brooks, *Report from Part One*, pp. 133–4.
97. Newquist, 'Gwendolyn Brooks', p. 32.
98. Henri Lefebvre, *Critique of Everyday Life: Volume II: Foundations for a Sociology of the Everyday*, trans. John Moore (London: Verso, 2002), p. 310.
99. Brooks, *Report from Part One*, p. 71.
100. Patricia Hill Collins, *Black Feminist Thought: Knowledge, Consciousness, and the Politics of Empowerment* (New York: Routledge, 2009), p. 62.
101. Schlabach, *Along the Streets of Bronzeville*, p. 22.
102. Kent, *A Life of Gwendolyn Brooks*, p. 210; Jackson, *A Surprised Queenhood in the New Black Sun*, p. 101.
103. Margo Natalie Crawford, 'Black Light on the *Wall of Respect*: The Chicago Black Arts Movement', in Lisa Gail Collins and Margo Natalie Crawford, eds, *New Thoughts on the Black Arts Movement* (New Brunswick: Rutgers University Press, 2006), pp. 23–42 (p. 27).
104. Lowney, *History, Memory, and the Literary Left*, pp. 153–4.
105. Marable, *Race, Reform, and Rebellion*, pp. 82–3.
106. Brooks, *Report from Part One*, p. 83.
107. Brooks, *Report from Part One*, p. 183.
108. Shockley, *Renegade Poetics*, p. 40.
109. Brooks, *Report from Part One*, p. 183.
110. See Julia Bloch, '"Shut your rhetorics in a box": Gwendolyn Brooks and Lyric Dilemma', *Tulsa Studies in Women's Literature* 35.2 (2016), 439–62 (pp. 439–40); Ford, 'The Sonnets of Satin-Legs Brooks', 346–8; Carl Phillips, 'Brooks's Prosody: Three Sermons on the Warpland', *Poetry* 210.3 (2017), 246–52 (pp. 246–7).
111. Kent, *A Life of Gwendolyn Brooks*, pp. 232, 260; Haki Madhubuti, 'Black Books Bulletin Interviews Gwen Brooks', in *Conversations with Gwendolyn Brooks*, pp. 74–84 (p. 76). See also James D. Sullivan, 'Killing John Cabot and Publishing Black: Gwendolyn Brooks's *Riot*', *African American Review* 36.4 (2002), 557–69.
112. Madhubuti, 'Black Books Bulletin Interviews Gwen Brooks', p. 74; Marable, *Race, Reform, and Rebellion*, pp. 42–3.
113. Christopher Metress aptly describes Brooks's 'A Bronzeville Mother Loiters in Mississippi' as 'the first serious work by an African American to re-imagine Till as a figure of disruption'. Christopher Metress, '"No Justice, No Peace": The Figure of Emmett Till in African American Literature', *MELUS* 28.1 (2003), 87–103 (p. 90).
114. Brooks, *Report from Part One*, p. 165; Tate, 'Interview with Gwendolyn Brooks', p. 107.
115. Martin Luther King, Jr, *Why We Can't Wait* (London: Penguin, 2018), pp. 6, 19; Brooks, *Report from Part One*, p. 187.
116. Tate, 'Interview with Gwendolyn Brooks', p. 106.
117. Kent, *A Life of Gwendolyn Brooks*, pp. 118, 141.
118. Marable, *Race, Reform, and Rebellion*, p. 65; Annette Debo, 'Reflecting Violence in the Warpland: Gwendolyn Brooks's *Riot*', *African American Review* 39.1/2 (2005), 143–52 (p. 144).

119. Jeni Rinner, 'From Bronzeville to the Mecca and After: Gwendolyn Brooks and the Location of Black Identity', *MELUS* 40.4 (2015), 150–72 (p. 151).
120. Brooks, *Report from Part One*, p. 45. See Annette Debo, 'Signifying *Afrika*: Gwendolyn Brooks's Later Poetry', *Calalloo* 29.1 (2006), 168–81.
121. Marable, *Race, Reform, and Rebellion*, pp. 92, 93.
122. Brooks, *Report from Part One*, p. 152.
123. Rinner, 'From Bronzeville to the Mecca and After', p. 168.
124. Debo, 'Reflecting Violence in the Warpland,' p. 150.
125. Michel de Certeau, *The Practice of Everyday Life*, trans. Steven Rendall (Berkeley: University of California Press, 1988), p. 18.
126. Sullivan, 'Killing John Cabot and Publishing Black,' 566.

Conclusion: After Late Modernism

1. Peter Howarth, *The Cambridge Introduction to Modernist Poetry* (Cambridge: Cambridge University Press, 2012), p. 220.
2. Marjorie Perloff, *21st-Century Modernism: The 'New' Poetics* (Oxford: Blackwell, 2002), p. 164.
3. Anthony Mellors, *Late Modernist Poetics: From Pound to Prynne* (Manchester: Manchester University Press, 2005), p. 42.
4. Anthony Mellors, 'Modernism after Modernism', in Alex Davis and Lee M. Jenkins, eds, *A History of Modernist Poetry* (Cambridge: Cambridge University Press, 2015), pp. 481–502 (p. 482).
5. Perloff, *21st-Century Modernism*, pp. 164, 5.
6. Eric Mottram, 'The British Poetry Revival, 1960–75,', in Robert Hampson and Peter Barry, eds, *New British Poetries: The Scope of the Possible* (Manchester: Manchester University Press, 1993), pp. 15–50 (pp. 27, 39).
7. Robert Sheppard, *The Poetry of Saying: British Poetry and its Discontents, 1950–2000* (Liverpool: Liverpool University Press, 2005), p. 36.
8. Sheppard, *The Poetry of Saying*, p. 39; Mottram, 'The British Poetry Revival,' p. 13.
9. Drew Milne, 'Neo-Modernism and Avant-Garde Orientations', in Nigel Alderman and C. D. Blanton, eds, *A Concise Companion to Postwar British and Irish Poetry* (Chichester: Wiley Blackwell, 2009), pp. 155–75 (pp. 165, 161).
10. Milne, 'Neo-Modernism and Avant-Garde Orientations', p. 161.
11. Redell Olsen, 'Postmodern Poetry in Britain,' in Neil Corcoran, ed., *The Cambridge Companion to Twentieth-century English Poetry* (Cambridge: Cambridge University Press, 2007), pp. 42–56 (pp. 43–4).
12. Mark Scroggins, 'US Modernism II: the Other Tradition – Williams, Zukofsky, Olson', in Alex Davis and Lee M. Jenkins, eds, *The Cambridge Companion to Modernist Poetry* (Cambridge: Cambridge University Press, 2007), pp. 181–94 (p. 189); Tom Clark, *Charles Olson: The Allegory of a Poet's Life* (New York: W. W. Norton, 1991), pp. 254–5.
13. Sheppard, *The Poetry of Saying*, p. 58.
14. Harriet Tarlo, 'Radical British Landscape Poetry in the Bunting Tradition'. in Richard Price and James McGonigal, eds, *The Star You Steer By: Basil Bunting and British Modernism* (Amsterdam: Rodopi, 2000), pp. 151–81;

Edward Dorn, *Ed Dorn Live: Lectures, Interviews, and Outtakes*, ed. Joseph Richey (Ann Arbor: University of Michigan Press, 2007), p. 85.
15. Maggie O'Sullivan, 'To the Reader', in Maggie O'Sullivan, ed., *Out of Everywhere: Linguistically Innovative Poetry by Women in North America & the UK* (London/Benhall: Reality Street Editions, 1996), pp. 9–10 (p. 10).
16. Iain Sinclair, 'Introduction', in Iain Sinclair, ed., *Conductors of Chaos* (London: Picador, 1996), pp. xiii– xx (p. xix).
17. Evie Shockley, *Renegade Poetics: Black Aesthetics and Formal Innovation in African American Poetry* (Iowa City: University of Iowa Press, 2011), pp. 109–12.
18. Clark, *Charles Olson*, pp. 323–5; Peter Barry, *Poetry Wars: British Poetry of the 1970s and the Battle of Earl's Court* (Great Wilbraham: Salt, 2006), p. 19.
19. David Harvey, *The Condition of Postmodernity: An Enquiry into the Origins of Cultural Change* (Oxford: Basil Blackwell, 1989), p. 284.
20. Eric Falci, 'Place, Space, and Landscape', in *A Concise Companion to Postwar British and Irish Poetry*, pp. 200–20 (p. 201).
21. Wendy Mulford, *and suddenly supposing: Selected Poems* (Buckfastleigh: Etruscan books, 2001), p. 160.
22. Harriet Tarlo, 'Introduction', in Harriet Tarlo, ed., *The Ground Aslant: An Anthology of Radical Landscape Poetry* (Exeter: Shearsman, 2011), pp. 7–18 (pp. 7, 14).
23. See Neal Alexander, 'Senses of place', in Robert T. Tally Jr, ed., *The Routledge Handbook of Literature and Space* (Abingdon: Routledge, 2017), pp. 39–49.
24. Lytle Shaw, *Fieldworks: From Place to Site in Postwar Poetics* (Tuscaloosa: The University of Alabama Press, 2013), pp. 4, 6, 7.
25. Susan Howe, *Singularities* (Middletown, CT: Wesleyan University Press, 1990), p. 40.
26. Ian Davidson, *Ideas of Space in Contemporary Poetry* (Basingstoke: Palgrave Macmillan, 2007), p. 59.
27. Edward Dorn, *Collected Poems*, ed. by Jennifer Dunbar Dorn (Manchester: Carcanet, 2012), pp. 160–1.
28. Jim Cocola, *Places in the Making: A Cultural Geography of American Poetry* (Iowa City: University of Iowa Press, 2016), pp. 4, 78.
29. Simon Gikandi, *Writing in Limbo: Modernism and Caribbean Literature* (Ithaca, NY: Cornell University Press, 1992), pp. 4–5, 16.
30. Jahan Ramazani, 'Modernist Bricolage, Postcolonial Hybridity', *Modernism/modernity* 13.3 (2006), 445–63 (p. 448).
31. Jahan Ramazani, 'Modernist Inflections, Postcolonial Directions', in *A History of Modernist Poetry*, pp. 459–78 (pp. 470–1).
32. Nathaniel Mackey, 'An Interview with Kamau Brathwaite', in Stewart Brown, ed., *The Art of Kamau Brathwaite* (Bridgend: Seren, 1995), pp. 13–32 (p. 13).
33. Laurence A. Breiner, 'Postcolonial Caribbean Poetry', in Jahan Ramazani, ed., *The Cambridge Companion to Postcolonial Poetry* (Cambridge: Cambridge University Press, 2017), pp. 19–30 (p. 23).
34. Edward [Kamau] Brathwaite, *The Arrivants: A New World Trilogy* (Oxford: Oxford University Press, 1996), p. 40.

35. Matthew Hart, *Nations of Nothing But Poetry: Modernism, Transnationalism, and Synthetic Vernacular Writing* (New York: Oxford University Press, 2010), pp. 112, 113.
36. M. NourbeSe Philip, *She Tries Her Tongue, Her Silence Softly Breaks* (Middletown, CT: Wesleyan University Press, 2014), p. 82.
37. Philip, *She Tries Her Tongue*, p. 32.
38. Kristen Mahlis, 'A Poet of Place: An Interview with M. NourbeSe Philip', *Callaloo* 27.3 (2004), 682–97 (p. 683).
39. Mandy Bloomfield, *Archaeopoetics: Word, Image, History* (Tuscaloosa: The University of Alabama Press, 2016), p. 200.
40. M. NourbeSe Philip, *Zong!* (Middletown, CT: Wesleyan University Press, 2008), pp. 39, 201–2.
41. Edward Kamau Brathwaite, *X/Self* (Oxford: Oxford University Press, 1987), p. 128.
42. Mackey, 'An Interview with Kamau Brathwaite', p. 25.

Bibliography

Primary Texts

Brathwaite, Edward [Kamau], *The Arrivants: A New World Trilogy* (Oxford: Oxford University Press, 1996).
Brathwaite, Edward Kamau, *X/Self* (Oxford: Oxford University Press, 1987).
Brooks, Gwendolyn, *Blacks* (Chicago: Third World Press, 1987).
Brooks, Gwendolyn, *Report from Part One* (Detroit: Broadside Press, 1972).
Brooks, Gwendolyn, 'They Call it Bronzeville', *Holiday* (October 1951), 61–7, 112–16.
Bunting, Basil, *Basil Bunting on Poetry*, ed. Peter Makin (Baltimore: The Johns Hopkins Press, 1999).
Bunting, Basil, *Briggflatts* (Tarset: Bloodaxe Books, 2009).
Bunting, Basil, *Bunting's Persia*, ed. Don Share (Chicago, IL: Flood Editions, 2012).
Bunting, Basil, *The Poems of Basil Bunting*, ed. Don Share (London: Faber, 2016).
Dorn, Edward, *Collected Poems*, ed. Jennifer Dunbar Dorn (Manchester: Carcanet, 2012).
Eliot, T. S., *Collected Poems 1909–1962* (London: Faber, 1974).
Graham, W. S., 'from Poetry Society Bulletins', *Edinburgh Review* 75 (1987), 37.
Graham, W. S., *New Collected Poems*, ed. Matthew Francis (London: Faber, 2004).
Graham, W. S., *The Nightfisherman: Selected Letters*, eds Michael and Margaret Snow (Manchester: Carcanet, 1999).
Hesiod, *Theogony; Works and Days* / Theognis, *Elegies*, trans. Dorothea Wender (London: Penguin, 1973).
Hopkins, Gerard Manley, *Selected Poetry*, ed. Catherine Phillips (Oxford: Oxford University Press, 1996).
Howe, Susan, *Singularities* (Middletown, CT: Wesleyan University Press, 1990).
Jones, David, *Epoch and Artist: Selected Writings*, ed. Harman Grisewood (London: Faber and Faber, 1959).
Jones, David, *In Parenthesis* (London: Faber and Faber, 1963).

Jones, David, *The Anathémata: Fragments of an Attempted Writing* (London: Faber, 1972).
Jones, David, *Letters to Vernon Watkins*, ed. Ruth Pryor (Cardiff: University of Wales Press, 1976).
Jones, David, *The Dying Gaul and Other Writings*, ed. Harman Grisewood (London: Faber and Faber, 1978).
Jones, David, *Dai Greatcoat: A Self-portrait of David Jones in his Letters*, ed. René Hague (London: Faber and Faber, 1980).
Jones, David, *Letters to a Friend*, ed. Aneurin Talfan Davies (Swansea: Triskele Books, 1980).
Jones, David, *The Roman Quarry and Other Sequences*, eds Harman Grisewood and René Hague (London: Agenda Editions, 1981).
Jones, David, *The Sleeping Lord and Other Fragments* (London: Faber and Faber, 1995).
Joyce, James, *Finnegans Wake*, 3rd edn (London: Faber and Faber, 1975).
Joyce, James, *Ulysses: The 1922 Text*, ed. Jeri Johnson (Oxford: Oxford University Press, 2008).
Mulford, Wendy, *and suddenly supposing: Selected Poems* (Buckfastleigh: Etruscan Books, 2001).
Niedecker, Lorine, 'Extracts from Letters to Kenneth Cox,' in Peter Dent, ed., *The Full Note: Lorine Niedecker* (Budleigh Salterton: Interim Press, 1983), pp. 36–42.
Niedecker, Lorine, *'Between Your House and Mine': The Letters of Lorine Niedecker to Cid Corman, 1960–1970*, ed. Lisa Pater Faranda (Durham, NC: Duke University Press, 1986).
Niedecker, Lorine, 'Lake Superior Country' in Jenny Penberthy, ed., *Lorine Niedecker: Woman and Poet* (Orono, ME: National Poetry Foundation, University of Maine, 1996), pp. 311–26.
Niedecker, Lorine, 'Local Letters,' in Jenny Penberthy, ed., *Lorine Niedecker: Woman and Poet* (Orono, ME: National Poetry Foundation, University of Maine, 1996), pp. 88–99.
Niedecker, Lorine, *Collected Works*, ed. Jenny Penberthy (Berkeley: University of California Press, 2002).
Olson, Charles, *The Special View of History*, ed. Ann Charters (Berkeley: Oyez, 1970).
Olson, Charles, *The Maximus Poems*, ed. George F. Butterick (Berkeley: University of California Press, 1983).
Olson, Charles, *Collected Prose*, ed. Donald Allen and Benjamin Friedlander (Berkeley: University of California Press, 1997).
Olson, Charles, *Selected Letters*, ed. Ralph Maud (Berkeley: University of California Press, 2000).
Olson, Charles, *Muthologos: Lectures and Interviews*, ed. Ralph Maud (Vancouver: Talonbooks, 2010).
Philip, M. NourbeSe, *Zong!* (Middletown, CT: Wesleyan University Press, 2008).
Philip, M. NourbeSe, *She Tries Her Tongue, Her Silence Softly Breaks* (Middletown, CT: Wesleyan University Press, 2014).
Pound, Ezra, *The Cantos of Ezra Pound* (New York: New Directions, 1970).

Williams, William Carlos, *I Wanted to Write a Poem: The Autobiography of the Works of a Poet*, ed. Edith Heal (New York: New Directions, 1978).
Williams, William Carlos, *Paterson*, ed. Christopher MacGowan (New York: New Directions, 1992).

Secondary Texts

Absher, Amy, *The Black Musician in the White City: Race and Music in Chicago, 1900–1967* (Ann Arbor: The University of Michigan Press, 2014).
Adorno, Theodor W., *Notes to Literature: Volume One*, ed. Rolf Tiedemann, trans. Shierry Weber Nicholsen (New York: Columbia University Press, 1991).
Adorno, Theodor W., *The Jargon of Authenticity*, trans. Knut Tarnowski and Frederic Will (London: Routledge, 2003).
Adorno, Theodor W., *Aesthetic Theory*, ed. Gretel Adorno and Rolf Tiedemann, trans. Robert Hullot-Kentor (London: Continuum, 2004).
Aldritt, Keith, *The Poet as Spy: The Life and Wild Times of Basil Bunting* (London: Aurum Press, 1998).
Alexander, Neal, 'On Literary Geography', *Literary Geographies* 1.1 (2015), 3–6.
Alexander, Neal, 'Senses of Place', in Robert T. Tally Jr, ed., *The Routledge Handbook of Literature and Space* (Abingdon: Routledge, 2017), pp. 39–49.
Alexander, Neal and James Moran, 'Introduction: Regional Modernisms', in Neal Alexander and James Moran, eds, *Regional Modernisms* (Edinburgh: Edinburgh University Press, 2013), pp. 1–21.
Allen, John, Doreen Massey and Allan Cochrane, *Rethinking the Region: Spaces of Neo-Liberalism* (London: Routledge, 1998).
Anderson, Jon, 'Towards an Assemblage Approach to Literary Geography', *Literary Geographies* 1.2 (2015), 120–37.
Anderson, Perry, 'Modernity and Revolution', *New Left Review* 1.144 (1984), 96–113.
Anderson, Perry, *The Origins of Postmodernity* (London: Verso, 1998).
Armantrout, Rae, 'Darkinfested', in Elizabeth Willis, ed., *Radical Vernacular: Lorine Niedecker and the Poetics of Place* (Iowa City: University of Iowa Press, 2008), pp. 103–12.
Armstrong, Tim, *Modernism: A Cultural History* (Cambridge: Polity Press, 2005).
Arrighi, Giovanni, *The Long Twentieth Century: Money, Power and the Origins of our Times* (London: Verso, 2010).
Bachelard, Gaston, *The Poetics of Space*, trans. Maria Jolas (Boston: Beacon Press, 1994).
Bachelard, Gaston, *Water and Dreams: An Essay on the Imagination of Matter*, trans. Edith Farrell (Dallas: The Dallas Institute of Humanities and Culture, 1999).
Badiou, Alain, *Theoretical Writings*, ed. and trans. Ray Brassier and Alberto Toscano (London: Bloomsbury, 2015).
Baker, Houston A., Jr, *Modernism and the Harlem Renaissance* (Chicago: The University of Chicago Press, 1989).

Balshaw, Maria, *Looking for Harlem: Urban Aesthetics in African American Literature* (London: Pluto Press, 2000).
Baker, Denys Val, *The Timeless Land: The Creative Spirit in Cornwall* (Bath: Adams & Dart, 1973).
Bambach, Charles, *Heidegger's Roots: Nietzsche, National Socialism, and the Greeks* (Ithaca, NY: Cornell University Press, 2003).
Barker, George, 'Tribute', in Ronnie Duncan and Jonathan Davison, eds, *The Constructed Space: A Celebration of W. S. Graham* (Lincoln: Jackson's Arm, 1994), p. 98.
Barry, Peter, *Poetry Wars: British Poetry of the 1970s and the Battle of Earl's Court* (Great Wilbraham: Salt, 2006).
Barthes, Roland, *S/Z*, trans. Richard Miller (New York: Hill and Wang, 1974).
Benjamin, Walter, *Illuminations*, ed. Hannah Arendt, trans. Harry Zohn (London: Pimlico, 1999).
Benjamin, Walter, *The Writer of Modern Life: Essays on Charles Baudelaire*, ed. Michael W. Jennings, trans. Howard Eiland (Cambridge, MA: The Belknap Press of Harvard University Press, 2006).
Bennett, Jane, *Vibrant Matter: A Political Ecology of Things* (Durham, NC: Duke University Press, 2010).
Berman, Jessica, 'Modernism's Possible Geographies', in Laura Doyle and Laura Winkiel, eds, *Geomodernisms: Race, Modernism, Modernity* (Bloomington: Indiana University Press, 2005), pp. 281–96.
Berman, Marshall, *All That is Solid Melts into Air: The Experience of Modernity* (London: Verso, 1983).
Bernstein, Michael André, *The Tale of the Tribe: Ezra Pound and the Modern Verse Epic* (Princeton: Princeton University Press, 1980).
Berry, Eleanor, 'Paradoxes of Form in the Poetry of Lorine Niedecker', in Eric Haralson, ed., *Reading the Middle Generation Anew: Culture, Community, and Form in Twentieth-Century American Poetry* (Iowa City: University of Iowa Press, 2006), pp. 203–32.
Bezner, Kevin, 'A Life Distilled: An Interview with Gwendolyn Brooks', in Gloria Wade Gayles, ed., *Conversations with Gwendolyn Brooks* (Jackson: University Press of Mississippi, 2003), pp. 117–24.
Bhabha, Homi K., *The Location of Culture* (Abingdon: Routledge, 2004).
Bird, Michael, *Bryan Wynter* (Farnham: Lund Humphries, 2010).
Bird, Michael, *The St Ives Artists: A Biography of Place and Time* (Aldershot: Lund Humphries, 2008).
Blanchot, Maurice, *The Space of Literature*, trans. Ann Smock (Lincoln, NE: University of Nebraska Press, 1982).
Blanchot, Maurice, *Friendship*, trans. Elizabeth Rottenberg (Stanford: Stanford University Press, 1997).
Blanton, C. D., *Epic Negation: The Dialectical Poetics of Late Modernism* (New York: Oxford University Press, 2015).
Bloch, Julia, '"Shut your Rhetorics in a Box": Gwendolyn Brooks and Lyric Dilemma', *Tulsa Studies in Women's Literature* 35 2 (2016), 439–62.
Bloomfield, Mandy, *Archaeopoetics: Word, Image, History* (Tuscaloosa: The University of Alabama Press, 2016).
Bluestone, Daniel, 'Chicago's Mecca Flat Blues', *Journal of the Society of Architectural Historians* 57.4 (1998), 382–403.

Bolster, W. Jeffrey, *The Mortal Sea: Fishing the Atlantic in the Age of Sail* (Cambridge, MA: The Belknap Press of Harvard University Press, 2012).
Bone, Robert, and Richard A. Courage, *The Muse in Bronzeville: African American Creative Expression in Chicago, 1932–1950* (New Brunswick: Rutgers University Press, 2011).
Boym, Svetlana, *The Future of Nostalgia* (New York: Basic Books, 2001).
Bradbury, Malcolm, 'The Cities of Modernism', in Malcolm Bradbury and James Macfarlane, eds, *Modernism, 1890–1930* (Harmondsworth: Penguin, 1991), pp. 96–104.
Bradbury, Malcolm and James Macfarlane, eds, *Modernism 1890–1930* (Harmondsworth: Penguin, 1991).
Brannigan, John, *Archipelagic Modernism: Literature in the Irish and British Isles, 1890–1970* (Edinburgh: Edinburgh University Press, 2015).
Breiner, Laurence A., 'Postcolonial Caribbean Poetry', in Jahan Ramazani, ed., *The Cambridge Companion to Postcolonial Poetry* (Cambridge: Cambridge University Press, 2017), pp. 19–30.
Brooker, Peter and Andrew Thacker, eds., *Geographies of Modernism: Literature, Cultures, Spaces* (Abingdon: Routledge, 2005).
Brosseau, Marc, 'Geography's Literature,' *Progress in Human Geography* 18.3 (1994), 333–53.
Brousseau, Marc, 'In, Of, Out, With, and Through: New Perspectives in Literary Geography', in Robert T. Tally Jr, ed., *The Routledge Handbook of Literature and Space* (Abingdon: Routledge, 2017), pp. 9–27.
Brown, Dennis, 'Basil Bunting: *Briggflatts*', in Gary Day and Brian Docherty, eds, *British Poetry from the 1950s to the 1990s: Politics and Art* (Basingstoke: Macmillan, 1997), pp. 23–32.
Buell, Lawrence, *The Environmental Imagination: Thoreau, Nature Writing, and the Formation of American Culture* (Cambridge, MA: Harvard University Press, 1995).
Burton, Richard, *A Strong Song Tows Us: The Life of Basil Bunting* (Oxford: Infinite Ideas, 2013).
Butler, Christopher, *Early Modernism: Literature, Music, and Painting in Europe 1900–1916* (Oxford: Clarendon Press, 1994).
Butterick, George F., *A Guide to the Maximus Poems of Charles Olson* (Berkeley: University of California Press, 1980).
Butterick, George F., *Editing The Maximus Poems: Supplementary Notes* (Storrs: The University of Connecticut Library, 1983).
Byrd, Don, *Charles Olson's* Maximus (Urbana: University of Illinois Press, 1980).
Caddel, Richard, 'Consider: Lorine Niedecker and her Environment,' in Jenny Penberthy, ed., *Lorine Niedecker: Woman and Poet* (Orono, ME: National Poetry Foundation, University of Maine, 1996), pp. 281–6.
Caddel, Richard, 'Bunting and Welsh', in Alex Davies and Lee M. Jenkins, eds, *Locations of Literary Modernism: Region and Nation in British and American Modernist Poetry* (Cambridge: Cambridge University Press, 2000), pp. 57–66.
Caddel, Richard and Anthony Flowers, *Basil Bunting: A Northern Life* (Newcastle-upon-Tyne: Newcastle Libraries & Information Centre, 1997).
Carr, Helen, '*Poetry: A Magazine of Verse* (1912–36), "Biggest of the Little

Magazines"', in Peter Brooker and Andrew Thacker, eds, *The Oxford Critical and Cultural History of Modernist Magazines: Volume II: North America 1894–1960* (Oxford: Oxford University Press, 2012), pp. 40–60.

Casey, Edward S., *Getting Back into Place: Toward a Renewed Understanding of the Place-World* (Bloomington: Indiana University Press, 1993).

Casey, Edward S., *The Fate of Place: A Philosophical History* (Berkeley: University of California Press, 1997).

Casey, Edward S., *Representing Place: Landscape Painting and Maps* (Minneapolis: University of Minnesota Press, 2002).

Casey, Edward S., *The World on Edge* (Bloomington Indiana University Press, 2017).

Causey, Andrew, *Peter Lanyon: Modernism and the Land* (London: Reaktion Books, 2006).

Challinor, John, *A Dictionary of Geology*, 5th edn (Cardiff: University of Wales Press, 1978).

Clark, Timothy, *The Theory of Inspiration: Composition as a Crisis of Subjectivity in Romantic and Post-Romantic Writing* (Manchester: Manchester University Press, 1997).

Clark, Timothy, *Martin Heidegger* (London: Routledge, 2002).

Clark, Tom, *Charles Olson: The Allegory of a Poet's Life* (New York: W. W. Norton, 1991).

Cockin, Katharine, 'Introducing the Literary North', in Katharine Cockin, ed., *The Literary North* (Basingstoke: Palgrave Macmillan, 2012), pp. 1–21.

Cocola, Jim, *Places in the Making: A Cultural Geography of American Poetry* (Iowa City: University of Iowa Press, 2016).

Cohen, Margaret, 'Literary Studies on the Terraqueous Globe', *PMLA* 125.3 (2010), 657–62.

Collins, Patricia Hill, *Black Feminist Thought: Knowledge, Consciousness, and the Politics of Empowerment* (New York: Routledge, 2009).

Conte, Joseph, 'Natural Histories: Serial Form in the Later Poetry of Lorine Niedecker', in Jenny Penberthy, ed., *Lorine Niedecker: Woman and Poet* (Orono, ME: National Poetry Foundation, University of Maine, 1996), pp. 347–60.

Corcoran, Neil, *English Poetry Since 1940* (London: Longman, 1993).

Corcoran, Neil, *The Song of Deeds: A Study of The Anathémata of David Jones* (Cardiff: University of Wales Press, 1982).

Corman, Cid, 'A Footnote to *With Lorine*', in Peter Dent, ed., *The Full Note: Lorine Niedecker* (Budleigh Salterton: Interim Press, 1983), pp. 54–5.

Cox, Kenneth, 'The Longer Poems', in Jenny Penberthy, ed., *Lorine Niedecker: Woman and Poet* (Orono, ME: National Poetry Foundation, University of Maine, 1996), pp. 303–10.

Crase, Douglas, 'Niedecker and the Evolutional Sublime', in Jenny Penberthy, ed., *Lorine Niedecker: Woman and Poet* (Orono, ME: National Poetry Foundation, University of Maine, 1996), pp. 327–46.

Crawford, Margo Natalie, 'Black Light on the *Wall of Respect*: The Chicago Black Arts Movement', in Lisa Gail Collins and Margo Natalie Crawford, eds, *New Thoughts on the Black Arts Movement* (New Brunswick: Rutgers University Press, 2006), pp. 23–42.

Crawford, Robert, 'MacDiarmid in Montrose', in Alex Davis and Lee M.

Jenkins, eds, *Locations of Literary Modernism: Region and Nation in British and American Modernist Poetry* (Cambridge: Cambridge University Press, 2000), pp. 33–56.

Cresswell, Tim, *The Tramp in America* (London: Reaktion Books, 2001).

Cresswell, Tim, *On the Move: Mobility in the Modern Western World* (Abingdon: Routledge, 2006).

Cresswell, Tim, *Geographical Thought: A Critical Introduction* (Chichester: Wiley-Blackwell, 2013).

Cresswell, Tim, *Place: An Introduction*, 2nd edn (Chichester: Wiley-Blackwell, 2015).

Cresswell, Tim, 'Towards *Topopoetics*: Space, Place and the Poem', in Bruce B. Janz, ed., *Place, Space and Hermeneutics* (Cham: Springer, 2017), pp. 319–31.

Culler, Jonathan, *Theory of the Lyric* (Cambridge, MA: Harvard University Press, 2015).

Cummings, Alison, 'Public Subjects: Race and the Critical Reception of Gwendolyn Brooks, Erica Hunt, and Harryette Mullen', *Frontiers: A Journal of Women's Studies* 26.2 (2005), 3–36.

Davidson, Ian, *Ideas of Space in Contemporary Poetry* (Houndmills: Palgrave Macmillan, 2007).

Davidson, Michael, *On the Outskirts of Form: Practicing Cultural Poetics* (Middletown, CT: Wesleyan University Press, 2011).

Davidson, Peter, *The Idea of North* (London: Reaktion Books, 2005).

Davidson, Robin, *Cornwall* (London: B. T. Batsford, 1978).

Davie, Donald, 'Lorine Niedecker: Lyric Minimum & Epic Scope', in Peter Dent, ed., *The Full Note: Lorine Niedecker* (Budleigh Salterton: Interim Press, 1983), pp. 64–73.

Davie, Donald, *Under Briggflatts: A History of Poetry in Great Britain 1960–1988* (Manchester: Carcanet, 1989).

Davies, John, *A History of Wales* (London: Penguin, 1994).

Davis, Alex and Lee M. Jenkins, eds, *Locations of Literary Modernism: Region and Nation in British and American Modernist Poetry* (Cambridge: Cambridge University Press, 2000).

De Certeau, Michel, *The Practice of Everyday Life*, trans. Steven Rendall (Berkeley: University of California Press, 1988).

De Man, Paul, *Blindness and Insight: Essays in the Rhetoric of Contemporary Criticism*, 2nd edn (London: Methuen, 1983).

Debo, Annette, 'Reflecting Violence in the Warpland: Gwendolyn Brooks's Riot,' *African American Review* 39.1/2 (2005), 143–52.

Debo, Annette, 'Signifying *Afrika*: Gwendolyn Brooks's Later Poetry,' *Calalloo* 29.1 (2006), 168–81.

Derrida, Jacques, *Of Grammatology*, trans. Gayatri Chakravorty Spivak (Baltimore: The Johns Hopkins University Press, 1978).

Derrida, Jacques, *Monolingualism of the Other; or, The Prosthesis of Origin*, trans. Patrick Mensah (Stanford: Stanford University Press, 1998).

Devine, T. M., *The Scottish Nation 1700–2000* (London: Penguin, 1999).

Dickie, Margaret, *On the Modernist Long Poem* (Iowa City: University of Iowa Press, 1986).

Dilworth, Thomas, 'David Jones and Fascism', *Journal of Modern Literature* 13.1 (1986), 49–62.

Dilworth, Thomas, *The Shape of Meaning in the Poetry of David Jones* (Toronto: The University of Toronto Press, 1988).
Dilworth, Thomas, 'Antithesis of place in the poetry and life of David Jones', in Alex Davis and Lee M. Jenkins, eds, *Locations of Literary Modernism: Region and Nation in British and American Modernist Poetry* (Cambridge: Cambridge University Press, 2000), pp. 67–88.
Dilworth, Thomas, *Reading David Jones* (Cardiff: University of Wales Press, 2008).
Dilworth, Thomas, *David Jones in the Great War* (London: Enitharmon Press, 2012).
Dilworth, Thomas, *David Jones: Engraver, Soldier, Painter, Poet* (London: Jonathan Cape, 2017).
Dobran, Ryan, ed, *The Collected Letters of Charles Olson and J. H. Prynne* (Albuquerque: University of New Mexico Press, 2017).
Doreski, C. K., *Writing America Black: Race Rhetoric in the Public Sphere* (Cambridge: Cambridge University Press, 1998).
Dorn, Edward, *Ed Dorn Live: Lectures, Interviews, and Outtakes*, ed. Joseph Richey (Ann Arbor: University of Michigan Press, 2007).
Drake, St Clair and Horace R. Clayton, *Black Metropolis: A Study of Negro Life in a Northern City*, 2 vols (New York: Harper & Row, 1967).
Dueck, Daniela and Kai Brodersen, *Geography in Classical Antiquity* (Cambridge: Cambridge University Press, 2012).
Duncan, Andrew, *Origins of the Underground: British Poetry between Apocryphon and Incident Light, 1933–79* (Cambridge: Salt, 2008).
DuPlessis, Rachel Blau, 'Lorine Niedecker's "Paean to Place" and Its Fusion Poetics', *Contemporary Literature* 46.3 (2005), 393–421.
DuPlessis, Rachel Blau, *Blue Studios: Poetry and its Cultural Work* (Tuscaloosa: University of Alabama Press, 2006).
DuPlessis, Rachel Blau, 'Lyric and Experimental Long Poems: Intersections', in J. Mark Smith, ed., *Time in Time: Short Poems, Long Poems, and the Rhetoric of North American Avant-Gardism, 1963–2008* (Montreal: McGill-Queens University Press, 2013), pp. 22–50.
DuPlessis, Rachel Blau, 'Olson and his *Maximus Poems*', in David Herd, ed., *Contemporary Olson* (Manchester: Manchester University Press, 2015), pp. 135–48.
Edson, Evelyn, *The World Map, 1300–1492: The Persistence of Tradition and Transformation* (Baltimore: Johns Hopkins University Press, 2007).
Eifert, Virginia S., *Journeys in Green Places: The Shores and Woods of Wisconsin's Door Peninsula*, rev edn (Sister Bay, WI: Wm. Caxton Ltd., 1989).
Eliot, T. S., *Selected Prose*, ed. Frank Kermode (London: Faber and Faber, 1975).
Ellmann, Richard, *James Joyce*, 2nd edn (Oxford: Oxford University Press, 1982).
Epstein, Josh, *Sublime Noise: Musical Culture and the Modernist Writer* (Baltimore: Johns Hopkins University Press, 2014).
Errington, Paul L., *Of Men and Marshes* (Iowa City: University of Iowa Press, 2012).
Esty, Jed, *A Shrinking Island: Modernism and National Culture in England* (Princeton: Princeton University Press, 2004).

Falci, Eric, 'Place, Space, and Landscape', in Nigel Alderman and C. D. Blanton, *A Concise Companion to Postwar British and Irish Poetry* (Oxford: Wiley-Blackwell, 2009), pp. 200–20.

Falci, Eric, *The Cambridge Introduction to British Poetry, 1945–2010* (Cambridge: Cambridge University Press, 2015).

Felski, Rita, *Doing Time: Feminist Theory and Postmodern Culture* (New York: New York University Press, 2000).

Fisher, Michael H., *Migration: A World History* (New York: Oxford University Press, 2014).

Ford, Karen Jackson, 'The Sonnets of Satin-Legs Brooks', *Contemporary Literature* 48.3 (2007), 345–73.

Forde, Victoria, *The Poetry of Basil Bunting* (Newcastle-upon-Tyne: Bloodaxe Books, 1991).

Francis, Matthew, *Where the People Are: Language and Community in the Poetry of W. S. Graham* (Cambridge: Salt, 2004).

Friedman, Susan Stanford, *Planetary Modernisms: Provocations on Modernity Across Time* (New York: Columbia University Press, 2015).

Fuller, Hoyt, Eugenia Collier, George Kent and Dudley Randall, 'Interview with Gwendolyn Brooks', in Gloria Wade Gayles, ed., *Conversations with Gwendolyn Brooks* (Jackson: University Press of Mississippi, 2003), pp. 67–73.

Gardner, Dana and Nancy Overcott, *Fifty Common Birds of the Upper Midwest* (Iowa City: University of Iowa Press, 2006).

Genette, Gérard, *Paratexts: Thresholds of Interpretation*, trans. Jane E. Lewin (Cambridge: Cambridge University Press, 1997).

Gikandi, Simon, *Writing in Limbo: Modernism and Caribbean Literature* (Ithaca, NY: Cornell University Press, 1992).

Giles, Paul, *The Global Remapping of American Literature* (Princeton: Princeton University Press, 2011).

Gillis, John R., *The Human Shore: Seacoasts in History* (Chicago: The University of Chicago Press, 2012).

Gillott, Brendan C., 'The Depth of Charles Olson's *Maximus Poems*', *English* 66.255 (2017), 351–71.

Gilroy, Paul, *The Black Atlantic: Modernity and Double Consciousness* (London: Verso, 1993).

Gohau, Gabriel, *A History of Geology*, trans. Albert V. Carozzi and Marguerite Carozzi (New Brunswick: Rutgers University Press, 1990).

Gregory, Derek, *Geographical Imaginations* (Oxford: Blackwell, 1994).

Gregson, Ian, '"Adult Male of a Merciless Species": Basil Bunting's Rueful Masculinity', in James McGonigal and Richard Price, *The Star You Steer By: Basil Bunting and British Modernism* (Amsterdam: Rodopi, 2000), pp. 109–22.

Habermas, Jürgen, 'Modernity versus Postmodernity,' trans. Seyla Ben-Habib, *New German Critique* 22 (1981), 3–14.

Haffenden, John, '"I Would Say I Was a Happy Man"': W. S. Graham interviewed by John Haffenden', *Poetry Review* 76.1/2 (1986), 67–74.

Hague, René, *David Jones* (Cardiff: University of Wales Press, 1975).

Hague, René, *A Commentary on* The Anathémata *of David Jones* (Wellingborough: Christopher Skelton, 1977).

Hair, Ross, *Avant-Folk: Small Press Poetry Networks from 1950 to the Present* (Liverpool: Liverpool University Press, 2016).
Halliday, F. E., *A History of Cornwall*, 2nd edn (London: Duckworth, 1975).
Hampson, Robert and Will Montgomery, 'Innovations in Poetry', in Peter Brooker, Andrzej Gąsiorek, Deborah Longworth and Andrew Thacker, eds, *The Oxford Handbook of Modernisms* (Oxford: Oxford University Press, 2010), pp. 63–84.
Hardt, Michael and Antonio Negri, *Empire* (Cambridge, MA: Harvard University Press, 2000).
Harley, J. B., *The New Nature of Maps: Essays in the History of Cartography*, ed. Paul Laxton (Baltimore: Johns Hopkins University Press, 2001).
Harrison, Andrew, 'The Regional Modernism of D. H. Lawrence and James Joyce,' in Neal Alexander and James Moran, eds, *Regional Modernisms* (Edinburgh: Edinburgh University Press, 2013), pp. 44–64.
Hart, Matthew, *Nations of Nothing But Poetry: Modernism, Transnationalism, and Synthetic Vernacular Writing* (New York: Oxford University Press, 2010).
Harvey, David, *The Condition of Postmodernity: An Enquiry into the Origins of Cultural Change* (Oxford: Basil Blackwell, 1989).
Harvey, David, *Justice, Nature and the Geography of Difference* (Oxford: Blackwell, 1996).
Harvey, David, *The Enigma of Capital and the Crises of Capitalism* (London: Profile, 2010).
Harvie, Christopher, *No Gods and Precious Few Heroes: Twentieth-century Scotland*, 3rd edn (Edinburgh: Edinburgh University Press, 1998).
Hatlen, Burton, 'A Poetics of Marginality and Resistance: The Objectivist Poets in Context', in Rachel Blau DuPlessis and Peter Quartermain, eds, *The Objectivist Nexus: Essays in Cultural Poetics* (Tuscaloosa: University of Alabama Press, 1999), pp. 37–55.
Hatlen, Burton, 'Regionalism and Internationalism in Basil Bunting's *Briggflatts*', *The Yale Journal of Criticism* 13.1 (2000), 49–66.
Hay, Pete, 'A Phenomenology of Islands', *Island Studies Journal* 1.1 (2006), 19–42.
Hegglund, Jon, *World Views: Metageographies of Modernist Fiction* (New York: Oxford University Press, 2012).
Heidegger, Martin, *Discourse on Thinking*, trans. John M. Anderson and E. Hans Freund (New York: Harper & Row, 1966).
Heidegger, Martin, *The Question Concerning Technology and Other Essays*, trans. William Lovitt (New York: Harper Perennial, 1977).
Heidegger, Martin, *Poetry, Language, Thought*, trans. Albert Hofstadter (New York: Harper Collins, 2001).
Heller, Michael, *Conviction's Net of Branches: Essays on the Objectivist Poets and Poetry* (New York: Spuyten Duyvil, 1985).
Heller, Michael, *Uncertain Poetries: Selected Essays on Poets, Poetry and Poetics* (Cambridge: Salt, 2005).
Hendy, David, *Noise: A Human History of Sound and Listening* (London: Profile Books, 2013).
Herd, David, 'The View from Gloucester: Open Field Poetics and the Politics

of Movement', in David Herd, ed., *Contemporary Olson* (Manchester: Manchester University Press, 2015), pp. 272–85.

Hindrichs, Cheryl, 'Late Modernism, 1928–1945: Criticism and Theory', *Literature Compass* 8.11 (2011), 840–55.

Hones, Sheila, 'Text as It Happens: Literary Geography', *Geography Compass* 2.5 (2008), 1301–17.

Hones, Sheila, *Literary Geographies: Narrative Space in* Let the Great World Spin (Basingstoke: Palgrave Macmillan, 2014).

Hooker, Jeremy, 'David Jones and the Matter of Wales', in Belinda Humfrey and Anne Price-Owen, eds, *David Jones: Diversity in Unity: Studies of his Literary and Visual Art* (Cardiff: University of Wales Press, 2000), pp. 11–25.

hooks, bell, *Yearning: Race, Gender, and Cultural Politics* (London: Turnaround, 1991).

hooks, bell, *Belonging: A Culture of Place* (Abingdon: Routledge, 2008).

Howarth, Peter, *British Poetry in the Age of Modernism* (Cambridge: Cambridge University Press, 2005).

Howarth, Peter, *The Cambridge Introduction to Modernist Poetry* (Cambridge: Cambridge University Press, 2012).

Howarth, William, 'Imagined Territory: The Writing of Wetlands', *New Literary History* 30.3 (1999), 509–39.

Hughes, Langston, 'The Negro Artist and the Racial Mountain', in Angelyn Mitchell, ed., *Within the Circle: An Anthology of African American Literary Criticism from the Harlem Renaissance to the Present* (Durham, NC: Duke University Press, 1994), pp. 55–9.

Huyssen, Andreas, 'Geographies of Modernism in a Globalizing World,' in Peter Brooker and Andrew Thacker, eds, *Geographies of Modernism: Literatures, Cultures, Spaces* (Abingdon: Routledge, 2005), pp. 6–18.

Jackson, Angela, *A Surprised Queenhood in the New Black Sun: The Life and Legacy of Gwendolyn Brooks* (Boston: Beacon Press, 2017).

James, David and Urmila Seshagiri, 'Metamodernism: Narratives of Continuity and Revolution', *PMLA* 129.1 (2014), 87–100.

Jameson, Fredric, *Postmodernism, or, The Cultural Logic of Late Capitalism* (London: Verso, 1991).

Jameson, Fredric, 'Notes on Globalization as a Philosophical Issue', in Fredric Jameson and Masao Miyoshi, eds, *The Cultures of Globalization* (Durham, NC: Duke University Press, 1998), pp. 54–77.

Jameson, Fredric, *A Singular Modernity: Essay on the Ontology of the Present* (London: Verso, 2002).

Jameson, Fredric, *The Modernist Papers* (London: Verso, 2007).

Jencks, Charles, *Late-Modern Architecture and Other Essays* (London: Academy Editions, 1980).

Jencks, Charles, *Modern Movements in Architecture*, 2nd edn (Harmondsworth: Penguin, 1985).

Johnes, Martin, *Wales Since 1939* (Manchester: Manchester University Press, 2012).

Jones, Huw Ceiriog, *The Library of David Jones: A Catalogue* (Aberystwyth: The National Library of Wales, 1995).

Kahn, Charles H., *The Art and Thought of Heraclitus* (Cambridge: Cambridge University Press, 1979).

Kearns, Gerry, 'The Spatial Poetics of James Joyce', *New Formations* 57 (2006), 107–25.
Kent, George, *A Life of Gwendolyn Brooks* (Lexington: The University Press of Kentucky, 1990).
King, Martin Luther, Jr., *Why We Can't Wait* (London: Penguin, 2018).
Kline, Naomi Reed, *Maps of Medieval Thought: The Hereford Paradigm* (Woodbridge: The Boydell Press, 2001).
Knox, Jane Shaw, *Lorine Niedecker: An Original Biography* (Fort Atkinson, WI: Dwight Foster Public Library, 1987).
Kristeva, Julia, *Strangers to Ourselves*, trans. Leon S. Roudiez (New York: Columbia University Press, 1991).
Kukrechtová, Daniela, 'The Death and Life of a Chicago Edifice: Gwendolyn Brooks's "In the Mecca"', *African American Review* 43.2/3 (2009), 457–72.
Latter, Alex, *Late Modernism and the English Intelligencer: On the Poetics of Community* (London: Bloomsbury, 2015).
Lawson, Andrew, 'Basil Bunting and English Modernism', *Sagetrieb* 9.1/2 (1990), 95–121.
Lefebvre, Henri, *The Production of Space*, trans. Donald Nicholson-Smith (Oxford: Blackwell, 1991).
Lefebvre, Henri, *Critique of Everyday Life: Volume II: Foundations for a Sociology of the Everyday*, trans. John Moore (London: Verso, 2002).
Lefebvre, Henri, *Critique of Everyday Life: Volume I: Introduction*, trans. John Moore (London: Verso, 2008).
Lefebvre, Henri, *Rhythmanalysis: Space, Time and Everyday Life*, trans. Stuart Elden and Gerald Moore (London: Bloomsbury, 2013).
Leighton, Angela, *On Form: Poetry, Aestheticism, and the Legacy of a Word* (Oxford: Oxford University Press, 2007).
Linnard, W., *Welsh Woods and Forests: A History* (Llandysul: Gomer, 2000).
Livingstone, David N., *The Geographical Tradition: Episodes in the History of a Contested Enterprise* (Oxford: Blackwell, 1992).
Loloi, Parvin and Glyn Purslove, 'Basil Bunting's Persian Overdrafts: A Commentary', in Carroll F. Terrell, ed., *Basil Bunting: Man and Poet* (Orono, ME: The National Poetry Foundation, 1981), pp. 343–53.
Lopez, Tony, *The Poetry of W. S. Graham* (Edinburgh University Press, 1989).
Lopez, Tony, 'Graham and the 1940s', in Ralph Pite and Hester Jones, eds, *W. S. Graham: Speaking Towards You* (Liverpool: Liverpool University Press, 2004), pp. 26–43.
Lopez, Tony, *Meaning Performance: Essays on Poetry* (Cambridge: Salt, 2006).
Lorde, Audre, *Your Silence Will Not Protect You* (London: Silver Press, 2017).
Lowney, John, *History, Memory, and the Literary Left: Modern American Poetry, 1935–1968* (Iowa City: University of Iowa Press, 2006).
Luchetta, Sara, 'Literary Mapping: At the Intersection of Complexity and Reduction', *Literary Geographies* 4.1 (2018), 6–9.
Lukács, Georg, *The Theory of the Novel: A Historico-philosophical Essay on the Forms of Great Epic Literature*, trans. Anna Bostock (London: The Merlin Press, 1978).
Lutwack, Leonard, *The Role of Place in Literature* (Syracuse, NY: Syracuse University Press, 1984).

Maber, Peter, '"The Poet or Painter Steers his Life to Maim": W. S. Graham and the St Ives Modernist School,' *Word & Image* 25.3 (2009), 258–71.

Maber, Peter, '"Strange to language": W. S. Graham's Bryan Wynter and the Problematics of Verbal-Visual Communication', *Journal of British and Irish Innovative Poetry* 4.1 (2012), 33–49.

Macauley, David, *Elemental Philosophy: Earth, Air, Fire, and Water as Elemental Ideas* (Albany: State University of New York Press, 2010).

McCulloch, Margery Palmer, *Scottish Modernism and its Contexts 1918–1959: Literature, National Identity and Cultural Exchange* (Edinburgh: Edinburgh University Press, 2009).

Mack, John, *The Sea: A Cultural History* (London: Reaktion Books, 2011).

MacKay, Marina, *Modernism and World War II* (Cambridge: Cambridge University Press, 2007).

Mackey, Nathaniel, 'An Interview with Kamau Brathwaite', in Stewart Brown, ed., *The Art of Kamau Brathwaite* (Bridgend: Seren, 1995), pp. 13–32.

McManis, Douglas R., *Colonial New England: A Historical Geography* (New York: Oxford University Press, 1975).

McPhail, Cameron, 'Pytheas of Massalia's Route of Travel', *Phoenix* 68.3/4 (2014), 247–57.

Madhubuti, Haki, 'Black Books Bulletin Interviews Gwen Brooks', in Gloria Wade Gayles, ed., *Conversations with Gwendolyn Brooks* (Jackson: University Press of Mississippi, 2003), pp. 74–84.

Mahlis, Kristen, 'A Poet of Place: An Interview with M. NourbeSe Philip', *Callaloo* 27.3 (2004), 682–97.

Makin, Peter, *Bunting: The Shaping of His Verse* (Oxford: Clarendon Press, 1992).

Malpas, J. E., *Place and Experience: A Philosophical Topography* (Cambridge: Cambridge University Press, 1999).

Mao, Douglas and Rebecca Walkowitz, 'The New Modernist Studies', *PMLA* 123.3 (2008), 737–48.

Marable, Manning, *Beyond Black and White: From Civil Rights to Barack Obama* (London: Verso, 2016).

Marable, Manning, *Race, Reform, and Rebellion: The Second Reconstruction in Black America, 1945–1990* (Jackson: University Press of Mississippi, 1991).

Massey, Doreen, *Space, Place and Gender* (Cambridge: Polity Press, 1994).

Massey, Doreen, *for space* (London: Sage, 2005).

Maud, Ralph, *Charles Olson's Reading: A Biography* (Carbondale: Southern Illinois University Press, 1996).

Maud, Ralph, *Charles Olson at the Harbor* (Vancouver: Talonbooks, 2008).

Mellors, Anthony, *Late Modernist Poetics: From Pound to Prynne* (Manchester: Manchester University Press, 2005).

Mellors, Anthony, 'Modernism after Modernism', in Alex Davis and Lee M. Jenkins, eds, *A History of Modernist Poetry* (Cambridge: Cambridge University Press, 2015), pp. 481–502.

Merrill, Thomas F., *The Poetry of Charles Olson: A Primer* (East Brunswick, NJ: Associated University Presses, 1982).

Merriman, Peter, *Mobility, Space and Culture* (Abingdon: Routledge, 2012).

Metress, Christopher, '"No Justice, No Peace": The Figure of Emmett Till in African American Literature', *MELUS* 28.1 (2003), 87–103.

Middleton, Peter, 'Lorine Niedecker's "Folk Base" and Her Challenge to the American Avant-Garde', in Rachel Blau DuPlessis and Peter Quartermain, eds, *The Objectivist Nexus: Essays in Cultural Poetics* (Tuscaloosa: University of Alabama Press, 1999), pp. 160–88.

Middleton, Peter, 'Discoverable Unknowns: Olson's Lifelong Preoccupation with the Sciences', in David Herd, ed., *Contemporary Olson* (Manchester: Manchester University Press, 2015), pp. 38–51.

Middleton, Peter and Tim Woods, *Literatures of Memory: History, Time and Space in Postwar Writing* (Manchester: Manchester University Press, 2000).

Miles, Jonathan, *Backgrounds to David Jones: A Study in Sources and Drafts* (Cardiff: University of Wales Press, 1990).

Miles, Jonathan, *Eric Gill & David Jones at Capel-y-Ffin* (Bridgend: Seren, 1992).

Miller, Tyrus, *Late Modernism: Politics, Fiction, and the Arts Between the World Wars* (Berkeley: University of California Press, 1999).

Mills, A. D., *A Dictionary of British Place Names*, rev edn (Oxford: Oxford University Press, 2011).

Milne, Drew, 'Modernist Poetry in the British Isles', in Alex Davis and Lee M. Jenkins, eds, *The Cambridge Companion to Modernist Poetry* (Cambridge: Cambridge University Press, 2008), pp. 147–62.

Milne, Drew, 'Neo-Modernism and Avant-Garde Orientations', in Nigel Alderman and C. D. Blanton, eds, *A Concise Companion to Postwar British and Irish Poetry* (Chichester: Wiley Blackwell, 2009), pp. 155–75.

Mitsch, William J. and James G. Gosselink, *Wetlands*, 5th edn (Hoboken, NJ: Wiley, 2015).

Moody, A. David, *Ezra Pound: Poet: Volume One: The Young Genius 1885–1920* (Oxford: Oxford University Press, 2007).

Moretti, Franco, *Atlas of the European Novel 1800–1900* (London: Verso, 1998).

Morgan, Edwin, 'The Poetry of W. S. Graham', in Ralph Pite and Hester Jones, eds, *W. S. Graham: Speaking Towards You* (Liverpool: Liverpool University Press, 2004), pp. 186–94.

Morrison, Toni, *Mouth Full of Blood: Essays, Speeches, Meditations* (London: Vintage, 2020).

Motte, Warren, *Small Worlds: Minimalism in Contemporary French Literature* (Lincoln: University of Nebraska Press, 1999).

Mottram, Eric, 'The British Poetry Revival, 1960–75', in Robert Hampson and Peter Barry, eds, *New British Poetries: The Scope of the Possible* (Manchester: Manchester University Press, 1993), pp. 15–50.

Müller, Timo, 'The Vernacular Sonnet and the Resurgence of Afro-Modernism in the 1940s', *American Literature* 87.2 (2015), 253–73.

Munro, David and Bruce Gittings, *Scotland: An Encyclopedia of Places & Landscape* (Glasgow: Collins, 2006).

Musgrove, Frank, *The North of England: A History from Roman Times to the Present* (Oxford: Basil Blackwell, 1990).

Nail, Thomas, *The Figure of the Migrant* (Stanford: Stanford University Press, 2015).

Nail, Thomas, *Theory of the Earth* (Stanford: Stanford University Press, 2021).

Nairn, Tom, *The Break-up of Britain: Crisis and Neo-Nationalism*, 2nd edn (London: Verso, 1981).

Najar, Lubna, 'The Chicago Poetry Group: African American Art and High Modernism at Midcentury', *Women's Studies Quarterly* 33.3/4 (2005), 314–23.

Newquist, Roy, 'Gwendolyn Brooks', in Gloria Wade Gayles, ed., *Conversations with Gwendolyn Brooks* (Jackson: University Press of Mississippi, 2003), pp. 26–36.

Nicholls, Peter, *Modernisms: A Literary Guide* (Basingstoke: Macmillan, 1995).

Nicholls, Peter, 'Lorine Niedecker: Rural Surreal', in Jenny Penberthy, ed., *Lorine Niedecker: Woman and Poet* (Orono, ME: National Poetry Foundation, University of Maine, 1996), pp. 193–217.

Nichols, Miriam, 'Myth and Document in Charles Olson's *Maximus Poems*', in David Herd, ed., *Contemporary Olson* (Manchester: Manchester University Press, 2015), pp. 25–37.

Niemann, Michelle, 'Towards an Ecopoetics of Food: Plants, Agricultural Politics, and Colonized Landscapes in Lorine Niedecker's Condensery', *Modernism/modernity* 25.1 (2018), 135–60.

Niven, Alex, 'The Formal Genesis of Basil Bunting's *Briggflatts*', *Cambridge Quarterly* 42.3 (2013), 203–24.

Niven, Alex, 'Towards a New Architecture: Basil Bunting's Postwar Reconstruction', *ELH* 81.1 (2014), 351–79.

North, Michael, *Reading 1922: A Return to the Scene of the Modern* (Oxford: Oxford University Press, 1999).

O'Driscoll, Denis, 'W. S. Graham: Professor of Silence', in Ronnie Duncan and Jonathan Davidson, eds, *The Constructed Space: A Celebration of W. S. Graham* (Lincoln: Jackson's Arm, 1994), pp. 51–65.

Olsen, Redell, 'Postmodern Poetry in Britain', in Neil Corcoran, ed., *The Cambridge Companion to Twentieth-century English Poetry* (Cambridge: Cambridge University Press, 2007), pp. 42–56.

Olson, Liesl, *Chicago Renaissance: Literature and Art in the Midwest Metropolis* (New Haven, CT: Yale University Press, 2017).

O'Sullivan, Maggie, 'To the Reader', in Maggie O'Sullivan, ed., *Out of Everywhere: Linguistically Innovative Poetry by Women in North America & the UK* (London/Benhall: Reality Street Editions, 1996), pp. 9–10.

Parsons, James J., '"Mr Sauer" and the Writers', *Geographical Review* 86.1 (1996), 22–41.

Pattison, Reitha, '"Empty Air": Charles Olson's Cosmology', in David Herd, ed., *Contemporary Olson* (Manchester: Manchester University Press, 2015), pp. 52–63.

Penberthy, Jenny, *Niedecker and the Correspondence with Zukofsky 1931–1970* (Cambridge: Cambridge University Press, 1993).

Penberthy, Jenny, 'Writing Lake Superior', in Elizabeth Willis, ed., *Radical Vernacular: Lorine Niedecker and the Poetics of Place* (Iowa City: University of Iowa Press, 2008), pp. 61–79.

Perloff, Marjorie, *21st-Century Modernism: The 'New' Poetics* (Oxford: Blackwell, 2002).

Peters, Margot, *Lorine Niedecker: A Poet's Life* (Madison, WN: The University of Wisconsin Press, 2011).

Phillips, Carl, 'Brooks's Prosody: Three Sermons on the Warpland', *Poetry* 210.3 (2017), 246–52.
Piette, Adam, '"Roaring between the lines": W. S Graham and the White Threshold of Line-Breaks', in Ralph Pite and Hester Jones, eds, *W. S. Graham: Speaking Towards You* (Liverpool: Liverpool University Press, 2004), pp. 44–62.
Pinard, Mary, 'Niedecker's Grammar of Flooding', in Elizabeth Willis, ed., *Radical Vernacular: Lorine Niedecker and the Poetics of Place* (Iowa City: University of Iowa Press, 2008), pp. 21–30.
Pite, Ralph, 'Abstract, Real and Particular: Graham and Painting', in Ralph Pite and Hester Jones, eds, *W. S. Graham: Speaking Towards You* (Liverpool: Liverpool University Press, 2004), pp. 65–84.
Pocock, D. C. D , ed., *Humanistic Geography and Literature: Essays on the Experience of Place* (London: Croom Helm, 1981).
Pollard, Natalie, *Speaking to You: Contemporary Poetry and Public Address* (Oxford: Oxford University Press, 2012).
Porteous, J. Douglas, 'Literature and Humanist Geography', *Area* 17.2 (1985), 117–22.
Porter, Roy, *The Making of Geology: Earth Science in Britain 1660–1815* (Cambridge: Cambridge University Press, 1977).
Pound, Ezra, *ABC of Reading* (London: George Routledge & Sons, 1934).
Pound, Ezra, *Literary Essays of Ezra Pound*, ed. T. S. Eliot (London: Faber and Faber, 1985).
Presson, Rebekah, 'Interviews with Gwendolyn Brooks', in Gloria Wade Gayles, ed., *Conversations with Gwendolyn Brooks* (Jackson: University Press of Mississippi, 2003), pp. 133–9.
Price-Owen, Anne, 'Feminist Principles in David Jones's Art', in *David Jones: Diversity in Unity*, ed. Belinda Humfrey and Anne Price-Owen (Cardiff: University of Wales Press, 2000), pp. 91–106.
Pringle, J., and T. Neville George, *British Regional Geology: South Wales*, 3rd edn (London: Her Majesty's Stationery Office, 1970).
Prynne, J. H., 'On *Maximus IV, V, VI*', *Minutes of the Charles Olson Society* 28 (1999), 3–13.
Quartermain, Peter, *Basil Bunting: Poet of the North* (Durham: Basil Bunting Poetry Archive, 1990).
Quartermain, Peter and Warren Tallman, 'Basil Bunting Talks about *Briggflatts*', *Agenda* 16.1 (1978), 8–19.
Ramazani, Jahan, 'Modernist Bricolage, Postcolonial Hybridity', *Modernism/modernity* 13.3 (2006), 445–63.
Ramazani, Jahan, *A Transnational Poetics* (Chicago: The University of Chicago Press, 2009).
Ramazani, Jahan, 'Modernist Inflections, Postcolonial Directions', in Alex Davis and Lee M. Jenkins, eds, *A History of Modernist Poetry* (Cambridge: Cambridge University Press, 2015), pp. 459–78.
Rancière, Jacques, *The Aesthetic Unconscious*, trans. Debra Keates and James Swenson (Cambridge: Polity, 2009).
Reagan, Dale, 'Basil Bunting obiter dicta', in Carroll F. Terrell, ed., *Basil Bunting: Man and Poet* (Orono, ME: The National Poetry Foundation, 1981), pp. 229–74.

Riach, Alan, 'W. S. Graham and his Scottish Contemporaries', *Journal of British and Irish Innovative Poetry* 4.1 (2012), 65–75.

Ricoeur, Paul, *Memory, History, Forgetting*, trans. Kathleen Blamey and David Pellauer (Chicago: The University of Chicago Press, 2004).

Rinner, Jeni, 'From Bronzeville to the Mecca and After: Gwendolyn Brooks and the Location of Black Identity', *MELUS* 40.4 (2015), 150–72.

Robichaud, Paul, *Making the Past Present: David Jones, the Middle Ages, & Modernism* (Washington, D.C.: The Catholic University of America Press, 2007).

Rogers, Samuel, '"Local Site and Historical Depth": *Briggflatts*, *A Drunk Man*, and British Modernist Poetics of Place', *English* 65.251 (2016), 332–62.

Roller, Duane W., *Through the Pillars of Herakles: Greco-Roman Exploration of the Atlantic* (New York: Routledge, 2006).

Roub, Gail, 'Getting to Know Lorine Niedecker', in Jenny Penberthy, ed., *Lorine Niedecker: Woman and Poet* (Orono, ME: National Poetry Foundation, University of Maine, 1996), pp. 79–86.

Russell, Dave, *Looking North: Northern England and the National Imagination* (Manchester: Manchester University Press, 2004).

Said, Edward W., *On Late Style: Music and Literature Against the Grain* (London: Bloomsbury, 2006).

Samuel, Raphael, *Island Stories: Unravelling Britain: Theatres of Memory, Volume II* (London: Verso, 1998).

Sauer, Carl Ortwin, *Land and Life*, ed. John Leighly (Berkeley: University of California Press, 1963).

Saunders, Angharad, *Place and the Scene of Literary Practice* (Abingdon: Routledge, 2018).

Scafi, Alessandro, 'Mapping Eden: Cartographies of the Earthly Paradise', in Denis Cosgrove, ed., *Mappings* (London: Reaktion Books, 1999), pp. 50–70.

Schafer, R., Murray, *The Soundscape: Our Sonic Environment and the Tuning of the World* (Rochester, VT: Destiny Books, 1994).

Schlabach, Elizabeth Schroeder, *Along the Streets of Bronzeville: Black Chicago's Literary Landscape* (Urbana: University of Illinois Press, 2013).

Scroggins, Mark, *Louis Zukofsky and the Poetry of Knowledge* (Tuscaloosa: University of Alabama Press, 1998).

Scroggins, Mark, 'US Modernism II: the Other Tradition – Williams, Zukofsky, Olson', in Alex Davis and Lee M. Jenkins, eds, *The Cambridge Companion to Modernist Poetry* (Cambridge: Cambridge University Press, 2007), pp. 181–94.

Scroggins, Mark, 'Objectivist Poets', in Alex Davis and Lee M. Jenkins, eds, *A History of Modernist Poetry* (Cambridge: Cambridge University Press, 2015), pp. 381–97.

Serres, Michel, with Bruno Latour, *Conversations on Science, Culture, and Time*, trans. Roxanne Lapidus (Ann Arbor: The University of Michigan Press, 1995).

Sharp, William, *Literary Geography* (London: Pall Mall, 1904).

Shaw, Lytle, *Fieldworks: From Place to Site in Postwar Poetics* (Tuscaloosa: The University of Alabama Press, 2013).

Sheppard, Robert, *The Poetry of Saying: British Poetry and its Discontents 1950–2000* (Liverpool: Liverpool University Press, 2005).

Sherry, Vincent B. Jr, 'A New Boast for *In Parenthesis*: The Dramatic Monologue of David Jones' *Notre Dame English Journal* 14.2 (1982), 113–28.
Shields, Rob, *Places on the Margin: Alternative Geographies of Modernity* (London: Routledge, 1991).
Shockley, Evie, *Renegade Poetics: Black Aesthetics and Formal Innovation in African American Poetry* (Iowa City: University of Iowa Press, 2011).
Sinclair, Iain, 'Introduction', in Iain Sinclair, ed., *Conductors of Chaos* (London: Picador, 1996), pp. xiii–xx.
Skinner, Jonathan, 'Particular Attention: Lorine Niedecker's Natural Histories', in Elizabeth Willis, ed., *Radical Vernacular: Lorine Niedecker and the Poetics of Place* (Iowa City: University of Iowa Press, 2008), pp. 41–60.
Sloterdijk, Peter, *In the World Interior of Capital: For a Philosophical Theory of Globalization*, trans. Wieland Hoban (Cambridge: Polity, 2013).
Smethurst, James, *The African American Roots of Modernism: From Reconstruction to the Harlem Renaissance* (Chapel Hill: The University of North Carolina Press, 2011).
Smith, James L., 'Europe's Confused Transmutation: the Realignment of Moral Cartography in Juan de la Cosa's *Mappa Mundi* (1500)', *European Review of History – Revue européene d'histoire* 21.6 (2014), 799–816.
Smith, Preston H., *Racial Democracy and the Black Metropolis: Housing Policy in Postwar Chicago* (Minneapolis: University of Minnesota Press, 2012).
Sorrentino, Gilbert, 'Misconstruing Lorine Niedecker', in Jenny Penberthy, ed., *Lorine Niedecker: Woman and Poet* (Orono, ME: National Poetry Foundation, University of Maine, 1996), pp. 287–92.
Spengler, Oswald, *The Decline of the West: Vol. I: Form and Actuality*, trans. Charles Francis Atkinson (London: George Allen & Unwin, 1926).
Stafford, Fiona, *Local Attachments: The Province of Poetry* (Oxford: Oxford University Press, 2010).
Stannard, Julian, *Basil Bunting* (Tavistock: Northcote House, 2014).
Staudt, Kathleen Henderson, *At the Turn of a Civilization: David Jones and Modern Poetics* (Ann Arbor: The University of Michigan Press, 1994).
Stephens, Chris, *Peter Lanyon: At the Edge of Landscape* (London: 21 Publishing, 2000).
Sullivan, James D., 'Killing John Cabot and Publishing Black: Gwendolyn Brooks's *Riot*', *African American Review* 36.4 (2002), 557–69.
Sutton, Walter, 'A Visit with William Carlos Williams', in Linda Welshimer Wagner, ed., *Interviews with William Carlos Williams: Speaking Straight Ahead* (New York: New Directions 1976), pp. 38–47.
Tally, Robert T. Jr, *Spatiality* (Abingdon: Routledge, 2013).
Tarlo, Harriet, 'Radical British Landscape Poetry in the Bunting Tradition', in Richard Price and James McGonigal, eds, *The Star You Steer By: Basil Bunting and British Modernism* (Amsterdam: Rodopi, 2000), pp. 151–81.
Tarlo, Harriet, 'Introduction', in Harriet Tarlo, ed., *The Ground Aslant: An Anthology of Radical Landscape Poetry* (Exeter: Shearsman, 2011), pp. 7–18.
Tate, Claudia, 'Interview with Gwendolyn Brooks', in Gloria Wade Gayles, ed., *Conversations with Gwendolyn Brooks* (Jackson: University Press of Mississippi, 2003), pp. 104–10.
Thacker, Andrew, *Moving Through Modernity: Space and Geography in Modernism* (Manchester: Manchester University Press, 2003).

Thacker, Andrew, 'The Idea of a Critical Literary Geography', *New Formations* 57 (2005), 56–73.
Thacker, Andrew, *Modernism, Space and the City: Outsiders and Affect in Paris, Vienna, Berlin and London* (Edinburgh: Edinburgh University Press, 2019).
Thorsson, Courtney, 'Gwendolyn Brooks's Black Aesthetic of the Domestic', *MELUS* 40.1 (2015), 149–76.
Tomaney, John, 'Keeping a Beat in the Dark: Narratives of Regional Identity in Basil Bunting's *Briggflatts*', *Environment and Planning D: Society and Space* 25 (2007), 355–75.
Tuma, Keith, *Fishing by Obstinate Isles: Modern and Postmodern British Poetry and American Readers* (Evanston: Northwestern University Press, 1998).
Waldman, Anne, 'Who Is Sounding? Awakened View, Gaps, Silence, Cage, Niedecker' in Elizabeth Willis, ed., *Radical Vernacular: Lorine Niedecker and the Poetics of Place* (Iowa City: University of Iowa Press, 2008), pp. 207–22.
Walsh, Rebecca, *The Geopoetics of Modernism* (Gainesville: University Press of Florida, 2015).
Ward, Elizabeth, *David Jones: Mythmaker* (Manchester: Manchester University Press, 1983).
Westphal, Bertrand, *Geocriticism: Real and Fictional Spaces*, trans. Robert T. Tally Jr (New York: Palgrave Macmillan, 2011).
Whittaker, David, *Give Me Your Painting Hand: W. S. Graham & Cornwall* (Charlbury: Wavestone Press, 2015).
Whittier-Ferguson, John, *Mortality and Form in Late Modernist Literature* (Cambridge: Cambridge University Press, 2014).
Williams, Jonathan, 'Some Jazz from the Baz: The Bunting-Williams Letters', in James McGonigal and Richard Price, eds, *The Star You Steer By: Basil Bunting and British Modernism* (Amsterdam: Rodopi, 2000), pp. 253–88.
Williams, Keith, and Steven Matthews, *Rewriting the Thirties: Modernism and After* (London: Longman, 1997).
Williams, Raymond, *The Country and the City* (London: Hogarth Press, 1973).
Williams, Raymond, *Politics of Modernism: Against the New Conformists* (London: Verso, 2007).
Willis, Elizabeth, 'Introduction', in Elizabeth Willis, ed., *Radical Vernacular: Lorine Niedecker and the Poetics of Place* (Iowa City: University of Iowa Press, 2008), pp. xiii–xxiii.
Wilson, J. Tuzo, 'Continental Drift', *Scientific American* 208.4 (1963), 86–103.
Withington, John, *Flood: Nature and Culture* (London: Reaktion Books, 2013).
Woods, Tim, '"Moving Among my Particulars": the "Negative Dialectics" of *The Maximus Poems*', in David Herd, ed., *Contemporary Olson* (Manchester: Manchester University Press, 2015), pp. 233–51.
Woolf, Virginia, 'Literary Geography', in Andrew McNellie, ed., *The Essays of Virginia Woolf: Volume 1* (Oxford: Oxford University Press, 1986), pp. 32–5.
Wooten, William, 'Basil Bunting, British Modernism and the Time of the Nation', in James McGonigal and Richard Price, eds, *The Star You Steer By: Basil Bunting and British Modernism* (Amsterdam: Rodopi, 2000), pp. 17–34.
Wright, David, 'W. S. Graham in the Forties: Memories and Conversations', *Edinburgh Review* 75 (1987), 49–56.

Wright, Richard, 'Blueprint for Negro Writing', in Angelyn Mitchell, ed., *Within the Circle: An Anthology of African American Literary Criticism from the Harlem Renaissance to the Present* (Durham, NC: Duke University Press, 1994), pp. 97–106.

Wright, Richard and Edwin Rosskam, *12 Million Black Voices* (New York: Thunder's Mouth Press, 1988).

Wynne-Jones, Nancy, 'W. S. Graham in Cornwall', *Edinburgh Review* 75 (1987), 66–9.

Zukofsky, Louis, *A Test of Poetry* (New York: Jargor/Corinth Books, 1964).

Zukofsky, Louis, *Prepositions: The Collected Critical Essays* (London: Rapp & Carroll, 1967).

Index

Aberfan disaster, 50, 218n
abjection, 186
abstract expressionism, 6, 7
Adorno, Theodor, 4, 17, 23, 37, 50, 56, 67, 84, 126
Africa, 19, 64, 165, 166, 167, 172, 195, 198, 204, 205
African Americans, 20, 171–2, 174, 175, 176–7, 178, 179, 182, 183, 186, 188, 191, 193, 195, 198
Afrocentrism, 182, 189, 193, 194, 198
Alabama, 178
Aldritt, Keith, 63
Alexander the Great, 62–3, 75
Algonquins, 153–5, 203
Alighieri, Dante, 55
alliterative verse, 69
Anderson, Perry, 6, 209n
Angles, 24, 30–1, 35, 61
Anglesey, 48
Aneurin, 24, 73, 76
Antarctica, 81, 109
anthropology, 4, 29
Arabic, 64
archaeology, 21, 38–9, 46, 146
architecture, 5, 82, 186–7
Arctic, 66, 81, 108–9
Armantrout, Rae, 122
Armstrong, Tim, 7
Arrighi, Giovanni, 14
Arthurian tales, 22, 24–5, 27–8, 31–2, 34, 48–50
Ashbery, John, 200
Asia, 166
Athens, 34
Atkinson, Henry, 117
Atlantic Ocean, 19, 21, 33, 34, 36, 74, 87, 142, 144, 146, 147–8, 150, 152–3, 156–60, 161, 162, 164, 165, 168, 169, 172, 201, 204
autobiography, 52, 56–7, 65, 67, 76, 77, 78, 79, 114, 123, 124–6, 127–30, 138, 141, 148, 171, 181
Avicenna (Ibn Sina), 65

Babbitt, Milton, 6, 7
Bach, Johann Sebastian, 113, 227n
Bachelard, Gaston, 93, 116, 185
Badiou, Alain, 83
Baghdad, 63
Bahamas, 159, 205
Bailey's Harbor, 139
Baker, Denys Val, 96
Balshaw, Maria, 184–5
Baraka, Amiri (LeRoi Jones), 173, 192, 200, 203
Barbados, 205
Barker, George, 88
Barnes, Djuna, 3
Barthes, Roland, 84
Basra, 65
Beat poetry, 200, 202
Beckett, Samuel, 3, 6, 7
Behaim, Martin, 152
Belafonte, Harry, 192
Belgium, 22, 23
Benjamin, Walter, 77, 158–9, 187
Bennett, Jane, 135
Berkeley, 145, 202
Berkshire, 74
Berlin, 53, 57
Berman, Jessica, 18
Berman, Marshall, 53
Bernstein, Charles, 200
Bernstein, Michael André, 158, 159
Berry, Eleanor, 115–16, 126
Bhabha, Homi, 187
Bird, Michael, 97
Black Arts Movement, 172, 180, 194, 200, 202
Black Hawk, 117
Black Mountain College, 9, 143, 145, 200, 201–2
Blackhawk Island, 13, 111, 113, 116, 117, 119, 120, 121, 122, 125, 128, 130, 131, 132, 140, 141
blackness, 172, 173, 174, 182, 192, 194, 195, 196, 197
Blanchot, Maurice, 102
Blanton, C. D., 10, 67
Blaser, Robin, 145, 200
Bletsoe, Elisabeth, 203
Bloodaxe, Eric, 68, 73, 76
Bolster, Jeffrey, 159

Bone, Robert, 175, 177
borders, 22, 44, 50, 120, 126, 132, 135, 137, 141, 204
Borges, Jorge Luis, 6
Boston, 150, 168
Botallack, 96, 99
botany, 116, 138–9, 140, 141
boundaries, 112, 116–17, 120–1, 123–5, 126, 129, 130, 132, 141, 177
Boym, Svetlana, 93
Bradbury, Malcolm, 53
Brancusi, Constantine, 55
Brannigan, John, 33
Brathwaite, Kamau, 204, 205–6, 207
Brigflatts, 74–5, 77, 222n
Bristol, 152
Britain, 12, 18, 19, 20, 21, 23, 24, 25, 27, 28–32, 33, 35–6, 42, 46, 47, 51, 53, 54, 74, 76, 88, 95, 199, 201, 202, 207
British Empire, 4, 29, 39
British Poetry Renaissance, 9, 200–1, 202
Broadside Press, 194
Brockley, 22
Bronzeville, 12, 20, 171, 172, 174, 175–80, 181, 182, 184, 185–6, 187, 190, 191, 192, 193, 195, 196, 197, 198, 207
Brooks, David, 178
Brooks, Gwendolyn, 2, 9, 10, 12, 18, 19, 20, 171–98, 199, 200, 201, 202, 207, 238n, 240n
Brooks, Keziah (Wims), 178
Broonzy, Bill, 178
Brosseau, Marc, 18
Brown, Dennis, 55–6
Brown, Sterling, 173
Buell, Lawrence, 28, 138
Buffalo, 143
Bulman, O. M. B., 44
Bunting, Basil, 1, 7, 8, 9, 10, 13, 18–19, 52–80, 112, 139, 199, 200, 201, 202, 203, 207, 218n, 221n
Burton, Richard, 54, 64, 66, 218n
Byrd, Don, 144, 147, 167
Byrd, William, 68
Byzantium, 63

Cabot, John, 168
Caddel, Richard, 56, 219
Cadiz, 148, 153
Caldey Island, 22
Canada, 116, 132, 135, 141, 206
Canary Islands, 52, 57, 166
Cape Ann, 142, 150, 153, 154, 156, 157, 158, 160, 164, 165, 166
Cape Juby, 166
Capel-y-ffin, 22
capitalism, 2, 6–7, 14–15, 36, 50, 57, 65, 119–20, 139, 144, 158, 159, 161, 201, 204
Caribbean, 20, 199, 201, 204–7
Carmichael, Stokely, 192
Carswell, Catherine, 89
Casey, Edward, 11, 38, 59, 105, 120–1, 125, 135
Castries, 205

Catterick, 24, 76
Causey, Andrew, 98
Celts, 23, 28, 31, 33, 35, 39, 40, 41, 42, 43, 48, 51, 61, 95
Champlain, Samuel de, 150, 154–5, 234n
Chicago, 9, 171, 174, 175, 176, 177, 178, 180, 186, 189, 191, 193, 194, 196, 197, 198, 205, 238n
Chicago Black Renaissance, 171, 172, 174–5, 177, 179
Chicago Poetry Group, 173–4
Chōmei, Kamo no, 58–9
cities, 12–13, 17, 19, 20, 23, 25, 36, 38–9, 41, 51, 53, 55, 82, 112, 120, 143–4, 146 149, 151, 155, 157, 159, 160–1, 166, 169, 171, 174, 175, 176, 178, 179, 183, 184, 186, 189–94, 197–8, 200, 203, 204, 205, 216n
Civil Rights Movement, 12, 172, 193, 194–5, 196, 198
Clark, Thomas A., 203
Clark, Timothy, 107
Clark, Tom, 145
class, 111–12, 115, 117, 172, 174, 180–1, 184, 185–6, 187, 191
Clayton, Horace, 175, 184
Cleaners Press, 19
Clydeside, 13, 31, 82, 85, 87, 88, 91, 94, 95, 207
Cockin, Katharine, 61
Cocola, Jim, 11, 153–4, 204
Coffey, Brian, 2, 7
Cold War, 6, 14, 111, 140, 201
colorism, 181, 182
Columbus, Christopher, 147 159, 205
community, 23, 28, 40–3, 50, 88, 90–1, 98–9, 103–4, 111–12, 115, 119, 120, 131, 139, 149, 160–1, 164, 171–2, 175, 177, 178, 180, 181, 187, 189, 192, 197, 198
Connecticut, 143, 150
Conte, Joseph, 134
continental drift, 142, 165–70
Corcoran, Neil, 21, 29, 30, 45, 46, 54
Corman, Cid, 112, 115, 124, 125, 132, 133, 139
Cornwall, 19, 34–5, 50, 81, 82, 88, 95–101, 110
cosmopolitanism, 29, 43, 53, 55–6, 58, 80, 160–1, 201, 216n
Courage, Richard, 175, 177
Cox, Kenneth, 113, 117
Crane, Hart, 12
Crawford, Margo Natalie, 192–3
Crawford, Robert, 54
Creeley, Robert, 200, 202, 203
Cresswell, Tim, 14, 17, 57, 156
Crete, 165
Cullen, Countee, 173
Culler, Jonathan, 92
Cumbria, 48, 60, 73, 74
cummings, e. e., 173
cynghanedd, 69

Dahlberg, Edward, 130
Darwin, Charles, 133, 139, 140

Davidson, Ian, 107–8, 203
Davidson, Michael, 119–20, 140, 149
Davidson, Peter, 60–1
Davidson, Robin, 95
Davie, Donald, 55, 137
Davies, Aneurin Talfan, 37
Dawson, Christopher, 25
De la Cosa, Juan, 150, 152–3, 159
De Man, Paul, 86
decolonisation, 4, 14, 29, 202, 204
Debo, Annette, 197
Depression (1930s), 1, 5, 59, 87, 111, 115, 120, 174, 175, 179, 200
Derbyshire, 53
Derrida, Jacques, 70, 72, 88–9
devolution, 74
Di Prima, Diane, 200
Dickens, Charles, 15
Dickinson, Emily, 132
Dilworth, Thomas, 26, 28, 39, 41, 42, 213n
disability, 128–9
displacement, 19, 38, 41, 46, 48, 51, 52, 56, 71–2, 75–6, 80, 81, 90–1, 93–4, 96, 119, 128, 141, 143, 148, 154, 164, 169, 170, 202, 205, 206
Dollase, Florence, 125
Doolittle, Hilda (H. D.), 1, 7, 10, 13, 18, 202
Door County, 138, 141
Dorchester, 157, 158, 163, 165
Dorn, Edward, 9, 145, 146, 169, 200, 202, 203–4
Dorset, 155
Dos Passos, John, 12
Drake, St Clair, 175, 184
Drerup, Karl, 55
Dublin, 38, 45, 49, 53, 73
Duncan, Andrew, 73
Duncan, Robert, 200, 202
Dunsmuir, Nessie, 87, 96
DuPlessis, Rachel Blau, 10, 116, 125, 126, 127, 160, 168
dwelling, 38, 58–9, 79, 80

Earth, 45, 48, 91, 134–5, 144, 146–7, 151–2, 162, 165, 166, 167–8, 169
ecology, 27–8, 50, 67–8, 111, 112, 115, 117, 118–19, 120, 121, 123–4, 127, 128–9, 130, 135, 137, 138–41, 207
Ede, Jim, 33, 214n
edges, 19, 111, 112, 116–17, 120–1, 123–5, 126, 129, 131, 141
Edinburgh, 87
Egypt, 65, 164
Eifert, Virginia, 138, 139, 141
Einstein, Albert, 146
elegy, 98–101, 125, 128, 130, 172, 178, 187
Eliot, T. S., 3, 4, 8, 10, 12, 23, 24, 26, 27, 29, 53, 54, 66, 67, 82–3, 104, 139, 173, 184, 191, 196, 199, 200, 205–6
England, 4, 5, 18, 19, 22, 28, 30, 36, 48, 54, 60, 119, 203
epic poetry, 10, 19, 63, 67, 142, 146, 151, 156, 158, 162, 165, 167, 172, 186, 188
Eratosthenes, 146–7, 148

estrangement, 88–9, 90, 92, 96, 103, 111–12, 128, 143, 190, 192, 193
Esty, Jed, 4–5, 29–30, 209n
ethnography, 203
ethnology, 136
Eurocentrism, 2
Europe, 2, 21, 33, 36, 53, 57, 61, 65, 74, 147, 152, 157, 158, 165, 169, 204, 205
Evans, I. O., 44
Evers, Medgar, 196
evolution, 46, 116, 138, 139, 140–1
exile, 41, 53, 54, 56, 72, 76, 80, 89–90, 174, 183, 205, 206
existentialism, 56
everyday life, 20, 55, 73, 171, 173, 177, 179, 180–3, 184–5, 188, 189, 194, 198

Faber, 66, 96
Falci, Eric, 56, 202
fascism, 36, 38, 43, 200
Fearnsides, W. G., 44
Felski, Rita, 181, 183
Ferdowsi, 55, 62, 63
Ferlinghetti, Lawrence, 200
Ferrini, Vincent, 143, 149, 155
feudalism, 57
First World War, 19, 22, 23, 25, 29, 171
Fisher, Allen, 200, 202, 203
Fisher, Roy, 9, 202, 203
fishing, 87, 102, 103, 104–5, 111, 117, 128, 131, 152–3, 154–5, 156, 157, 158–60, 163, 165, 169
floods, 120, 121–5, 130–1, 141
Flowers, Anthony, 56
Flynn, Dallam, 19
folk poetry, 115, 117, 119–20
Ford, Karen Jackson, 173
Forde, Victoria, 59, 70
Forster, E. M., 4
Fort Atkinson, 112, 113, 117, 132
Foster, Norman, 5, 7
France, 22, 23, 24, 27, 52
Francis, Matthew, 81, 86, 90, 97, 101, 109
Franz Josef Land, 109
Frazer, J. G., 27
Fulcrum Press, 9, 19, 201

Gabo, Naum, 97
Galveston, 19
Galway, 162
Gascoyne, David, 202
Gauls, 23
gender, 40–2, 51, 93, 131–2, 160, 168, 177, 181, 182, 183, 190–1, 198
geocriticism, 17
geography, 10, 11–14, 15–18, 21, 22, 24, 27, 28, 29, 32–3, 35, 48, 49, 50, 51, 52, 53, 57, 58, 60, 64, 65, 74, 78, 79, 82, 84–5, 86, 105, 111, 117, 119, 120, 131, 132, 134, 136, 137, 138, 141, 142, 144, 145–9, 150, 151–2, 154, 156, 157, 158, 167, 169, 172, 174, 176, 177, 187, 195, 196, 197, 198, 200, 202, 203, 204, 205, 207, 210n

geology, 12, 21, 22, 44–51, 85, 126, 132–3, 134–6, 137, 138, 140–1, 145, 165–70, 207
geometry, 145
Germany, 1, 19, 36
Germoe, 88, 95, 96
Ghana, 19
Gibbon, Lewis Grassic, 89
Gibson, Morgan, 134
Gikandi, Simon, 204
Giles, Paul, 157
Gillis, John, 156–7
Gillott, Brendan, 167
Gilroy, Paul, 172
Ginsberg, Allen, 200, 202
Giovanni, Nikki, 200
Glasgow, 65, 81, 82, 87, 223n
globalisation, 14–15, 39, 40, 43–4, 60, 80, 119–20, 202, 204
Gloucester, Massachusetts, 12, 19, 142, 143, 144, 145, 146, 147, 148–9, 150, 151, 153, 154, 155, 156–60, 161, 162, 163, 164, 165–6, 167, 168, 169, 170
Godard, Jean-Luc, 6, 7
Goliard Press, 201
Goodison, Lorna, 204
Gorton, John, 22
Gosnold, Bartholomew, 159
Graham Land, 109
Graham, W. S., 1, 8, 9, 10, 11, 13, 18, 19, 54, 81–110, 199, 200, 202, 207, 223n, 224n, 225n, 226n
Greece, 33–4
Greenberg, Clement, 6
Greenock, 19, 81, 82, 85, 87–8, 90–4, 95, 96, 101, 102, 110
Gregson, Ian, 68
Grieg, Edvard, 191
Gropius, Walter, 5
Guest, Barbara, 200
Gunn, Neil M., 89
Gurnard's Head, 96, 98, 99, 102
Gwent, 50
Gwynedd, 48

Hafez, 63
Hague, René, 30
Hair, Ross, 119
Hampson, Robert, 10
Hardt, Michael, 44
Hardy, Thomas, 54
Harlem, 174
Harlem Renaissance, 171, 172, 173, 174, 194, 200
Harley, J. B., 153, 154
Hart, Matthew, 8, 67, 70, 172
Harvey, David, 13
Harwood, Lee, 200
Hatlen, Burton, 74, 77, 114
Hawes, 75
Hay, Peter, 32–3
Heezen, Bruce, 167
Hegglund, Jon, 12, 35, 150
Heidegger, Martin, 37–8, 56, 58, 108, 226n

Hejinian, Lyn, 200
Heller, Michael, 113, 139
Hendry, J. F., 202
Hepworth, Barbara, 97
Heraclitus, 83, 84, 223n
Herd, David, 161
Herodotus, 142
Heron Bay, 132
Heron, Patrick, 97
Hesiod, 164–5
Hilton, Roger, 97
Hilton, Ruth, 50
Hindrichs, Cheryl, 3
Hines, Jack, 162
history, 4, 6–7, 10, 14–15, 19, 21, 24, 25–6, 27, 28, 30, 35, 42, 45, 48, 50, 51, 52, 56, 60, 61, 63, 74, 76, 78, 79, 93, 99, 110, 111, 113, 119–20, 131, 132, 134, 136, 137, 138, 139, 140, 142, 144, 146, 147, 148–9, 151, 155, 156, 158, 160, 162, 163–4, 165, 169, 170, 172, 179, 183, 188, 195, 196, 198, 200, 202, 203, 204, 205, 206, 207, 233n
home-place, 22, 41, 51, 52, 56–7, 58–60, 63, 66, 74, 75–6, 88–91, 92–4, 96, 104, 111, 115, 117, 119–20, 121–2, 123, 128, 129, 132, 141, 143, 149, 161, 168, 174, 175, 177, 178, 182, 183, 188, 191, 216n
Homer, 142, 164
Hones, Sheila, 15, 16–17
Hocker, Jeremy, 38
hooks, bell, 183
Hopkins, Gerard Manley, 32, 41, 82, 104
Horace, 55
housing, 176–7, 179, 180, 183–9, 190, 192–3, 198
Howarth, Peter, 54, 199
Howe, Susan, 200, 203
Hughes, Langston, 171, 173, 180–1, 190, 200
Hunt, Erica, 172
Huyssen, Andreas, 2

Iceland, 147, 163
Idaho, 204
Illinois, 176, 178
Imagism, 116
imperialism, 4, 21, 23, 24, 29, 39–40, 41, 43–4, 51, 53, 62–3, 132, 135, 136, 137, 142, 150, 152–5, 158, 159, 195, 202, 203, 204, 205, 209n 233n
India, 166, 204
industrialism, 27–8, 36, 41, 50, 81, 87–8, 91–4, 95, 99, 134–5, 143, 159, 174, 176, 180, 203
integrationism, 173, 182, 189, 194
Iraq, 63, 65
Iran, 52, 63–4, 218n
Ireland, 22, 25, 27, 53, 75, 164, 165
Irish Sea, 47
Isfahan, 57, 63, 64, 65
islands, 29, 32–3, 34, 51, 73, 143–4, 157, 163, 166
Isle of Man, 48
Isle of Wight, 35

Israel, 65
Italy, 52, 57, 71–2, 73, 74, 75

Jackson, Angela, 175, 186
Jamaica, 206
James, Henry, 139–40
James, Henry Sr, 140
Jameson, Fredric, 5–7, 13, 43, 82
Japan, 59, 115, 119
Jefferson, Thomas, 133
Jencks, Charles, 5, 6
Jerusalem, 39
Johnson, Fenton, 173
Johnson, James Weldon, 173
Joliet, Louis, 137
Jones, David, 1, 8, 9, 10, 11, 12, 18, 19, 21–51, 54, 199, 200, 201, 202, 207, 213n, 214n, 215n, 216n
Joyce, James, 1, 11, 37, 38, 45, 49, 53, 82, 145, 199, 216n, 217n
Jung, Carl, 142

Kansas, 178
Kent, 22
Kenya, 19
King, Martin Luther Jr, 192, 195, 196, 197
Kingston, 205
kitchenette apartments, 171, 172, 177, 180, 181, 183–6, 187, 193, 198
Kristeva, Julia, 96
Kukrechtová, Daniela, 189
Kyger, Joanne, 203
Kyoto, 58, 59

Lake Huron, 135
Lake Michigan, 132, 138
Lake Superior, 12, 132, 134–7
Land's End, 95
landscape, 15, 27–8, 35, 46, 48, 49–50, 51, 52, 54, 56, 65–6, 67, 69, 75, 78, 81, 85, 86, 88, 95–6, 97–9, 101, 109, 110, 136, 137, 141, 145, 148, 149, 150, 156, 167, 195, 202, 203, 204, 207
language, 9, 11–12, 19, 22, 28, 30–1, 42–3, 44–5, 48, 49, 52, 55, 67, 69, 70, 71, 81, 82–7, 88–9, 90–1, 101, 102–4, 105–6, 107–8, 109, 136, 153, 158, 172, 184, 203, 205–7, 224n
Language poetry, 200
Lanyon, Peter, 97–9
Larkin, Philip, 54, 201
Latin, 30, 42–3, 57, 144
Lawrence, D. H., 53, 140
Lawson, Andrew, 77
Le Corbusier, 5
Lebanon, 163
Lefebvre, Henri, 11, 60, 182, 189
Leighton, Angela, 100, 104
Levant, 99
Levertov, Denise, 200
Lewis, Wyndham, 3
Libya, 65
Lindisfarne, 73, 75
Linnaeus, Carl, 139

literary geography, 1, 15–18, 35, 118, 190, 211n
literary history, 1–9, 15, 53, 55, 112, 118, 208n
Little Rock, 194, 195
living spaces, 171, 179, 182, 183–9, 190, 193, 198
Lobeck, A. K., 145, 146
locality, 4, 11, 13, 14, 19, 21, 23, 25, 29, 36–44, 51, 52–6, 59–60, 74, 79–80, 113, 118, 119–20, 131–2, 144, 145, 150, 157, 161, 175, 200
Lofoten, 66
London, 19, 22, 24, 38, 39, 44, 53, 57, 74, 75, 82, 119, 223n
Lopez, Tony, 74, 81, 86, 87, 96, 97, 106
Lorde, Audre, 182
Los Angeles, 18
Lowney, John, 186, 188
Loy, Mina, 3, 55, 202
Lucca, 78
Lucretius, 132
Lukács, György, 52
Lundy Island, 22
lyric poetry, 10, 83–4, 86, 92, 114, 186, 203, 204

Mack, John, 101, 156, 160
McCaffery, Steve, 200
McCullough, Margery Palmer, 89
MacDiarmid, Hugh, 1, 7, 9, 44, 53, 54, 74, 89–90, 201
Macedonia, 63, 75
MacGreevy, Thomas, 7
McKay, Claude, 173
MacKay, Marina, 4–5
Mackinder, Halford, 18, 22
McManis, Douglas, 154
MacSweeney, Barry, 200, 202
Madhubuti, Haki (Don Lee), 189, 194, 200, 202
Madron, 96, 100
Magellan, Ferdinand, 147
Maine, 153, 159
Makin, Peter, 62, 75–6
Malcolm X, 192, 196
Malherbe, François de, 55
Malory, Thomas, 24–5, 26
Malpas, J. E., 40, 118
Malta, 163, 165
Manuchehri, 55, 63
maps, 16, 18, 19–20, 22, 36, 133, 136–7, 142–3, 145, 146, 150–6, 159, 161, 164, 166–7, 169–70, 192, 207, 234n
Marable, Manning, 176
Marinus of Tyre, 146–7, 148
Marquette, Jacques, 137
Marseille, 163
Martin, John Bartlow, 186–7
Massachusetts, 150, 165
Massey, Doreen, 14, 46, 135, 137, 179
materialism, 41, 67, 71, 73, 82, 109, 113–14, 116, 126–7, 132, 134–5, 136, 138–9, 140–1, 155–6, 158, 160, 184

mathematics, 145
Maud, Ralph, 150
Maximus of Tyre, 143
Mediterranean Sea, 19, 21, 33–4, 45, 75, 142, 144, 147–8, 152, 153, 161, 164, 165, 218n
Meek, Russell, 187
Mellors, Anthony, 8, 167, 200
Melville, Herman, 145, 150
memory, 21, 40, 76–80, 81, 86, 87, 90, 91–4, 99, 100–1, 125, 130–1, 148–9, 172, 185, 187–8, 195, 196
Memphis Minnie, 178
Merriman, Peter, 179
Mevagissey, 95, 96, 101
MI6, 52
Michigan, 135
Middle East, 60, 62–6, 75
Middleton, Peter, 78, 115, 148
Midwest (United States), 111, 113, 116, 130, 174, 176, 195, 230n
Mies van der Rohe, Ludwig, 5, 186
migration, 19–20, 142, 143, 146, 147, 148–9, 155, 158, 160–5, 166, 169–70, 171, 174, 176–9, 186, 191, 198, 205, 206, 207
Miles, Jonathan, 38, 46
Miller, Tyrus, 3, 5
Milne, Drew, 55, 56, 201
Milwaukee, 111, 140
Miners' strike (1980s), 74
minimalism, 115–16
Minnesota, 132
Minton, John, 95
Mississippi, 176, 188, 195, 240n
mobility, 14–15, 17, 19, 38, 46, 52, 56–8, 66, 75–6, 80, 81–2, 86, 98, 105–6, 110, 132–3, 134–5, 137, 138, 140, 141, 142–3, 144, 148–9, 157, 161, 162, 163–4, 165, 168, 169–70, 177, 178, 190, 207
modernism, 1–9, 10, 12, 13–14, 15, 16, 18, 21, 29–30, 33, 53, 58, 67, 76, 77, 82, 87, 89, 97, 109, 112, 119, 132, 137, 150, 172, 173, 174, 175, 184, 186, 188, 189, 193, 194, 199, 200, 201, 204, 207, 208n, 209n, 210n
   African American modernism, 171, 172–4, 186
   American modernism, 157, 173–4
   archipelagic modernism, 33–6
   British modernism, 54–6
   Caribbean modernism, 204–7
   high modernism, 3, 4, 8, 18, 33, 54, 82, 172, 173, 174, 200, 206, 207
   late modernism, 1–13, 16, 17, 18, 20, 22, 33, 43, 46, 51, 54, 55, 82, 83, 112, 119, 142, 143, 171, 172, 174, 175, 189, 194, 198, 199, 200, 201, 203, 207, 209n
   neo-modernism, 9, 20, 172, 201–7
   regional modernism, 52–5, 62, 80
modernity, 2, 14–15, 23, 25–6, 36–7, 40, 41, 43–4, 51, 52, 53, 147–8, 172, 174, 183, 202, 204, 205
Money, Mississippi, 195
Montana, 204

Monteverdi, Claudio, 68, 73
Montgomerie, William, 85
Montgomery, 194
Montgomery, Stuart, 19
Montgomery, Will, 10
Montrose, 53
Moore, Marianne, 1
Moore, Nicholas, 202
Moretti, Franco, 16
Morgan, Edwin, 82, 86, 95, 103
Morocco, 166
Morrison, Toni, 183
Morvah, 96, 99
Mossadeq, Mohammad, 64
Motion, Andrew, 54
Mottram, Eric, 70
mountains, 13, 22, 47–8, 49, 58–9, 67–8, 73, 74, 75, 77, 78, 84–6, 94
Muccioli, Marcello, 59
Muir, Edwin, 89
Muir, Willa, 89
Mulford, Wendy, 200, 202–3
Mullen, Harryette, 172, 202
music, 47, 66–72, 79, 82, 113, 178, 191, 193, 205, 221n, 227n
myth, 8, 21, 23, 24, 25–6, 29, 31, 33, 34, 35, 42, 45, 48–9, 63, 75, 113, 118, 127–8, 142, 151, 160, 161, 164, 165, 167, 198, 204, 214n

Nabokov, Vladimir, 6
Nail, Thomas, 163, 178
Nairn, Tom, 74
Najar, Lubna, 174
nation, 4, 14, 21, 22, 28–32, 33–5, 42, 44–5, 51, 54–5, 60, 74, 79, 89–90, 135, 136, 144, 157, 158, 182, 189, 192, 194, 195, 196, 206, 207
natural history, 125, 132, 138
Negri, Antonio, 44
New Critics, 6
New Directions, 2
New England, 142, 145, 146, 153–4, 156, 158, 159, 165, 203
New Jersey, 13, 17
New York, 13, 18, 19, 53, 57, 59, 82, 111, 112, 119, 120, 174, 177, 203, 223n
New York poets, 200
Newcastle, 66
Newfoundland, 157, 159, 161, 163, 168
Newlyn, 97
Newman, Barnett, 7
Nichols, Miriam, 164
Nicholson, Ben, 97
Niedecker, Daisy, 122–3, 127–8, 129
Niedecker, Henry, 111, 122, 123, 127, 128, 129, 229n
Niedecker, Lorine, 2, 7, 9, 10, 11, 12, 13, 18, 19, 44, 55, 111–41, 199, 200, 201, 202, 203, 207, 228n, 229n
Niemann, Michelle, 113
night, 92–3, 94, 99, 101–2, 103, 104, 105
Nipigon, 132
Niven, Alex, 64

non-metropolitan places, 12–13, 23–4, 29, 33, 36–44, 54–5, 56, 58–9, 82, 113, 119–20, 200, 207
Norse, 34, 61, 68, 69, 156–7, 163
North Carolina, 143
North Sea, 35–6, 75
northernness, 52, 56, 60–2, 67, 69, 76, 78, 88, 132
Northumberland, 52, 60, 64, 66, 75
Northumbria, 13, 19, 54, 55, 56, 58, 59, 60, 61, 62, 63, 68, 69, 71, 72, 73, 74, 75–6, 77, 79, 218n
Norway, 66, 147
nostalgia, 93–4, 117, 180
Nottinghamshire, 53
nuclear weapons, 14, 111, 140

Objectivism, 112, 113–16, 200
oceanography, 22, 166–7
O'Donnell, George Marion, 70
O'Driscoll, Denis, 101
O'Hara, Frank, 200, 203
Oklahoma, 178
Olsen, Carl, 160
Olsen, Redell, 201
Olson, Betty, 150
Olson, Charles, 1, 6, 7, 8, 10, 11–12, 18, 19–20, 44, 142–70, 199, 200, 201–2, 203, 207, 232n, 233n, 234n
Olson, Karl, 161–2
Olson, Liesl, 174, 180, 187
Ontario, 135
Oppen, George, 1–2, 7, 10, 112
Örebro, 161
Orkney Isles, 73, 75
O'Sullivan, Maggie, 202

painting, 6, 7, 82, 95, 96–101, 150
Palestine, 22, 23, 39
Pangaea, 150, 166–7
Paris, 38, 53, 57
Paterson, 13, 17
Pembrokeshire, 22
Penberthy, Jenny, 112, 114, 138
Penzance, 95
periodisation, 3–9
Perloff, Marjorie, 199, 200
Perse, Saint-John, 26
Persia, 55, 62–5, 68, 73
Peters, Margot, 117, 130
phenomenology, 11, 120
Philip, M. NourbeSe, 204, 206–7
Phoenicians, 34, 147, 148, 156, 163, 165
Piano, Renzo, 5
Picasso, Pablo, 97, 145, 193
Pickard, Tom, 66, 202
Pinard, Mary, 121, 124
Pite, Ralph, 97
place, 10–15, 16, 17, 19, 20, 21, 22, 29, 35, 36–44, 45–6, 48, 52, 54, 55, 56, 57, 58–60, 61, 62, 63, 64, 66–72, 73–6, 77, 78, 81, 86–7, 88, 91, 94, 96, 98, 99–100, 102, 105–6, 107–8, 109–10, 111, 112, 116, 117–18, 119, 120–1, 123, 125–31, 132, 133, 135, 136, 137, 141, 142, 144, 145, 148–9, 150, 153, 154, 156, 157, 159, 161, 163, 166, 168, 169, 170, 171, 175, 176, 179, 182, 183, 186, 187, 191, 196, 198, 200, 202–7
plate tectonics, 167
Pleistocene, 12, 46–7
Plymouth, Massachusetts, 158
poetic sequences, 10, 91, 92, 104, 133, 172
poetics of place, 10–15, 18–20, 22, 24, 44, 52, 59–60, 62, 63, 72–3, 77, 78, 79, 81, 86–7, 97, 110, 116, 117, 119, 120, 141, 143, 144, 175, 177, 194, 198, 200, 207
Poland, 1
politics, 2, 3, 4–5, 6–7, 8, 14, 23, 29–30, 36–7, 39, 43–4, 54–5, 63–4, 74, 111, 115, 119–20, 130, 135, 162, 171, 172, 175, 181, 182, 186, 192, 193, 194–5, 198, 200, 215n
Pollard, Natalie, 98
Pollock, Jackson, 7
Pope, Alexander, 191
Port Arthur, 132
Port of Spain, 205
postcolonialism, 204–7
postmodernism, 3, 5, 6, 43, 201, 207
Pound, Dorothy, 54
Pound, Ezra, 2, 8, 9, 10, 18, 19, 23, 53, 54, 55, 57, 58, 62, 67, 70, 82–3, 113, 143, 144, 162, 173, 199, 200
Presley, Frances, 203
Presocratic philosophy, 126
Price-Owen, Anne, 42
primitivism, 174
Pring, Martin, 159
Proust, Marcel, 145
provincialism, 13, 53, 97, 119
Prynne, J. H., 8, 166, 168, 200, 202
psychology, 142, 184
Ptolemy, 146–7, 148
Pytheas of Massalia, 146–8, 163, 165

Quartermain, Peter, 69

racism, 20, 25, 162, 171, 174, 176–7, 182–3, 185–6, 187, 188, 193, 196, 198, 200
Rakosi, Carl, 112
Ramazani, Jahan, 15, 204
Rancière, Jacques, 46
Rapallo, 9, 57
region, 15, 19, 44, 52, 53–6, 58, 59–61, 63, 74, 76, 79–80, 97, 99, 116, 119, 132, 133, 135, 136, 140, 141, 150, 154, 200
religion, 21, 23, 24, 26, 32, 35, 40–1, 42, 45, 46, 48, 50, 64, 73, 74–5, 136, 151, 158, 196, 205
Renfrewshire, 87
Reznikoff, Charles, 1, 10, 112
Rhodes, 165
Ricoeur, Paul, 91
Riley, Denise, 200
Riley, Peter, 203
Rimbaud, Arthur, 82, 87
Rinner, Jeni, 196

rivers, 24, 48, 50, 61, 67–8, 69, 71, 76–7, 81, 82, 84, 91–2, 111, 114, 117, 120, 121–6, 129, 130–1, 135, 141, 156, 223n
ritual, 24, 25, 26, 46
Roberts, Lynette, 1, 8, 10, 54
Robichaud, Paul, 36
Rogers, Richard, 5, 7
Rogers, Samuel, 56
Roman Empire, 21, 23, 24, 39–40, 41, 42, 43, 51, 61
Romanticism, 83, 96, 125–6, 201
Rome, 39, 40
rootedness, 37–8, 56–60, 62, 63, 79, 131–2, 175
Roub, Bonnie, 115
Roub, Gail, 115, 118
Roxburghshire, 48
Rudaki, 63
Ruhrmund, Frank, 96
Rutherford, 13

Saadi, 63
Said, Edward, 4, 76, 133
Saint Aidan, 73
Saint Buryan, 99, 100
Saint Columba, 73
Saint Columbanus, 73
Saint Cuthbert, 73
Saint Ives, 95, 97
Saint Just, 99
Saint Malo, 152
Saint Petersburg, 53
Saint-Saëns, Camille, 191
San Francisco Renaissance, 9, 200, 202
Sanchez, Sonia, 200, 202
Sauer, Carl, 12, 145, 232n
Sault Sainte Marie, 132, 134–5
Saville, William, 156
Schafer, Murray, 68
Schlabach, Elizabeth Schroeder, 175, 192
Schmidt, Michael, 88
Schoenberg, Arnold, 68
Schoolcraft, Henry Rowe, 136, 137
Scotland, 19, 36, 44, 47, 48, 66, 77, 85, 87, 88, 95, 96, 110, 119, 168, 218n, 224n
Scots language, 88, 89–90, 95, 103
Scotswood-on-Tyne, 57, 218n
Scottish Renaissance, 39–90, 95
Scroggins, Mark, 112
sea, 81, 92, 97, 101, 102–6, 144, 147, 148, 152, 156–60, 166, 167, 169, 206–7
sea coasts, 19, 32–6, 51, 65–6, 72, 79, 96, 98, 101–2, 103, 110, 146, 150, 152, 153, 154, 156–8, 203
sea voyages, 19, 33–6, 57–8, 65–6, 69–70, 74, 76, 78–9, 86, 104–6, 142, 146–9, 152–5, 162–3, 164–5, 169, 206–7
Second World War, 1, 2, 4, 5, 8, 9, 15, 36, 63, 65–6, 95, 97, 162, 165, 176, 179, 200, 201, 204, 207, 218n
segregation, 20, 171, 174, 176–9, 182, 186, 194, 198
Semple, Ellen Churchill, 18
serial poetry, 10, 133–4, 141

Serly, Tibor, 55
Serres, Michel, 79
Shakespeare, William, 168, 196
Sharp, William, 15
Shaw, Lytle, 203
Shelley, Percy, 126
Shetland Isles, 53, 75, 147
Shockley, Evie, 172, 194
Sinclair, Iain, 202
site, 19, 21, 28, 29, 37, 38–9, 45, 51, 91, 146, 192, 203
Situationists, 6
Skinner, Jonathan, 132
slavery, 172, 133, 188, 195, 205, 206–7
Sloterdijk, Peter, 147, 152
Smethurst, James, 174
Smith, James, 152
Smith, John, 150, 153–4
Smith, Sydney Goodsir, 90
Snyder, Gary, 9, 203
social realism, 173, 174, 175, 198
sociology, 175
Sorrentino, Gilbert, 132
soundscape, 68–70, 71, 113, 124, 128–9
South Africa, 196
South Shields, 57
South Side Writers Group, 175
space, 11–12, 14–15, 16, 35, 36, 51, 52, 53, 58, 60, 61, 62, 73, 75, 77, 78, 79, 81, 84, 85, 86–7, 91, 97, 98, 101, 102, 106–9, 120, 137, 143, 145–6, 147, 149, 150, 151, 155–6, 161, 162, 168, 169, 171, 174, 177, 189, 190, 191, 195, 196, 198, 202, 204, 205, 207
spatial scales, 13–14, 35–6, 47–8, 52–6, 58, 60, 62, 73, 75, 79–80, 97, 119–20, 137, 140, 143, 146, 150, 167, 168, 207
Spengler, Oswald, 25–6, 27, 214n, 216n
Spenser, Edmund, 55
Spicer, Jack, 200
Spitzbergen, 66
Stafford, Fiona, 74
Stamp, L. Dudley, 22
Stannard, Julian, 62, 65
Stark, Inez Cunningham, 173
Staudt, Kathleen Henderson, 24, 26
Stein, Gertrude, 3, 4, 53, 202
Stevens, Wallace, 1, 7, 104
Stokes, Adrian, 97
streets, 171, 172, 174, 178, 189–94
Sullivan, James D., 198
Surrealism, 99, 115, 116
survival, 3, 6, 7, 8–9, 141, 197, 199, 207
Swansea, 50
Sweden, 161
Syria, 165

Taliesin, 73, 76
Tally, Robert T. Jr, 17, 136–7
Tampa Red, 178
Tanzania, 19
Tarlo, Harriet, 203
technology, 23, 25, 27–8, 36–7
Tehran, 57, 63

Texas, 19
Thacker, Andrew, 12, 13, 15, 16, 24
Thackeray, William, 15
Tharp, Marie, 167
Third World Press, 194
Thoreau, Henry David, 140
Thorsson, Courtney, 175, 184
throwntogetherness, 20, 179–80, 183, 184, 186, 187, 198
Till, Emmett, 194–5, 240n
Till, Mamie, 195
time, 12, 21, 45–8, 52, 58, 59, 64, 72–3, 76–80, 93, 101, 120, 132, 135, 136, 137, 138, 139, 140, 141, 143, 146, 148, 151, 156, 162, 165–6, 167, 168, 169, 192, 195, 202, 204
Tobago, 206
Tolson, Melvin, 1, 9, 10, 172
Tomaney, John, 58, 59–60
Topeka, 178, 238n
toponyms, 35, 36, 42–3, 48, 74–5, 85, 99, 105, 133, 137, 153–4, 155, 175–6, 203, 233n
Torrey Canyon oil spill, 50
Toyama, 58
translation, 55, 58–9, 62–3, 89
transnationalism, 2, 4–5, 11, 14, 36, 52, 53–6, 58, 74, 76, 79–80, 89, 97, 119, 132, 140, 158, 193
Trieste, 38
Tripoli, 65
Trueman, A. E., 22
Tuma, Keith, 58
Tyre, 147, 153, 163, 165

United Nations, 14
United States of America, 6, 11–12, 14, 18, 20, 52, 57, 112, 119, 132, 135, 141, 143, 144, 145–6, 147, 157, 158, 159, 161, 162, 172, 182, 183, 189, 196, 199, 200, 201, 202, 207
urban redevelopment, 171, 180, 186, 187–8, 198
utopia, 7, 144, 149, 157, 158, 159–60, 189

vagabond poetics, 57–8, 79
Vidal de la Blanche, Paul, 18
Vietnam, 132, 140, 196
Vikings, 68, 69, 73, 76, 156–7
Villon, François, 55, 57

Walcott, Derek, 204
Wales, 13, 21, 22, 24, 27–8, 29, 30, 38, 39, 44, 47, 48, 49, 50, 51, 73, 75
walking, 57, 82, 85–6, 101, 171, 177, 189, 191, 192, 224n, 238n
Walsh, Rebecca, 13

Ward, Elizabeth, 23, 39, 43, 44
Ward, Val Gray, 197
Washington, D. C., 133, 143
Washington, Richard 'Peanut', 187
waste lands, 24–8, 51, 196
water, 33, 73, 103, 106, 111, 112, 116–31, 134–5, 141, 228n
Watts, W. W., 44
Welsh language, 22, 28–9, 30–1, 42–3, 49
Wegener, Alfred, 150, 166
West Penwith, 13, 82, 95, 96, 97, 98–9, 100, 110
Western culture, 6–7, 21, 25–7, 31, 45, 72, 183
Westphal, Bertrand, 17
wetlands, 19, 75, 116–21, 123–5, 127, 128, 130–1, 138, 141, 230n
Whitehead, A. N., 148
Whitman, Walt, 13, 55
Whittier-Ferguson, John, 3–4
Williams, Jonathan, 74, 132, 202
Williams, Raymond, 2, 6, 82, 112
Williams, William Carlos, 1, 7, 8, 9, 10, 11, 12–13, 17, 18, 55, 66, 113, 114, 133, 143–4, 199, 203
Wilson, Tuzo, 166, 167, 168
Winthrop, John, 150
Wisconsin, 9, 13, 19, 111, 112, 119, 132, 229n
Woods, Tim, 78, 155, 156
Woolf, Virginia, 3, 4, 12, 15, 29
Wooten, William, 54, 76
Worcester, Massachusetts, 143
Wordsworth, William, 55, 125
work, 57, 70–2, 82, 86, 87–8, 92–3, 101–2, 104–5, 113, 135, 159–60, 161, 162, 182, 188
World Bank, 14
Wright, David, 86
Wright, John Kirtland, 17
Wright, Richard, 175, 176, 184
Wyatt, Thomas, 55
Wylam, 57, 66
Wynne-Jones, Nancy, 96, 97
Wynter, Bryan, 97, 99–101

Yeats, W. B., 8, 23, 54, 63, 200
York, 73
Yorkshire, 61, 74, 75

Zennor, 96, 99–100
Zionism, 65
Zukofsky, Louis, 1, 6, 7, 8, 9, 10, 19, 55, 63, 66, 112, 113, 114, 115, 118, 121, 125, 128, 133, 199, 227n, 228n
Zukofsky, Paul, 115
Zurich, 38

EU representative:
Easy Access System Europe
Mustamäe tee 50, 10621 Tallinn, Estonia
Gpsr.requests@easproject.com

www.ingramcontent.com/pod-product-compliance
Lightning Source LLC
Chambersburg PA
CBHW051112230426
43667CB00014B/2545